Lady Wisdom,
Jesus,
and the Sages

Lady Wisdom, Jesus, and the Sages

METAPHOR AND SOCIAL CONTEXT IN MATTHEW'S GOSPEL

Celia M. Deutsch

TRINITY PRESS INTERNATIONAL
Valley Forge, Pennsylvania

Trinity Press International, P.O. Box 851, Valley Forge, PA 19482-0851
Trinity Press International is part of the Morehouse Publishing Group

Library of Congress Cataloging-in-Publication Data

Deutsch, Celia.
    Lady Wisdom, Jesus, and the sages : metaphor and social context in
  Matthew's Gospel / Celia M. Deutsch.
        p.   cm.
    Includes bibliographical references and index.
    ISBN 1-56338-163-X
    1. Wisdom (Biblical personification) 2. Bible. N.T. Matthew —
  Criticism, interpretation, etc. 3. Jesus Christ — History of
  doctrines — Early church, ca. 30-600.   I. Title.
  BS2575.6.W45   1996
  226.2′064–dc20   96-32904
                                                                CIP

Printed in the United States of America

96   97   98   99   10   9   8   7   6   5   4   3   2   1

To

Sr. Mary Winifred McAnany, n.d.s.

(1910–1995)

Friend, Sister, Wise Woman

Contents

Acknowledgments

This book has been, for me, an extended conversation over the course of its writing. My primary conversation partners have been the texts themselves, and the sages behind them who first gave to us the portrait of Lady Wisdom. The inspiration of those usually unnamed figures, as well as the debt to the many who continue to interpret the literature of early Judaism and early Christianity, is apparent throughout the body of the text as well as the notes.

Others have enlivened the conversation. There is my religious congregation, the Sisters of Our Lady of Sion, who give me the companionship of wise women. I am particularly grateful to my own community in Brooklyn, N.Y. Thanks, too, are due to the communities of Montreal and the Convent of the Ecce Homo (Jerusalem), where I spent two memorable summers writing.

Many others have been conversation partners. Alexandra Brown (Washington and Lee University), Claudia Setzer (Manhattan College) and Joann Spillman (Rockhurst College, Kansas City, Mo.) — first friends, then colleagues of many years — have offered their inspiration and perspectives in the course of innumerable discussions. And I am grateful to my colleagues in the joint religion department at Barnard College/Columbia University, particularly Angela Zito, Judith Weisenfeld, David Weiss Halivni, Sara Winter (the New School for Social Research, New York City) and John Stratton Hawley. Kate Cooper (University of Manchester), Alan Segal, and Robin Scroggs (Union Theological Seminary/New York) read the entire manuscript and offered their insights and criticism. Dirk Obbink (Cambridge University) and Holland Hendrix (Union Theological Seminary/New York) helped me with Greco-Roman materials. Colleagues in the SBL, the Christian Scholars Group on Judaism and the Jewish People, the Union Theological Seminary New Testament Seminar and the Columbia University Hebrew Bible Seminar have provided lively exchange.

Barnard College awarded me a grant for the preparation of the manuscript, and Susan Schafer, Rachel Winer, Jenny Knust, and Tamara Fish gave cheerful and efficient help as research assistants. Professor Deidre Good (General Theological Seminary) directed me to Trinity Press International, and Dr. Harold Rast has given me not only a warm reception, but helpful criticism. Laura Barrett, Therese Boyd, and John Eagleson have enabled this project to reach completion.

Finally, the Camoldolese Benedictine nuns of Transfiguration Monastery (Windsor, N.Y.) have frequently offered me hospitality for concentrated periods of work.

As I write these words, I am thus aware of a large circle of intellectual "ancestors," of friends and colleagues who have been part of this project. My thanks to all for inspiration, encouragement and criticism. The mistakes are my own.

Introduction

Raising the Question

Since the early part of this century scholars have demonstrated repeatedly that Matthew portrays Jesus as personified Wisdom.[1] Most studies have focused on a specific passage or unit, although some have surveyed the complete range of relevant texts.[2] All observe, at least in passing, similarities to Jewish materials in which Wisdom likewise appears as personified.

Scholars, then, have given a great deal of attention to Matthew's use of the Wisdom metaphor.[3] Indeed, one might note a certain fascination with the matter. Why then examine the question yet again? I believe the matter worth pursuing because even after writing a doctoral thesis on a related subject there remain for me a good many unanswered questions: Why does Matthew use *Lady Wisdom* as a trope for speculation on Jesus' life and teaching? By what process does Matthew transform the symbol of Lady Wisdom so that its referent becomes Jesus? Whom does this serve? In other words, in which social context does this occur? And how does a metaphor shift so that the content is located not in an imaginary woman but in a historical, if exalted, male?

Use of the Wisdom metaphor is not central to Matthew's thought. However, these questions yield an example of the relationship between metaphor and social context, and of the ways in which a metaphor is transformed to meet new situations. Specifically, Matthew's usage illustrates ways in which Jews who followed Jesus transformed traditional metaphors to account for their understanding of Jesus and to legitimate social structures.

In addition to the very real intellectual questions, I must admit to having succumbed to my own fascination with the use of the metaphor Lady Wisdom. The texts in which Lady Wisdom appears often possess a grace and beauty that draw me to pore over them and to wonder what the use of such a metaphor might tell us about the people who wrote these texts, their understanding of self, community, and the transcendent. And I have not yet exhausted the meaning of the metaphor's use in early Christian texts.

1

The metaphor of Lady Wisdom emerges in the context of Jewish learned circles during the Restoration, the period following the return of Jews to Judea from Babylonia in the late sixth century B.C.E. Use of the metaphor develops under the impulse of the cult of the virtues as well as the cult of Isis, in the context of the Greco-Roman world. It serves to articulate certain concerns in the learned circles where the metaphor originates, and to legitimate the authority of the sages who use it.

The metaphor is female, in most cases clearly delineated with a variety of roles, and often erotic. It becomes a point of convergence for religious concerns as well as for social questions, specifically those of gender and social function. The metaphor especially allows members of predominantly male learned groups to speculate on questions of revelation, cosmogony, social order, and theodicy. And it legitimates their authority in relationship to disciples, both prospective and actual.

Matthew, as we shall see, is a learned person, and perceives reality through the lens of a member of a learned group.[4] Thus, he identifies the metaphor with Jesus. I believe he enhances the identification, already present in the Sayings Source, because it allows him to articulate earlier concerns and locate them in the figure of Jesus. It also allows him to legitimate the teaching of Jesus and that of his own community's leadership, specifically a male teaching group. Matthew is able to identify a hitherto female metaphor with a male historical figure because of the tensive quality of metaphor, which permits usage to expand under new circumstances and to include new content, as well as to acquire and abandon various features. Matthew is able to represent Jesus as Wisdom also because of the widespread practice of identifying female deified virtues with male charismatic figures.

With the exception of Matt. 11:19 and possibly 11:28–30, I do not believe that one can prove that the evangelist identifies Jesus with Wisdom. Nor can I establish the use of that identification to legitimate the authority of the teaching group in the Matthean community. I hope simply to show the plausibility for such assertions.

I shall proceed by studying use of the metaphor in earlier and contemporary Jewish literature, as well as by examining the way in which Matthew uses the material from his sources, and the literary contexts in which the Wisdom passages occur in his gospel. Various aspects of the discussion will be familiar to those who are specialists in Second Temple Jewish literature, feminist biblical studies, the synoptic gospels, and Matthew. I intend to bring together insights from those specializations in order to cast new light on an interesting phenomenon in the development of early Christian thought.

Procedure

The fundamental methodologies employed in examination of the New Testament materials in this study are redaction criticism and composition criticism. Certainly, we use methods and insights from literary criticism, as well as from the social sciences and feminist biblical studies. But composition and redaction criticism constitute the framework for our investigation.

The first chapter examines the texts in late biblical and early Jewish literature where Lady Wisdom appears. It discusses the function of Lady Wisdom against the backdrop of the nature of metaphor itself, and in the context of the learned groups in which Lady Wisdom appears. Then we study the relevant passages in Matthew's gospel and Matthew's use of the metaphor to express his understanding of Jesus' life and ministry in chapter 2. Chapter 3 examines Matthew's portrayal of Jesus as teacher and the ways in which the evangelist uses the Wisdom metaphor to articulate his interpretation of Jesus' teaching. And chapter 4 presents the figure of the teacher in Matthew's community and the relationship between those teachers, Jesus-Wisdom, and the portrayal of Jesus' disciples in Matthew's gospel. We conclude with a summary chapter.

My reading of Matthew and the comparative literature have shaped each other. Thus, I have read and discussed Matthew's gospel in light of other Jewish literature, canonical and noncanonical. And I have discussed that literature in terms of the First Gospel and its use of the Wisdom metaphor. Consequently, there is, for example, no exploration of the relationship of Wisdom and Logos in Second Temple literature.[5]

In most cases, the nature of the comparative literature — composite documents or collections — has required that I present a synthesized discussion of that material. This is particularly true in chapter 1. I do not use the term *class* to describe the groups in which the metaphor found a home, because I understand *class* as "an aggregation of persons in a society who stand in a similar position to some form of power, privilege, or prestige."[6] Such a term might imply a single group, whereas the metaphor is used by a variety of learned groups over a period of several hundred years. Moreover, these groups had such varied positions in relation to power as the Qumran sectarians and the tannaim. Thus, I have judged it less confusing to speak simply of "learned groups" until I reach the discussion of Matthew and his community.

I have used the terms *scribe, sage,* and *teacher* according to the usage found in the particular document or collection. At times, according to the document under examination, I have used all three. All, however, represent the ideal of the learned as students and interpreters of the tradition.

Matthew and His Gospel

I assume that Matthew is a redactor and has edited earlier sources, namely Mark, the Sayings Source (Q), and M.[7] While I do not believe one can impose a rigid structure on Matthew's gospel, one can discern a pattern of alternating narrative and discourse within the text. Each discourse ends with a formulaic statement that serves as a transition to the narrative section that follows.[8]

I believe that the editor of Matthew's gospel was a Jew who believed in Jesus, and was a member of a community with similar beliefs. Matthew's interests in legal matters, his knowledge of Jewish exegetical techniques and nonbiblical Jewish traditions, his concern to place Jesus among the Jewish people — all these suggest someone who was Jewish.[9] And those same elements suggest that the redactor possessed expert knowledge of Jewish tradition.[10]

I assume also that the community for whom Matthew wrote was predominantly Jewish. There were members of gentile origin; passages like Matt. 8:5–13, 15:21–28, and 28:16–20 suggest such a presence.[11] But the majority of Matthew's audience was Jewish. Moreover, they were Torah-observant. While the gospel certainly reflects disputes over *how* to observe *halachah* (12:1–8, 9–14; 15:1–20), and in what circumstances, nowhere does Matthew suggest — or describe Jesus as suggesting — that members of the community should abrogate Torah. Nowhere, for example, does the text indicate that baptism has replaced circumcision.[12]

But, one might object, what of the use of *ethnikoi* in Matt. 5:47, 6:7, and 18:17 — does not the use of such a slur indicate that Matthew's community had no gentile members?[13] Matthew's community had no gentile members simply because members of gentile origin in his community, as Torah-observant, would have undergone Jewish conversion and thus been considered Jews. However, this does not rule out the possibility of tensions in the Matthean community between ethnically Jewish members and those born of gentile parentage.

Matthew's insistence on the importance of love of neighbor suggests internal conflict (7:12, 19:19, 22:34–40), as does his provision for community order in chapter 18.[14] Tensions within the Matthean community include the influence of false prophets and expectations regarding the end-time (which Matthew viewed as wrong-headed; 7:15–20, 24:23–24), and the threat of "lawlessness" (5:17–20).[15] And while converted

Gentiles would have been considered Jews, texts such as 15:21–28 and 28:16–20 suggest an internal debate concerning the gentile mission.

But the most significant source of pressure appears to be that presented by teachers in the parent community. There seems to be a struggle about who will control teaching authority in Matthew's community: the "scribes" of Matthew's choosing (reflected in 13:52, 23:34, and so on) or the teachers of the broader Jewish community represented by the "scribes and Pharisees" of such passages as chapter 23. The latter are members of formative Judaism, a reform movement that included successors to the Pharisees.[16] Their power, authority, and influence have implications in the broader political realm, for some among them are lower-level bureaucrats, retainers in government administrative service.[17]

The center of the symbol system in first-century Judaism was Torah. For Matthew and others like him, that center shifted so that it was located in the person of Jesus, his teaching and life, death and resurrection. Even Torah was interpreted in light of that shift, and so Matthew presents Jesus as its definitive teacher,[18] and identifies personified Wisdom with Jesus.

Matthew disparages his opponents' symbol system in the attempt to offer an alternative understanding. In this manner he seeks to legitimate the teaching authority of his own "scribes" and "prophets" in the face of the tensions *within* his community. The fierce rhetoric suggests that in the struggle for the allegiance of the members, as well as in attracting new recruits, Matthew perceives the opposition to have the upper hand.[19]

There is no indication that Matthew's group had been expelled from "the synagogue," if one understands that word to be a synonym for "Judaism."[20] On the contrary, the evangelist usually reserves his invective for leadership groups.[21] The references to judicial flogging indicate that he and his community were still considered by the parent group to be subject to the discipline of the broader community, as they so considered themselves.[22] The bitter conflict echoed in phrases like "their synagogues"[23] suggests separate institutions in Matthew's city, whether by expulsion or by choice. But certainly other Jewish communities before and since have undergone such division and continued to consider themselves and each other as Jewish. Perhaps not "good" Jews — but Jewish.[24]

The fierce debates between Jesus and the opposing teachers are better explained by the nature of polemic in Greco-Roman literature[25] and in Second Temple Jewish literature than by some formal expulsion. The bitterness of the invective in the comparative literature, as well as within

Matthew's gospel itself, reflects conflict between groups in particularly close relationship, for the social sciences suggest that "the closer the relationship, the more intense the conflict."[26]

Certain scholars cling to the notion of a decisive separation between the Matthean community and the broader Jewish community, some on the grounds that followers of Jesus would not have been able to pray the *bîrkhat ha-mînîm*.[27] Recent studies, however, cast serious doubt on whether the prayer referred to *Christians* at this early date.[28] Moreover, it is not certain that the prayer was in use in the first century, or in what way it was eventually promulgated.[29]

I believe it best to view Matthew's community as a sect within first-century Judaism. That is, it was a minority group that stood over against the parent group while understanding itself to be subject to it. Moreover, it made exclusive claims to be what the parent group itself claimed to be.[30]

The evangelist represented the learned class in his community,[31] a group in competition with the opposition for the allegiance of new re-cruits as well as of present members in his community. That struggle occurred at the end of the first century, after the destruction of Jerusalem and the Second Temple. Learned groups emerged as would-be leaders of the Jewish community as it underwent the long process of restructur-ing and consolidation. In competition with one another, these various groups made claims to revelatory learning which guaranteed the authen-ticity of their interpretations of Torah. Thus, 4 Ezra presents a chosen leader whose visionary experience insures not only the text of the canon, but the legitimacy of esoteric learning as well.[32] And 2 *Apoc. Baruch* promises that Israel will always have a "wise man ... a son of the Law" (45:4), teachers who can be "shepherds and lamps and fountains" for the people (77:15).[33] Matthew represents a learned group, competing for the leadership of a Jewish community going through the process of self-definition in light of their understanding of Jesus and in the train of the destruction of the Second Temple. Conflict with the leadership of the parent community may have served in that process as the group and its leaders articulated their identity. Indeed, sectarian conflict with the par-ent group may have increased cohesion in the Matthean community, or at least its leadership, as it consolidated its norms in the confrontation with a perceived threat.[34]

Matthew and his colleagues faced a conflict concerning authority over interpretation of Torah with opposing teachers. Matthew's use of the Wisdom metaphor legitimated the authority of his group, not only in face of external opposition, but in relationship to internal opposition as well, which may have included women teachers.

Matthew and his community lived in Syria or northern Palestine. A document such as the First Gospel would seem to be most at home in an environment where Greek was spoken and written, and where a significant number of both Jews and Gentiles lived. The town or city would need to be large enough to include at least two opposing Jewish parties, one led by the "scribes and Pharisees" and one led by Matthew and his colleagues.[35] It would also need to be large enough and have sufficient economic and intellectual means to provide the resources necessary for a learned group. And finally, the document requires an environment where certain kinds of halachic discussion as well as apocalyptic usage of the sort familiar in Palestinian contexts would be "at home." Antioch would be a likely candidate for Matthew's city, but so would centers like Sepphoris and Tiberias.[36]

The specific social structure within which and for which Matthew wrote his gospel is not clear. Matthew was a learned person, writing for his audience's instruction.[37] His reference to "their synagogues" suggests that his audience was a synagogue of Jews who followed Jesus. Archaeological evidence, in the land of Israel as well as the Diaspora, indicates that the community may have gathered in a modest building constructed expressly for worship and study.[38] But synagogues also met in households, whether that of a teacher or a more well-to-do patron.[39] The Matthean community may also have been composed of several smaller households based in a larger one.[40] In the case of a large establishment, a single household — with its immediate family members, servants, retainers, and clients — might have constituted the "synagogue." Or it might have served as a gathering place for members of other households. Both synagogue and urban household served as centers for education, both more and less formal.[41]

Matthew and his colleagues served as leaders and teachers of such a community. As had the metaphor Lady Wisdom, so the portrayal of Jesus-Wisdom emerged in a learned circle, articulated their understanding not only of Jesus' story but of their own, and legitimated their authority within the community and in face of their external opponents.

Chapter 1

The Metaphor of Lady Wisdom

A PROLOGOMENON

The Nature of Metaphor[1]

Matthew uses the metaphor of Lady Wisdom to interpret the significance of Jesus and his teaching. That metaphor was familiar to him through the traditions of biblical, Second Temple, and tannaitic Judaism. Thus, a brief discussion of the nature of metaphor and then an examination of Lady Wisdom's appearance in the earlier and contemporary materials will allow us to understand more completely what Matthew is trying to do.

Metaphor is a mode of symbolic language that "conjoins the semantic fields of two words in such a way as to create new meaning."[2] Metaphor brings together two thoughts, two fields of meaning, to create new meaning. The two ideas presented are tenor and vehicle. Tenor is the "underlying idea or principal subject which the vehicle or figure means." We describe or qualify the tenor by describing the vehicle.[3] There is a conjoining of the two, not merely of single words, but of contexts, of systems of "associated commonplaces."[4]

Metaphor is *interactive*.[5] Therefore, the new meaning it creates resides in vehicle as well as tenor. In other words, *both* terms of the metaphor, tenor (content, the less familiar) and vehicle (the more familiar), acquire new meaning.[6] And because metaphor includes the associated commonplaces of both tenor and vehicle, not only the individual words but whole ranges of meaning and feeling come together and mutually inform each other.

Metaphor is a form of symbol.[7] It is tensive and may "have a set of meanings that can neither be exhausted nor adequately expressed by any one referent."[8] It transforms itself to "accommodate new experience and shift in community setting."[9] Metaphorical activity is "intrinsically perspectival."[10] It asserts, sometimes only by implication, that something is "like this" or "not like that."[11] One thus ascertains a particular meaning by looking to context.[12]

9

Personification is a form of metaphor that gives "attributes of a human being to an animal, an object or a concept."[13] In other words, it treats the nonpersonal as personal.[14] The vehicle of the metaphor is, thus, a human figure. And so, in the literature we shall study, Woman, or — to use the honorific — Lady, is the vehicle for the tenor wisdom, an abstract concept.[15]

Lady Wisdom

The metaphor of Lady Wisdom appears in a wide range of literature throughout the Second Temple and tannaitic periods: biblical and apocryphal wisdom literature, pseudepigrapha, Qumran texts, Philo, and tannaitic sources.[16] Examination of relevant materials discloses the richness of the image and allows us to perceive something of its hold on the imagination of those who wrote and used it. Study of Lady Wisdom's roles and attributes enables us to understand the significance of Matthew's usage.

But what is wisdom? *Ḥokmâh* bears a variety of meanings.[17] Ultimately, of course, wisdom in human matters is God's wisdom, as we see in Solomon's prayer in 1K 3:3–14. God creates the world by divine wisdom.[18] Beginning with Ben Sira, Jewish authors identify divine Wisdom with Torah.[19] Other Second Temple authors associate her with apocalyptic mysteries.[20] Divine Wisdom, working in creation and in the social order, present in Israel's history and revealed in Torah, is the tenor of the metaphor.[21]

As one would expect, the vehicle assumes a variety of forms, depending on context. Thus, Lady Wisdom appears in a variety of roles, both public and domestic.[22] In this chapter we will examine the ways in which she is portrayed, as well as the relationship of the metaphor Lady Wisdom to the learned groups in which she appears, the ways in which she articulates the religious understanding of those groups and serves to legitimate their authority. This discussion of Lady Wisdom's functions will allow us to propose in the following chapter that Matthew uses the metaphor to describe Jesus because he understands Jesus to exercise the same functions as Wisdom.

Teacher, Prophet, and Hymnist

Lady Wisdom's most dominant role is that of teacher, a public role ordinarily associated with males.[23] This is already apparent in Proverbs, where the metaphor appears for the first time. There Lady Wisdom

speaks in public places where passersby can easily hear her mes-
sage:[24] streets, marketplaces, city walls, crossroads, gates, and portals
(Prov. 1:20–21, 8:2–3, 9:3). In the conclusion to the Wisdom poem in
Proverbs 8, she exhorts, as would a teacher:

> And now, my children, listen to me: happy are those who keep my
> ways. Hear instruction and be wise, and do not neglect it. Happy
> is the one who listens to me, watching daily at my gates, waiting
> beside my doors. For whoever finds me finds life and obtains favor
> from the Lord; but those who miss me injure themselves; all who
> hate me love death. (8:32–36)[25]

One of the most evident features of Lady Wisdom's teaching role, that
of disciplinarian, is most clearly exemplified in Sirach, where Lady Wisdom the teacher accompanies her "sons" along the "tortuous paths"
of instruction (Sir. 4:17).[26] Her instruction is a stern business: Lady
Wisdom admonishes, tests, and disciplines the student. That is to be
expected, for *mûsār* and *paideia* both imply discipline, including physical discipline. Ben Sira emphasizes the labor associated with obtaining
her. "She seems very harsh to the undisciplined,"[27] he says, bidding his
hearers to submit to her fetters, collar, bonds, and yoke (6:20, 23–31).[28]

But there is another side to Lady Wisdom's manner of teaching.
Ben Sira, for instance, also stresses the paradoxical nature of the quest
for Lady Wisdom. Her instruction occurs in a context of relationship
between herself and her students. The students are Lady Wisdom's "children" (4:11), and the one "who loves her loves life" (4:12). Her collar
becomes a "glorious robe," her yoke a golden ornament (6:29–30). And
the author of the acrostic can say that he has labored but little in return
for his reward (51:27). Indeed, Lady Wisdom finishes by exalting her
sons and giving them rest (6:28, 15:5, 51:27).

Several of our texts portray Lady Wisdom in the role of householder. In Proverbs she is a householder whose seven-pillared home
bespeaks her wealth.[29] Lady Wisdom invites the ignorant, the simple
(*pethî, aphrōn*) into her house to share a banquet. She dispatches servants to proffer the invitation, but she herself also goes out to cry her
summons from the town's high places (Prov. 8:1–2; 9:1–6).

Ben Sira speaks of Lady Wisdom as having a house (Sir. 14:24–25).
He describes vividly the would-be disciple peering through the win-
dows and listening at the doors of her house (14:23–24). As welcoming
householder, Lady Wisdom invites people to eat and drink (24:19–22).[30]
One also finds the image of Lady Wisdom the householder in 11QPsa
18.8. Given the fact that sages often gathered disciples for instruction in
their homes, I believe that the image of Lady Wisdom the householder is

best understood in the context of her role as teacher.[31] This image may
be related, then, not only to roles usually exercised by women but to the
description of Lady Wisdom as a teacher. Her house would thus be the
place of instruction.

In a few instances, Lady Wisdom is prophet and/or preacher — roles
often associated with teachers in the Second Temple and tannaitic periods, as later discussion will suggest. These were public roles usually
reserved for males.[32] As prophet, Lady Wisdom reproves her audience
and calls them to repentance in the Book of Proverbs (1:22).[33] And she
warns those who refuse to heed her that she will withdraw (v. 28).

The Wisdom of Solomon also implies that Lady Wisdom is a prophet.
She "knows the things of old and infers the things to come." Furthermore, she has "foreknowledge of signs and wonders, and of the outcome
of seasons and times" (8:8). However, there is no trace of prophetic
warning as in Proverbs, or description of her stern ways as in Sirach.

Later discussion will show that one of the sage's functions in the Second Temple era was that of hymnist.[34] In 11QPsa 18, Lady Wisdom
appears as a hymnist. She has a voice, a song (l. 12).[35] She is given by
God to recount God's deeds (l. 6), to make known God's might and
greatness to the simple and senseless (l. 7). This echoes the descriptions
of the community meal in lines 12–14, where the righteous recite hymns,
making known God's might. It is there that Lady Wisdom's voice is
heard (l. 12).[36]

Lady Wisdom's public roles find parallels in the descriptions of the
sages, and later, in Matthew, of Jesus as teacher, prophet, and hymnist.
Indeed, the functions of prophet and teacher will dominate Matthew's
use of the metaphor.

Bride, Wife, and Lover

Lady Wisdom, then, acts in two public roles usually associated with
males — teacher and prophet. But she also acts in domestic roles. She
is frequently described in erotic imagery, appearing as bride, wife, and
lover. In Proverbs the sage exhorts the student not to forsake her; he
describes the rewards for those who love and embrace her (4:6–9).[37]
She will give the sage a "beautiful crown" (4:9).[38] The sage is to call
Wisdom by the bridal title "sister" (7:4).[39] Ties of affection and fidelity
bind Lady Wisdom to those who respond to her; she loves those who
love her.[40]

Later sources develop the erotic imagery already present in Proverbs.[41] In the Sirach acrostic (Sir. 51:13–30) as well as 14:20–15:8,

Lady Wisdom is lover, object of the sage/student's pursuit.[42] And in 14:20–15:8, the quest is actually compared to a hunt (14:22).[43]

The erotic language of Wisdom of Solomon 6–9 depends, of course, on Proverbs and Sirach.[44] But Wisdom of Solomon surpasses its sources, and Sophia appears in this text with a "luminous and passionate intensity."[45] The description of the sage's union with Wisdom corresponds to the descriptions of Lady Wisdom's union with God;[46] union between the sage and Lady Wisdom imitates God's union with her. And it is precisely because of the union between Lady Wisdom and God that Lady Wisdom can impart to the sage revelation and salvation.[47]

Philo develops further the portrayal of Lady Wisdom as bride, wife, and lover, both of God and of the *sophos*.[48] His use of the metaphor is of particular interest for our study. The personification of Wisdom alternates between male and female.[49] On the one hand, Wisdom is usually female — daughter and wife of God, mother and nurse of the universe, kinswoman to the progressive, and wife to the *sophos*. But Philo sometimes reverses the sexual roles, portraying Wisdom as male and the *sophos* as female.[50] Thus he speaks of Wisdom as impregnating the *sophos* (*Congr.* 9; *Fug.* 52).[51] As for the wise, "when souls become divinely inspired, from being women they become virgins, throwing off the womanly corruptions which are [found] in sense-perception and passion" (*QE* 2.3).

Philo is himself aware of the confusion of sexual roles in the imagery through which he personifies Wisdom. He does not explain or resolve it. Rather, he says, "Let us, then, pay no heed to the discrepancy in the gender of the words, and say that the daughter of God, even Wisdom, is not masculine, but father, sowing and begetting in souls aptness to learn, discipline, knowledge, sound sense, good and laudable actions" (*Fug.* 52).

The qualities of Wisdom as father as well as mother serve to illustrate the generative qualities of Wisdom on the one hand, and the passivity of the person receiving it on the other.[52] The ways in which Philo uses male and female erotic imagery in his use of the Wisdom metaphor is of particular interest for our study because they illustrate the extent to which metaphor is tensive with regard to both vehicle and tenor.

Tannaitic sources use erotic language to describe Torah, which is synonymous with ḥokmâh.[53] In some texts, Wisdom-Torah is God's daughter or bride, or Israel's bride.[54] For example, one source likens early study of Torah to the erotic attraction between a young man and a young woman: "He that studies Torah as a child is like a young man who needs a maiden: for she is suited to him and he is suited to her, and she is drawn to him and he is drawn to her" (*'Abot R. Nat. a*

23). Torah is personified as God's daughter who is given as "bride" to Israel in the "marriage" at Mount Sinai, according to a tradition ascribed to R. Meir in *Lev. Rab.* 20:10.[55] This imagery conveys Torah's pre-eminence as cherished by God, and the intimacy of the relationship between Israel and Torah.

The use of erotic imagery in these texts suggests qualities of affective appeal, intimacy, union. This is true of the sage's relationship to Lady Wisdom or to Torah, and of God's relationship to sage, Israel and Torah. The intersection of the relationship of God to Lady Wisdom on the one hand, and of the sage to Lady Wisdom on the other, creates the locus for the sage's own union with God and for his receiving revelation.

Mother and Nurse

One also finds maternal imagery associated with Lady Wisdom. Ben Sira likens her explicitly to a mother, paralleling the image to that of a bride (Sir. 15:2–3):

> She will come to meet him like a mother,
> and like a young bride she will welcome him.
> She will feed him with the bread of learning
> and give him the water of wisdom to drink.

Philo develops the image, telling us that God has begotten the universe through Lady Wisdom; so she is not only God's wife, but mother and nurse of the created order, of humankind, and especially of the sage.[56] Indeed, Philo says, God's wisdom

> feeds and nurses and rears to sturdiness all who yearn after imperishable sustenance. For this divine Wisdom has appeared as mother of all that are in the world, affording to her offspring, as soon as they are born, the nourishment which they require from her own breasts. (*Det.* 115–16)[57]

Two texts from the Septuagint convey the maternal imagery less directly, implicitly likening Wisdom to a mother bird.[58] Prov. 16:16 (LXX) compares the nests of wisdom and those of insight to gold and silver respectively.[59] And Sir. 1:15 tells us that Lady Wisdom has made her nest an eternal foundation among humankind.[60] The parallel indicates that the image is meant to suggest not only the nurturance of maternal Wisdom, but her fidelity.[61]

The likeness of the mother bird and the maternal imagery occur in reference to the figure of the sage. These images will be significant for our examination of Matt. 23:37–39.

God's Daughter

Lady Wisdom has her source in God. Thus, the Book of Proverbs tells us that she is the daughter of the One who begets her[62] and brings her forth (8:23f).[63] She is present as "darling child" (*'āmôn*, 8:30a)[64] when God creates the universe (*shām 'ānî*, v. 27). Present to God, created order, and humankind, Wisdom plays a mediative role. The author does not define that role, however, for the emphasis in 8:22–30 is not on Wisdom's activity, but rather on her antiquity.[65]

The tannaim use Prov. 8:22–30 when they describe Torah-Wisdom as God's daughter. For example, there is a *baraita* in *b. Sanh.* 101a which portrays her as God's daughter, citing Prov. 8:22 as a proof-text.[66] The role of God's daughter implies that Lady Wisdom's source is divine and that she is subordinate to that source. It also implies that she is God's intimate. Her mediating function in creation and revelation is possible because Lady Wisdom is at the same time divine in origin and subordinate to God. In particular, she can mediate relationship with the divine to the sage. Matthew's use of the motif of sonship in 11:25–27 will likewise suggest origin and intimacy with God, and a role in mediating revelation.

Transcendent, Pre-existent, and Hidden

The description of Lady Wisdom as God's daughter conveys not only the notions of her intimacy with and subordination to Israel's God but also her *divine* origin. She is, in other words, transcendent. Ben Sira begins his book telling us that God created Wisdom and that she remains with God forever (1:1). And the author of the Wisdom of Solomon tells us that she stands beside the throne of glory (9:10) and lives with God as the divine consort (8:3).

Our texts also imply Lady Wisdom's transcendence by describing her as pre-existent, that is, existing before creation. This appears first in the poem in Proverbs 8, which tells us that she was present as God's "darling child" when God created the universe (vv. 27, 30a). The motif is adopted by Second Temple traditions.[67]

Tannaitic literature sometimes describes Torah as one of several pre-existent beings. *'Abot* 6:10, for example, tells us, "Five possessions did the Holy One, blessed be He, take to Himself in His world; and these are they: Torah is one possession, heaven and earth is one possession, Abraham is one possession, Israel is one possession, and the house of the sanctuary is one possession." The saying cites Prov. 8:22 to support the assertion regarding Torah.[68]

Certain traditions reflect the notion of Wisdom's transcendence by speaking of her as hidden, thus the query in the Book of Job, "But where shall wisdom be found?" (28:12; cf. v. 20), with its response, "Mortals do not know the way to it" (v. 13).[69] The author compares Wisdom to gold, silver, and jewels (vv. 15–19), and parallels Wisdom's hiddenness with the inaccessibility of treasure (vv. 1–11). God alone knows where Lady Wisdom is to be found; it is God who, at creation, "saw it and declared it" (v. 27).[70] As God is hidden beyond the limits of the earth (26:2–14), so is Wisdom.

Philo implies Wisdom's transcendence and the passivity of her reception by human beings. He speaks in terms of a sudden and unexpected illumination in which the *sophos* receives Lady Wisdom in "bright and pure rays," allowing the *sophos* to see God and the divine powers (*dynameis, Deus* 3).[71] The illumination, which is a gift of God's own wisdom, allows the person to see and apprehend "things divine and human" (*Sacr.* 78–80).[72]

Matthew will use the motif of hiddenness and transcendence in his description of Jesus as Wisdom. It is, however, the quality of immanence that dominates that portrait.

Immanent in Creation, History, and Torah

Lady Wisdom is indeed transcendent. She is pre-existent, hidden with God, inaccessible to human beings unless granted by divine gift. But according to most of our texts she is also immanent. This is apparent in several ways. For example, various traditions understand Lady Wisdom to have been present at creation when God fashioned the universe, as poured out on God's works and given to humankind.[73] She is present as God's word.[74] She is also present as the instrument, the worker, the blueprint of creation.[75]

Lady Wisdom is immanent in the cosmic order, at the moment of creation and in the ongoing existence of the universe. As metaphor, however, Lady Wisdom is tensive and thus has more than one referent. She is also immanent in the sages' teaching. And so, for example, in the Book of Proverbs we might say that Lady Wisdom actually personifies the wisdom taught in the schools and articulated in that book.[76] One acquires her through hard work in attending to the sages' instruction.[77] Use of the metaphor thus legitimates the sages' teaching function.

The Wisdom of Solomon identifies Wisdom with philosophy, science, and the arts in passages such as 7:22–8:15.[78] Lady Wisdom reveals the hidden things through the labor of the human mind,[79] including the structure of social order and the secrets of the universe, all of which are the objects of study in the classical curriculum.

Some traditions describe Lady Wisdom as immanent in history. For Ben Sira, she is not only present at creation, poured out in some manner on all humankind, but she is associated with Israel in a particular way. She accompanied Israel in her desert wandering, with her throne in the pillar of cloud (24:4);[80] at God's bidding she has made her dwelling in Jacob — in the Temple, to be specific (24:8–12).[81] Similarly, the Wisdom of Solomon describes Lady Wisdom not only in the primeval and patriarchal histories, but in the wonders of the Exodus events (10:15–11:20).

Lady Wisdom is immanent in history, not only in the collective sphere, but also individually in her relationship to the sage. The Wisdom of Solomon tells us that "in every generation she passes into holy souls and makes them friends of God and prophets" (7:27). Precisely because of her intimacy with God, Lady Wisdom mediates relationship with the divine to the sage.

Finally, Lady Wisdom is immanent in the cosmic and social orders and in Israel's history in her identification with Torah. The earliest indication of this is Sirach 24, where the author describes Wisdom as being "the book of the covenant of the Most High God" (24:23). Ben Sira cites Deut. 33:4 (LXX) to describe it as "the law that Moses commanded us as an inheritance for the congregations of Jacob."[82] He likens Wisdom-Torah to the rivers flowing from Eden (vv. 23–27).[83] And, while Baruch speaks of Wisdom's inaccessibility, the poem ends with a clear assertion that Wisdom is ultimately found in Torah (Bar. 4:1–4). Indeed, the statement of Wisdom's inaccessibility serves rhetorically to underscore the magnitude of the gift of Torah given to Israel.[84]

Lady Wisdom's immanence, then, is not simply a general presence in creation. It is localized specifically in Israel and particularly as Torah. As Torah, Lady Wisdom is one with the Word of creation and dwells in Israel's midst. Thus, the Word that contains the way of life for the covenant community is one with the primal Word of cosmic life and order.

The tannaim, as indeed later rabbinical authorities, assumed the identification of Torah and *ḥokmâh*.[85] In fact, the two terms became synonymous. This is clear from the personification of Torah, and from the way in which texts where Proverbs personifies wisdom are explicitly interpreted to refer to Torah. For example, *Sifre Deut.* 48 cites Proverbs 3, 4, and 8 — among other materials — to describe the properties of Torah. Thus, "just as water is priceless, so are words of Torah priceless, as it is said, 'She (wisdom) is more precious than rubies'" (Prov. 3:15).

And "just as ointment is beneficial for the head and beneficial for the body, so are words of Torah beneficial for the head and beneficial for the body, as it is said, 'For they shall be a chaplet of grace unto thy head and chains about thy neck' (Prov. 1:9), and 'she will give to thy head a chaplet of grace' (Prov. 4:9)."[86]

Lady Wisdom thus represents the wisdom of human experience present in the social order, as well as God's pre-existent wisdom, which is present in the primeval cosmic order.[87] She is thus immanent, and she is accessible through the sages' instruction, particularly through the study of Torah. Indeed, for authors like Ben Sira and the pseudonymous Baruch, even statements about Lady Wisdom's transcendence serve to display the gift of her immanence.

Matthew's gospel will present Wisdom as immanent in Jesus, accessible through his teaching as well as through the continuation of that teaching in the scribal leadership of the Matthean community.

Lady Wisdom's Withdrawal

The dominant note in these traditions is that transcendent Wisdom is immanent in creation, in history, and in Torah. There is another tradition, however, in which Lady Wisdom withdraws or is hidden. In Prov. 1:28 Lady Wisdom calls her audience to repentance (v. 22), as we noted earlier. She warns that, should they refuse to heed her, she will withdraw (v. 28).

1 Enoch represents a clear example of the use of the motif of Lady Wisdom's withdrawal in the Second Temple era.[88] In *1 Enoch* 42, Lady Wisdom goes forth from the heavens to take her dwelling among humankind but, finding no habitation, she returns to the heavens (vv. 1–2). At this point personified Iniquity seeks a home with humankind — and finds it (v. 3). The passage implies that Wisdom and Iniquity are mutually exclusive; Lady Wisdom is unable to dwell with people because they have chosen Iniquity. Conversely, evil is deployed in the world by Wisdom's withdrawal. Lady Wisdom does not remain hidden because she is transcendent. On the contrary, she seeks a dwelling among human beings, but is *forced* to withdraw.[89]

What is the content of the metaphor in *1 Enoch* 42? Chapters 37–72, the context of this passage, do not specify the content of "wisdom," but do suggest that wisdom is revealed knowledge of the apocalyptic realities, including visions of the final times and apocalyptic judgment (chaps. 38, 55, 56, 62–64), the new heaven and new earth (chaps. 39, 45), the cosmic secrets (41:3–9, 43:1–44:1), and Enoch's vision of the

Son of Man (chaps. 46, 48, 61), the vision of the heavenly court.[90] The heavenly places contain fountains of wisdom from which the thirsty drink (48:1). The teaching contained in the visions is revealed to Enoch, who then transmits it to the community (37:5).

The figure of the Son of Man is a significant element of Enoch's vision of wisdom.[91] Like Wisdom, the Son of Man is pre-existent (*1 Enoch* 48:3), both hidden and revealed (62:7).[92] He is himself a wisdom figure, given the spirit of wisdom, understanding, and might (49:3). He is also the revealer of God's wisdom (48:7), the source of the "secrets of wisdom" (51:3).[93] And the Son of Man is apocalyptic judge.[94] The elements of revealer, wisdom figure, and judge actually converge in various ways in the Similitudes.[95] The immediate context of *1 Enoch* 42 — chapters 37–72 — thus suggests that the tenor of the metaphor Wisdom is knowledge of apocalyptic realities. It also suggests that, even while Wisdom withdraws, she remains with the wise, paralleled in chapter 71 with the apocalyptic Son of Man. Moreover, looking to the broader context, one sees that in chapters 92–105 wisdom refers to the teaching of the "wise," the teachers of the author's community. That teaching is their interpretation of Torah, and the righteous follow it.[96] In 104:9–12 we learn that the teaching of the wise is contained in scripture.

In *1 Enoch*, then, the apocalyptic nature of Wisdom does not exclude the fact that the understanding appropriate to apocalyptic mysteries still has to do with the meaning of history, with the cosmic order, and with Torah. Indeed, Wisdom is identified with the teaching of sages who define themselves and their community in sectarian fashion.[97]

Matthew will describe Jesus-Wisdom in relation to revealed knowledge. He will describe him as Son of Man and he will tell of his withdrawal in the face of rejection. He will also speak of the coming at the Parousia of Jesus-Wisdom, Son of Man, as apocalyptic judge.

Metaphor and Hypostasis

Second Temple and tannaitic literature, then, provide many examples of the metaphor of Lady Wisdom. One perceives a variety of roles attributed to Lady Wisdom. Some are the domestic roles customarily assigned to women, such as daughter, wife, mother, lover, nurse, householder. Others, however, are public roles usually assigned to men, such as prophet, teacher. *All* of this is contained in the vehicle (the more familiar element) of the metaphor Lady Wisdom, that is, "Lady" (or Woman).

The content — the tenor — of the metaphor is wisdom. It includes one or more of the following referents: the order of creation, the social order, apocalyptic mysteries, Torah. Earlier we observed that the interactive nature of metaphor joins the semantic fields of vehicle and tenor. Thus, in the context of the metaphor as it occurs in these materials, one cannot understand "Wisdom" without "Woman" or "Woman" without "Wisdom." And the specific nature of this metaphor as personification means that it renders concrete what would ordinarily be abstract — that is, wisdom — and calls attention to the unity of the whole.

The sages use the vehicle's roles to convey the nature of the content wisdom. As God's daughter, Lady Wisdom is clearly dependent on and subordinate to God. As mother and nurse, she is creative and nurturing of life, the life of the cosmos and that of the social order. As prophet, Lady Wisdom calls people to repentance and teaches them how to live. She is stern disciplinarian. Paradoxically, she is also the source of rest and delight.

The quest for wisdom engages the student/sage on the imaginative and affective levels as well as the intellectual level. As lover, Lady Wisdom is object of the sage's passion. Because she is wife, a relationship with her is enduring. Because of her relationship to God, Lady Wisdom can mediate revelation, understanding, intimacy with the divine to the sage. In other words, as God's daughter, God's wife, and lover of God as well as of the sage, Lady Wisdom enjoys a particular intimacy with God and can thus introduce the sage into similar intimacy with the divine. The relationship among God, Lady Wisdom, and the sage is the locus of knowledge and understanding.

The semantic field of the metaphor conveys Wisdom's nature as being on the one hand transcendent, sometimes hidden or withdrawing, and on the other as revealed, accessible through prayer, study, knowledge of the cosmic order, and discipline.

Can we speak of "hypostasis" in reference to Lady Wisdom? That is, has the metaphor acquired the quality of personal entity?[98] Admittedly, it is not clear whether some texts — particularly those in which the representation is attenuated — represent solely a literary personification, or whether Wisdom there has a kind of quasi-independent existence. But it would appear that in most texts the metaphorical process has gone beyond personification. There, Wisdom has acquired the property of a personal entity, thus rendering concrete God's wisdom.[99]

Has the result been a separate divinity? It is difficult to establish clear boundaries between personification, hypostasis, and divinity.[100] Certainly most of our texts would subordinate Wisdom to the God of Israel. Lady Wisdom is *God's* wisdom. There is no direct literary evidence that Lady Wisdom was a separate divinity, no trace of cult or iconography. Nor do these traditions propose "Lady Wisdom" as an equivalent to "God of Israel."[101] Nonetheless, certain features suggest that for some Jews Lady Wisdom was indeed a separate divinity,[102] hence the frequency with which the authors insist on Wisdom's subordinate position. Moreover, Job and Baruch hint of earlier traditions that held that Wisdom was not only pre-existent but *independent* of God.[103] But in most of our texts Lady Wisdom plays an intermediary role while at the same time possessing both origin and continued existence in dependence on God. And it is very possible that the insistence on the subordination of Wisdom, the awareness that Woman Wisdom is *God's* wisdom, may indeed echo a polemic against a cult to a goddess Wisdom.[104]

The metaphor, the hypostasis of Lady Wisdom, bears an implied narrative. As we have observed, Wisdom is divine and therefore hidden. Thus she must be both revealed by God *and* sought actively by the human person. Wisdom revealed is described variously as either accepted or rejected. Accepted, Wisdom takes her dwelling place among humankind. Rejected, she returns to her heavenly dwelling. And the rejection of Wisdom results in judgment.

Insofar as the metaphor of Lady Wisdom indeed implies a narrative, we can speak of a Wisdom myth.[105] Jewish writers did not use mythical imagery in a naive manner, however. Rather, they used it reflectively to respond to certain basic questions.[106] Mythical language became a vehicle for theological speculation.[107]

One must be careful in speaking of a Wisdom myth. We are dealing with a *composite* picture, for individual documents and traditions deal with the individual elements in various ways, and more or less completely. However, taken as a whole, we might say that this "myth" provided a vehicle for reflection on questions crucial to Israel's existence, particularly after the Exile, during the suffering of the Maccabean era and that of the first century, culminating in the fall of the Second Temple.

People asked, "How did the world come to be?" "How does the human person know God and the divine will, and thus respond?" "Why does evil happen to Israel?" The writers using the Wisdom myth would have answered: The world comes to be because God creates through Wisdom-Torah. God is known, and the divine will is understood, through the revelation of pre-existent Wisdom (Torah). The individual, as well as the community, knows God and understands God's will, responding to it by receiving Wisdom as a gift and actively pursuing it.[108] Evil happens to Israel because Israel rejects Wisdom.

The imagery objectifies and distances Wisdom from the human person, and it emphasizes the difficulty in finding knowledge or understanding of God.[109] However, the terms of that imagery (bride, daughter, mother, mistress, teacher) equally suggest intimacy and affective attraction. Wisdom is not only free, transcendent, and difficult to find, but she is near as nurturer, lover, wife, and instructor, engaging the commitment of those who seek her. Although free gift, she is also the sure reward of those who engage themselves in quest of her.

The metaphor Lady Wisdom serves to articulate and respond to a number of questions regarding cosmogony, revelation, and theodicy. She reflects the influence of the cult of Isis during the Hellenistic age.[110] Hellenistic sources call Isis "mother of all" and describe her as active in creation.[111] In Palestine, she was identified with Astarte, which may have lent the erotic quality in some portrayals of Lady Wisdom.[112]

Isis is lawgiver.[113] Moreover, she is the wise one who possesses knowledge (*eidēnai*) and understanding (*epistēmē*).[114] And she is associated with abstract titles, like Righteousness (*dikaiosynē*), Wise (*sophēn*), and Prudent (*phronimēn*).[115] Texts such as Proverbs 8 and Sirach 24 suggest a polemic against the Isis cult, but the impact of assuming the Isis myth to describe divine Wisdom far exceeds the function of polemics. Our examination of the Wisdom texts suggests that use of the Isis myth allowed for a new range of categories in which Israel could pose questions of God's relationship to creation and to humankind.

The interactive nature of the metaphor Lady Wisdom brings together two otherwise separate fields of meaning, woman and wisdom. In the texts in which Lady Wisdom appears, the metaphorical process has so joined the vehicle (woman) with the tenor (wisdom) that the two are inseparable. Thus, in these texts, if one would know what wisdom is, one must look to woman. And if one would know what woman is, one must look to wisdom. The ways in which the metaphor Lady Wisdom brings together vehicle and tenor will be significant for our discussion of Matthew's portrayal of Jesus as Wisdom. As we shall see, that portrait will include many of the elements found in earlier appearances of Lady Wisdom. And Matthew will use the Wisdom metaphor to articulate his understanding not only of Jesus, but of revelation, history, divine immanence, and transcendence.

The Social Nature of Metaphor

The metaphor Lady Wisdom is most adequately understood under the broader categories of symbol and myth, which are inherently social in nature. They order experience.[116] Sacred symbols and religion express a community's or group's values, what it fears and hates.[117] They function to synthesize a people's ethos — the tone, character, and quality of their life, its moral and aesthetic style and mood and their worldview — the picture they have of the way things are.[118]

But symbol works in another direction as well. Not only does it express a community's reality, but it also shapes and transforms that reality.[119] Symbol and myth portray values "not as subjective human preferences but as the imposed conditions for life implicit in a world with a particular structure."[120]

Myth is, in a profound sense, a "plan of action" for a given society.[121] That is, it tells a community what it needs to know about cosmic and collective origins, the community's gods, history, laws, and class structure.[122] Myth actually serves to legitimate the socially constructed world of the everyday by describing the social order as reflecting the divine.[123]

Increasing development of the mythological — and, eventually, theological — tradition implies socially segregated subuniverses of meaning and concomitant institutional segmentation.[124] Specific groups within the collective whole transmit the community's religious tradition, its sacred symbols.[125] Members of those groups occupy a particular place in the community's social structure.

The evolution of more complex forms of knowledge requires the development of a cadre of experts who will devote themselves full-time to the development and transmission of knowledge in their respective areas. Thus, the development of specialized knowledge requires a certain level of division of labor.[126]

Lady Wisdom and the Sages

The literary evidence suggests that the metaphor of Lady Wisdom and its implied myth emerged from the learned class, those cadres of experts engaged in the transmission of the community's tradition. With the exception of Job, all our texts refer explicitly to scholars or sages. Some are attributed to scribes (e.g., Baruch, *2 Apoc. Baruch*, 4 Ezra, *1 Enoch*). Others describe the wise person, or *sophos* (Wisdom of Solomon, Philo). Then there are those texts attributed to Solomon, the wise man *par excellence* (Proverbs, Wisdom of Solomon). Finally, many of the texts describe the teacher and the pedagogical process (Sirach, Qumran, rabbinical texts).

Our texts indicate that not only did the metaphor serve to articulate the class's religious questions, but it also exercised a social function. That is, it both reflected and legitimated the role of the scholar and sage in Jewish society. The metaphor functioned in this way directly, through the explicit association of Wisdom with the sage's instruction. And it functioned indirectly through parallels between the figure of Lady Wisdom and that of the sage. This is true of the metaphor as it functioned in Second Temple and tannaitic literature, and in its usage in Matthew's gospel.

At this point we shall examine the ways in which our texts reflect the sages' role(s). I do not attempt a thorough discussion of the roles of scholar and teacher in the Second Temple and tannaitic eras — that would require its own book-length study.[127] Rather, I shall attend to those aspects of the matter which illuminate our understanding of the metaphor Lady Wisdom and/or pertain to the ways in which Matthew uses the metaphor and describes the teaching function of Jesus and the disciples.

The Sage's Invitation and Exhortation

Some texts describe the teacher as inviting or exhorting people to study with him, for example, the sage's exhortations to heed his instruction in the Book of Proverbs.[128] The Sirach 51 acrostic includes the sage's invitation, "Draw near to me, you who are uneducated, and lodge in the house of instruction" (51:23). And, in 4Q185, the speaker exhorts the community: "And now listen, my people, pay attention to me" (1.13–14).

In Proverbs and Sirach, the sage's invitation or exhortation is paralleled by those of Lady Wisdom.[129] In Proverbs 1–9, the context of Lady Wisdom's speeches which directly precede or follow those of the sage suggest that her speeches support the sage's. Clearly, for the authors Lady Wisdom is closely associated, if not identified with, the sage's teaching.[130]

In other instances the association between Lady Wisdom and the sage's instruction is less explicit. Proverbs contains a number of parallels between Lady Wisdom and the sage. Lady Wisdom's message is associated with security, life, and longevity, as is the teacher's instruction.[131] She addresses the simple,[132] and she uses the teacher's address "my child."[133] Her words are righteous.[134] Indeed, they are of incomparable worth, far more valuable than jewels or precious metals.[135] Wisdom enters the heart,[136] the depths of a person's being and the seat of understanding.[137] She confers wealth and happiness,[138] and offers adornment to the person — crown, garland, necklace.[139] And if reward and life are associated with heeding Lady Wisdom's message, then death and disaster are the consequences of ignoring it.[140] In all of these aspects, the description of Lady Wisdom parallels that of the teacher.

Ben Sira also associates Lady Wisdom with the sage's teaching. Sir. 24:30–34 implies that Lady Wisdom who is God's Word present at creation and among the people Israel, identified with Torah, is accessible through the sage's instruction.[141] The author of the appendix makes this explicit: "I have opened my mouth and spoken about her. Acquire for yourselves wisdom without silver" (51:25).[142] Moreover, Ben Sira tells us that the one who seeks Lady Wisdom submits to a discipline precisely in the study of Torah with the sages.[143] Wisdom (*ḥokmâh*) and Discipline (*mūsâr*)are associated, if not identified, both with Torah and the sage's instruction.

Three texts that speak of Wisdom's withdrawal also associate wisdom with the figure of the teacher. *1 Enoch* identifies Enoch's teaching, the revelation made to him, as "wisdom" (37:2, 82:1–6, 92:1). 4 Ezra does not identify the metaphor Lady Wisdom with the sage's teaching. Nonetheless, it presents Ezra as possessing wisdom and understanding.[144] Those instructed by Ezra will in turn become a source of wisdom for the community (14:47). *2 Apoc. Baruch* associates Torah with Wisdom.[145] He commissions his successors, who will be the guides to the future life assured by Torah observance.[146]

In the context of these documents, the metaphor Lady Wisdom serves three functions. It reassures the readers that, despite its apparent inaccessibility, wisdom can be found;[147] it suggests that wisdom is accessible in the scribe's teaching;[148] and it legitimates the teaching presented.

Later discussion will indicate that Matthew presents Jesus-Wisdom as inviting and exhorting would-be disciples. It will suggest that Matthew associates the Wisdom metaphor with Jesus' teaching and with the ongoing scribal function in his community.

Learning as Relationship

The sources describe the process of learning in the context of a relationship between sage and disciple and frequently allude to that relationship in parental language, recalling the fact that Lady Wisdom sometimes occurs in the role of mother. This is evident in Proverbs, where the sage addresses his students in parental terms, as we noted above. He speaks of himself as "father," and speaks also of a "mother" (1:8, 5:20).

Parental language also occurs in Qumran texts. The Damascus Document says, "He [the Guardian] shall love them as a father loves his children" (CD 13.9–10). The *maskîl* likens himself to a father and a wet-nurse (1QH 7.20–22). The imagery alludes to the discipline, nurturance, and tenderness associated with the roles of parent and teacher.[149] And it reflects an understanding of the instructional role that is both personal and affective.[150]

The tannaitic sage is father to his disciples, and they are his "sons."[151] The sages believed that just as a father gives life in this world, so the sage brings the students to life in the world-to-come.[152] And because Torah represents life not only in this world but in the world-to-come, there are instances when the sage's rights precede those of the birth-father (*m. B. Meṣ.* 2:11).[153]

The use of paternal language reflects the sage's understanding of his role. As we have seen, wisdom, contained in the teacher's instruction, is associated — even identified with — life.[154] So the teacher becomes a father (or mother) in a metaphorical sense, giving those under his or her tutelage the life of wisdom.

Finally, the teacher describes himself as a "father" because it is his task to give *mûsār*. *Mûsār* can indeed signify "instruction"; however, its primary meaning is "discipline." It can also mean "physical discipline." It was the father's duty to discipline an unruly child, and the teacher reinforced instruction with the stick.[155] The sage considers himself "father" because he exercises the father's role of instruction and discipline.

The sources, then, reflect a relational understanding of teaching through their use of parental language. But they reflect that understanding in other ways as well. They tell us of the ways in which sages taught and disciples learned. For example, Philo tells us that the good teacher is not so concerned with giving the pupil all that he can, but with giving what the pupil needs and is able to receive. Thus, "the teacher comes down to the learner and attentively studies him as one with whom he is intimately concerned" (*Post* 142ff.).[156]

The tannaim clearly understand the sage's function in relational terms. The sage delivers his instructions in formal classes, of course. But the disciple learns Torah equally from constant companionship with and attendance upon the sage. Thus, the disciples hear "words of Torah" and see them embodied in the life of the sage in all possible situations in daily life: at meals (*Sifre Deut.* 38; 41), visiting the master while he was sick (*Sifre Deut.* 32) or dying (*'Abot R. Nat. a* 25), visiting the sage to console him on the loss of his son (*'Abot R. Nat. a* 14), traveling with him as he journeyed on his ass through the countryside (*Sifre Deut.* 305; *t. Ḥag* 2:1), watching a wedding procession (*'Abot R. Nat. a* 4). The disciple might even sleep under his master's bed (*m. Sukk.* 2:1). Indeed one expression for "study" is "to serve the sages" (*shămôsh ḥŏkāmîm*).[157]

Constant attendance upon the sage provides the disciple not only with the opportunity to hear the sage's instruction under the widest possible variety of circumstances. It also allows the disciple to observe the sage's *actions*, for the sage is a "living Torah." His gestures and actions become a source of Torah instruction.[158]

The understanding of learning in the context of a relationship will be significant for Matthew. In the framework of his use of the Wisdom metaphor, this is most apparent in the invitation (11:28–30), and in the use of maternal imagery in the lament over Jerusalem (23:37–39).

The Sage

Prophet

Many of our texts associate the sage with prophecy as they do Lady Wisdom.[159] Ben Sira speaks of his own work, saying that he "will again pour out teaching like prophecy" (24:33).[160] He tells us that the scholar meditates on God's mysteries under the guidance of God's spirit (39:6–8). The prophetic tone of his words suggests that for Ben Sira the scribe has succeeded to the prophets.[161]

Moreover, the Qumran documents speak of the *maskîl*'s task in prophetic terms.[162] Thus, the *maskîl* describes his call in ways that recall the great prophets of Israel's past, Jeremiah and Isaiah: "For Thou hast known me from (the time of) my father (and hast chosen me) from the womb. (From the belly of) my mother Thou hast dealt kindly with me" (1QH 9.29–31).[163] Then he tells us that he is to "rebuke the creature of clay for his ways." He is to be a messenger of God's goodness "that to the humble he might bring glad tidings of thy great mercy, [proclaiming salvation] from out of the fountain [of holiness to the contrite] of spirit and everlasting joy to those who mourn" (1QH 18.10–15).[164] He is to care for community members and "shall carry them in all their distress like a shepherd his sheep" (CD 13.9–10).[165] Finally, laments such as 1QH 5.32–39 recall not simply the Psalms of lament, but also prophetic texts such as Jer. 15:10–21, 17:14–18, 18:19–23, and 20:7–18.

1 Enoch 12–14 suggests the prophetic quality of the seer's function by using the prophetic commissioning form.[166] Furthermore, the texts associate Enoch with some of the same concerns one meets in classical prophecy: social justice (94:6–11, 96:4–8, 98:1ff.), blasphemy (96:4–8), idolatry (46:7), sexual mores (8:2), magic (8:3, 94:1), and warfare (8:1, 52:8–9). Finally, the author of chapters 92–105 uses literary forms common in the prophets, as well as expressions such as "know," "be it known," "I say to you," and "I swear to you." All of this suggests that the authors of the pertinent texts and the final redactor(s) are presenting their message as revelation.[167] Once again, the seer and his teaching are legitimated. By associating Enoch with the prophets, the author not only makes a statement about the revelatory nature of that message but also places it in continuity with tradition.[168]

The tannaitic sage's position in the chain of tradition made of him a successor to the prophets, for Moses was not only the "wisest of the wise" (*ḥkm gdl shbgdlm*), but "father of the prophets" (*'b lnbi'm, 'Abot R. Nat. a* 1).[169] Certainly, the sages *act* like prophets. Shimeon b. Shetah, for example, challenges the political establishment.[170] The sources attribute prophetic activity to Hillel (*t. Soṭa* 13:3) and Shmuel the Small (*t. Soṭa* 13:4) — they "are designated by the Holy Spirit" (*r'ûi lruaḥ hqôdsh*). Indeed, it is said that the latter foretold on his deathbed the martyrdom of R. Ishmael and R. Simeon (*t. Soṭa* 13:4). R. Gamaliel II even makes a halachic decision through prophecy (*t. Pesaḥ.* 1:27).[171]

Chapters 3 and 4 will indicate that Matthew also understands the sage's function to be prophetic. This will be apparent not only in his portrayal of Jesus-Wisdom, but in his description of the disciples.

Visionary

Many of our texts present sages as visionaries. For example, the *Songs of the Sabbath Sacrifice*, which are attributed to the *maskîl*, describe the heavenly sanctuary, its angelic priesthood, and their worship.[172] The Sabbath Songs appear to be intended to induce in the community a sense of presence in the heavenly Temple and to allow them to unite themselves to the angelic worship.[173] All of this is reminiscent of the references to angelic presence in other Qumran texts.[174]

Philo believes that Sophia, wisdom, is indeed a God-given illumination, perception. And the passion with which Philo speaks of the sage's relationship to Lady Wisdom, as well as his description of the sage's illumination, suggests that the sage is a mystic, an ecstatic.[175] Philo tells us that he himself is often "god-possessed" (*theolēpteisthai, Cher.* 27).[176] He says that, even beset by community concerns, he is "irradiated by the light of wisdom" as he studies the sacred texts and he thanks God for that gift (*Spec.* 3.6). Philo describes an ecstasy that implies departure from body, senses, speech, from the soul and the mind itself.[177] Indeed, he describes the experience of heavenly ascent.[178]

In *1 Enoch* the description of Wisdom's descent and withdrawal occurs in the context of the account of Enoch's ascent to the heavenly throne room in which he sees the secrets of the cosmos (*1 Enoch* 39:3; chaps. 41, 43–44).[179] And in Book 1 appears the account in 14:8–16:3.

The visions of ascent, throne, and chariot link Enoch to visionary elements of the prophetic tradition in their reliance on Isaiah 6, Ezekiel 1–2, 8, 40–48, and, in the case of the vision in Book 2, Daniel 7.[180] But a number of features also recall the accounts of the burning bush and of Sinai, for example, references to the divine glory, fire, cloud, the seer's altered face, an angelic or divine voice, a commissioning.[181]

In 60:10 and 71:14, Enoch is addressed as "Son of Man." These sources parallel the figure of Enoch, transported into the celestial realms, with the heavenly wisdom figure.[182] The ascent narratives provide the setting for Enoch's receiving instruction in "hidden things" (*1 Enoch* 60:10): the judgment of the Watchers (chapters 12–16), the secrets of the cosmos (chapters 41, 43–44, 60:7–25). These narratives serve to legitimate the teacher's instruction, demonstrating that the teaching is not Enoch's; it is *revealed* to him, and he is therefore a "mouthpiece" with heavenly authority.

It is possible that those who used *1 Enoch* regarded Enoch's visionary experience as a paradigm of their own.[183] *1 Enoch* 13:7–8 reflects practices such as gazing at water and reading a text to induce visionary experience. There Enoch induces a dream vision by sitting on a riverbank and reading the Watchers' prayers.[184]

Tannaitic sources suggest that some of the tannaim were seers who engaged in *Merkabah* speculation. Amoraic as well as tannaitic sources associate Johanan ben Zakkai and his disciples, especially Eleazar ben Arak,[185] with *Merkabah* traditions.[186] Particularly relevant for our study is the material commenting on *m. Ḥag* 2:1, which restricts the expounding or exegeting of certain biblical texts (Leviticus 18; Genesis 1; Ezekiel 1 and possibly 10). These sources contain several passages that show the master with one or more disciples.[187] All contain elements of the visionary, and all contain Sinai-Moses typology in reference to the sages and their disciples.

In the first of these accounts, R. Johanan b. Zakkai is journeying with R. Eleazar b. Arak, his disciple. With Johanan ben Zakkai's permission, Eleazar interprets the "Work of the Chariot" (Ezekiel 1). Fire descends from heaven, and the trees begin to praise God (*b. Ḥag* 14b).[188] An angel out of the fire confirms Eleazar's discourse. Johanan ben Zakkai blesses Eleazar ben Arak's interpretation and acknowledges him.[189]

In another account, R. Johanan recounts a dream (keep in mind that "dream" is the equivalent of "vision"),[190] where he is reclining at a banquet on Mount Sinai. A *bat qôl* invites him and his disciples to ascend higher (*b. Ḥag* 14b). The invitation echoes God's invitation to Moses, "Come up to me on the mountain" (Exod. 24:12).

And finally, in the Palestinian Talmud is the story of R. Eliezer and R. Joshua, present at the circumcision of Elisha ben Abuyah. When the other guests exhibit unseemly behavior, the two sages withdraw and begin to study together. Fire descends from heaven and surrounds them. The two sages say, "The words were as alive as when they were given from Mount Sinai. And the fire shone around us as it shone from Mount Sinai" (*j. Ḥag* 2:1). The account links the study of Torah to Sinai by naming the mountain of revelation, as well as the fire that descended upon it (Exod. 19:18). A tradition of visionary experience articulated in Sinai typology is, then, associated with R. Johanan ben Zakkai and his disciples, which lends authority to their interpreting Torah by forming a metaphorical "chain of tradition." In addition, miracles possibly suggest that R. Johanan and his disciples have "inherited the mantle of Moses."[191]

Tannaitic — and later, amoraic — involvement in mystical speculation, or the attribution of such involvement to those sages, served a social function. It signaled "the 'charisma' of this newly formed class of spiritual leaders."[192] Ecstatic experience legitimates the authority of those who have access to heavenly realities and therefore possess information not available to those who are not adepts, whether other sages or general populace.

Visionary experience is a component of the sage's activity according to many early Jewish sources. The significance of this for Matthew's portrait of Jesus-Wisdom and his disciples will become clear in chapters 3 and 4.

Hymnist

As noted earlier, in 11QPsa 18 Lady Wisdom appears as a hymnist. This finds its parallel in the sages' activity as composer of hymns. Ben Sira exhorts his audience to join him in praising God and then proffers his long hymn of praise (39:12–43:33).[193] The author of Wisdom of Solomon has the sage make a prayer of petition for the gift of wisdom (9:1–18). The seer of *1 Enoch*, in his ascent to the heavens, praises God, joining his praise to that of the heavenly beings (*1 Enoch* 39:11–14).[194]

Furthermore, the *maskîl* of Qumran recites hymns of several kinds. The long hymn in 1QS 9.20–11.22 likely served as a model for hymns that the *maskîl* was to recite twice daily, as well as at the beginning and end of each month (10.1–5). The *hôdāyôt*, of uncertain authorship but ascribed by many to the Teacher of Righteousness, are characterized by the themes of salvation and knowledge.[195] It is not known what function these hymns served. The Sabbath Songs, assigned to the *maskîl*, appear to be liturgical hymns, through which the community members, under the *maskîl*'s leadership, united themselves with the angelic liturgy.[196] They thereby legitimated their sectarian priestly status. The mantra-like nature of these hymns suggests that community members may possibly have used them to induce trance.

Philo describes the worship of the Therapeutics. After the leader expounded on a matter pertaining to scripture and just before the ritual foods were brought in, the head of the congregation led the members in taking turns singing hymns. He might have sung one of his own compositions or a traditional hymn. Presumably the members had a similar freedom of choice (*Cont.* 80–81). After the ritual meal, the whole congregation sang hymns and sometimes broke into dance. This was a night-long vigil which Philo likened to the ecstasy (*enthousiōntes*) of those who sang at the Red Sea under Moses and Miriam's leadership (87). It would appear, then, that the Therapeutics used singing and dancing as means to altered states of consciousness.

The relevance of this material for Matthew will be apparent in his description of Jesus, Wisdom and Sage, as reciting a hymn of thanksgiving for revealed knowledge.

Wonder-Worker

Some of our texts portray the sage as wonder-worker, yet another way in which to legitimate the sage's authority.[197] At Qumran, the *maskîl* seems to have been an exorcist, for he proclaims

> the majesty of his beauty to frighten and ter[rify] all the spirits of the destroying angels and the spirits of the bastards, the demons, Lilith, the howlers (?)...they who strike suddenly to lead astray the spirit of understanding and to appal their heart. (4Q 510)[198]

The *maskîl*'s access to esoteric knowledge allowed him to offer community members protection against demonic powers.[199] Freedom from demons and power over them, as well as companionship with heavenly spirits, characterize the holy man during the Hellenistic period and late antiquity.[200] The *maskîl*'s role as exorcist was thus a counterpart to his role as leader in the worship articulated in the Sabbath Songs.[201]

Philo describes, in cautious terms, Moses as wonder-worker. As king, Moses is God's "fellow" — he enjoys *koinōnia* with the Divine. In that context he is a wonder-worker; he is God's friend, in the terms of a Stoic sage (*Mos.* 1.156), and thus shares that which belongs to God. Philo does not, however, signal wonder-working as demonstrating Moses' superiority. Rather, that superiority is due to his excellence in virtue and wisdom (1.148, 154).[202] It is, moreover, related to the cosmic nature of Moses' rule, a notion influenced by the Cynic-Stoic understanding of the philosopher-king. Accordingly, "Philo says that God gave Moses *ton plouton tēs physeōs*, i.e., mastery over *physis*, which the Stoics conceived of materialistically."[203]

In *2 Apoc. Baruch* there is no account of a heavenly ascent or reference to any kind of transformation of the seer. Instead, when Baruch asks God what will be the form of the living in the final times, he is told that their faces will be transformed and that miracles will "appear at their own time to those who are saved because of their works and for whom the Law is now a hope, and intelligence, expectation, and wisdom a trust" (51:3, 7). In the final times, then, *all* those faithful to Torah will experience apocalyptic transformation and become wonder-workers.

Tannaitic sources reflect little concern for miracle working and/or exorcism.[204] There are some exceptions.[205] For example, Honi the Circle-Drawer prayed for rain for his people — a prayer that was answered.[206] Hanina ben Dosa prayed for the healing of the son of Johanan ben Zakkai and the boy, healed at a distance, lived.[207] The request for rain and the healing powers recall the figure of Elijah — despite Hanina's disclaimer. And the latter assumes the posture attributed to Elijah when he prays for Johanan ben Zakkai's son; he places his head between his knees.[208]

Many of our sources thus describe teachers as wonder-workers. Their deeds attest to their authority, for miracles are evidence of the "charisma" of spiritual leaders.[209] They demonstrate that the holy man is intimate with the divine world.[210] Matthew's Jesus will also exhibit the features of a wonder-worker. And the disciples commissioned by Jesus-Wisdom will receive authority to exercise similar powers.

The Sage's Authority:
Continuity with Tradition

The sage of late antiquity possessed authority only to the degree that he stood in a relationship of continuity with his tradition. Our texts express this in a variety of ways. In the Book of Proverbs, the teacher's instruction is legitimated by the fact that it stands in a line of tradition: "I give you good precepts: do not forsake my teaching" (4:2). He continues, "When I was a son with my father, tender, and my mother's favorite, he taught me, and said to me, 'Let your heart hold fast to my words; keep my commandments and live' " (Prov. 4:3–4). In other words, the sage's teaching has authority because he has received it from his predecessors.

Some texts express the sage's continuity with the tradition by describing him in language that recalls the figure of Moses. Thus, the author of 4 Ezra parallels Moses when he describes Ezra and his teaching.[211] For example, a voice from a bush calls Ezra twice by name (14:1–2), he spends forty days apart from the people (vv. 23, 37), and receives a "new Law" — the twenty-four books and the seventy books (vv. 43–48).

The author(s) of 2 *Apoc. Baruch* also legitimate the teaching and leadership of Baruch by likening him to Moses. The parallels between Moses and Baruch are perhaps clearest and most focused in chapter 84, part of Baruch's letter (chapters 78–86),[212] which recalls explicitly the renewal of the covenant by Moses in Deut. 33:19–20, calling on heaven and earth as witnesses (2 Bar. 84:2). Baruch instructs the people in "Babylon" to "learn my mighty commandments which he has instructed you" (84:1).[213] He tells the people to remember Moses' words about the consequences of fidelity and infidelity to Torah. Baruch, as Moses, is both intermediary and intercessor. Following visionary experiences he brings instruction back to the people. It seems clear that in paralleling Baruch with Moses the authors have vested Baruch the apocalyptic prophet-scribe with authority over Torah.

Tannaitic sages express the continuity between themselves and the past by describing the process of Torah study as repeating the experience of Sinai. And so it was said that the student was to sit in the dust at his master's feet and listen to his words "with awe, fear, dread, and trembling — the way our fathers received (the Torah) from Mount Sinai" (*'Abot R. Nat. a* 6).

The sage could also claim authority, or his students and successors could claim that authority for him, by invoking the chain of tradition, that is, by placing his teaching in the context of his teachers'.[214] Ultimately, that chain makes the sage the successor to the prophets, and even to Moses himself (*'Abot* 1:1; *'Abot R. Nat. a* 1). Sinai is the ultimate starting point of the chain of tradition, and the sage claims its authority by locating himself in that lineage.[215]

Matthew will place Jesus-Wisdom and his disciples in a chain of tradition, and use the framework of Moses and Sinai imagery to describe teaching authority. Thus the redactor will claim authority for them by establishing their continuity with the tradition and with the sources of revelation.

The Sages and Their Social Settings

Speaking in the most general terms, one can say that the sages occupied a relatively high status. To be sure, they were not all born into the upper classes.[216] But, generally speaking, the sages were involved in advanced study of their tradition, a work that required specialized training and some access to written material, an expensive commodity in the Greco-Roman world.[217] Moreover, that work required *time*. Little wonder that Ben Sira believed that only a person of independent means could become a sage (Sir. 38:24).

Some would have been quite affluent. Ben Sira provides us with a case in point. He recommends travel, which permits the widest possible range of experiences, thereby allowing the sage to study human behavior and interpret the tradition.[218] Manual labor, Ben Sira tells us, does not allow for the leisure necessary to pursue serious study. The sage, then, must be from the upper classes — an aristocrat, priest, or retainer.[219]

In the Wisdom of Solomon the sage's knowledge and instruction encompass not only Jewish tradition, but also the full range of scientific and philosophical learning (7:14–22) — "ontology, cosmology, physics, astronomy, biology, botany, esoteric knowledge."[220] Given the content of the instruction to which the texts alludes, it is likely, though not certain, that the author speaks to an educated and presumably affluent audience, probably in Alexandria.[221] The setting of that instruction might be private or public.[222]

Some of the sages belonged to the retainer class, and thus to that group serving the ruler and the governing class in "a variety of more or less specialized capacities."[223] Ben Sira, for example, implies that study of proverbs functions as a training in reasoning with public service as its goal (8:8–9, 18:28–29). Public service likely meant involvement in government bureaucracy, possibly as a jurist in a tribunal under the Seleucid administration.[224]

Ben Sira's frequent references and allusions to the priesthood suggest that he was a priest.[225] Membership in the priestly class would have meant belonging to a group favored for administrative and judicial appointment under the Ptolemies and Seleucids, and thus would have allowed him to pursue a scholar's role.[226]

Ben Sira was not the only member of a learned group to act as a retainer. Josephus's descriptions of the Pharisees most often place them in relation to the governing class, as well as to the people at large.[227] Some of the tannaim appear to have been members of the retainer class as well. Certainly by the middle of the third century C.E. many of their number had assumed the role of village administrator, "with general responsibility for the oversight of village affairs, in particular finances, including the distribution of public charity and the supervision of building projects."[228] Their salaries came not from public funds but from the patriarch.[229]

The sources suggest that tannaitic sages came from a wide spectrum of socioeconomic backgrounds. Some were priests.[230] Others, such as R. Simeon, were from wealthy families.[231] And still others, such as R. Akiba and R. Eliezer ben Hyrcanus, came from impoverished backgrounds.[232] The priests among the sages would have received tithes.[233] Most, however, appear to have come from the artisan, peasant, and retainer classes. They would have farmed or practiced a trade or profession part of the time and devoted the rest of their time to study.

The sources indicate that some considered concern with "worldly matters" (derek 'ereṣ) to be inappropriate to the sage ('Abot R. Nat. a 1). Others, such as the wealthy R. Gamaliel, son of Jehudah ha-Nasi, advised study along with worldly occupation — presumably even when not financially necessary — for "toil in them both puts sin out of mind" ('Abot 2:2).

At times we perceive the tension between the call to study and the all-too-real demand of earning a living. Disciple and sage were reminded to make Torah primary and worldly occupation secondary ('Abot R. Nat. a 28). Simeon ben Yohai queried plaintively, "There is no end to it. If one harvests at harvest time, ploughs at ploughing time, threshes in the hot season, and winnows in the windy season, when can one (find time to) study Torah?" (Sifre Deut. 42).

The sages' and disciples' involvement in "worldly occupations" explains the "many traditions which tell of the gathering of the disciples in the evenings, on the sabbath and on festivals."[234] Beyond the concern for earning a living, however, was the fact that sages and their disciples sometimes served as administrators and bureaucrats, both for the Jewish community and for the Roman provincial government. In other words, some of the sages formed the retainer class.[235] This is not surprising. The sages and disciples' education, their ability to read well and often write, made them fitting candidates for public service. The sages and disciples, then, often were engaged in some form of labor outside of Torah study for financial necessity, service to the community, and as a fitting balance to study. However, it would appear that even scholars who refused reimbursement for instruction accepted hospitality when on a journey (Sifre Deut. 1).[236]

The texts in which the metaphor of Lady Wisdom appears, then, reflect a relatively elevated social status in which members were highly literate. They were often from the priestly class and/or served as retainers. Some, to be sure, were from economically poor backgrounds. But the very fact of acquiring the learning reflected in these sophisticated texts suggests that those involved had access to a degree of upward mobility unusual in traditional societies.[237]

The setting of advanced instruction seems to have been varied.[238] Schools may have existed at court or in the Temple. And there is evidence for instruction taking place in synagogues[239] or in sages' homes.[240] In more hellenized settings, it might occur under the guidance of a private tutor in the student's home.[241]

Almost always, Israelite and Jewish sages appear to have been male. There are exceptions, of course: the women sages behind the early strata of Proverbs 1–9,[242] the Therapeutae,[243] and the wife of Rabbi Meir, called Beruriah in Amoraic sources.[244] Among the Qumran texts, 1QSa 1.4–11 refers explicitly to the instruction of women.[245] Certain of the pseudepigraphical texts suggest that women visionaries had received the sort of training required for apocalyptic visions,[246] and that some women, particularly among the upper classes, were highly educated. In certain instances, it seems, women formed part of the learned classes, or learned groups with recognizable social functions or lifestyles. For the most part, however, those groups were dominated by men.

The personification of Wisdom as a *woman* reflects something about women's roles as wives, mothers, daughters, and lovers, and so on. It may also reflect their presence as prophets and learned women. Does the evidence indicate that the metaphor originated with women, sages or otherwise? Could that metaphor have acted to empower them in their study and/or in their religious quest? While the answer to these questions is a tentative "possibly," there is nothing in the material available to allow more than speculation.

Predominantly, male social contexts — the scribal or scholarly groups — provide the literary evidence for use of the metaphor. The texts available to us reflect that metaphor as it was used by males. The metaphor, occurring as it does in frequently erotic terms, conveys to a male audience the nature of the quest for wisdom as intimate, engaging the depths of human affectivity. And it implies that intimacy with Wisdom will also bring the person into intimacy with God.[247] Finally, the use of a *female* personification allows the sages, members of a patriarchal social structure and an overwhelmingly, usually exclusively, male teaching class, to bring the female into themselves through use of erotic language and thereby to appropriate it.[248] That process means that it is primarily male scribes who mediate female Lady Wisdom for the community.

The texts say nothing of the ways in which the metaphor of Lady

Wisdom may have impacted on actual women. Many of these texts, such as Proverbs and Sirach, were originally addressed to male circles. Through the canonization process, however, some of the texts acquired a broader audience. And the texts suggest women's presence in some learned groups. Thus the metaphor would have been familiar to some women. Is it possible that even though male learned groups subverted the metaphor to their own ends, it still might have enhanced women's understanding of their roles as wives, mothers, counselors, prophets, and teachers? Or would the metaphor, in its insistence on the sage as the one who unites with Lady Wisdom, have served further to exclude women?[249] Examination of the relevant materials leads me to conclude that these questions must remain unanswered. It is most likely that the metaphor functioned according to context, sometimes positively in relationship to women's experience, and at other times negatively. While the portrayal of Lady Wisdom in our texts certainly reflects the many roles women exercised in late Israelite and early Jewish society — including occasional public roles — it says nothing of the significance of the metaphor for their religious experience or of their understanding of their roles.

The Sages, Wisdom, and Language of the Margin

Given the relative affluence that characterized those belonging to learned classes, one is struck by the attitudes to material wealth in some of these texts,[250] and the language of humility and poverty in others.

Philo was a man of wealth and high social status, likely of the governing class.[251] Nonetheless, his ideal of the sage proffers an ascetical ideal and a critique of material wealth. He tells us that young Moses viewed luxury with scorn, preferring a frugal life.[252] Elsewhere, he describes the sage's life as marked by detachment from material possessions.[253] Philo's thoughts on the subject form part of his descriptions of the Essenes and the Therapeutae.[254] But Philo holds out to *all* who seek wisdom the challenge to renounce created things "on the ground of that intimate association with the Uncreated (*agenēton*), to possess whom, they are convinced, is the only wealth, the only gauge of consummate happiness" (*Plant.* 65–66). Such detachment is the result of being "enraptured by the beauty of Wisdom, as by that of some distinguished lady" (*Plant.* 65).[255]

Tannaitic sources, for the most part, do not suggest that wealth is undesirable, even for a sage, but it is to be shared with the poor. Certain traditions, however, associate Hillel with actual poverty.[256] And we are told that R. Eleazar of Modi'im held up R. Hanina ben Dosa as a model in his poverty and disdain for money (*Mek. Amalek* 4:63–70).[257] Other traditions recommend detachment from possessions.[258] One tradition tells us that satiety can lead to pride, self-sufficiency, and rebellion against God (*Sifre Deut.* 43). Some sources, moreover, associate the sages with asceticism regarding such matters as speech, the schedule of one's day, and eating habits.[259] And some students of the tannaitic era appear to have used a common fund, a practice possibly reflective of ascetical attitudes.[260]

Members of the Qumran community also held their goods in common.[261] They believed that material wealth was suspect and they described themselves in terms of poverty and lowliness.[262] Wealth, however, was not simply counter to the ascetical ideal. It characterized the enemy camp. The Habakuk pesher speaks of the Wicked Priest as having been corrupted by riches (1QpHab 8.10–11), as having robbed the Poor (1QpHab 12.10). Scribe and community behind *1 Enoch* 92–105 eschew material wealth as the product of violence and oppression.[263] And in chapters 92–108 unrighteousness is defined with respect to material wealth.

In the Qumran literature and in *1 Enoch*, it does not appear that poverty is to be taken literally, that is, to signify deprivation of the necessities. Indeed, a group that produced a written literature of the quantity and sophistication reflected in these texts would have required access to resources beyond those necessary for mere subsistence. Rather, poverty is to be taken in a relative sense as signifying *perceived* deprivation.[264] It functions as a boundary between the communities and sages of the texts and those of the opposing groups.

The language of poverty and lowliness is joined to wisdom vocabulary in some Second Temple traditions. For example, the founders of the Qumran community are called "men of discernment" (*nbônîm*) and "wise" (*ḥkmîm*, CD 6.2–3). The same terms are used in 1QSa 1.28–2.3 to refer to groups of leaders eligible for membership in the community council (1QSa 1.28–2.3). The community is characterized by wisdom and knowledge, and thus blessed by the sovereign Princes, that is, by the archangels (4Q403 1.1.1–29). Such qualities not only characterize the community, but are conditions for membership (1QH 8.12–13).[265]

At Qumran, as elsewhere in Second Temple literature, *anawim* language, the vocabulary of lowliness, came to signify an inner attitude. It did not, however, lose its social significance.[266] The Qumran community lived in a sectarian atmosphere, cut off from the majority of the Jewish community which it understood as unfaithful. The group defined itself over and against the broader community, in wisdom and *anawim* vocabulary or terms of humility and lowliness. The language of poverty, lowliness, and humility functioned with wisdom categories as boundary markers, setting the members over against those outside the community.

A number of Second Temple texts encourage an ideal of humility. Humility makes Ezra worthy to receive revelation. He compares himself to the unrighteous, an act of humility acknowledged by God as praiseworthy (4 Ezra 8:47–49). Ezra has forsaken his own ways in obedience to God, and in persistent study of Torah and in devotion to wisdom and understanding (13:53–55). Humility, wisdom, and devotion to Torah are interrelated. The true sage is marked not only by learning but by humility.[267]

Over against this ideal of humility one sees the Messiah condemning the enemy: "And you have judged the earth, but not with truth; for you have afflicted the meek and injured the peaceable; you have hated those who tell the truth, and have loved liars" (4 Ezra 11:41–42). One is reminded of the Qumran sect's description of its enemies. Not only the sages, but the entire community is characterized in terms of humility, meekness, truthfulness. They stand over against and are oppressed by the proud, exalted, deceitful.

The language of lowliness and humility functions in a sectarian manner in texts such as the Qumran literature and 4 Ezra. It also can reflect an ascetical ideal. The tannaim enjoin meekness and humility.[268] Torah is like wine — it keeps well only in the lowliest of vessels (*Sifre Deut.* 48). Even prophecy was contingent upon humility (*Sifre Deut.* 95).[269] A saying attributed to Ben Azzai advises, "Come down from where thou art two or three steps and take thy place: better is it for thee to be told to go up than to be told to come down" (*'Abot R. Nat. a* 25). And, when R. Simeon ben Gamaliel queries why he is being martyred by the Romans, R. Ishmael responds, "Perhaps when you sat holding a discourse on the Temple mount and all the force of Israel sat before you and your mind was proud."[270] Simeon acknowledges that this is the case and that martyrdom is punishment for his pride (*'Abot R. Nat. a* 38).

Certain tannaitic traditions refer to Moses as the paradigm of humility, citing Num. 12:3. Thus, in *'Abot R. Nat. a* 23, one finds a reference to this text inserted into the citation of *'Abot* 4:1. And, in *Mek. ba-Hodesh* 9:99–116 we read that Moses was allowed to enter the cloud on Sinai precisely because of his humility.

One finds in tannaitic sources frequent reminders, then, of the excellence of humility. These texts imply that humility is a hallmark of the true sage. However, they do not use it in the sectarian fashion found in other Second Temple materials.

Many Second Temple and tannaitic texts reflect an ascetical approach to material goods and use language of poverty and/or humility to describe the sages and their communities. And yet few among these people come from situations of physical deprivation. Indeed, findings from other contexts would suggest that poverty, asceticism, humility can be a religious response "only to those with some wealth to renounce."[271] The vocabulary of marginalization that characterizes many of these texts thus indicates origin in high or "solidly respectable, structural status."[272]

This language does not necessarily reflect *actual* powerlessness, at least on the perceptual level.[273] On the contrary, it reflects a highly stratified and hierarchical society in which the religiously powerful idealize poverty and humility. In such a society religious specialists may lead ascetical lives.[274] The language of powerlessness, then, is used in an ironic fashion. In the case of a millenarian sect like the Qumran community, it expresses the perception that community members are the ones in possession of the *real* power because they alone have access to the truth, to the divine. Such usage reverses the normal categories of contemporary social thought.[275] In the case of nonsectarian materials, such as Philo's *opus* or the rabbinic texts, use of such categories reflects the position of those who have *actual* power, religious, political, and — often — economic.

Our discussion of the sages' social locations and functions, as well as the relationship of the language of powerlessness to those factors, allows us to understand Matthew's portrayal of Jesus-Wisdom and his disciples as sages who are described in terms of deprivation, humility, and powerlessness.

Conclusion

The metaphor Lady Wisdom appears in a number of instances in Second Temple and tannaitic literature. She represents divine wisdom present in the cosmic and social orders, and appears in a variety of roles: teacher, prophet, householder, mother and nurse, lover, bride and wife, daughter. Each of those roles tells us something about the nature of Wisdom.

The metaphor emerged from learned circles in which sages spoke of themselves as being in continuity with their tradition. For the most part, they were upper-class males who expressed themselves in terms of status reversal. The erotic and parental language suggests that the sages understood themselves as enjoying the most intimate of relationships with Lady Wisdom. Ultimately Lady Wisdom is identified or associated with the sage's instruction, and the sage is ascribed roles that parallel those of Lady Wisdom. This leads one to believe that the metaphor served not only to articulate the sages' questions about cosmology, ethics, and revelation, but also to legitimate their functions by describing their role(s) as reflecting a divine order of things. That divine order included a predominantly male learned elite.

Chapter 2

Jesus as Wisdom

MATTHEW TRANSFORMS A METAPHOR

The metaphor of Lady Wisdom carries a wide range of meanings. But metaphor is tensive; it is able to expand to bear yet new meaning, as required by new situations and circumstances. Thus, early Christians used the metaphor of Wisdom to reflect on the significance of Jesus' life, work, death, and resurrection.[1] One sees evidence of this in Paul,[2] and it is present implicitly in Q.[3] John's Gospel likewise provides an example of early Christian usage,[4] and the Gospel of Thomas appears to have used it as well.[5]

Matthew also portrays Jesus as personified Wisdom, and describes him as sage.[6] In this chapter and in the following, we will turn to the Matthean Wisdom passages, keeping in mind the discussion in chapter 1. In other words, we will undertake a detailed exegesis of the relevant materials in their immediate and remote contexts, that is, the Gospel of Matthew as well as biblical, Second Temple, and tannaitic literature. While other studies have presented exegeses of these materials, examining the texts again will help us to arrive at a new perspective on the question of Matthew's portrait of Jesus-Wisdom.

In the present chapter we will suggest that Matthew presents Jesus as Wisdom by ascribing to Jesus qualities and roles attributed to Lady Wisdom in other Jewish sources. For example, Jesus is hidden and revealed, accepted and rejected. He is teacher and prophet. Our study will show the rhetorical function of Matthew's use of the Wisdom metaphor in legitimating Jesus' teaching over against those who would reject it, particularly the opposing teachers, namely, the scribes and Pharisees.

Almost all examples of Matthew's use of the Wisdom metaphor occur in two major sections of his gospel: 11:2–13:58 and 19:1–25:46. Only 8:18–22 lies outside either of these two larger units. In each case, we will begin with a description of the larger section and proceed to examine the individual passages in question.

Matthew 8:18–22

Context

The first text under consideration is Matt. 8:18–22, which occurs in the Matthean context in the block of materials consisting largely of miracle stories, chapters 8–9. That section follows immediately the Sermon on the Mount and precedes the section on commissioning and discipleship in chapter 10.

In chapters 8–9, Matthew has assembled material from Mark and Q. The miracle stories include accounts of healings (8:1–4, 5–13, 14–17; 9:2–8, 18–26, 27–31), exorcisms (8:28–34, 9:32–34), and a nature miracle (8:23–27). Matthew proves to be a careful editor, omitting material that he considers to be extraneous. The result is that the narratives focus on dialogue between Jesus and the persons involved, and ultimately draw attention to the response of faith called forth in the context of the miracle.[7]

Matthew's redactional activity in chapters 8–9 thus highlights Jesus' miracle-working activity, emphasized by the evangelist's inclusion of the traditional summary statement in 8:16–17 and his construction of the one in 9:35–38. But I believe that Matthew's redaction of the material in chapters 8–9 discloses other interests as well.

Here, as elsewhere in his gospel, Matthew portrays Jesus as teacher, sage. We will discuss in detail that feature of Matthew's description of Jesus in a later chapter. But it is of immediate interest to note that in 8:18–22 Jesus' interlocutor is called a scribe (*grammateus*), and he addresses Jesus as "Teacher" (*didaskale*). Both titles are Matthean insertions into the Q logion (Luke 9:57). In 9:11 Matthew inserts "your teacher" into the Pharisees' challenge about Jesus' practice of eating with tax collectors and sinners. Matthew thus makes it clear that the debate is between Jesus the teacher and the opposing teachers.

Finally, in the closing summary statement (9:35–38), Matthew has constructed a summary of traditional materials (Mark 6:6b, 34; Luke 10:2). In doing so, he has added a reference to Jesus' teaching "in their synagogues" to the references to his bearing the gospel of the kingdom and "curing every disease and every sickness." Matthew thus places Jesus' function as teacher in tandem with that of miracle-worker, as do some earlier and contemporary Jewish sources.

Matthew is also interested in saying something about discipleship in chapters 8–9. Thus he includes not only the Q double logion in 8:18–22, but the brief account of the call of Matthew (9:9; Mark 2:13–14), and the dispute over fasting in 9:14–17 (Mark 2:18–22). He closes the section by including the Markan description of Jesus' compassion on the crowds (9:36), emphasizing the traditional description by adding "they were harassed and helpless" (*eskylmenoi kai errimmenoi*). The evangelist adds the Q saying about the need of laborers for the harvest (9:37; Luke 10:2) immediately preceding the section on the commissioning of the disciples in chapter 10.

The interest in discipleship disclosed in Matthew's editing of chapters 8–9 is related directly to his interest in Jesus' function as teacher. After all, in the context of Greco-Roman antiquity and first-century Judaism, sages trained disciples. Matthew's editing of chapters 8–9 certainly emphasizes Jesus' function as miracle-worker. But his editorial activity also reflects a correlative concern about discipleship, disclosed in a context of thaumaturgical activity exercised precisely in the teaching function. This may reflect the broader milieu where the teacher was sometimes described as a wonder-worker.

Wisdom, Discipleship, and Homelessness

> Now when Jesus saw great crowds around him, he gave orders to go over to the other side. A scribe then approached, and said, "Teacher, I will follow you wherever you go." And Jesus said to him, "Foxes have holes, and birds of the air have nests; but the Son of Man has nowhere to lay his head." Another of his disciples said to him, "Lord, first let me go and bury my father." But Jesus said to him, "Follow me, and let the dead bury their own dead."

At first glance, Matthew 8:18–22 appears to be a straightforward double logion about discipleship which Matthew has taken from Q (Luke 9:57–60).[8] Matthew has changed the introduction to fit his literary context (8:18). More important for our purposes, he has, as we have already noted, designated the interlocutor a scribe, and placed the direct address "teacher" on his lips. Otherwise, he has retained the logion about the Son of Man's homelessness as it exists in Q. Matthew has edited the second half of the pericope more extensively. He has abbreviated the longer Q response to the would-be disciple's request to bury his father before following Jesus: "Let the dead bury their own dead; but as for you, go and proclaim the kingdom of God" (Luke 9:60). Matthew has simply "Follow me, and let the dead bury their own dead" (8:22). By adding the phrase "Follow me" and abbreviating the Q material, Matthew focuses even more sharply on the radicality of discipleship.

All of this is clear from an attentive reading of the text. But why would one think Matt. 8:18–22 to be a text about Jesus-Wisdom? The pericope nowhere includes the terms *sophia* or *sophos*. There are actually several indications that this pericope is not only about discipleship but also about discipleship to Wisdom. In the first place, the statement about the homelessness of the Son of Man recalls the references to the rejection of Wisdom and her resultant homelessness on earth in such traditions as those reflected in Prov. 1:20ff; *1 Enoch* 42, 94:5; *2 Apoc. Bar.* 48:36; and Sir. 24:7.[9]

The second indication that Matt. 8:18–22 is a passage about personified Wisdom is that, in the original Q context, it follows directly Luke 7:31–35, and precedes the block of material about discipleship in Luke 10.[10] That context emphasizes the rejection of Wisdom and the acceptance of Jesus-Wisdom by those who become his disciples. Finally, the Q saying identifies Jesus as the Son of Man, recalling our earlier discussion of the association of Wisdom with the Son of Man in *1 Enoch*.[11]

Matthew, however, has loosened the pericope from its context in Q. Does this indicate that he considers it to be a saying about discipleship rather than Wisdom? I do not believe that one can make a definitive statement about this matter. Certainly, Matthew edits the pericope in such a way as to draw attention to Jesus' function as teacher and to the nature of discipleship. Elsewhere Matthew *heightens* those traces in Q which suggest that Jesus is personified Wisdom, as we will see in the course of this chapter.

But these facts need not exclude Matthew's understanding 8:18–22 as a pericope about Wisdom. Our study of earlier materials shows us that Wisdom is a teacher (e.g., Sir. 4:11), and that at least one tradition describes the Son of Man as a wisdom figure.[12] All of this suggests that Matthew may well have considered 8:18–22 to be a passage about discipleship to personified Wisdom. And this conclusion will be confirmed by a study of the way in which the evangelist treats other Wisdom materials. Jesus' identity as Wisdom as well as Son of Man would lend the authority to utter such austere words as we find in this passage. Such a designation would, of course, give Jesus the "upper hand" as authoritative teacher in opposition to his rivals such as the scribes and Pharisees of 9:3, 11, 34. Study of the way in which the evangelist treats other materials about Wisdom will confirm this.

Matthew 11:2–13:58

Context

The remaining Wisdom passages occur in the contexts of two broader sections: 11:2–13:58 and 19:1–25:46. We turn to Matt. 11:2–13:58.[13] Most authors consider the focus of this section to be the rejection of Jesus.[14] The material, however, is far too complex to speak of its being dominated by any *one* theme. Rather, it portrays Jesus as teaching, preaching, and healing, and describes a variety of responses to that ministry.

The teaching and "deeds" of Jesus are the point of reference throughout the section. Thus, immediately after the transition in 11:1, Matthew tells us, "Now when John heard in prison about the deeds (*ta erga*) of the Christ, he sent word by his disciples and said to him, 'Are you he who is to come, or shall we look for another?' " (11:2–3).[15] And in the closing scene of the section (13:54), after Jesus has taught them, the people in the synagogue ask, "Where did this man get this wisdom and these deeds of power (*hē sophia hautē kai hai dynameis*)?" Indeed, Matthew's abbreviation of the longer Markan version of that question (Mark 6:2), as well as his removing it from the Markan context, emphasizes Matthew's attention to *sophia* and *dynameis* not only in 13:53–58, but in the entire preceding section.

In the opening dialogue with John's disciples, Matthew has Jesus describe his deeds, his mighty works in healing the infirm, raising the dead, preaching the good news to the poor (vv. 4–6). These words refer to the miracles and teaching of chapters 8–9. However, 11:2–13:58 will again show Jesus working "deeds of power": healing a man with a withered hand in 12:9–14 and a blind and mute demoniac in 12:22–30.

We see Jesus preach and teach. He speaks to the crowds about John and the meaning of John's ministry (11:7–19a). He proclaims judgment on the Galilean cities (11:20–24). Jesus teaches about the *basileia tōn ouranōn* (kingdom or reign of Heaven) in parables (13:1–52), and he teaches in the synagogue (13:53–58).[16] Moreover, Jesus enters into controversy with "Pharisees" — other teachers — and defends his actions using the rabbinic principle of *qal ve-homer* (12:1–8, 9–14), or a fortiori argument.[17]

Matthew shows a variety of responses to Jesus' words and deeds. There are questions. John and his disciples ask, "Are you he who is to come?" (11:3). In reaction to the Sabbath healing, Matthean redaction in 12:10 changes Mark 3:2 to read, "Is it lawful to heal on the Sabbath (*eksestin*)?" And, after the healing of the blind and mute demoniac, the people ask in amazement, "Can this be the Son of David (*mēti houtos estin ho huios Dauid*)?" (12:23).[18] Jesus' disciples often ask, "Why do you speak to them in parables?" (13:10). And there is that final question in 13:54–56, in fact a whole series of questions: "Where did this man get this wisdom and these deeds of power? Is not his mother called Mary? And are not his brothers James and Joseph and Simon and Judas? And are not all his sisters with us?" Matthew underscores all of this by adding, "Where then did this man get all this?" (13:56b; cf. Mark 6:3).

The questions could be rephrased: "Who is Jesus? What is the significance of his deeds and his teaching?" Matthew uses the questions, moreover, to provide occasions in which to elucidate the answers. To the question, "Are you he who is to come?" Matthew has Jesus respond with a list of deeds which in this context indicate that he is indeed the Coming One (11:4–6). To the Pharisees' question about the lawfulness of curing a man on the Sabbath, Jesus gives halachic justification for his actions (12:9–14). And in response to the disciples' question, Jesus explains both his reason for teaching in parables and the parable of the sower (13:10–17, 18–23).

The question central to the material is, "Who is Jesus?" Jesus' works tell us that he is the Coming One (11:4–6), Son of David (12:22–30), Wisdom (11:19), and Servant (12:15–21). And his words, his teaching, show him to be Son of Man (12:8) and sage (11:28–30; 12:1–8, 9–14; 13). Confronting the Pharisees' accusation that Jesus exorcises by demonic power, Jesus responds, "But if it is by the Spirit of God that I cast out demons, then the Kingdom of God has come to you" (12:28). He implies, of course, that the *basileia tou theou* has indeed come in his ministry.

The questions of Jesus' identity and the significance of his deeds and teaching thus stand at the heart of 11:2–13:58. And the responses to those questions vary. There are the responses of misperception, opposition, rejection, and unbelief. Thus Jesus chastises the crowd for misperceiving the true identity of John the Baptist (11:7–15). It is necessary for Jesus to speak in parables to the crowds because they are "dull" of heart (*epachynthē gar hē kardia*) and cannot "see" or "hear" (13:15).

Opposition, rejection, unbelief come from various quarters and often meet with Jesus' condemnation. Despite the mighty works (*dynameis*) Jesus has performed in the Galilean cities, those cities do not repent (11:20–24). The woes Jesus pronounces make it clear that, indeed, they have *refused* to do so. Opposing teachers challenge Jesus regarding Sabbath observance (12:1–8, 9–14) and accuse Jesus of exorcising by demonic power (12:22–30). Moreover, scribes and Pharisees ask for a sign: "Teacher, we wish to see a sign from you" (12:38). And this de-

spite the *erga* and *dynameis* that have already been worked! In chapter
13, as we have seen, we are told that Jesus must speak in parables because of the crowds' "dullness" of heart, because of their failure to see
and hear and understand (13:10–17). And, finally, we are told that Jesus
is greeted with skepticism, unbelief, and rejection on the part of his fellow townspeople who are offended by him (13:57): *kai eskandalizonto
en autō*. Indeed, skepticism and unbelief are literally the "last words"
of 11:2–13:58.

Such opposition meets with unequivocal response on Jesus' part. He
challenges the dissatisfied people of "this generation" and pronounces
woes on the Galilean cities. He accuses opposing teachers of rejecting the
very Reign of God (12:28), and of blasphemy against the Spirit (12:31–
37). He meets the request for a sign with the promise of the "sign of
Jonah" and declares that the queen of the South will condemn "this
generation" (12:38–42). Moreover, Jesus teaches the crowds in abstruse
parables. And because of their unbelief (*apisteia*), Jesus is unable to do
many "deeds of power" for his townspeople (13:58).

Conflict reaches a climax in 12:1–14, 15–21. At that point, in reaction to Jesus' defense of a Sabbath cure, the Pharisees plot to kill him
and he withdraws. Matthew here describes the Pharisees exclusively as
plotting to kill Jesus, changing the Markan reference to a plot between
the Pharisees and Herodians.[19] He thereby heightens the tension between
Jesus and the Pharisees.[20]

Opposition, unbelief, lack of perception are indeed dominant motifs
in 11:2–13:58. They are not, however, of sole import. Equally significant are contrasting motifs of acceptance, perception, understanding.
John and his disciples query in good faith (11:2–6), as indicated by
Jesus' response and his subsequent praise of John (vv. 7–15), and the
"little ones" receive the divine revelation of "these things" (11:25). All
the people (*pantes hoi ochloi*) are amazed at the exorcism of the blind
and mute demoniac (12:23). Also, the disciples do the will of the Father in heaven (12:49–50). They have been given the "mysteries of the
Kingdom of Heaven" (13:11); they "see" (*horaō, blepō*), "hear" (*akouō,*
13:17), and "understand" (*syniēmi*, 13:23, 51).

Just as Jesus condemns opposition and rejection, so he acknowledges
those who receive him. He blesses those who take no offense in him
(11:6) and praises John the Baptist. He acknowledges the "infants"
who, in contrast to the "wise and understanding,"[21] have received the
revelation of "these things" (11:25). Those who do the Father's will —
that is, the disciples — are his "family," his mother and brothers (12:46–
50). They are blessed because they have received the mysteries of the
kingdom of heaven, because they "see" and "hear" (13:16). The one

who hears the word of the *basileia* and understands it is a seed sown on good soil (13:23). And the scribe trained for the *basileia* is like one who draws new and old out of his treasure (13:52).

Parallel, or congruent with, the themes of opposition and acceptance are themes of revelation and concealment. Jesus reveals who he is through word and deed (11:2–6; 12:15–21, 22–30; 13:53–58). And the Father reveals "these things" and the Son to whom he wills (11:25–27). It is given to the disciples to know the secrets of the *basileia tōn ouranōn* ("reign of heaven," 13:11), and Jesus explains to them the parables of the seed and the weeds (13:18–23, 36–43). Even the parables are vehicles for the disclosure of "hidden things" (*kekrymmenoi*, 13:35). The content of that revelation, as will be clear, is eschatological and apocalyptic. That is, it has to do with the disclosure of a new order, the *basileia tou theou*, or the *basileia tōn ouranōn*, in Matthew's term.

Matthew 11:19: Jesus-Wisdom's Deeds

> But to what will I compare this generation? It is like children sitting in the marketplaces and calling to one another, "We played the flute for you and you did not dance; we wailed, and you did not mourn." For John came neither eating nor drinking, and they say, "He has a demon"; the Son of Man came eating and drinking, and they say, "Look, a glutton and a drunkard, a friend of tax collectors and sinners!" Yet wisdom is vindicated by her deeds.

The most explicit reference to Jesus as Wisdom in this section of Matthew's gospel occurs at 11:19, "Yet wisdom is vindicated by her deeds" (*kai edikaiōthē hē sophia apo tōn ergōn autēs*). The saying appears at 11:19b, the end of the parable of the children in the marketplace and its interpretation (11:16–19a). Comparison with Luke shows that the logion occurs in Q in the same context, but in a slightly different form (Luke 7:35): "wisdom is vindicated by all her children" (*apo pantōn tōn teknōn autēs*). The Lukan form is most likely closest to the Q saying.[22] Examination of Matthew's use of the saying will suggest not only his explicit identification of Jesus with Wisdom, but it will also indicate his understanding of the role of Jesus-Wisdom as rejected eschatological prophet and wonder-worker.[23] And it will suggest a rhetorical function in that portrayal.

In both Matthew and Q, the saying and parable appear at the end of a block of sayings about Jesus and John the Baptist (Matt. 11:2–19; Luke 7:18–35). The occurrences of *erga tou christou* in 11:2 and *apo tōn ergōn autēs* in 11:19 suggest that Matthew considered these materials to be a unit.[24] And the fact that the materials exist in substantially the same order in Luke implies that they had probably already achieved that order and were handed on as a unit by the redactor of Q.[25]

Certain differences between the Matthean version of the parable and that in Luke are significant for our study. One of these is Matthew's use of *ekopsasthe* (11:17) rather than Luke's *eklausate*. Matthew uses *koptō* only in two other places. At 21:8, it means "to cut," but that has no significance for our text. At 24:30, however, Matthew uses *koptō* in the sense of "to mourn," inserting it into a Markan passage (Mark 13:26), which is part of the "Little Apocalypse." So the use of the verb at 11:17, as in the apocalyptic context of 24:30, may suggest that Matthew is heightening the mood of eschatological urgency associated with the mission of John the Baptist (cf. 11:7–15).[26]

The parable may have stood by itself, independent of its application to John the Baptist and the Son of Man, in the pre-Q stratum.[27] In Q it probably had a double referent: primarily to the Son of Man and John the Baptist, who are the "children" or envoys of Wisdom, but also, by extension, to those who recognize Wisdom's messengers, that is, the "tax collectors and sinners" as in Luke 7:34, with the latter being contrasted to the children (*paidioi*) in the marketplace.[28]

We have already noted that Matthew's version of the saying reads, "Yet wisdom is vindicated by her deeds," rather than "by all her children." At first glance, the Matthean saying seems to be loosened from its point of reference, namely, John the Baptist and Jesus, and those who accept or reject them. Verse 19, in fact, presents us with a saying about Wisdom's *deeds* rather than about Wisdom's *children* or *envoys*, that is, John the Baptist and Jesus.

Study of the larger unit (vv. 2–19) confirms the redactional interest in the deeds of Jesus-Wisdom. Comparison with Luke 7:18–23 indicates that Q has a longer version of the introduction to the opening pericope of the unit.[29] That version includes a description of John's disciples approaching Jesus and an account of Jesus' works. Matthew, however, follows his usual practice of condensing extraneous material to underscore what he considers to be the main point, and eliminates the narrative contained in Luke 7:20–21. He introduces John's question to Jesus (11:2) with "Now when John heard in prison about the deeds of the Christ" (*ta erga tou christou*).[30] Matthew then eliminates the account of Jesus' miracles which follows the disciples' question about Jesus' identity ("Are you he who is to come [*ho erchomenos*], or shall we look for another?" 11:3 ‖ Luke 7:19). He has Jesus respond to the question about his identity with the words, "Go and tell John what you hear and see" (*ha akouete kai blepete*, 11:4), rather than "what you have seen and heard" (*ha eidete kai ēkousate*, Luke 7:22).[31] Matthew changes the "hear" and "see" from the aorist to the present tense, thus stressing the contemporaneous quality of Jesus' words and deeds. Matthew implies that those words and deeds are addressed not simply to Jesus' hearers in the historical past but to the audience of the redactor's own day. Furthermore, he changes *ha eidete kai ēkousate* to *ha akouete kai blepete*, thus conforming it to 11:15 and to the citation of Isa. 6:9 in 13:14, and corresponding to the stress on perception and understanding that characterizes the longer literary unit of 11:2–13:58.[32]

Matthew's shorter form of the pericope, by eliminating repetition, focuses on Jesus' response to John's disciples and on Jesus' deeds: healing, raising the dead, preaching. Those deeds hail the presence of the Messiah and Coming One. So, through his editorial changes, Matthew tells us that Wisdom's deeds are the deeds of Jesus, who is the Messiah and Coming One.[33] In the Matthean context this description echoes the miracles recounted in chapters 8 and 9.

The next pericope honors John the Baptist (Matt. 11:7–19 ‖ Luke 7:24–35) as "more than a prophet" and the greatest of those born of women (Matt. 11:9, 11 ‖ Luke 7:26, 28).[34] Matthew both underscores John's honored place and parallels him to Jesus. So he changes the saying in 11:11 to read "no one has arisen" (*ouk egēgertai*) rather than "no one is" (*oudeis estin*, Luke 7:28). And just as Jesus is *ho erchomenos*, so John the Baptist is "Elijah who is to come" (*ho mellōn erchesthai*, 11:14) — thereby rendering explicit the allusion in Mal. 3:1 (Matt. 11:10 ‖ Luke 7:27).[35] Furthermore, Matthew calls attention to John's eschatological role with the words, "Let anyone with ears listen" (*ho echōn ōta akouetō*, v. 15).

Although Matthew emphasizes the honor accorded to John the Baptist, he also makes it clear that the latter's role is subordinate to that of Jesus. It is Jesus who is the Christ, the Coming One (vv. 2–3), while John the Baptist is the messenger (11:10), the Elijah figure. And though John the Baptist is greater than other people, Jesus as the "least" (*mikroteros*) is still greater (11:11).[36]

In the closing verse of 11:2–19, Matthew shifts the significance of the Wisdom saying. Whereas in Q, John the Baptist and Jesus are Wisdom's "children" (although Jesus' status is that of *primus inter pares*),[37] by his redactional work — especially in verses 2–6 and verse 19 — Matthew makes it clear that he considers Jesus as the Christ to be identified with Wisdom. It is the "deeds of Wisdom" — healing, raising the dead, preaching the good news to the poor, and table fellowship with tax collectors and sinners — which vindicate Wisdom and so reveal and verify

Jesus' identity as the Christ, the eschatological Son of Man.[38] Matthew does not understand Jesus to be *primus inter pares* among Wisdom's envoys. Rather, he understands Jesus to be Wisdom itself. And so as a conclusion to the parable of the children in the marketplace and its interpretation, the saying focuses on the rejection of Jesus-Wisdom rather than on the rejection of both John and Jesus.

Matthew's change, with its allusion to the work of the Christ in 11:2, thus makes more explicit the identification of Jesus with Wisdom.[39] The evangelist emphasizes the identification between *Wisdom's* deeds and those of Jesus; in the process he shifts the point of reference, relativizes the place of John the Baptist, and emphasizes the rejection of Jesus-Wisdom.

In Matthew, the woes on Chorazin and Bethsaida (11:20–24) follow the long section on John the Baptist and Wisdom's deeds. The introduction of verse 20 makes it clear that the focus of this passage is, for Matthew, deeds of power (*dynameis*) and repentance, or lack thereof. Matthew takes the noun *dynameis* and the verb *metanoeō* from the Q passage (vv. 21, 23; Luke 10:13) to construct the introduction: "Then he began to reproach the cities in which most of his deeds of power had been done, because they did not repent." But Matthew's context makes it clear that he considers *dynameis* to be the "works of wisdom."[40]

Furthermore, Matthew highlights by his redaction "deeds of power," repentance," and "deeds of Wisdom." The importance of those motifs for the longer section becomes clear with the double logion of 12:38–42, which compares Jesus to Jonah, the prophet of repentance, and to the wise Solomon, and declares Jesus to be greater than both.[41] In the conclusion of the longer section, Matthew has the people ask, "Where did this man get this wisdom and these deeds of power?" (13:54).

In the parable of 11:16–19a, the saying of 11:19b, and the woes of 11:20–24, Jesus-Wisdom calls to repentance those who witness his mighty works, specifically Chorazin and Bethsaida, but more generally the "crowds" (v. 7). The juxtaposition of the parable of the children with the woes, a prophetic form, suggests that the redactor understands Jesus-Wisdom to be prophet.[42] It indicates to what degree Wisdom is not heeded. Matthew thus emphasizes the rejection of Wisdom in the context of Wisdom's deeds, as well as the prophetic call to repentance in the face of the approaching apocalyptic moment.

Why is Jesus-Wisdom rejected? Because he is "a glutton and a drunkard, a friend of tax collectors and sinners!" (11:19).[43] This accusation would seem to exclude Jesus from Wisdom, mark him as fool and as godless.[44] But according to some traditions, Wisdom invites and exhorts the foolish, the simple, the uninstructed.[45] And the works of Jesus-

Wisdom are visible to all, justifying the one who does them.[46] It is, the parable tells us, precisely those gluttons and drunkards, tax collectors and sinners — whom some conventions would exclude from Wisdom — that accept Jesus as Wisdom. Thus, the redactor implies, it is actually those who reject Jesus-Wisdom who exclude *themselves* from Wisdom.

Why does Matthew describe Jesus as personified Wisdom in 11:19? He does so because, for him, Jesus, like Wisdom, is prophet of repentance and sage. Like Wisdom he, too, is both accepted and rejected. The identification of Jesus as Son of Man precisely in 11:16–19 echoes 8:18–22 and recalls the association of the Son of Man with Wisdom in earlier apocalyptic literature,[47] an association we have described in the preceding chapter as well as elsewhere.[48] This description of Jesus as rejected Wisdom is in line with the pattern of the rejection of Wisdom which we observed in Second Temple literature in the previous chapter.

The portrayal of Jesus-Wisdom says something about the way in which Matthew interprets Jesus' identity, teaching, and work. But that interpretation has a social context, and a rhetorical function. Matt. 11:2–19, 20–24 is set in the framework of popular preaching: crowds (v. 7), "this generation" (v. 16), and the cities of Chorazin, Bethsaida, and Capernaum (vv. 21, 23). Use of the present instead of the aorist in 11:4 suggests that Matthew is describing Jesus' words and deeds as contemporaneous with his own community. The crowds represent those who are not part of the community, but who are open to Jesus' message.[49] "This generation" and the Galilean cities represent those who reject Jesus-Wisdom.[50]

Matthew may have used the Wisdom metaphor to persuade the uncommitted as well as to heighten the condemnation of those who rejected Jesus, his words and deeds. The metaphor would have suggested that *Jesus* is Wisdom precisely because he — like Lady Wisdom — is rejected.

There is a specific reference, however, to the followers of John the Baptist. Matthew, while honoring John, furthers the relativization of the prophet already present in Q. Thus, use of the Wisdom metaphor may have served a specific purpose in subordinating John the Baptist to Jesus, the Coming One, Son of Man, Wisdom. It is, then, possible that Matthew's portrayal of Jesus as Wisdom served in part as a polemic against those proposing John's equality with or superiority to Jesus. He may also have used the Wisdom metaphor to persuade those in his community who might have been attracted by a Baptist group.

The evangelist may have directed his version of 11:16–19 particularly to those offended by Jesus' consorting with socially and religiously marginalized groups represented by the tax collectors and sinners or by those in the Matthean community who ministered to such groups. This certainly appears to have been the reference in Q.

Matthew may also have had opposing teachers in mind when he redacted the parable in 11:16–19a and its closing Wisdom logion. One notes the sitting position of the children in 11:16, which may refer to the teaching function or to authority.[51] More significantly, one recalls the Pharisees' challenge to Jesus' disciples that their teacher eats with tax collectors and sinners (9:9–13). So portrayal of Jesus as Wisdom may have served as a rhetorical maneuver to counter opposing teachers' charges against practices in the Matthean community, particularly by its leadership.[52]

Use of the Wisdom metaphor to describe Jesus thus explains the rejection he meets.[53] It legitimates his preaching as well as his mighty works, whether miracles or attention to the marginalized. It situates Jesus in his proper relationship to John the Baptist and his followers, as well as to the populace and to opposing teachers. And, as we have already suggested and will discuss more fully in a later chapter, such use of the Wisdom metaphor also reflects Matthew's own social setting.

Matthew 11:25-30: Wisdom's Hymn, Wisdom's Invitation

> At that time Jesus said, "I thank you, Father, Lord of heaven and earth, because you have hidden these things from the wise and understanding[54] and have revealed them to infants; yes, Father, for such was your gracious will. All things have been handed over to me by my Father; and no one knows the Son except the Father, and no one knows the Father except the Son and anyone to whom the Son chooses to reveal him. Come to me, all you that are weary and are carrying heavy burdens, and I will give you rest. Take my yoke upon you, and learn from me; for I am gentle and humble in heart, and you will find rest for your souls. For my yoke is easy, and my burden is light."

The next Wisdom passage is 11:25–30, which includes a Q thanksgiving (vv. 25–26) and revelation saying (v. 27),[55] as well as the invitation from M (vv. 28–30). Our discussion will indicate the ways in which Matthew's joining the two units makes explicit the implicit Wisdom motif in verses 25–27. His treatment serves to show Jesus-Wisdom to be the sage who teaches the apocalyptic mysteries, interprets Torah, and calls disciples.

For the moment, we shall confine our observations to verses 25–27. There are several relevant differences between the Matthean and Lukan versions of this material. First is the question of context. Both versions follow the woes on the Galilean cities (Matt. 11:20–24 ‖ Luke 10:13–15), although Luke has Jesus receiving the disciples and the return of the seventy between the woes and the blessing (Luke 10:16, 17–20). Thus, the blessing and revelation saying probably followed the woes in Q.

Luke 10 has the blessing and revelation saying in the section on the mission of the disciples. This material contains the sending of the disciples (vv. 1–12),[56] the woes on the Galilean cities (vv. 13–15),[57] the saying about hearing and rejecting the disciples and Jesus (v. 16),[58] the return of the disciples (vv. 17–20). Luke 10:21–22 is followed immediately by the macarism in verses 23–24.[59] Acceptance and rejection are important motifs focused on the disciples' mission of healing, preaching the nearness of the *basileia tou theou*, and exorcism. Luke 10:21–22 applies equally to those who receive the disciples, recognizing the significance of their words and deeds, and to the disciples themselves.

Matthew, however, has placed 11:25–27 in a long section dominated by motifs of acceptance and rejection, revelation and concealment. These motifs refer primarily to *Jesus* and his identity, and the significance of his words and deeds, as we have seen above. Thus, Matt. 11:25–27 refers to those who receive *Jesus*, who perceive correctly his identity, words, and deeds.

Within the passage itself, several differences between the Matthean and Lukan versions are significant for our discussion. The introduction differs markedly. In fact, the word *eipen* is the sole feature common to Luke and Matthew. It may have been present in an introduction to the Q saying.[60]

As for the Matthean version, the phrase *en ekeinō tō kairō* occurs in the New Testament only in our passage and in Matt. 12:1 and 14:1, which allows us to conclude that it is redactional in our passage. Similarly, *apokritheis . . . eipen* occurs several times in Matthew with *ho Iēsous*.[61] Thus the entire introduction to the Matthean logion, with the possible exception of *eipen*, is due to Matthean redactional activity. It functions not only to introduce the passage but to link it to the preceding material in 11:20–24 in which Jesus castigates the Galilean cities for failing to recognize the mighty works done in their midst.

There are differences between the Lukan and Matthean versions in the body of the passage as well. In verse 25, Matthew has *ekrypsas*, whereas Luke has *apekrypsas* (Luke 10:21). It is likely that *apekrypsas* was present in Q, for it is the sole Lukan usage of the verb, although he does use *kryptō* elsewhere (Luke 13:21, 18:34, 19:42). Matthew changed the verb to the simpler form, possibly to correspond to the usage in 13:35 and 13:44, where the verb refers to the teaching about the *basileia tōn ouranōn* and to the *basileia* itself. Matthew's redaction suggests the apocalyptic nature of revelation in relation to God's final reign.

In verse 27 Matthew has *epiginōskei* whereas Luke 10:22 has *ginōskei*.[62] Both verbs signify "to know" or "to perceive" or "to recognize." Which represents the more original reading? Matthew displays a certain preference to *epiginōskō*, as evidenced by his redactional usage in 7:16, 20; 17:12. Is that preference simply stylistic, or is there also a theological significance?

Matthew's use of the verb connotes recognition: of the good and bad news (7:16, 20), or of John the Baptist as Elijah returned (17:12). And so, in our passage *epiginōskō* connotes recognition of Jesus' identity as Son and the messianic significance of his words and deeds. Again, the change emphasizes the eschatological and the apocalyptic.

There is a further significant difference between the Matthean and Lukan parallels. Matthew has "no one knows the Son except the Father, and no one knows the Father except the Son" (*oudeis epiginōskei ton huion ei mē ho patēr oude ton patera tis epiginōskei ei mē ho huios*). Luke, however, has "no one knows who the Son is except the Father or who the Father is except the Son" (*oudeis ginōskei tis estin ho huios ei mē ho patēr kai tis estin ho patēr ei mē ho huios*).[63] Matthew thus has an accusative as object of the verb, whereas Luke has an indirect question. In this instance, it is likely that Matthew has preserved the more original wording, for Luke frequently uses the phrase *tis estin* with reference to Jesus' identity.[64] Thus, in the Lukan parallel to Matthew 11:27, the Lukan redactor would have changed the accusative to an indirect question to underscore the question of Jesus' identity.

Despite the absence of the word *sophia*, Matt. 11:25–27 presents Jesus as personified Wisdom. How can we justify such a claim? With regard to the Q saying, the material pertaining to Jesus bears certain similarities to the various descriptions of personified Wisdom. Wisdom is hidden, transcendent, known only to God. So, too, Jesus is known only to the Father and to those chosen to become privy to that knowledge. Wisdom is God's child. Wisdom knows the hidden things of God, and mediates that knowledge to the wise. So, too, Jesus is God's son. He alone knows the Father and mediates that knowledge to others. Q describes Jesus in terms reserved elsewhere for personified Wisdom.[65]

Q thus implies that Jesus is personified Wisdom through assigning him Wisdom's properties and functions. In Matt. 11:25–27, Q also describes Jesus with the contours of Wisdom's features as teacher and hymnist. Matthew's redaction of the saying emphasizes in several respects the apocalyptic nature of the revelation, a disclosure of hidden things to sages who are "infants" (*nēpioi*), who contrast with the "wise and intelligent" (*sophōn kai synetōn*). All of this will be significant not only for Matthew's interpretation of Jesus and his message, but also for his understanding of community leadership, past and contemporaneous.

The most obvious — and the most significant — difference between the Matthean and the Lukan versions of the thanksgiving and revelation saying is the fact that the Matthean version is followed immediately by the invitation in verses 28–30. Is the invitation part of the original Q passage and was it then omitted by Luke? Or was it added by the Matthean redactor?

The absence of the invitation in Luke leads us to believe that the logion was not part of the Q passage, for Luke would have had no reason to omit this material.[66] Moreover, a variant of verses 28–30 independent of the thanksgiving and revelation sayings exists in the *Gospel of Thomas* 90.[67] There the logion is far simpler in form than Matt. 11:28–30, and reads "Jesus said, 'Come to me because my yoke is easy and my mastery is gentle and you will find your rest.'" This fact, and the early date of the *Gospel of Thomas* — probably first century C.E.[68] — suggest that the logion probably circulated independent of verses 25–27 in the early Matthean community.[69] It may have come into the Matthean *vorlage* through the *Gospel of Thomas* or one of the sources of the latter document.

The invitation itself bears redactional traces — namely, *pantes*[70] and *praus*.[71] Matthew probably added the invitation to verses 25–27 because of the *anawim* language in both (*nēpios, tapeinos, praus*), and because both of the smaller units are concerned with revelation and its recipients.[72] Matthew, then, brings together two traditional units, one a thanksgiving prayer and revelation saying, the other an invitation. His redactional use of *kryptō* and *epiginōskō* suggests an apocalyptic emphasis, and the addition of the invitation highlights the relationship between revelation and discipleship.

In the Q saying, the traces of Wisdom speculation remain implicit; however, they become explicit in Matthew, with the addition of verses 28–30 to verses 25–27.[73] How can we make this claim when, as in verses 25–27, neither *sophos* nor *sophia* appears? What specifically justifies this assertion?

If we recall the literature surveyed in the previous chapter, we will remember that Wisdom is often associated with rest and/or refreshment. Specifically, in Sir. 51:13–20, we find a sage's invitation to come to him for instruction coupled with the exhortation to submit to Wisdom's yoke. And in Sir. 6:18–37, we find the image of Wisdom's yoke and the promise of rest.[74] Elsewhere we find that not only the sage, but Wisdom herself, utters invitations.[75]

Matthew's use of the motifs of invitation, yoke, and promise of rest allows us to say that in 11:28–30 he is making explicit the portrayal of Jesus as personified Wisdom, already implicit in 11:25–27 and elsewhere in Q. This is particularly clear in the occurrence of the possessive pronoun with "yoke," for in Sirach the yoke belongs only to Wisdom, and elsewhere in early Jewish literature the possessor is God.

Matt. 11:28–30 shows Jesus to be not only Wisdom but Sage. This is clear in the invitation "Come to me" so reminiscent of Sir. 51:23,[76] and in the command "Learn from me" (*mathete ap'emou*, v. 29), which implies that the speaker is a teacher calling would-be disciples.

Matthew 11:25–30, the Q passage with the appended invitation, describes Wisdom as hidden and revealed. This is associated with the concealment of "these things" from the wise and understanding and disclosure to the "infants." The invitation in verses 28–30 suggests to us that it is precisely in discipleship, in learning from the sage who is personified Wisdom, that revelation occurs. Both disciples and sage are described in the *anawim* language common in the Second Temple era.

Matt. 11:19 describes Jesus as Wisdom in his functions as prophet and preacher, as doer of mighty deeds, and the context of that logion portrays the rejection of Wisdom (11:2–19, 20–24). Matt. 11:25–30 highlights the acceptance of Wisdom by the "infants," and stands in stark contrast to the rejection prevalent in the preceding material, the conflict with the leaders illustrated in chapter 12, and the dullness of heart exhibited by the crowds in 13:10–17.

What does the context tell us about the exhortations, "Learn of me" and "take my yoke upon you"? The Wisdom passage in Sir. 6:18–37 gives an indication, for the references to Wisdom's yoke and the promise of rest are set in a passage that ends with the exhortation, "Reflect on the statutes of the Lord and meditate at all times on his commandments. It is he who will give insight to your mind, and your desire for wisdom will be granted" (v. 37). Wisdom and her yoke are thus associated with Torah.[77] Elsewhere Wisdom *is* Torah, and the yoke is that of Torah, or of God and God's reign.[78]

Biblical and Second Temple usage describe Wisdom as a teacher. Thus, Jesus' identity as Wisdom is not to be separated from his function as sage. As in Second Temple literature, here, too, Wisdom is a teacher. This is made yet more clear in chapter 13 where he teaches the mysteries of the *basileia*.

To learn of Jesus-Wisdom the sage, to take up his yoke, is to learn Torah. Matthew indicates that this is his understanding by placing

11:25–30 in the context of two controversy stories (12:1–8, 9–14) and by the way in which he edits those stories. Both of these pericopae have to do with proper interpretation of Torah, as is clear in Mark as well as from the manner in which Matthew edits Mark. We will explore more fully in chapter 3 the significance of Jesus' interpretation of *halachah* and his function as apocalyptic teacher.

Jesus invites those who are "weary and are carrying heavy burdens" (*kopiōntes kai pephortismenoi*) to take up his yoke. Who are they? We will discuss the identity of the addressees, as well as that of the *nēpioi*, in a later chapter. But study of the presentation of Jesus as Wisdom and sage requires a few words at this point. Within the Matthean narrative, the presence of *phortion* in 23:4 indicates that they are people who follow other teachers. Those teachers do not stand with their people; while they lay heavy burdens on their people, "they themselves are unwilling to lift a finger to move them" (23:4). The burden is that of the halachic interpretation of these teachers.[79] In the context of 11:25–30, it is illustrated by the position taken by Jesus' opponents in the Sabbath controversies (12:1–8, 9–14).

Just as Wisdom is associated with rest and refreshment in the earlier literature, so Jesus as personified Wisdom provides rest (*anapausis*) to those who labor and are burdened. He tells them that his "yoke is easy" and his "burden is light" (v. 30). But how can that be, in light of the radical ethical demands of the Son of Man, and of the prediction of persecution in chapter 10?

We recall that earlier literature associated Wisdom simultaneously with rest and refreshment, and with labor and discipline. Despite the labor of study and discipline, Wisdom is also rest and refreshment because she is Torah, that is, the word of revelation that embodies the socioreligious order. So, for Matthew, despite the demands of discipleship, Jesus' yoke is sweet, and he gives rest because through him God is revealed. Just as Wisdom remains with Israel (Sir. 24; Wis. Sol. 10–13), Jesus, who is Wisdom, is also "God with us" (Matt. 1:23) who remains with his disciples until the consummation of the age (28:20).

What, then, does Matthew tell us about Wisdom in 11:25–30? Matthew tells us that Jesus is Wisdom hidden and revealed. In him are disclosed the "hidden things," the apocalyptic secrets regarding his identity as Son and the presence of God's reign in his words and deeds. Jesus' identity as Wisdom legitimates his teaching. The passage tells us that revelation and understanding occur in discipleship to Jesus, and that to come to Jesus is to take up his yoke, that is, his interpretation of Torah. Revelation and discipleship both present demands and provide rest. So 11:2–30 presents Wisdom revealed and accepted, in contrast to the conflict and rejection present throughout the larger section of 11:2–13:58.

Does Matthew imply that Jesus *is* Torah by identifying him with Wisdom? I do not believe so. In Matthew, as will become increasingly clear, Torah exists outside of Jesus and is interpreted by him.[80] Rather than identifying Jesus with Torah precisely as Wisdom, Matthew has presented us with an analogy: As Wisdom is identified with Torah, embodied in it, so is Wisdom identified with Jesus who, as apocalyptic preacher and prophet, and interpreter of Torah, is its personification.[81]

Matthew, in 11:25–30, thus ascribes to Jesus many of the same characteristics ascribed to Wisdom in the earlier literature: hiddenness and revelation, transcendence and immanence, the paradox of the easy yoke and light burdens, the promise of rest, the roles of prophet, preacher, and teacher. That earlier literature suggested that Wisdom is accessible in the relationship between sage and disciple. So, too, Matthew implies that revelation and learning occur in the relationship between Jesus-Wisdom and his disciples.

The sages of biblical and Second Temple Judaism used the metaphor of Lady Wisdom to legitimate their teaching authority. The metaphor served a rhetorical function, to persuade disciples and would-be disciples. So, too, the identification of Jesus with Wisdom serves to legitimate his teaching and to persuade disciples and would-be disciples. In relationship to the implied audience, Matt. 11:25–30, with its motifs of acceptance, revelation, and discipleship, contrasts sharply with the emphasis on rejection in the section immediately preceding. It endorses the position of the "infants," and with the promise of rest serves as an attempt to persuade the "burdened" to come to the sage who is Wisdom. Finally, the text legitimates the sage's interpretation of Torah, even in controversial instances, in face of challenge from other teaching authorities, represented by the "wise and understanding" (11:25), the Pharisees (12:2).[82] It does so with a note of irony, implying that the wise and understanding are not *really* wise and understanding at all.[83] And, as we will see, the rhetorical function of the Wisdom metaphor within the narrative also reflects the social setting of Matthew and his community.

Matthew 12:38–42, Wisdom: "Something greater than Jonah, . . . something greater than Solomon"

> Then some of the scribes and Pharisees said to him, "Teacher, we wish to see a sign from you." But he answered them, "An evil and adulterous generation asks for a sign, but no sign will be given

to it except the sign of the prophet Jonah. For just as Jonah was three days and three nights in the belly of the sea monster, so for three days and three nights the Son of Man will be in the heart of the earth. The people of Nineveh will rise up at the judgment with this generation and condemn it, because they repented at the proclamation of Jonah, and see, something greater than Jonah is here! The queen of the South will rise up at the judgment with this generation and condemn it, because she came from the ends of the earth to listen to the wisdom of Solomon, and see, something greater than Solomon is here!"

The next Wisdom passage to occur in our context (11:2–13:58) is 12:41–42 (Luke 11:31–32),[84] another text made up of Q material.[85] Matthew accepts the Markan tradition about the request for a sign (Mark 8:11–12), and combines it with the Q tradition about the sign of Jonah the prophet and the wisdom of Solomon (Luke 11:30–32).[86] There are three sayings in the Q context: the first comparing the Son of Man to Jonah (Luke 11:30), the second comparing the wisdom of Solomon to that of the Son of Man (Luke 11:31), and the third comparing Jonah's preaching of repentance to that of the Son of Man (Luke 11:32).

Q understands the sign of Jonah to refer to Jesus' preaching.[87] Matthew, however, understands the "sign of Jonah" to be the Son of Man's three days and nights in the tomb.[88] Furthermore, his version has the saying about the conversion of Nineveh at Jonah's preaching follow immediately after the saying about the sign of Jonah (12:41), whereas Q has the saying about Nineveh's repentance follow the saying about the wisdom of Solomon (Luke 11:31, 32). The saying about the Queen of the South and the wisdom of Solomon is the last of the series in the Matthean order. Matthew has changed the order of the sayings, evidently so that the two sayings about Jonah might be juxtaposed.[89]

Matthew indeed considers the "sign of Jonah" to be the Son of Man's three days and nights in the tomb. But in juxtaposing the two sayings about the sign of Jonah, he has paralleled more clearly the preaching of Jonah and the wisdom of Solomon, and has emphasized the wisdom of Solomon by placing it last. The broader Matthean context (11:2–13:58) suggests that it is as Wisdom itself that Jesus surpasses Solomon's wisdom.[90]

Both Q and Matthew present Jonah's preaching of repentance and Solomon's wisdom as points of comparison with Jesus, the Son of Man. So Jesus' preaching and Wisdom are the "something greater" than those of Jonah and Solomon. Although these sayings in Q and Matthew do not explicitly depict Jesus as personified Wisdom, they do place him in the context of Q's historical consciousness, wherein John the Baptist and Jesus are set forth as the culminating figures in the whole line of salvation history.[91] Allusions to that history are reflected not in direct citations but in references to the history of the Hebrew Bible: Solomon and the Queen of the South (Matt. 12:42 || Luke 11:31), Jonah and the Ninevites (Matt. 12:40ff || Luke 11:30, 32), Noah and the flood (Matt. 24:37–39 || Luke 17:26ff), Sodom (Matt. 10:15; 11:24 || Luke 10:12), Tyre and Sidon (Matt. 11:21ff || Luke 10:13ff), and, in fact, the entire history (Matt. 23:35 || Luke 11:51).[92]

Q's version of history follows the deuteronomistic tradition, which interprets Israel's history as being one of continued disobedience to God. In that tradition, God sends his prophets to call Israel to repentance. Having rejected the prophets, suffered punishment, and responded to a new call to repentance, Israel is saved and her enemies are judged.[93] This view of history is assumed in the literature of the Second Temple period, and it converges there with the Wisdom tradition.[94]

In Q, Wisdom sends the prophets and the sages, which line culminates in John the Baptist and Jesus.[95] And here, in 12:41–42, we have Jesus presented specifically as the prophet greater than Jonah and the sage greater than Solomon.[96]

While Matt. 12:38–42 does not identify Jesus with personified Wisdom, the Matthean context highlights the association of Jesus with Wisdom by alluding to the association with Solomon. In 12:23 the people respond to the healing of the blind and mute demoniac with the exclamation, "Can this be the son of David?"[97] It is not likely that in this context "son of David" is a messianic title. Rather it is a reference to Solomon, David's son and sage *par excellence*.[98]

Biblical texts already describe Solomon's wisdom,[99] and that tradition was developed in the Second Temple era.[100] Many of the pertinent texts associate Solomon's wisdom particularly with the ability to exorcise and to heal.[101] We see the Matthean context of 12:38–42 describing Jesus the son of David as an exorcist. And Matthew moves the Q parable about the return of the unclean spirit so that it follows immediately the saying about the "something greater than Solomon" (12:43–45; Luke 11:24–26).

Matthew further associates Jesus with Wisdom by assuming the Q title "Son of Man" in 12:40 (Luke 11:30). As we have already seen, the Son of Man is a wisdom figure. Matthew develops the relationship between Jesus and Wisdom through the insertion of the fulfillment citation in 12:18–21, which interprets Jesus' healing activity, with its reference to the presence of God's Spirit with the prophet.[102] Matthew also develops the association of Jesus with Wisdom by speaking of him as exorcising by "the Spirit of God" (12:28), a phrase that represents a redactional change of Q's "finger of God."[103] For the redactor, those references echo the association of Wisdom with God's Spirit in earlier tradition.[104] And they recall the figure of Solomon who receives the Spirit who is God's Wisdom (Wis. 9:17), as well as the Son of Man in whom God's Spirit also resides (e.g., *1 Enoch* 49:1–4).

Once again, as in 11:19, there is the convergence of Wisdom and the prophetic call to repentance in Jesus, and there is also the association of Wisdom with the Son of Man present in 8:18–22, as well as in 11:19.[105] The comparison here of Jesus to Jonah the prophet and to Solomon the sage recalls not only the deuteronomistic interpretation of history assumed in Second Temple Jewish literature and Q, but also the figure of Lady Wisdom as prophet and street preacher, which first appears in Proverbs 1 and 8.[106]

In 12:41–42, Matthew changes the context of his material as well as the order of the sayings. Luke has the sayings addressed to the crowds whom Jesus calls "an evil generation" and "this generation" (Luke 11:29, 31, 32).[107] Matthew presents the sayings as a response to the request for a sign by some of the scribes and Pharisees (12:38 ‖ Luke 11:29). They signal him as the opposition, casting him in the outsider's role and accusing him of exorcising by demonic power.[108] But in calling Jesus "teacher" (*didaskale*), the scribes and Pharisees cast the debate in scholastic terms. Thus, in the Matthean context these sayings function rhetorically in a polemic between Jesus the sage and his opponents. Jesus' preaching challenges them, for his wisdom, identified with God's very Spirit, is even greater than that of Solomon — and, a fortiori, that of the "Scribes and Pharisees."[109] In the context of 12:18, 21, the sayings about the repentance of Nineveh and the Queen of the South indicate an opening to the Gentiles. That would contrast with attitudes of opposition and rejection exemplified by "scribes" and "Pharisees."

Matthew 13:53–58: Words of Wisdom, Deeds of Power

He came to his hometown and began to teach the people in their synagogue, so that they were astounded and said, "Where did this man get this wisdom, and these deeds of power? Is not this the carpenter's son? Is not his mother called Mary? And are not his brothers James and Joseph and Simon and Judas? And are not all his sisters with us? Where then did this man get all this?" And they took offense at him. But Jesus said to them, "Prophets are not without honor except in their own country and in their own house." And he did not do many deeds of power there, because of their unbelief.

The last reference to Wisdom in 11:2–13:58 occurs at the conclusion, 13:53–58.[110] Matthew adapts Mark 6:1–6a, which in Mark follows the healing of Jairus' daughter. But Matthew places the pericope after the parables of the *basileia* and as the conclusion to his entire literary unit of 11:2–13:58.

In 13:53–58, Jesus teaches in "their synagogue." The Matthean addition of the possessive pronoun *autōn* at verse 54 alerts one to the polemical note.[111] The people exclaim at his teaching, "Where did this man get this wisdom and these deeds of power?" (*pothen toutō hē sophia hautē kai hai dynameis*). The Markan pericope has "Where did this man get all this? What is this wisdom that has been given to him? What deeds of power are being done by his hands!" (6:2). Matthew has shortened the exclamation. He has divided and abbreviated the Markan explanation, placing the reference to Jesus' wisdom and mighty works in verse 54. And he has repeated the question, *pothen . . . toutō*, after the reference to the presence of Jesus' family, adding the typically Matthean "all" (*panta*) after "these things" (*tauta*) in verse 56.[112]

Matthew's reworking of the Markan pericope emphasizes the exclamation about Jesus' wisdom and mighty works occasioned by his teaching. And it brings to a conclusion the emphasis on Wisdom and mighty works, which are important themes in 11:2–13:52.[113] It also serves rhetorically to place in relief the general rejection of Jesus by the community at large, a rejection rendered inexplicable in the presence of wisdom and mighty deeds.

Our investigation of 11:2–13:58, therefore, reveals that this unit contains several passages in which Jesus is either identified with Wisdom (11:2–19, 25–30) or described as possessing wisdom in a preeminent way (12:41–42, 13:53–58). In the Q materials, Jesus as Son (11:25–27) or Son of Man (11:16–19a, 12:41–42) is Wisdom's preeminent envoy, who preaches the presence of the eschatological moment and calls his hearers to repentance. The call to repentance is heightened by Matthew in placing the pericope concerning woes on Chorazin and Bethsaida (11:20–24) directly after the parable in 11:16–19,[114] and in placing the saying about Jonah and Solomon in the context of a conflict with the scribes and Pharisees.

While Q implicitly identifies Jesus with Wisdom in 11:25–27, as we observed, Matthew goes beyond Q. In reworking the saying about Wisdom's children (11:19b) and in adding the invitation (11:28–30) to the prayer of thanksgiving, Matthew identifies Jesus with Wisdom in an explicit way. Jesus is not simply the most important of Wisdom's envoys; he is Wisdom itself. Yet Matthew's portrayal also includes the identification of Jesus as the Teacher of Wisdom. He illustrates the significance of this in his depiction of Jesus as interpreting Torah (12:1–8, 9–14) and as disclosing the mysteries of the *basileia tōn ouranōn* (chap. 13). Thus Matthew's adaptation shows Jesus, as the Son or the Son of Man, to be not only the envoy of Wisdom and therefore the eschatological prophet and preacher, but also Wisdom personified and the Teacher of Wisdom — and so the interpreter of Torah and the revealer of eschatological mysteries.

But what does it mean that Matthew has identified Jesus with Wisdom? In the preceding chapter, we observed that Lady Wisdom is a symbol, a metaphor for the divine presence, and revelation in human history. As such, it responded to certain underlying questions among Jews of the Second Temple and tannaitic periods.

In 11:2–13:58, the metaphor, symbol, myth is transformed so that it now applies to Jesus. Jesus is prophet and preacher calling people to repentance and to discipleship. He is God's presence, both transcendent and immanent, and he is the vehicle of revelation. In the relationship with Jesus in discipleship, one responds to the prophetic call to repentance, learns the proper interpretation of Torah, and receives knowledge of the "hidden things."

By appropriating the metaphor of Wisdom that is traditional in Second Temple Judaism and present in Q, in 11:2–13:58 Matthew presents a focus for his presentation of Jesus as apocalyptic preacher and prophet, and the sage who interprets Torah and calls disciples. And he does so in language that evokes not only challenge and judgment, but invitation and nurturance. Within the narrative, Matthew's portrayal of Jesus-Wisdom functions rhetorically in the debate between Jesus and opposing teachers, as well as the more generalized rejection present in this material. It offers a contrast between Jesus-Wisdom and the opposing teachers, the "wise and understanding" who are, in fact, without Wisdom. And the metaphor acts as a device of persuasion to appeal to would-be disciples as well as to encourage those already present in the community.

Matthew 23:34–36, 37–39

Context

The Wisdom sayings of 23:34–36, 37–39 conclude the woes addressed to the "scribes" and "Pharisees," who are called "hypocrites" (23:13–33).[115] And the woes are preceded by verses 1–12, a passage in which Jesus contrasts the manner of leadership exercised by the scribes and Pharisees to that required of the leaders of the Matthean community. The Wisdom sayings are followed by Jesus' departure from the Temple in 24:1 and the apocalyptic discourse in 24:3–25:46, the latter of which describes the events to occur at the "end of the age" (24:3; *synteleia tou aiōnos*).

The extended context of the Wisdom sayings is the unit 19:1–25:46. Conflict between Jesus and opposing leaders dominates this unit. The opponents include Herodians (22:16) and Sadducees (22:23), chief priests (20:18; 21:23, 45) and elders (21:23). Most frequently, however, they are Pharisees (19:3; 21:45; 22:15, 34, 41) and scribes (20:18; 21:15).

The conflict between Jesus and his opponents has to do with Jesus' teaching. The debate is halachic in the instances of the discussion of divorce and remarriage (19:3–9), the payment of Caesar's tax (22:15–22), the question of the woman married successively to seven brothers (22:23–33), and the great commandment (22:34–40).

Chief priests and elders challenge Jesus' authority to teach, and to heal, and to perform other "amazing things" (*thaumasia*, 21:15; cf. vv. 14–22, 23). There are political connotations to their opposition, suggested by the chief priests' and scribes' indignation at the acclamation "Hosanna to the Son of David" (21:14–16),[116] which culminates in the chief priests' and Pharisees' attempt to arrest Jesus when he predicts that leadership will be wrested from them (21:45–46).

Prior to chapter 23, Jesus challenges the opposing leadership in the parable of the wicked husbandmen (21:33–43). There, in the editorial conclusion, Matthew has Jesus predict that leadership will be given to others who will produce "fruits" from the vineyard (21:43).[117] And Jesus stills his opponents by insinuating that he is somehow "more" than David's son (22:46). The note of conflict will reach its climax in 24:1 when Jesus leaves the Temple.

While conflict dominates the mood of the unit, other motifs exist as well, such as the incident in which the departure of the would-be disciple occasions conversation on the exigencies of discipleship (19:16–22, 23–30), the reception of Jesus by the Jerusalem crowds (21:1–17) and by the blind man of Jericho (20:29–33), as well as the willingness of the disciples. All this contrasts with the opposition of the leaders.

Discipleship coincides with entry into the *basileia tōn ouranōn* (cf. 19:23). The disciple is one who is as the child (19:14; cf. 18:1–4), and who is willing to leave all to follow Jesus (vv. 23–30). Jesus is the "humble" one (21:5; cf. 11:28–30) who has come to serve (20:28). Thus discipleship and leadership mean that the follower likewise becomes a "slave" (*doulos*, 20:26–27; 23:11–12).[118] Entry into the *basileia* is available to all — even tax collector and sinner — on the condition of repentance and faith (21:31).

There is also a motif of perception in this unit (21:28–32). It is not so dominant as in 11:2–13:58, but it is nonetheless significant. Following the story of the Zebedee's sons and their mother, Matthew presents us with the story of two blind men who ask Jesus to open their eyes.[119] To be sure, this is a miracle story, and therefore it concerns a physical healing. Nonetheless, certain features indicate that Matthew considers this to be a story about faith, an inner "sight," as well. The two men call on Jesus not only as "Son of David" (cf. Mark 10:47–48), but also as "Lord" (*kyrie*), thereby using a title reserved by Matthew for disciples or those seeking Jesus' help.[120] Matthew eliminates all extraneous material to focus on the restoration of sight and on the blind men's following Jesus in the conclusion to the pericope (vv. 32–34).[121] Finally, the request of the blind men and their "perception" contrasts with the story of Zebedee's sons and their mother in 20:20–28.

The motif of perception recurs in chapter 24. The verbs *blepō* and *horaō*[122] are to be understood on two levels: that of physical sight and that of inner perception. This is indicated by the relationship of sight to signs (*sēmeion*) in chapter 24, for signs must be understood with regard to outward appearance and to inner significance.[123]

While the chief priests and Pharisees perceive (*egnōsan*) that the parable of the wicked husbandmen is directed at them (21:45), they are actually "blind" (*typhloi* — 23:16, 17, 19, 24, 26).[124] That is, they do not perceive the inner meaning of *halachah* and thus they lead their people incorrectly.[125]

The conflict signaled earlier is between Jesus and the leaders of the opposition; however, in chapter 24, conflict also becomes a matter internal to the Matthean community. Matthew shows Jesus as warning against false leaders in the chaos of the apocalyptic time: the false Messiahs (v. 5)[126] and false prophets (v. 11)[127] who will lead people astray (v. 24). Matthew warns that, because of the hostility of "all nations" (*pantōn tōn ethnōn* — 24:9),[128] the community will be divided by mutual betrayal and hatred (24:10). He associates this with the rise of

false prophets, the spread of lawlessness (*anomia*), and the cooling of
communal love (vv. 11–12).

As we noted earlier, "lawlessness" is not to be identified necessarily
with antinomian tendencies. Rather, it is part of contemporary Jewish
sectarian language and designates all who would subvert God's will,
particularly those who present or follow an interpretation of Torah at
variance with that of the accuser.[129] Over against those who would lead
people astray, into lawlessness and lack of charity on the one hand
(24:9–14), or into false expectations on the other (24:23–28), Jesus
stands as apocalyptic teacher who tells his disciples that the day and
hour of the final time is hidden with the Father, undisclosed even to
himself (24:32–36). His message is one of endurance (24:13) and readiness (24:36–51; 25:1–13, 14–30), and the community is to exercise that
readiness in communal concern (24:31–46).

Conflict marks 19:1–25:46. On the one side stand leaders of the
opposition. These include Jewish leaders: chief priests, elders, scribes,
Sadducees, and Herodians, but predominantly the Pharisees. These are
meant to refer not only to leaders of the community contemporary with
Jesus, but also the opposing leadership of the broader Jewish community
contemporary with the Matthean community. Leaders of the opposition
also include false prophets, those in Matthew's community who would
lead people into lawlessness, the cooling of communal charity, and false
expectations.

On the other side stand Jesus and his disciples, with the latter representing the teachers of Matthew's community. Jesus is the "humble" one
(21:5) who instructs his disciples in a pattern of leadership like his own
(20:20–28, 23:1–12). As teacher he is concerned with the inner meaning of *halachah* (23:13–33) and proper apocalyptic instruction (chaps.
24–25).

Conflict thus dominates this section. The conflict between Jesus and
his opponents is underscored by motifs of perception and discipleship.
These serve to contrast the unperceptive opposing leadership with those
who perceive the true meaning of Jesus' identity and the significance of
his teaching with those who do not do so.

Matthew 23:34–36, 37–39: Wisdom's Oracle, Wisdom's Lament

Therefore I send you prophets, sages, and scribes, some of whom
you will kill and crucify, and some you will flog in your synagogues
and pursue from town to town, so that upon you may come all the
righteous blood shed on earth, from the blood of righteous Abel
to the blood of Zechariah son of Barachiah, whom you murdered

between the sanctuary and the altar. Truly I tell you, all this will come upon this generation.

Jerusalem, Jerusalem, the city that kills the prophets and stones those who are sent to it! How often have I desired to gather your children together as a hen gathers her brood under her wings, and you were not willing! See, your house is left to you, desolate. For I tell you, you will not see me again until you say, "Blessed is the one who comes in the name of the Lord."

At the end of the woes in chapter 23, we find another Wisdom passage. This is the saying about Wisdom's envoys (23:34–36), another Q logion.[130] In both Matthew and Luke, the saying occurs immediately after the woe on the slaying of the prophets (Matt. 23:29–31 ‖ Luke 11:47–48), suggesting that this was likewise its order in Q. They differ, however, in that Luke has the saying as part of a series of woes which are woven into a conflict narrative (11:37–54), whereas Matthew has it as part of an extended series of woes without such a narrative.[131]

Matthew's expansion begins with the instruction about the authority of scribes and Pharisees, and the exhortation to follow their teaching but not their practice (23:2–3). It heightens the note of conflict between Jesus and the opposing teachers already present in Q. The significance of this will become evident in the ensuing discussion.

Luke, who probably reproduces Q at 11:49, has, "Therefore also the Wisdom of God said, 'I will send them prophets and apostles, some of whom they will kill and persecute'" (*dia touto kai hē sophia tou theou eipen apostelō eis autous prophētas kai apostolous*). Matthew redacts the Q saying, using the second-person plural rather than the third-person plural, thus placing Wisdom's words on Jesus' lips.[132] Thus, in 23:34–36, Jesus assumes the function possessed by Wisdom in Q, as well as in certain Second Temple Jewish texts, when he sends envoys. Once again, Matthew presents Jesus as personified Wisdom.[133]

The Q version of the saying evidently had Wisdom speak in the future tense: *apostelō eis autous*. Matthew's version, however, has Jesus speak in the present tense directly to his addressees: *egō apostellō pros hymas*. The use of the present tense and the additional *pros hymas*, as redactional changes, point beyond the narrative. They actualize the saying and relate it to the Matthean community, as well as to Jesus. The addition of *egō* emphasizes that the envoys are sent by Jesus-Wisdom rather than by the scribes and Pharisees. For Matthew Wisdom's envoys are not just — or even primarily — the prophets of old. They are the disciples of Jesus and the "messengers" of the Matthean community.[134]

Luke's version of the saying has "prophets and apostles" (*prophētas kai apostolous*) for Wisdom's envoys, while Matthew has "prophets, sages, and scribes" (*prophētas kai sophous kai grammateis*). It is likely that *prophētas* appeared originally in Q. *Apostolos*, however, is a term preferred by Luke and one he could easily have added.[135] Matthew seems to have retained *prophētas* from Q. While he may have found *sophous* in Q as well, since in his Gospel it occurs only once more (11:25, a Q saying),[136] it is equally likely that he inserted it here independent of Q. *Grammateis* is probably a Matthean addition[137] that (to anticipate a later discussion) reflects Matthew's interest in Christian scribes.[138]

The three terms — *prophētas, sophous*, and *grammateis* — probably reflect Matthew's ecclesiological interests, and likely correspond to various functions held by leaders in his community.[139] We will discuss these functions in a later chapter; for the moment it is sufficient to note that Matthew describes Jesus' disciples, Wisdom's envoys, as exercising teaching and prophetic functions both in Jesus' time and in that of the Matthean community. Those envoys are closely associated with Wisdom as the true teachers in contrast to the "scribes and Pharisees."

The saying about Wisdom's envoys occurs at the end of the woes, both in Q and in Matthew. In Matthew, the woes are preceded by a section in which Jesus is described as contrasting his model of discipleship and of the teaching office with that of the Pharisees (vv. 2–12). In this context, the prophets, wise men, and scribes of Matthew's community (v. 34) are set over against the teachers of the Pharisees. Unlike the latter, it is implied, the prophets, wise men, and scribes are to stand in solidarity with their disciples, bearing with them the "burden" of Torah.

Matthew's version of the saying about Wisdom's envoys expands the prediction of persecution. Whereas Luke has "some of whom they will kill and persecute," Matthew has "some of whom you will kill and crucify and some you will flog in your synagogues and pursue from town to town." The addition of the verbs *stauroō* and *mastigoō* recalls the passion predictions, the third of which occurs in our broader unit (20:19). And the "scourge in your synagogues" and "pursue from town to town" recall the fate of the disciples described in 10:17, 23.[140]

"Kill and crucify" (*apokteneite kai staurōsete*) is not to be taken literally here. Romans controlled the death penalty in the provinces, even though they seem to have allowed Jews to execute for certain religious offenses such as adultery and "violating the prohibitions against circulating in certain quarters of the Temple."[141] For the Romans, crucifixion was a sentence usually restricted to slaves and insurgents.[142] There is no evidence of the crucifixion of Christians because of any denunciation by Jews during the period.[143] The use of "crucify" and "scourge" (*stauroō, mastigoō*) in 23:34 recalls, as we have noted, the fate of the disciples described in 10:17, 23. That description, however, rests upon the description of Jesus' own fate in the passion prediction of 20:19.[144] Thus Matthew's description of the fate of Wisdom's envoys is governed by the fate of Wisdom personified. Although crucifixion is not to be taken literally, there is in verse 34 an echo of the conflict between the teachers of Matthew's community and the "scribes and Pharisees" — and perhaps also of persecution.[145]

The warning continues in 23:35–36. Luke 11:50–51 reads:

> so that this generation may be charged with the blood of all the prophets shed since the foundation of the world, from the blood of Abel to the blood of Zechariah, who perished between the altar and the sanctuary. Yes, I tell you, it will be charged against this generation.

Matthew has reworked this part of the saying, as he has the first section. Certain changes are of particular interest here. Matthew has *elthē eph'hymas* rather than *ekzētēthē ... apo tēs geneas tautēs* for two reasons: the reference to "this generation" in verse 36 would have rendered the first usage superfluous; and the use of *eph'hymas* conforms this part of the saying to verse 34, as well as to verses 29–32, and to the use of the second-person plural in that material. It emphasizes the fact that Matthew's reference is not simply to Jesus' audience, but to his own contemporaries, to his opponents.[146]

The deletion of "the prophets" in verse 35 parallels the saying more closely to Jesus' own death by emphasizing "the blood."[147] And the modification of "blood" by "righteous" links verse 35 to verse 29, where "prophets" and "righteous" are set in parallel.[148]

The use of *epi tēs gēs* represents a Matthean stylistic variant.[149] Moreover, Matthew calls Abel "the righteous," thus identifying him with those victims described in verses 29–31. He adds the patronymic "son of Berachiah" (*huiou Barachiou*) to Zechariah's name, following his tendency to use patronymics,[150] which clarifies the identification in Q of Zechariah as the prophet.[151] Again, he alters the verb from a middle-aorist participle (*apolomenou*, Luke 11:51) to a second-person-plural aorist (*ephoneusate*, Matt. 23:35).[152] The reference to Abel and Zechariah spans the entire Hebrew Scriptures,[153] the first and last mentioned murders there.[154] And through the use of the second-person plural throughout verses 34–36, Matthew takes over the deuteronomistic tradition regarding the rejection and killing of the prophets and applies it directly to the fate of the preachers sent by Jesus. This, however, extends beyond the narrative to the prophets, wise men, and scribes of his own community.[155]

Matthew has *hon ephoneusate* rather than *tou apolomenou* (Luke 11:51), another redactional change. As we have noted, he has placed the verb in the second-person plural to conform to the rest of the section and to emphasize the responsibility of his audience, thus heightening the tone of warning and the implication of the relationship of the audience's deeds to those of their ancestors. Furthermore, Matthew has changed the verb to *phoneuō*, a change that conforms to the usage in verse 31.[156]

The Matthean form of Wisdom's oracle concludes, "Truly I tell you, all this will come upon this generation" (*amēn legō hymin hēksei tauta panta epi tēn genean tautēn*), whereas Luke's version has "Yes, I tell you, it will be charged against this generation" (*nai legō hymin ekzētēthēsetai apo tēs geneas tautēs*, 11:51). Given Matthew's preference for the phrase *amēn legō hymin* one can conclude that its presence in 23:36 is due to redactional activity.[157] Similarly, the use of *hēksei* rather than *ekzētēthēsetai*, and the addition of *tauta panta* are due to Matthean redactional activity; *ekzēteō* occurs in the synoptics only in Luke 11:50–51.[158] Matthew's substitution heightens the note of judgment, and he underscores that tone by inserting *tauta panta*. *Hēksei tauta panta* is much more specific than the third-person passive future of *ekzēteō*, for it refers back to "all the righteous blood" of verse 35.[159] Moreover, it is clear from Matthew's use of the second-person plural throughout verses 34–36, and the references to persecution, that "this generation" extends beyond the limits of the narrative itself. It refers not only to those of Jesus' hearers who reject his call to repentance, but to those who oppose the evangelist and/or his community.

Matthew's redaction of the oracle of doom in 23:34–36 shows Jesus to be identified with Wisdom. As personified Wisdom, Jesus sends envoys, specifically, prophets, wise men, and scribes — offices that reflect those in Matthew's community, as we have noted. Furthermore, Matthew's redaction of the Q account of the envoys' fate, with its reference to persecution, hearkens to the experience of the disciples — that is, to his community — and parallels their fate to that of Jesus. The reference to Abel and Zechariah present in Q places the envoys in the context of Wisdom's history, a history that — at least as reflected in Wis. 7:27 and chapters 10–11 — includes her presence in Adam, Abel, Noah, the patriarchs, and Moses.[160] It recalls once again the traditional description of Wisdom's presence in Israelite and Jewish history exemplified in Sirach 24 as well as Wisdom of Solomon 10–11. And it places Wisdom's envoys in the broader context of the deuteronomistic understanding of the rejection of the prophets. Moreover, the Matthean use of the second-person plural, the addition of *tauta panta*, and the Q reference to "this generation" create and emphasize a continuity of deed and judgment between the past history of Israel, the rejection of repentance in Jesus' day, and the opposition experienced by the Matthean community.[161] For Matthew, just as Israel rejected the prophets sent by God, so too the opponents of his community reject and persecute the envoys sent by Jesus, who is Wisdom personified.[162]

Within the narrative, then, Matthew's use of the Wisdom metaphor gives Jesus authority in relationship to the scribes and Pharisees, the teachers who oppose him. And it legitimates the authority of the envoys sent by Jesus-Wisdom. Matthew's redaction of 23:34–36, however, points beyond the confines of the narrative to place this material in the context of Matthew's community in its attempts to understand the meaning of Jesus, their experience of conflict, and the authority of the teaching leadership.

Matthew 23:37–39

The oracle about Wisdom's envoys is followed in Matthew by the lament over Jerusalem (23:37–39),[163] which occurs in another context in Luke (13:34–35), where it follows the saying "it cannot be that a prophet should perish away from Jerusalem" (Luke 13:33b). In Matthew's context, however, the oracle and lament are bound together. Opinion is divided as to whether or not the two sayings were originally found together in Q,[164] joined together in Q, whether in the *Vorlage* or by the redactor,[165] or joined first by Matthew.[166] If one agrees with either of the first two positions, then one concludes that Matthew has preserved the order of Q.[167]

It is not at all clear to us that the two sayings did originally stand together.[168] Matt. 23:34–36 is an oracle of doom, which looks to the *future* sending of prophets (in Q), though with a reference to Israel's past history, whereas Matt. 23:37–39 is a lament that looks to the sending of prophets as a *past* event.[169] Although the presence of differing tenses does not rule out an original unity between the two sayings,[170] there is no positive evidence that the two sayings originally stood together, either in Q or in the *Vorlage* of Q.[171]

Nor is it completely clear that the lament was *originally* a lament of Wisdom.[172] Although certain Wisdom passages of Second Temple Jewish literature speak of Wisdom as sending prophets, of seeking a dwelling place among humankind, of being rejected and thus withdrawing, the presence of these motifs does not rule out the fact that verses 37–39 could represent a prophetic lament ascribed to God — a possibility suggested by the use of the theological passive in verse 38 (*aphietai*).[173]

Finally, there is no specific reference to Wisdom in the Q lament. All of this leads me to conclude that, in its original setting, Luke 13:34–35 was not a Wisdom saying, but a dominical saying or a prophetic lament in which God was intended as the speaker. Nonetheless, Wisdom's oracle and the lament *are* together in the Matthean context. And the fact that the lament follows the oracle immediately, without so much as a transitional phrase, indicates that Matthew considers the speaker of the lament to be Jesus as personified Wisdom.

Matthew would have placed these sayings together for several reasons. First, the terms *prophētes, apostellō,* and *apokteinō* are present in both sayings and thus serve as catchwords. Second, the motifs of the Temple and the slaying of the prophets are likewise present in both passages. And, finally, the motif of the sending of the prophets, the use of maternal imagery, and the theme of rejection are, in fact, applied to Wisdom in many of the traditions examined in the preceding chapter.

The text of the lament is almost identical in Matthew and Luke; however, the examination of the Matthean version shows minor stylistic variations.[174] The image of the mother bird gathering her brood recalls the allusions to Wisdom building a nest in Proverbs and Sirach. It also corresponds to Lady Wisdom's roles as mother and nurse in Second Temple literature. And it recalls the description of Lady Wisdom in Sir. 14:26.[175] Use of the image of a mother bird to represent God, as well as Lady Wisdom, suggests parental care, intimacy, and refuge.[176]

Some think that the reference to the wings of the mother bird implies a reference to the Shekinah.[177] The expression "the wings of the Shekinah" does, indeed, occur in Tannaitic and later rabbinic literature, where to be "under the wings of the Shekinah" signifies primarily to be "under God's protection."[178] "Shekinah" is thus a circumlocution for God. To be "under the wings of the Shekinah" is to be "under the wings of the heavenly Father" or "under the wings of Heaven."[179] There is in rabbinic thought, however, no instance in which the Shekinah addresses Israel. Furthermore, the Shekinah and Wisdom are not identified, nor does the Shekinah possess feminine qualities in our period.[180]

A close examination of Matt. 23:37–39 in the light of Second Temple and Tannaitic sources leads us to conclude that the saying was not originally the "lament of Wisdom," but rather a prophetic oracle in which the speaker is God Himself. It was attached to the saying about Wisdom's envoys (23:34–36) for the reasons noted above.

In joining the two sayings, Matthew shows Jesus as Wisdom incarnate who sends prophets, wise men, and scribes. These are slain in the pattern of all Wisdom's envoys from Abel to Zechariah.[181] Matthew extends that pattern to the death of Jesus and the persecution of his disciples and Matthew's community by redactional use of *stauroō, mastigoō*, and *apokteinō*. The lament suggests Wisdom's maternal care for those to whom the envoys are sent; but because Wisdom and her envoys are rejected Jesus-Wisdom pronounces a word of judgment and foretells his withdrawal from the Temple.

Earlier we noted the association of Wisdom with the Son of Man in the Similitudes of Enoch, as well as in Matt. 8:18–22 and 11:19. The context of Matt. 23:34–36, 37–39 suggests that in this case, too, the redactor associates the figure of Jesus-Wisdom with the Son of Man. While Jesus-Wisdom departs the Temple because of rejection, the apocalyptic Son of Man will come in judgment to gather the elect (24:30–31).[182] All of this indicates that Matthew believes the destruction of the Temple to be due to the rejection and execution of Jesus-Wisdom. Moreover, he locates Wisdom's presence not in the Temple and the teaching activity of the opponents, but in that of Wisdom's envoys, the teaching leadership of his own community. The righteousness of community and leaders will be vindicated in the end-time. We will explore the implications of this in chapter 4.

Jesus, Wisdom Incarnate

Comparison of the Wisdom passages in Q and in Matthew makes it evident that Q usually understands Jesus to be Wisdom's envoy, although the Sayings Source implicitly identifies him with Wisdom in Matt. 11:25–27 ‖ Luke 10:21–22. Matthew develops the tendency toward Wisdom speculation already present in Q. He consistently understands Jesus as actually being identified with Wisdom. Although this is overt only in 11:19, the evangelist expresses this elsewhere by allusion, through categories hitherto used of Lady Wisdom and now employed to articulate his understanding of Jesus' identity, life, and ministry.[183]

In other words, Matthew ascribes to Jesus characteristics and functions ascribed to Lady Wisdom in earlier and contemporary literature. Thus the identity of Jesus as Son is both hidden and revealed (11:25), as are the mysteries of the *basileia* he preaches (13:11, 35). As Wisdom, Jesus is a teacher — he teaches Wisdom or Torah, calls people to discipleship, and reveals the apocalyptic mysteries (13:35–38). He is hymn-singer, thanking God for revealing apocalyptic mysteries to the "infants" and hiding them from the "wise and understanding" (11:25–30). Jesus is also prophet, calling the people to repentance (11:20–24). Just as Wisdom is described as mother and nurturer, so the imagery of a mother hen is used of Jesus (23:37). Jesus is rejected, as are his envoys (11:20–24; 23:34–36, 37–39), and this rejection results in prophetic judgment on the guilty parties and — ultimately — Wisdom's withdrawal until the *parousia*.

Matthew identifies Jesus with Wisdom as Son or Son of Man (8:18–22; 11:19, 25–30; 23:34–39), and teacher of Wisdom (12:41–42, 13:53–58). He associates Jesus' identity as Wisdom or teacher of Wisdom with his eschatological deeds (11:2–19; 13:53–58; 12:1–8, 9–14, 15–22) and preaching (11:20–24, 23:37–39). Matthew, then, identifies Jesus as the embodiment of Wisdom because he perceives that many of the elements in the various descriptions of Wisdom actually belong to Jesus. Jesus' story is Wisdom's own and Wisdom's story is that of Jesus.

For Matthew, revelation occurs in discipleship to Jesus who is Son, Teacher, and Wisdom (11:25–30). It is no longer a matter of Jesus' being sent as Wisdom's envoy, but of his being Wisdom personified who calls disciples to himself and then sends them out. The disciples are to come to Jesus, take on his yoke, and, in turn, be sages themselves. In Matt. 23:34, the terms describing Jesus' envoys parallel the description of Jesus himself. They are prophets, as he is a prophet, uttering an eschatological call to repentance (11:20–24, 23:37–39) and condemning "this generation" (12:42), and they are sages, as he is a sage. Finally, they are scribes, a term synonymous with "sage." The Matthean treatment of Wisdom thus has implications for both his understanding of Jesus and his consideration of discipleship, which will be the focus of our discussion in chapter 4.

Matthew, then, ascribes to Jesus some of the roles given to Lady Wisdom in various biblical and Second Temple traditions. As it did in the earlier traditions, so too for Matthew the Wisdom metaphor plays a speculative role. Jesus assumes the functions of Wisdom in terms of the basic questions outlined in chapter 1. Thus, to the question, "Why has evil befallen the people? Why has the Temple been destroyed?" Matthew might respond, "Because the people and their teachers have not recognized Jesus-Wisdom," or "Because they have rejected him." To the question, "How do the people know God's will and respond to it?" Matthew would reply, "Through Jesus' teaching, which is the authoritative interpretation of our tradition." To the question, "How is God known?" Matthew would have replied, "Through the revelation which occurs in the context of discipleship to Jesus the Son, who is Wisdom." And if one had asked, "How does God respond to those who turn away from the divine presence and call to repentance?" Matthew would have answered, "As a mother who would gather and shelter her children."

Matthew thus has taken over many of the elements of Wisdom to describe Jesus, but he has not assumed certain other aspects. He does not speak of Jesus as pre-existent, or as the instrument of creation.[184] There is no *Logos* speculation in Matthew's use of the Wisdom metaphor, and Matthew does not identify Jesus with Torah. Some would say that Matthew has indeed made the latter identification. They would argue that because Wisdom is identified with Torah in Jewish literature and Jesus is identified with Wisdom in Matthew's gospel, Jesus must therefore be identified with Torah as well as with Wisdom.[185] This argument presupposes that, in adopting the Wisdom myth, Matthew has assumed it in *all* of its aspects. We have already observed that Matthew leaves aside such elements as pre-existence and *Logos* speculation. We believe that Matthew has similarly left aside the identification of Wisdom and Torah in his description of Jesus as Wisdom incarnate.

How can we explain the fact that Matthew at least appears to leave aside such important elements as speculation about Wisdom's pre-existence and role in creation, considerations about the *Logos*, and the identification of Wisdom with Torah? We can do so if we recall the tensive nature of metaphor, the fact that the vehicle expands to include new content, with changing contexts. Thus, one element or another is emphasized or abandoned according to need. We have already seen this to be the case with use of the metaphor Lady Wisdom in biblical and early Jewish literature. The metaphor, as it appears in *1 Enoch* and several of the Qumran texts, does not refer to Wisdom's role in creation. The content of the metaphor, the tenor, shifts.

But Matthew — expanding on his sources Q and M — has done something more radical. He has transformed the metaphor Lady Wisdom to present us with Jesus-Wisdom. Matthew has located the tenor, the content of "Wisdom," not in the female figure of *Lady* Wisdom, whether considered as "mere" poetic personification, as hypostasis, or as distinct goddess. Rather, he has located the tenor in a historical, if exalted, *male*. The interactive nature of metaphor means that Jesus the vehicle tells us something about the nature of Wisdom, and the tenor Wisdom tells us something about who Jesus is.

Thus, in the context of the materials examined in this chapter, if we would know who Jesus is, we must look to Wisdom. And if we would know the nature of Wisdom, we must look to Jesus. Just as the tensive nature of metaphor had allowed Philo occasionally to use a male personification for Wisdom, so Matthew has been able to identify the tenor of a hitherto female metaphor with a historical male figure. We will explore the social significance of the transformation of gender in chapter 4.

The tensive nature of metaphor, as well as literary and historical precedent, suggest that, in describing Jesus as Wisdom, Matthew has abandoned the female character of the vehicle,[186] just as he has abandoned, for example, cosmological speculation. For Matthew, Jesus is

Wisdom not because she has become male or because Jesus has become female, but rather because he *functions* as does Wisdom. And
Matthew's transformation of the metaphor has caused the female nature of that metaphor to be absorbed into the male figure of Jesus. All
of this is so because the center of Matthew's symbolic universe is no
longer Torah-Wisdom, but Jesus.[187]

This shift in gender may also have been facilitated by the association
of Wisdom with the apocalyptic Son of Man, exemplified in *1 Enoch*.
As we noted in chapter 1, the Enochian Son of Man is given the spirit of
wisdom, and functions as revealer of wisdom and as apocalyptic judge.
One finds parallels in Matthew's portrayal. The limitations of this study
prevent us from making an argument for literary dependence of Matthew on the *Similitudes*.[188] However, one can certainly observe that the
tradition articulated in *1 Enoch* may have served as a precedent for
Matthew. He may have believed that, just as the Son of Man is closely
associated with the spirit of Wisdom, so too is Jesus to be understood
as one with divine Wisdom.

Yet another element allows Matthew to identify Wisdom with Jesus.
In the previous chapter we observed that the metaphor Lady Wisdom,
as it occurs in late biblical and early Jewish sources, is usually best
understood as an hypostasis resembling the deified virtues of Greek and
Roman religions, which represented intermediary powers through whom
divine power acted in the world.[189]

Literary and epigraphical sources abound. Cicero, for example, gives
us a long list of deified virtues. They are gods named according to the
benefits they confer, according to the Greek sages and Roman ancestors,
he says: Ops, Salus, Libertas, Victoria,[190] Mens, Virtus, and Fides.[191] All
appear in female representations.

In the Greco-Roman world, deified virtues were sometimes identified
with charismatic leaders, especially the monarch.[192] For example, Romans believed that deified virtues such as Pax, Justitia, Concordia and
Providentia had their earthly manifestations in Caesar Augustus.

There is no evidence that Matthew had any intention of comparing Jesus with Caesar. However, the evangelist was a person of the
Greco-Roman world. He lived in a cultural and religious milieu in
which people thought that they had access to deified virtues through
charismatic figures, particularly the emperor, with whom those virtues
and powers were identified. Moreover, in Matthew's world, human
self-consciousness could be replaced by a spirit, either evil or good.
He — as Q or the *Gospel of Thomas* — may have believed that Jesus
was thus "possessed" by hypostatized Wisdom, a previously female
representation.[193]

Matthew's gospel is a polemical document. Does Matthew's identification of Jesus as Wisdom imply a polemic against a Wisdom
speculation that understands Wisdom to be a "supreme revealer figure"?[194] There is no evidence of a polemic against such speculation;
however, all of the Wisdom passages occur within a polemical setting.
Matt. 11:19 and 11:25–30 occur in the context of popular rejection of
Jesus. And the context, whether remote or immediate, of all of relevant
passages includes debate between Jesus and scribes and/or Pharisees.
Jesus, rather than opposing teachers, has authority to interpret the tradition, reveal apocalyptic mysteries, and to send forth prophets, wise
men, and scribes because he is Wisdom. Thus Matthew's identification
of Jesus with Wisdom is part of a polemic about authority over the
community and over the interpretation of Torah, rather than about a
"supreme revealer figure."

In chapter 1, we suggested that the metaphor of Lady Wisdom served
to legitimate the sages' teaching authority. Disciples might go to the
sages and find her because the sages were united with Lady Wisdom.
Matthew shows that Jesus' interpretation of Torah is authoritative because he is identified with Wisdom. Those who accept his invitation find
Wisdom because of that identification. Jesus' opponents, Matthew implies, cannot render a proper interpretation because in rejecting Jesus
they separate themselves from Wisdom. Within the confines of the narrative, Matthew tells us that the envoys sent by Jesus-Wisdom, the
prophets, sages, and scribes, are the legitimate authorities who correctly
interpret Torah and hand on the apocalyptic mysteries because they are
Wisdom's envoys.

Matthew, then, emphasizes and develops a trend toward Wisdom
christology already present in his sources. The redactor perceives that
Jesus is who Wisdom is, does what Wisdom does. But what takes precedence, the metaphor or the perception? In other words, does Matthew
reflect on Jesus' life and teaching as mediated through his sources and
then extend the application of the Wisdom metaphor? Or does he begin with the source and the metaphor available in Jewish sources and
appropriated by Q and M, and then develop his understanding of Jesus?

I do not believe that it is possible to resolve this matter, that it is a
matter of a circular process, with metaphor and perception generating
each other in much the same way that sacred symbols both express a
community's experience on the one hand, and shape and transform it
on the other.[195] I do think, however, that Matthew's social position as a
learned person, a sage in the community, would have made him alert to
the rhetorical and speculative possibilities offered by the Wisdom metaphor. Given the social nature of metaphor, the trope of Wisdom would

have expressed Matthew's reality and that of his community, both the scribal group of leaders and the community at large. The metaphor would also have served to shape that reality.

Matthew's editing of his sources, particularly the way in which he alters verb tenses and person, suggests that the rhetorical function of the Wisdom metaphor points beyond the narrative, beyond the story of Jesus-Wisdom and his envoys, to its social context in the Matthean community. Later discussion will explore the ways in which it serves to legitimate the authority of those Matthew recognizes as the community's authentic teachers.

Chapter 3

Jesus-Wisdom the Teacher

Matthew develops the use of the metaphor Lady Wisdom, transferring its content from a female image to a historical, if exalted, male, Jesus. He does this because he believes Jesus to possess some of the same attributes and perform some of the same functions as does Lady Wisdom in biblical, Second Temple, and tannaitic sources. And he uses the transformed metaphor to reflect on some of the issues addressed in those earlier traditions. Matthew is able to effect such a transformation for various reasons, for example, the tensive nature of metaphor and the contemporary practice of associating deified virtues with charismatic male figures.

Our findings in chapter 1 suggest that various features of the Wisdom metaphor correspond to aspects of the sage's role(s). And the contours of the portrait of Jesus-Wisdom, as it emerged in the previous chapter, suggest that Matthew is particularly interested in his subject's teaching role. The historical Jesus had been a teacher. Certainly, by the end of the first century various traditions described him as such, and Matthew highlights this in various ways. As we noted in the introduction, the redactor was involved in the scribal activity of interpreting and transmitting the tradition. In other words, Matthew himself was a teacher. He would, therefore, have had a particular sensitivity to this aspect of traditional understandings of Jesus' ministry, specifically, use of the Wisdom metaphor whose features corresponded to various aspects of the teacher's role.

In this chapter we will concentrate on the role of teacher which Matthew ascribed to Jesus-Wisdom. We will examine more closely the various facets of that role: prophet, wonder-worker, apocalyptic sage, teacher of Torah, and lowly one. Matthew draws clear parallels between the portrait of Jesus and that of the disciples, understood not simply as followers of Jesus but as leaders of the Matthean community.[1] Thus, a closer look at Matthew's description of Jesus-Wisdom the teacher will allow us to discuss more fully in chapter 4 his understanding of the disciples' role as sages. We will suggest that use of the Wisdom metaphor serves to legitimate Jesus' teaching, and — by extension — the teaching given in his name.

This chapter does not explore in depth all facets of Matthew's portrait of Jesus as teacher. Rather, I have chosen to concentrate on those elements that emerge specifically in the Wisdom passages themselves or in their contexts.

Ho Didaskalos

Matthew's vocabulary, both traditional and redactional, indicates that he considers Jesus to be teacher. This is readily apparent in the first Wisdom passage where the scribe addresses Jesus as *didaskale* (8:19), with the vocative a Matthean insertion.[2] While Matt. 8:18–22 is the only Wisdom passage where one finds *didaskale*, the noun occurs in the contexts of all these passages. For instance, Matthew again inserts the designation into 9:11, when he has the Pharisees ask Jesus' disciples, "Why does your teacher eat with tax collectors and sinners?"[3] And in 10:24–25, in the instruction on discipleship and the commissioning of the Twelve, Matthew will incorporate the use of the word from Q.[4] Then, in 12:38, he inserts the word into the scribes and Pharisees' request for a sign.[5] Matthew's M saying in chapter 23 has Jesus tell the disciples that they are not to be called "rabbi" because they have "one teacher" (v. 8). And in three of the controversy stories in chapter 22, opposing teachers address Jesus as *didaskale*.[6]

Use of *didaskalos* reflects Matthew's understanding of Jesus as teacher. The vocative serves occasionally to emphasize the motif of discipleship (8:19, 10:24–25, 23:8). It is usually uttered by Jesus' opponents, and it serves to place the conflict or challenge in the realm of scholastic debate. It implies that the opponents recognize Jesus' "credentials" as a teacher and thereby heightens the tone of conflict.

The verb *didaskō* appears in the context of the Wisdom passages as well. In fact, chapters 8–13, where much of the relevant material occurs, are bracketed by summary statements in which the verb or its cognate noun appears. The previous unit, Matt. 5:1–7:29, concludes with a summary taken from Mark:[7] "Now when Jesus had finished saying these sayings, the crowds were astounded at his teaching, for he taught them as one having authority, and not as their scribes."[8] Matthew focuses on the *fact* of Jesus' teaching by adding *tous logous toutous*, and omitting the reference to the Capernaum synagogue. The statement thereby points back to the teaching contained in the immediately preceding Sermon on the Mount. Moreover, Matthew inserts the possessive pronoun and thus emphasizes the polemic between Jesus the teacher and "their" scribes.

In 9:35, Matthew takes over the Markan statement about Jesus teaching in the villages. He expands the Markan text so that what he presents to us is "Then Jesus went about all the cities and villages, teaching in their synagogues, and proclaiming the good news of the kingdom, and curing every disease and every sickness." Matthew's editing of the remainder of 9:35–38 will form a bridge with the commissioning of the disciples in 10:1–42, which we will discuss in the next chapter. Chapter 10, and thereby the broader unit of 8:1–10:42, is delineated from the following section (11:2–13:58) with the transitional statement: "Now when Jesus had finished instructing his twelve disciples, he went on from there to teach and proclaim his message in their cities" (11:1).

Matthew does not indicate the content of *didaskō*[9] in the summary statements, although he does in other instances. There is no need to indicate the contents of the verb in 7:28–29, 9:35, and 11:1, for these are either transitional or summary statements.[10] The content is to be sought in the body of Matthew's gospel. However, through his redactional activity, Matthew tells us that he considers teaching as essential to Jesus' ministry as preaching the message of the *basileia tōn ouranōn* and healing the afflicted.

Jesus-Wisdom

Wonder-Worker

The summary statements, we noted, associate teaching and preaching with healing, and the Matthean narrative itself situates much of the Wisdom material in relationship to miracles. Most immediately, we recall the saying about Wisdom's deeds in 11:19 and its direct reference to the statement about the deeds of the Christ in verses 2–6. There, preaching and wonder-working are joined explicitly.

The parable and saying about Wisdom's deeds is followed immediately in Matthew by the woes on the Galilean cities (11:20–24). Matthew's redaction of the Q material, with his repetition of the word *dynameis*, emphasizes the relationship between Wisdom and wonderworking. That relationship is displayed in even sharper relief in the closing statement of the section, 13:54, "Where did this man get this wisdom and these deeds of power?"

If we examine the material more extensively, we will recall that Matthew joins preaching and teaching with healing in the summary

statement in 9:35. Indeed, the dominant feature of chapters 8 and 9 —
the context of the Wisdom passage Matt. 8:18–22 — is the collection
of miracle stories gathered from Mark and Q. As we have noted, those
stories include healing, exorcism, raising from the dead, and a nature
miracle. Matthew appears to attribute some diseases to demon possession (8:16; Mark 1:34). In any event, he interprets Jesus' activity
as healer and exorcist as fulfillment of prophecy, citing Isa. 53:4, the
Isaian servant song, in 8:17.[11] Matthew tells us that Jesus is wonder-
worker as Servant, following immediately with the passage in which
Jesus-Wisdom, sage and Son of Man, reminds a would-be disciple of
the cost of discipleship.

Moreover, as we noted earlier, the literature in which Lady Wisdom
appears sometimes refers to wonder-working. At Qumran, the *maskîl*
exorcises and the community expects victory over the evil spirit.[12]
1 Enoch 54:4–6 anticipates the apocalyptic victory over the evil spirits,
and 69:27–29 contrasts the downfall of the evil spirits with the triumph
of the Son of Man. 2 Baruch holds forth the promise of miracle-working
in conjunction with apocalyptic transformation in the coming age. And
some of the sages of the tannaitic era are described as wonder-workers.[13]
Finally, beyond the range of our specific texts, the figure of Solomon is
associated with exorcism and healing.[14] All of this suggests that in many
circles in the Second Temple and tannaitic eras, prophecy, healing, and
exorcism were considered to be related to the possession of wisdom and
the function of teaching. In other words, wisdom, learning, and wonder-
working were all part of being a sage, particularly in the context of a
belief in the presence of the apocalyptic end of days.

I believe that Matthew is working from this context when he describes Jesus' activity in chapters 8 and 9, as elsewhere in the first gospel.
The fact that the miracle cycle includes the story of the two blind men
confirms this. They address Jesus as "Son of David" (9:27). As we noted
in chapter 2, this is not a messianic title in this context, but a reference
to Jesus' status as successor to Solomon's healing function.

Jesus has disciples. As Wisdom he reminds the scribe in 8:18–22 that
if he follows Jesus, he is following Wisdom who is homeless. And he
calls a tax collector in 9:9.[15] Finally, in 10:1–16 he calls the Twelve and
commissions them to exorcise, heal, raise the dead, and preach the nearness of the kingdom of heaven. As we will see more fully in chapter 4,
they are to continue Jesus' mission as wonder-worker and preacher of
the kingdom.

There is a polemical quality in Matthew's description of Jesus calling
disciples. There is the reference to Jesus' homelessness, recalling the rejection of Wisdom. When Jesus has called the tax collector and is seen

eating with tax collectors and sinners, the Pharisees challenge Jesus' disciples about their master's behavior (9:10–13).[16] John's disciples query Jesus, contrasting his disciples who do not fast with the Pharisees and themselves who do fast (9:14–17).[17] The miracle stories function within that polemic, legitimating the authority of Jesus-Wisdom, verifying that the divine presence is indeed with him, inviting people to faith. The wonders worked by Jesus-Wisdom address the audience at large, as well as competing groups such as John the Baptist's disciples or Pharisees.

The sayings about the sign of Jonah and the wisdom of Solomon in chapter 12 respond to the scribes of the Pharisees' request for a sign (v. 38), following a healing story in which Jesus cures a blind and mute demoniac (12:22–30). Matthew's version has the people wonder if Jesus is the Son of David,[18] referring to Solomon the sage, exorcist, and healer. When the Pharisees accuse Jesus of exorcising by the power of Beelzebul (v. 24), it is the accusation of leaders of the dominant faction seeking to exercise social control.[19] Jesus' response indicates that he exorcises by the Spirit of God, an indication of the presence of God's reign (v. 28). Matt. 12:38–42 suggests that Jesus exorcises in his capacity as the sage greater than Solomon, himself known as healer and exorcist, and that activity calls people to repentance.

Matt. 13:53–58 closes the longer unit 11:2–13:58 in which occurs much of the Wisdom material. Matthew has taken the passage from Mark (6:1–6a). The way in which he has redacted the Markan material, however, is suggestive of his particular understanding of Jesus' teaching function.

Mark follows the parables of 4:1–34 and the miracles of 4:35–5:43 with a pericope about Jesus' teaching in the synagogue in "his hometown" (*tēn patrida autou*, Mark 6:1). When he has finished, his listeners exclaim, "Where did this man get all this? What is this wisdom that has been given to him? What deeds of power are being done by his hands!" (v. 2).[20] The listeners then refer to Jesus' parents and relatives as indicating the *impossibility* of his possessing such wisdom and mighty works, and they are scandalized (*kai eskandalizonto en autō*, v. 3). Jesus responds with a proverb about the prophet's reception. And Mark concludes the pericope with the observation that Jesus could work but few miracles there and that he marveled at his listeners' unbelief (vv. 4–6).

Matthew rearranges the material. To begin, he places the pericope immediately after the parables of the *basileia*, a collection that includes most of the Markan parallels.[21] Matthew includes the miracles of Mark 4:35–5:43 in chapters 8 and 9. Indeed, the only miracle accounts in Matt. 11:2–13:52 are the healing of the man with the withered hand in 12:9–14[22] and the healing of the blind and mute demoniac in 12:22–

23.[23] The section 11:2–13:52 begins with the pericope taken from Q
in which the disciples of John the Baptist question Jesus about his messianic identity and are given a reference to his preaching and miracles
as evidence.

Matthew's redaction of 13:53–58 summarizes the major themes of
the preceding section and the ways in which he views Jesus' teaching
role. Verses 53b–54a read, "He left that place. He came to his hometown and began to teach the people in their synagogue" (*kai elthōn eis
tēn patrida autou edidasken*). Matthew abbreviates the Markan version,
which reads, "He left that place and came to his hometown, and his
disciples followed him. On the sabbath he began to teach in the synagogue" (Mark 6:1–2). Matthew's editing of Mark accomplishes two
things. First, it concentrates the reader's attention on Jesus' teaching in
the synagogue. And, by referring to "their synagogue" (*synagōgē autōn*)
instead of "the synagogue" (*tē synagōgē*), Matthew injects a note of
polemic. This places Jesus' teaching over against that of the leaders of
"their synagogue," and it prepares the reader for the congregation's
response in verses 54b–57.

We see Matthew's editorial hand at work in the clause that records
the congregation's reaction: "so that they were astonished and said . . . "
(*hōste ekplēssesthai autous kai legein*, v. 54b). Mark has "And many
who heard him were astonished, saying . . . " (*kai hoi polloi akouontes
ekseplēssonto legontes*, 6:2). The Matthean change relates the crowd's
reaction more directly to Jesus' teaching and focuses the reader's attention on their response, which follows immediately: "Where did this man
get this wisdom and these deeds of power?" (*pothen toutō hē sophia
hautē kai hai dynameis*, v. 54b).

Once again, Matthew has edited the longer Markan version: "Where
did this man get all this? What is this wisdom that has been given to
him? What deeds are being done by his hands!" (*pothen toutō tauta;
. . . kai hai dynameis toiautai dia tōn cheirōn autou ginomenai*, Mark
6:2). Matthew's shorter version calls the reader's attention to Jesus' wisdom and mighty works. Given the context of this passage, "wisdom"
and "deeds of power" refer to Jesus' teaching — Torah interpretation,
prophetic warning, apocalyptic parable — as well as the miracles signaled in 11:2–13:52. The significance of Jesus' teaching and miracles is
understood by Matthew's insertion after the reference to Jesus' origins:
"Where then did this man get all this?" (*pothen oun toutō tauta panta*,
v. 56b).[24]

Matthew concludes the pericope: "And he did not do many deeds of
power there, because of their unbelief" (*kai ouk epoiēsen ekei dynameis
pollas dia tēn apistian autōn*) (v. 58). Again, he has shortened Mark,

which has: "And he could do no deed of power there, except that he laid his hands on a few sick people and cured them. And he was amazed at their unbelief" (*kai ouk edunato ekei poiēsai oudemian dynamin, ei mē oligois arrōstois epitheis tas cheiras etherapeusen. kai ethaumasen dia tēn apistian autōn*, Mark 6:5–6).

Matthew's editorial skill thus allows him to use this traditional pericope to describe Jesus' teaching activity as associating Torah, apocalyptic revelation, prophecy, and wonder-working. In his portrait of Jesus converge several of the functions associated with Jewish teachers of Second Temple and tannaitic Judaism. Moreover, Matthew's redaction of 13:53–58 places Jesus' teaching activity in a highly polemical context. Jesus the teacher and apocalyptic Son stands over against opposing teachers and is rejected by the membership of "their" synagogue as well.

Throughout Matthew's gospel, Jesus' miracles authenticate his identity and teaching, inviting people to faith. But they also suggest that responses of unbelief or opposition, whether by the general populace or competing teachers, are without excuse.

Prophet

In chapter 2 we observed that the texts suggest that, for Matthew, Jesus-Wisdom is a prophet. The word *prophētēs* is not used by Jesus' disciples in Matthew's gospel. Rather, "others" (*heteroi*, 16:14) or the "crowds" (*hoi ochloi*, 21:11, 46) call him a prophet.[25] Only in Matt. 13:57 (Mark 6:4) does Jesus use it of himself.

Other features of Matthew's gospel, however, indicate a prophetic quality to the identity of Jesus-Wisdom. Matthew takes over the traditional use of *kēryssō* to refer to Jesus' exhortation to repentance and announcement of the nearness of the *basileia* (4:17, 23; 9:35).[26] Matthew redacts his material in such a way that he refers the verb directly to the *basileia tōn ouranōn* in 4:17, 23; 9:35. And he redacts the report of John's preaching in 3:1 to make it identical with that of Jesus.[27]

But why does use of *kēryssō* imply that Jesus is a prophet? Most immediately, there is the parallelism with John's activity (3:1, 4:17). Also, while the ordinary meaning of the verb is "to announce" or "to proclaim,"[28] in the Septuagint it sometimes refers directly to prophetic activity.[29] It is particularly significant for our purposes that it describes Lady Wisdom's announcements in Prov. 1:21 and 8:1, and the noun *kērygma* is used similarly in Prov. 9:3.

The Wisdom passage of Matt. 8:18–22 recalls Elijah's call of Elisha (1K 19:19–21),[30] and thus models Jesus after that paradigmatic prophet. And the miracle stories of chapters 8 and 9 echo the miracle stories re-

counted in the Elijah and Elisha cycles in 1–2 Kings. Cleansing the leper
(8:1–4) and raising the dead child (9:18–26) confirm the impression that
Matthew uses Elijah and Elisha as models.[31]

The prophetic quality of Jesus-Wisdom's teaching role is also evident
in the fact that Matthew not only adopts the woes from Q, but expands
them, first in 11:20–24 and then in chapter 23, using and highlight-
ing a literary form common in classical prophecy as well as apocalyptic
literature.[32] Matthew suggests that Jesus-Wisdom is prophet in 11:16–
19 by following immediately with the woes on Chorazin and Bethsaida
(vv. 20–24). He emphasizes the prophetic call to repentance by adding
plēn legō hymin in verse 22, and then repeating the reference to the
mighty works and the day of judgment in verses 23b–24.[33]

Matthew expands the woes against the scribes and Pharisees in chapter 23. His version thus includes 23:15, 16–22, 24, 27b–28, 30, and
he rewrites Luke 11:39–41 as a woe (Matt. 23:25–26). Furthermore,
Matthew has the lament — another prophetic form[34] — in verses 37–39
follow directly the saying about Wisdom's envoys.[35] The lament speaks
of the rejection of Wisdom specifically in the context of the persecution
of Wisdom's envoys. And it forms a transition to the apocalyptic discourse of chapter 24, implying that the destruction of Jerusalem is due
to the rejection of Jesus-Wisdom.

Jesus' teaching in Matt. 12:41–42 is a prophetic warning. This time
it is directed to the "scribes and Pharisees" of "this generation" who
seek a sign (12:38–39). Matthew shows Jesus responding to their request by stating that no sign shall be given except that of Jonah, which
Matthew interprets to be the resurrection (vv. 39–40).[36] The significance
of Jonah's preaching as effecting repentance is not lost upon the evangelist, however. He follows the reference to the resurrection with the
saying about Jonah's preaching and Nineveh's repentance, and parallels these with Solomon's wisdom (v. 42). The conclusion of the two
sayings ("See, something greater than Jonah is here.... See, something
greater than Solomon is here") indicates that prophecy and Wisdom are
combined in the description of Jesus' eschatological role.[37]

Matt. 13:53–58 also presents us with the prophetic quality of Wisdom. The crowd takes offense (13:57; cf. Mark 6:3), and Jesus gives
a parting word: "A prophet is not without honor except in his own
hometown and in his own house."[38] Matthew has shortened the Markan
version (cf. Mark 6:4), but his adapting of the traditional proverb implies, as it does in Mark, that Jesus is not only teacher but also prophet.
Indeed, Matthew associates directly these various roles, and by doing so
in the context of Jesus' teaching in "their" synagogue, and by placing
that scene after the parabolic discourse of chapter 13, he tells us that

the teacher is also prophet and wonder-worker and that prophecy and wonder-working are actually corollaries of teaching.[39]

Jesus-Wisdom the prophet stands over against various groups — "this generation," the Galilean cities, the townspeople of Nazareth. Most often, scribes and Pharisees, opposing teachers, form either the primary focus of prophetic activity or, at the very least, form part of the "outside" group. Jesus-Wisdom's prophetic address castigates those who would reject him, announces judgment on the unrepentant, and predicts destruction.

Description of Jesus-Wisdom as prophet legitimates that address, since it places Jesus in continuity with the prophets of Israel's past. It explains why his word and works are rejected. After all, Wisdom is rejected and the prophets persecuted and killed.

The Lowly Sage

In the invitation issued by Jesus as both Wisdom and teacher of wisdom, Matthew describes Jesus as calling himself "gentle and humble of heart" (*praus eimi kai tapeinos tē kardia*, 11:29). As we have observed elsewhere, it is likely that in 11:29 *tapeinos* is traditional and *praus* is redactional.[40]

Neither of these terms nor their cognates appears frequently in Matthew or in the synoptic tradition. In the synoptic tradition, *tapeinos* appears only in Matt. 11:29 and in Luke 1:52, but these terms and their cognates are significant as forming part of the *anawim* vocabulary used for Jesus and his followers — both believers and leaders of the community — in early texts.[41]

Matthew usually retains such language when he finds it in the tradition.[42] He never omits traditional usage; moreover, he includes it from his special tradition in 11:29. Most interesting for our purposes is the fact that Matthew inserts these terms into traditional material.[43]

In 11:29 and 21:5, where he adds *praus*, it refers specifically to Jesus. What is Matthew telling us in these two instances? In 21:5, he uses it when citing Zech. 9:9 to provide prophetic legitimation for Jesus' triumphal ride into Jerusalem, which the evangelist interprets in messianic fashion: "Tell the daughter of Zion, Look your king is coming to you, humble and mounted on a donkey, and on a colt, the foal of a donkey." Both the Masoretic text and the LXX describe the messianic king as righteous and saving, meek (*ṣadîq wᵉnôšāʿ hûʾ ānî; dikaios kai sōzōn autos, praus*).[44] Matthew diverges from both the MT and the LXX on several points. For our purposes, however, most significant is the fact that Matthew has used a version of the Zechariah text that does not have the references to the king as righteous and saving as well as meek. I believe that Matthew has done so precisely to emphasize Jesus' messianic identity and ministry as one of meekness.[45]

In 12:15–21, Matthew uses Isa. 42:1–4, one of the Servant Songs, to interpret Jesus' healing activity.[46] As we have seen, that activity occurs in the context of teaching. Matthew's usage recalls the figures of the wise one in Wis. 2:12–20 and the Son of Man of *1 Enoch* (48:10, 52:4), both of whom are described as God's Servant.[47] The evangelist describes Jesus-Wisdom as teacher, Son of Man, and God's Servant. And his use of the Servant Song underscores the motif of meekness and humility found in 11:28–30.[48]

The use of *anawim* language in 11:28–30 may reflect the ideal of the sage found in some Second Temple and tannaitic sources. Some of these use Moses as the paradigm of the lowly sage. This would suggest that, in 11:28–30, Matthew uses the Moses typology to signal Jesus as authoritative teacher.[49]

In Matt. 11:29, Jesus' meekness is asserted specifically in reference to his role as teacher as well as Wisdom. The description of Jesus as "gentle and lowly of heart" is part of his invitation "Come to me.... Take my yoke upon you and learn from me" (vv. 28–29). Moreover, the designation of Jesus' gentleness actually legitimates Jesus' role as Teacher. "Take my yoke upon you and learn from me; *for* I am gentle and lowly in heart" (*arate ton zygon mou eph'hymas kai mathete ap'emou hoti praus eimi tapeinos tē kardia*). It is Jesus' meekness that signals him as the proper teacher.[50]

This validation of Jesus as teacher is all the more evident when one notes that the invitation is addressed to those who "labor and are carrying heavy burdens" (*kopiōntes kai pephortismenoi*, v. 28). As we have noted in the context of the whole passage, the "burden" to which verse 28 alludes is that of the scribes and Pharisees' failure to stand in solidarity with those whom they teach. In contrast to them, Matthew's Jesus not only promises instruction, but his continuing presence.[51] Thus, Matthew's use of *anawim* vocabulary to describe Jesus legitimates both Jesus' role as the *proper* teacher and the excellence of his teaching, in much the same fashion as meekness is attributed to sages like the Teacher of Qumran, or to certain tannaim.

Such vocabulary is particularly suitable in view of Jesus-Wisdom's audience, described in the Wisdom passage, Matt. 11:16–19. Matt. 11:19, the saying about Wisdom's deeds, occurs at the end of the parable of the children in the marketplace and its interpretation, which applies the parable to John the Baptist and Jesus (vv. 16–17, 18). Most immediately, Wisdom's deeds refer to Jesus' eating with tax collectors and sinners

(v. 19a). Wisdom invites her disciples to a banquet in the traditional texts (Prov. 9:1–6; Sir. 24:19–22). And Jesus-Wisdom participates in table fellowship with those he would have as his disciples. But in this case, the table partners are outcasts, not only those who have been termed such by dominant social groups, but those who have *placed themselves* on the margins of society by actively harming their fellows.[52]

The memory of such behavior, which appears to have caused scandal during the lifetime of the historical Jesus,[53] may have still been problematic in Matthew's day. Certainly describing that behavior as Wisdom's deeds would have been a theological justification for that memory and for the continued inclusion of outcasts in the Matthean community.

In Matt. 11:16–19, the polemic about Jesus' objectionable choice of table companions is between Jesus and "this generation" (v. 16). But the conflict recalls 9:11, where the Pharisees question Jesus' disciples about his behavior.[54] There they challenge the behavior of Jesus as a teacher: "Why does your teacher eat with tax collectors and sinners?"[55] In 11:19, however, Matthew's Jesus refers to himself as Wisdom, Jesus-Wisdom. The people of "this generation" have pitted themselves against one who is personified Wisdom, not merely a superior teacher.

Wisdom's deeds refer as well to the deeds of preaching, healing, and raising the dead heralded in 11:2–6. Most directly, these deeds signal Jesus as the "Christ" (v. 2) and the "Coming One" (v. 3). However, they also echo the miracles of chapters 8 and 9, as we observed in chapter 2. And we noted earlier that in the context of Second Temple and tannaitic Judaism, one must view teaching, wonder-working, and prophecy as interrelated in an apocalyptic expectation. And so, too, in 11:2–19.

But the kind of wonder-worker, teacher, prophet Matthew presents in the figure of Jesus, those to whom he directs his words and deeds, is also signaled in 11:2–6. The blind, lame, lepers, deaf, the poor — these receive the benefits of Jesus' powers as wonder-worker, in accord with prophetic expectation.[56]

The reference to the raising of the dead, already present in Q (Luke 7:22), in the Matthean context makes an even closer parallel with chapters 8 and 9. The allusion to Isaiah, in Matthew's consideration, may have served to legitimate Jesus' wonder-working, as being that of an apocalyptic sage, the Son of Man and Messiah, and not that of a magician.

Matthew, as had Q, presents Jesus in 11:2–6 as directing his activity to the needy and to the outcast. Of course, these would have been the "innocent," in contrast to the tax collectors and sinners of verse 19, but in both texts Jesus directs himself to those marginalized in some way: socially, economically, religiously.[57]

While the categories of marginalization probably were understood literally to some extent by Matthew and his community, our discussion in chapter 4 will suggest that they also served — as they did for the Qumran community, for example — as a boundary marker, designating those inside (the ones who accepted Jesus' message and his activity) against those outside (those who rejected Jesus, his message and works).

Jesus-Wisdom and Torah

In chapter 1 we observed the identification of Lady Wisdom with Torah in many of the texts in which the metaphor occurs. And in chapter 2 we noted that while Jesus-Wisdom is not identified with Torah he is associated with Torah as teacher. This is first apparent in 11:25–30, which includes the use of the verb *paradidōmi* and the invitation with its exhortation to take up Jesus' yoke.

In verse 27a Jesus says, "All things have been handed over to me by my Father" (*panta moi paredothē*). This refers primarily to the filial relationship of Jesus with the Father, which includes knowledge and revelation. Nonetheless, *paradidōmi* is a technical term for the transmission of tradition.[58] It grounds a teacher's authority, linking his instruction to that of his predecessors.[59] Furthermore, the context of 11:27, preceding immediately the invitation to take up Jesus' yoke and the two Sabbath controversies in chapter 12, suggests that, for Matthew *paradidōmi* refers to interpretation of Torah as well as revelatory knowledge. Indeed, the whole suggests that Jesus' interpretation of Torah is legitimated by the fact that he also receives such revelation. Revelation is the locus of the chain of tradition.

The invitation contains the exhortation "take my yoke." As we have demonstrated in chapter 2, the use of the image of the yoke in Second Temple and tannaitic literature suggests that its occurrence in Matt. 11:28–30 refers to Torah as interpreted by Jesus.[60] Thus the content of Jesus' teaching is also his teaching and interpretation of Torah, and acceptance of the yoke of that teaching is concomitant with discipleship.[61] Matt. 11:25–30 authenticates Jesus' teaching by placing it in the chain of tradition. Matthew's use of a "chain of tradition" allows the redactor to show Jesus as surpassing his opponents. It implies that while they might claim authority through a chain of human teachers Jesus receives authorization from the Divine.[62]

Matt. 11:25–30 is followed by 12:1–8, which preserves a controversy over the disciples' plucking grain on the Sabbath. Matthew follows Mark 2:25–26 in defending this action on the basis of the precedent set by David and his followers in 1 Sam. 21:1–6.[63] Matthew, however, bolsters the position in verse 5 by addressing a reference to Num. 28:9–10, which describes the burnt offerings made on the Sabbath, in a *qal ve-homer* argument (cf. v. 6).[64] The addition of the Num. 28:9–10 reference justifies argument from the perspective of (proto)rabbinic interpretation; such would require *legal* precedent.[65] Matthew further inserts in verse 7 a citation of Hos. 6:6 before concluding with the statement about the Son of Man's Lordship of the Sabbath (v. 8; cf. Mark 2:27).

Matthew shows Jesus interpreting Torah in 12:9–14, another Sabbath controversy. While Matthew has again received the narrative from Mark (3:1–6), he has recast the Markan version of the Pharisees' challenge. Whereas Mark has "They watched him to see whether he would cure him on the sabbath, so that they might accuse him" (Mark 3:2), Matthew has the Pharisees ask directly, "Is it lawful to cure on the sabbath?" The direct question immediately casts the controversy as a halachic debate. Moreover, in verse 11 Matthew inserts a reference to oral Torah and shows Jesus justifying his practice halachically.[66] Jesus heals the man, and the Pharisees, outdone, go out to plot Jesus' destruction; Matthew omits the Markan reference to the Herodians.

Matthew's stance on Torah, here and elsewhere, reflects a position parallel to that of other first-century Jewish groups, although not that of the Pharisees or Essenes. Law was the focus of polemic, with each group claiming proper understanding of law over against the others.[67] At this point, we note that the placing of these controversy stories immediately after 11:25–30 shows the manner in which Jesus, Wisdom personified, is also the sage par excellence who gives authoritative interpretation of *halachah*. His interpretation is seen in a relationship of conflict to that of opposing teachers.

The passages that follow the thanksgiving and invitation demonstrate that Jesus' teaching is interpretation of Torah (Matt. 12:1–8, 9–14) as well as disclosure of the apocalyptic mysteries of the *basileia* (13:1–52), for the Matthean redaction of 12:1–8 and 9–14 shows Jesus using rabbinic principles of exegesis to reinterpret *halachah* regulating Sabbath observance. He does so not only on the basis of Scripture, but also on his authority as Son of Man (12:8). While Matthew has taken the saying about the Son of Man from Mark (Mark 2:28), the context in the First Gospel associates the apocalyptic title with Jesus' identity as Wisdom, a factor we have already met in 8:18–22.

Jesus' interpretation of Torah is understood as a conflict with those whom Matthew calls "the Pharisees" (12:2). Matthew shows Jesus' interpretation of *halachah* to be legitimated not only by his identity as Son of Man but also by his exegesis of scripture, and by his identity as Wisdom.

In chapter 23, the immediate context of the saying about Wisdom's envoys and the prophetic lament, Matthew describes Jesus' criticism as directed against the opponents' discrepancy between teaching and practice (v. 3b), lack of solidarity with those whom they teach (v. 4), and ostentation in religious practice (vv. 5–6).

Chapter 23 contains an expanded version of the woes. These include a critique of scribes' and Pharisees' interpretation and observance regarding oaths (vv. 16–22), tithes (vv. 23–24), and ritual purity (vv. 25–26).[68] Here, as in 11:25–30, we see that Jesus' teaching in the context of the Wisdom passage refers not only to prophetic warning, but also to interpretation of Torah. Jesus does not challenge *halachah* itself, but rather insists on the inner intention of religious observance. Matthew implies that this in itself makes mockery of the Pharisees' interpretation of oaths with their various distinctions. (In 5:33–37 Matthew has already rejected altogether the custom of taking oaths.)[69] Matthew's Jesus implies that tithes are to be given while attending to justice, mercy, and faith (v. 23). Moreover, ritual purity is to be observed, but only after cleansing the "inside," as an outward expression of interior attitude (v. 26).[70]

The critique articulated by Matthew's Jesus can be summed up in one word: "hypocrisy." It signifies, for Matthew, a lack of attention to the inner meaning of things, a discrepancy between teaching and doing.[71] Matthew's invective associates that hypocrisy with "lawlessness" (*anomia*, v. 28) and blindness (vv. 16, 17, 19, 24, 26) — the Pharisees "do not discern and do the true will of God."[72] Such terms suggest not intellectual debate but an attempt to gain power by directing irony and ridicule at one's opponent.[73] They call into question not the community itself or its institutions but the moral integrity of its leaders. We will explore this further in chapter 4.

Despite the bitter polemic of this section, Matthew does not describe Jesus as abrogating oral tradition or even, with the exception of verses 16–22, criticizing his opponents' exposition of that tradition. Indeed, in verses 2–3, he tells his disciples, "The scribes and Pharisees sit on Moses' seat; so practice and observe whatever they tell you, but not what they do; for they preach, but do not practice." Matthew thus describes Jesus as acknowledging his opponents' authority to interpret Torah — they "sit on Moses' seat."[74]

The charge of hypocrisy is particularly evident in verses 16–33. In verses 16–22, Matthew describes Jesus as mocking his opponents' statements about which oaths are or are not binding. In verses 23–24, Matthew does not show Jesus as contradicting the law of tithes but, rather, as criticizing his opponents for ignoring the "weightier matters" of justice, mercy, and faith, which stand behind all authentic religious practice. In verses 25–26, Jesus criticizes the opponents for their lack of inward purification, which is symbolized in the laws of ritual purity. The hypocrisy that is the target of Jesus' criticism is described graphically in verses 27–28, where the opponents are compared to "whitewashed tombs." The criticism culminates in verses 29–33, where Matthew presents Jesus as declaiming the opponents' sentiments as murderous and comparing them to those ancestors who murdered the prophets.

In chapter 23, then, Matthew's Jesus upholds Torah — according to the evangelist's interpretation of it — while making a strong critique of the opponents who interpret it differently. The chapter concludes with the Wisdom passage (23:34–36, 37–39), thereby suggesting that Jesus upholds Torah in his identification with Wisdom.

We have already described in detail Matt. 19:1–25:46, the broader literary unit in which chapter 23 is situated. We noted the element of conflict that dominates that material. At this point it is of particular interest to recall that chapter 23 is preceded immediately by the controversy stories of 22:15–40, in which various opposing teachers challenge Jesus on taxes to Caesar (vv. 15–22), the resurrection of the dead and marriage in the afterlife (vv. 23–33), priority among the commandments (vv. 34–40), and David's son (vv. 41–46). The first three concern legal matters, in one way or another. The opponents include Sadducees (vv. 23–33) and Herodians (vv. 15–22). The Pharisees are present in all three of the stories, with the exception of the narrative about the resurrection of the dead. Jesus responds to all his challengers as a teacher, quoting the *Tanach* in the last three debates.

Thus, chapter 23 presents Jesus not addressing himself primarily to leaders of the Matthean community.[75] Nor does he attack Torah observance. Indeed the invective occurs *within* the halachic framework. In that context, Jesus levels his charges at the Pharisees and scribes, those leaders most vocal in their opposition to Jesus. We will explore the significance of this for Matthew's social situation in chapter 5.

Jesus' teaching in chapter 23 includes material on discipleship (vv. 8–12), as well as that about interiority in religious practice and prophetic warnings. Although we shall examine 23:8–12 more fully in the following chapter, at this point we must observe that the material illuminates the saying about Wisdom's envoys, for Matt. 23:8–12 contrasts Jesus' disciples with those of his opponents. Thus we again see Wisdom in a polemical context. The teaching of Jesus-Wisdom challenges that of his opponents, while the humility that characterizes Wisdom's disciples and the martyrdom that is their fate stand in sharp contrast to the honors sought by Wisdom's opponents.

Certainly the broader literary unit of 19:1–25:46 describes Jesus as teaching about the nature of discipleship (19:16–22, 23–30; 20:20–28). He is acknowledged to be a prophet (21:11).[76] And he is a healer (20:29–34). There is a prophetic element in chapter 23, with its use of woe, oracle, and lament. But Matthew uses the Wisdom metaphor in chapter 23 especially to legitimate Jesus' status as interpreter of Torah who sends disciples.

In an earlier chapter, we observed the identification of Wisdom and Torah in Second Temple and tannaitic literature. The association of Wisdom with prophets and prophecy derives from this identification.[77] For "when Torah is Wisdom and the prophets are seen primarily as calling men to return to Yahweh and, hence, to Torah, then the prophets can be regarded as the 'wise' and Wisdom as the sender of prophets."[78] This statement may be pressed yet further in Matthew's association of Jesus as personified Wisdom with his role as teacher of Torah. If Wisdom is Torah, and Jesus is personified Wisdom, then his role includes not only calling people to return to Torah in repentance, but also authoritatively interpreting Torah itself.

Our study thus far suggests that Matthew uses the Wisdom metaphor and transforms it in such a way as to legitimate his understanding of Jesus as authoritative interpreter of Torah. He does this in the context of Second Temple and tannaitic understanding of the roles of the sage. At this point we need to examine more closely Matthew's notion of Jesus' relationship to Torah, as well as his interpretation of Jesus as an apocalyptic figure.

Matthew 5:17–20

Jesus' relationship to Torah is played out in the ethical teaching of Matthew's gospel. That gospel is replete with passages illustrating the evangelist's understanding of that relationship. A thorough discussion of Matthew's understanding of Jesus' relationship to Torah is beyond the limitations of our task.[79] However, Matthew sets it forth most explicitly in 5:17–20 and in the antitheses that follow. For this reason, and because the woes of chapter 23 find their inverse in the Sermon on the Mount,[80] we will focus our attention on 5:17–20, 21–48.

Matt. 5:17–20 describes a positive relationship between Jesus and Torah.[81] In verse 17, Matthew describes Jesus as exhorting, "Do not think that I have come to abolish the law or the prophets; I have come not to abolish but to fulfill" (*mē nomisēte hoti ēlthon katalysai ton nomon ē tous prophētas. ouk ēlthon katalysai alla plērōsai*). The redactional "do not think" (*mē nomisēte*)[82] implies a contrary position, likely held by some in the Matthean community — namely, that Jesus has indeed abolished the Law and the Prophets.[83] In 5:17 and the following verses, however, Matthew states his perception of the relationship of Jesus' mission and the enduring validity of Torah, understood as the entire Hebrew scriptures.

What does the redactor mean by the verb *plēroō*?[84] Does he suggest that Jesus has replaced Torah, revoked it, brought it to completion? Matt. 5:17–20 serves as an introduction to the antitheses of verses 21–48. The immediate context of 5:17–20, then, suggests that Matthew intends the verb to signify that Jesus gives the proper understanding of Torah.[85] The reference to the prophets, along with the law refers to the entirety of the Hebrew Scriptures.[86] It implies as well that Jesus' relationship to Torah is also prophetic; that is, it corresponds to and fulfills God's promises to his people.[87]

In verse 18 Matthew emphasizes his understanding of the continuing validity of Torah. He binds the traditional saying about the eternal quality of Torah to verse 17 with the redactional "for truly I tell you" (*amēn gar legō hymin*) and draws our attention to his point by the redactional conclusion "until all is accomplished" (*heōs an panta genētai*).[88] But what is the referent of *panta genētai*?[89] Does it refer to the ethical "doing" of all that is required by Torah? In this case, verse 18 would be a statement that Torah will not pass away, either as a whole or in any of its details, until it is completely carried out in the lives of human beings.[90] But this meaning is excluded by the warning in verse 19. And it is also rendered unlikely by the fact that *genētai* rarely refers to "doing." Rather, it usually refers to events happening.[91]

One meets a similar expression in Matt. 24:34: *amēn legō hymin hoti ou mē parelthē hē genea hautē heōs an panta tauta genētai* ("Truly I tell you, this generation will not pass away until all these things have taken place"). There, in a saying about the second coming of the Son of Man, Matthew has substituted *heōs an* for the Markan *ou mē*.[92] In 24:34, *panta tauta* refers to the signs preceding the Parousia. Moreover, the apocalyptic language of Matt. 27:51–53 and 28:2–4 indicates that the evangelist considered the end-time to have begun with the death and resurrection.[93] But, as we will demonstrate more fully, this does not mean that Matthew considered Torah to have reached its end-point with the death and resurrection.[94] While the apocalyptic age has begun, "heaven and earth" have not passed away, for the end of the age (*synteleia tou aiōnos*) is yet to come.[95]

That the validity of Torah does not end with the death and resurrection of Jesus is further verified in verse 19: "Therefore, whoever breaks one of the least of these commandments and teaches others to do the same.... "[96] Once again, we find a traditional logion has been integrated into the whole by the Matthean redactional use of *oun*. By incorporating this sentence, and assimilating it to verses 17–18, Matthew shows Jesus as expanding his teaching about the enduring validity of Torah and his relationship to it, to extend to his disciples and their ministry. Moreover, the fact that this is the sole instance in which *didaskō* refers to the disciples prior to the post-Easter commissioning in 28:16–20 suggests that 5:19 likewise refers to the disciples' post-Easter ministry.

The reference to "the least of these commandments" can be understood within the context of rabbinic discussion about great or little commandments.[97] The teacher's position in the *basileia tōn ouranōn*, according to Matthew, depends upon the thoroughness with which he practices and teaches Torah. "These commandments," therefore, does not refer to the Sermon on the Mount to the exclusion of Torah.[98] Rather, in the context of 5:17–20, 21–48, it refers to the observance of "law and prophets" as interpreted by Jesus.

One might ask whether verse 19 implies that the one who relaxes a lesser command and teaches others to do so might still be admitted to the *basileia tōn ouranōn*.[99] Although this would certainly appear to be the case, thus differentiating the logion from parallel Jewish discussions, the student is well advised to attend to the *point* of the logion itself, that is, that Jesus' disciples are to do and to teach *all* of Torah as interpreted by Jesus.[100] This is not contradicted by texts such as 12:1–8, 9–14, in which exceptions are made in the case of Sabbath observance. There, Jesus does not relax the command of Sabbath observance per se. Rather, he interprets it in the light of a particular case.[101]

Matt. 5:20 is a redactional saying that forms a transition from 5:17–19 to the antitheses.[102] But it also corresponds to verse 17, for the greater righteousness of verse 20 parallels Jesus' fulfilling of law and prophets in verse 17. The vocabulary here recalls the redactional sentence in 3:15, referring to Jesus' baptism: "Let it be so now, for it is proper for us in this way to fulfill all righteousness" (*plērōsai pasan dikaiosynēn*). "Righteousness" is the will of God lived out in one's life.[103] But the greater righteousness required of the disciples, over against Matthew's "scribes and Pharisees," does not in any way mean a negation of literal observance of Torah. Rather, in the context of 5:17–20, it implies observance of Torah as interpreted by Jesus.

The Antitheses (Matt. 5:21–48)

Matt. 5:20 contrasts the righteousness expected of Jesus' disciples with that of the scribes and Pharisees. The antitheses that immediately follow (vv. 21–48) suggest that the disciples' righteousness consists in observing Torah as interpreted by Jesus and give examples illustrating that observance.[104] Thus, Matt. 5:17–20 illustrates a two-front polemic that prevails throughout the gospel: first against Christian antinomians, and second against those whom Matthew calls "Pharisees" or "scribes."[105]

In 5:21–48, Matthew presents six antitheses on murder, adultery, divorce, oaths, talion, and love of enemies. Much of the material in 5:21–48 is traditional — it is likely that the teaching contained in the antitheses on divorce, talion, and love of neighbor existed in Q.[106] Matthew, however, has assembled the traditional material and joined it to his own (the antitheses on murder, adultery, and oaths), unifying the whole through use of the antithesis form.[107]

This form may have been present in Q, because in Luke we have *alla hymin legō tois akouousin* (6:27).[108] Matthew, however, has developed the antithesis into the unifying element of the entire section and, in so doing, has told us something about the way in which he envisions Jesus' relationship to Torah. He formulates the first clause of the antithesis in various ways: "You have heard that it was said to those of ancient times" (*ēkousate hoti errethē tois archaiois*, vv. 21, 33), "you have heard that it was said" (*ēkousate hoti errethē*, vv. 27, 38, 43), and "it was also said" (*errethē de*, v. 31). Whatever the form, the first clause of the antithesis is followed by a citation or paraphrase from Torah,[109] and the second clause by "but I say unto you" (*egō de legō hymin*, vv. 22, 28, 32, 34, 39, 44).

One could understand the antitheses on divorce, oaths, and talion as actually revoking prohibition or permission given in Torah,[110] and the others as radicalizing the demand of Torah.[111] If this is the case, one is left with a contradiction between the antitheses and verses 17–20. One could resolve the contradiction in several ways. First, one might say that Matthew is unaware of the inconsistency.[112] Second, one might say that it is not a matter of inconsistency, but rather an "arbitrary manner of dealing with the Torah" due to the fact that Jesus is Wisdom-Torah, and that Matthew knows no problem here because "he appeals *always* to the Torah even when he appears to contradict it."[113] Finally, one might limit the duration of the validity of Torah by the "turning of the age" referred to in verse 18. Thus one would say that "prophecy has come to pass, and so the letter must fall in favor of the prophetic-eschatological fulfillment of God's will."[114]

Yet another option offers a way through the seeming inconsistency, one that takes us in the direction pointed out by Daube[115] and Smith.[116] Daube examines the significance of the verb *šm'* in tannaitic exegesis. In that literature, the verb means "to understand literally."[117] The narrow literal understanding is countered by a broader interpretation that is sometimes based on another part of scripture. One finds an example of this in *Mek. ba-Hodesh* 8:1–3 (on Exod. 20:12): "Honor thy father and thy mother." The interpretation follows: "I might understand it [*šm' 'nî*] to mean only with words, but Scripture says, 'Honor the Lord with thy substance'" (Prov. 3:9). Hence it must mean with food and drink and with clean garments.[118]

Smith, likewise, has isolated a form similar to the last half of the antithesis, "but I say to you." Prior interpretations or opinions are cited, and then countered by another. This form has some variety with respect to wording: *hû' 'mr . . . w'nî 'mr* (*t. Bik.* 1:2; *t. Mik.* 3:4) or simply *'mr 'nî* (*t. Bek.* 6:15).[119] But in all of the instances cited, the new opinion or interpretation stands on its own without citation of prior authority or proof-text; the prior opinion is simply stated and then countered by the new.

The countering of prior opinion extends to the text of Torah itself, and one sees a variety of examples in which principles from the Pentateuch are revoked.[120] All of the examples are attributed to first-century teachers. Thus there is precedent for Matthew's "arbitrary" handling of Torah in the tannaitic literature. Such practice extended to the Decalogue itself, as one observes in a second-century text, *Mek. ba-Hodesh* 7:8–12, which interprets Exod. 20:7 as meaning that one should not swear at all.[121] In the latter instance, admittedly, one finds neither *šm' 'anî* nor the *w'nî 'amr* forms and biblical support is given for the argument.

The literature surveyed does not disclose an exact parallel to Matthew's antithesis form, which consistently places the first clause in the second person, and the second clause in the first person. This is not of real significance, however. What is significant is the countering of prior opinion — even biblical practice — with a sage's new opinion stated emphatically in the first person, often without citation of prior authority or proof-text.[122]

One notices that in Matt. 5:21–48, only 5:27 and 5:38 are exact citations of the Pentateuch.[123] All of the other citations are actually paraphrases.[124] In every instance, the interpretation of *ēkousate* as corresponding to the verb *šm'* and signifying "to understand literally" allows us to make more sense of the antithesis. Thus, we might read 5:21 as "You have understood literally that it was said to the ancients, 'You shall not kill; and whoever kills shall be liable to judgment,'" imply-ing that the one who does not kill is not so liable. Verse 27 could be read, "You have understood literally [i.e., too narrowly] that it was said, 'You shall not commit adultery,'" implying that no sin exists apart from the physical act. And verse 33 could be understood, "Again, you have understood literally that it was said to the ancients, 'You shall not swear falsely, but shall perform to the Lord what you have sworn,'" imply-ing that a false oath is simply one in which the subsequent action is not performed. A literal understanding of verse 38 would require a per-son to take "measure for measure" rather than lead him to the mercy which is the intent of the command. Finally, a literal understanding of verse 43 ("You shall love your neighbor") might imply that one hate one's enemy.

Such a rereading of the Pentateuchal material cited in the antitheses allows us to see that in every instance Jesus' response counters the lit-eral understanding and extends the meaning of the original command. It is possible that, in three instances (divorce, oaths, and talion), Jesus actually revokes the letter of the Torah. In light of the material we have investigated, this is not unique to the New Testament. For while we have found no complete, literal parallels, we have discovered material suffi-cient to indicate that the debate reflected in Matt. 5:21–28 occurs in the ambience of tannaitic Judaism. For Matthew, as for his Jewish contem-poraries, "the Law remained even while it changed."[125] On the strength of the antitheses themselves, we can say that they do indeed present Jesus as upholder of Torah. Thus, one cannot make lavish christological statements on the basis of 5:17–48 alone, nor can one be reduction-istic by saying that Matthew describes Jesus' relationship to Torah as consisting solely in "the law of love."[126]

The Sermon on the Mount, which is the context for 5:17–20, is di-rected to the Matthean community, unlike chapter 23. Nonetheless, it too has a polemical note. Indeed, the very use of the antithesis form with its parallels in rabbinic usage establishes Jesus' role as teacher who stands in opposition to other teachers.[127] Matthew's Jesus exhorts mem-bers not to be like the Gentiles (6:7) or "hypocrites" in their religious praxis (6:2, 5). The latter is likely a reference to the "scribes and Phar-isees," since "hypocrite" elsewhere in Matthew always refers to those groups.[128]

The closing section of the Sermon on the Mount has "Now when Jesus had finished these things, the crowds were astounded at his teach-ing, for he taught them as one having authority, and not as their scribes" (7:28–29).[129] The salient feature of this text is not the crowds' aston-ishment — astonishment at the teaching of Menahem ben Sungai was

expressed by his peers (t. 'Ed. 3:1).[130] Nor is it the contrast between
Jesus' teaching over against that of the opponents whom Matthew terms
"scribes" or "Pharisees." Rather, the significant feature of this text is
the cause of the crowds' amazement — the *eksousia* with which Jesus
teaches. Matthew usually retains this word from his source,[131] and he
has done so here (Mark 1:22). But there is a marked difference between
the way in which Matthew has used *eksousia* and its use in the synagogue at Capernaum, whereas Matthew has used the description with
relation to the reaction to Jesus' teaching in the Sermon on the Mount.
While Mark has given but a laconic reference to Jesus' teaching, Matthew gives it a content that includes 5:17–48 on the fulfillment of Torah
as illustrated by the antitheses.

Matthew attaches *eksousia* to Jesus' teaching again in 21:23, 24,
27 — again retaining the word from his source (Mark 11:28, 29, 33).
Both Mark and Matthew locate the pericope in the Temple immediately following the incident of the withered fig tree. But, as we noted
above, the challenge of the chief priests and elders in Matt. 21:23 refers
to Jesus' teaching.

Finally, Matthew uses *eksousia* redactionally in 28:18. There the risen
Lord declares "all authority in heaven and on earth has been given to
me," and then commissions his disciples to go out and make disciples
of all nations, baptizing them and "teaching them to observe all that I
have commanded you" (vv. 19–20). Once again, *eksousia* is associated
with teaching, this time in the commission to teach all nations. As we
shall observe in the section on discipleship, the risen Lord's authority is
associated with the *disciples'* teaching.

In light of Matt. 28:18–20 and 7:28–29, we might say that in the Sermon on the Mount Jesus teaches and interprets Torah with the authority
of the apocalyptic Son of Man, and not simply as another sage. Thus,
while the antitheses resemble other discussions in contemporary Jewish
sources, Matthew presents Jesus' interpretation as decisive because it is
the teaching of the eschatological Son of Man.

The antitheses and their heading (5:17–20) show Jesus as a sage who
counters the accusation that he has come to destroy the Law and the
Prophets by demonstrating the way in which he has come to fulfill it —
by giving its true interpretation. This portrait corresponds to the image
set forth in the introduction to the Sermon on the Mount, where Jesus
ascends the mountain and sits down and begins to teach the crowds
and disciples — an allusion to Moses' ascent of Sinai and his role as
Israel's teacher and law-giver par excellence.[132] Matthew has already set
the stage for an understanding of Jesus as successor to Moses, by the
allusions in the infancy narrative,[133] and his redaction of the temptation

story.[134] And he lends emphasis to the allusion to Moses in the Sermon on the Mount and in the conclusion in 7:28,[135] and by referring to Jesus as descending from the mountain in 8:1, which is the transition between the Sermon on the Mount and the following section.

Matt. 5:18 tells us that Torah endures until "heaven and earth pass away." Does this moment occur at the death-resurrection of Jesus, which is understood by Matthew as an apocalyptic event (27:51–53, 28:2–4)? If so, Torah is no longer to be upheld. Or does the passing away of heaven and earth occur only at the second coming (24:24–36)? If so, Torah endures until the fullness of the eschatological age is established.

We believe the latter to be the case. Although the apocalyptic tones of 27:51–53 and 28:2–4 suggest that Matthew does indeed understand Jesus' death-resurrection as an apocalyptic event, he does so proleptically. Despite the fact that the risen Jesus comes to his disciples as the exalted Son of Man in 28:16–20,[136] heaven and earth have *not* passed away — that is, the full-scale cosmic cataclysm that is to precede the fullness of the Parousia (24:29–31) has not yet occurred. The fullness of the age (*synteleia tou aiōnos*) lies ahead in the future (13:39, 40, 49; 28:20). Thus Torah endures until a future — and final — completion of the event begun in Jesus' death and resurrection.

Furthermore, the risen Lord bids his disciples to teach all nations "to observe all that I have commanded you" (28:20).[137] Because these words form the conclusion of Matthew's gospel, it is difficult to understand what the reference point of this exhortation would be other than the entire teaching of Jesus as presented in the gospel itself. Much of that teaching is framed as the true interpretation of Torah, given by Jesus the sage in his authority as personified Wisdom and apocalyptic Son of Man.

Matthew's presentation of Jesus' relationship to Torah serves several rhetorical purposes. The redactor makes it clear to those who might wish to set it aside that Torah, including halachic observance, has ongoing validity. His position also counters charges — from sources within the community as well as from outside — that Jesus and his followers have broken with Torah or misinterpret it. Matthew confronts competing teachers ("scribes" and "Pharisees") as well as those within the community who might be attracted by those teachers.

Jesus-Wisdom, Apocalyptic Sage

Does Matthew portray Jesus the teacher as apocalyptic seer in the same way that other Jewish texts portray significant teachers? Yes and no.

Matthew understands Jesus to be at the center of apocalyptic revelation. In relationship to Wisdom, this view is apparent in Matt. 8:18–22 and 11:16–19, where Jesus-Wisdom is also the Son of Man. In 11:25–30, Jesus is both apocalyptic sage and teacher of Torah. There, as in certain Second Temple traditions where one of the sage's functions was to compose hymns, Jesus utters a thanksgiving hymn.[138] "All things" are handed over to Jesus the Son by the Father (v. 27a). Thus, Matthew follows the theme present in Second Temple literature linking filial relationship, knowledge, and/or revelation.[139] He not only mediates revelation but is its subject, for the apocalyptic and messianic identity of the Son is the content of the revelation of "these things" (*tauta*), and discipleship is its locus.

In the broader context of Matt. 11:25–30, revelation to the *nēpioi* includes the apocalyptic mysteries in the parables of the *basileia tōn ouranōn* in chapter 13, including the interpretation of the parable of the weeds in which the Son of Man appears in a function of judgment (13:36–43).[140] And, immediately following 23:34–36, 37–39, the lament describing Wisdom's disappearance, Matthew describes Jesus as leaving the Temple (*kai ekselthōn ho Iēsous apo tou ierou*, 24:1).[141] There follows the apocalyptic discourse of 24:3–25:46, where Jesus speaks, as in chapter 13, not only as an apocalyptic teacher but also as one who is himself the center of the apocalyptic event. And so Matthew edits Mark's version of the disciples' query — "Tell us when will this be, and what will be the sign that all these things are about to be accomplished?" (*eipon hēmin pote tauta estai; kai ti to sēmeion hotan mellē tauta synteleisthai panta?* Mark 13:4) — to read, "Tell us when will this be, and what will be the sign of your coming and of the end of the age?" (*eipe hēmin pote tauta estai, kai ti to sēmeion tēs sēs parousias kai synteleias tou aiōnos*, Matt. 24:3). Matthew emphasizes the coming of the Son of Man by enhancing the allusion to Dan. 7:13 in 24:29–31 (Mark 13:24–27).

Here, in the context of 23:34–36, 37–39, the prophetic and apocalyptic converge with wisdom considerations, as they did in the context of the Wisdom sayings of chapter 11, and as we have seen occur in the literature of the Second Temple and tannaitic periods. There, too, sages claimed to possess Wisdom. Even texts describing Wisdom's withdrawal implied that she was actually to be found in the sages' teaching, because they had access to heavenly things through their learning and through revealed knowledge. Matthew's Jesus, however, utters prophetic warning, interprets *halachah*, and teaches about the end-time as more than just prophet, Torah scholar, and apocalyptic seer. Matthew assigns to Jesus ultimate authority in his identity as Wisdom and the Coming One.

Jesus' authority thus surpasses that of opposing sages. They may indeed be wise; he is Wisdom.

Jesus is the apocalyptic teacher and the subject of revelation in other parts of Matthew's gospel as well. In Matthew's version of Peter's confession at Caesarea Philippi, for example,[142] Jesus asks Peter, "Who do people say that the Son of Man is?" instead of "Who do people say that I am?" in Mark (Matt. 16:13; Mark 8:27).[143] Whereas Mark has Peter say, "You are the Messiah" (*sy ei ho christos*, 8:29), Matthew has "You are the Messiah, the Son of the Living God" (*sy ei ho christos ho huios tou theou tou zōntos*, 16:16). A macarism sometimes accompanies revelation in Second Temple and tannaitic literature — as it did in Matt. 13:16 (Luke 10:23).[144] Matthew adds the macarism, "Blessed are you, Simon son of Jona! For flesh and blood has not revealed this to you, but my Father in heaven" (*makarios ei Simon Bariōna hoti sarks kai haima ouk apekalypsen soi all'ho patēr mou ho en tois ouranois*, Matt. 16:17).[145] The content of revelation and the source of Simon's blessedness is the apocalyptic identity of Jesus as Messiah and Son of the Living God.[146]

The apocalyptic nature of Matthew's understanding of Jesus' role also appears in the evangelist's account of the transfiguration.[147] Apocalyptic features in the narrative are present in the Markan tradition (Mark 9:2–10):[148] the mountain as a place of revelation,[149] Jesus' altered appearance,[150] and white garments,[151] the heavenly voice[152] and the cloud,[153] and the acknowledgment of Jesus as beloved Son.[154]

Matthew's editorial activity enhances the apocalyptic quality already present in Mark.[155] He adds to Mark's version of Jesus' transfiguration, "and his face shone like the sun" (*kai elampsen to prosōpon autou hōs ho hēlios*, Matt. 17:5).[156] And whereas Mark has an extended description of the whiteness of Jesus' garments, Matthew abbreviates and has simply "his garments became white as light" (*ta de himatia autou egeneto leuka hōs to phōs*, 17:2b).[157]

Matthew's editing has several effects. He makes a nice parallel between the shining of Jesus' face and the whiteness of his garments (*hōs ho hēlios* ‖ *hōs to phōs*). This in turn heightens the apocalyptic note already present in Mark, for brilliance of countenance and raiment was commonplace in apocalyptic literature.[158]

Matthew adds a further apocalyptic note. At God's words designating Jesus as the beloved Son, the disciples "fell on their faces and were filled with fear" (*hoi mathētai epesan epi prosōpon autōn kai ephobēthēsan sphodra*, 17:6). Jesus then touches them and says, "Rise, and have no fear" (*egerthēte kai mē phobeisthe*, 17:7).[159] Prostration occurs as a response to visionary experience in biblical and postbiblical Jewish literature,[160] as does awe or fear.[161] Then God or a heavenly visitor bids the visionary to have no fear, reassures the visionary,[162] and raises the prostrate figure or bids the person to stand.[163] Matthew's addition thus places the disciples' experience in continuity with the visionaries who have preceded them and confirms the apocalyptic nature of Jesus' sonship.

There are several allusions to Moses and the theophany on Sinai: the reference to six days, the ascent and descent from the mountain, the cloud and the heavenly voice from the cloud, the presence of companions.[164] And there is the reference not only to Moses but also to Elijah who also conversed with God on Sinai/Horeb.[165] Matthew emphasizes the typology by adding the reference to Jesus shining face (v. 2; Exod. 34:29, 33–35). He adds the adjective "bright" (*phōteinē*, v. 5) to describe the cloud. And he reverses the Markan "Elijah with Moses" to read "Moses and Elijah," thereby giving priority to Moses.[166]

Lawgiver and prophet, both associated with Sinai, disappear after the divine command "Listen to him" (vv. 5–8; Mark 9:7–8). The narrative implies that they are subordinate to Jesus the Son.[167] Moses typology and apocalyptic motifs thus both appear in the transfiguration story. Matthew heightens them in ways that recall such Second Temple literature as 4 Ezra and *2 Apoc. Baruch*.[168]

Matthew adds an apocalyptic note to the passion narrative in 27:51–53[169] when he tells us that not only was the temple curtain torn in two (cf. Mark 14:38), but that an earthquake occurred, tombs were opened and saints raised (27:51–52). Earthquakes signal the moment of apocalyptic tribulation or judgment.[170] The opening of tombs and raising of the saints echoes the expectation of resurrection present in Second Temple Judaism.[171] Matthew's addition alerts his audience to the fact that the apocalyptic moment has begun with the death of Jesus.

That motif continues in the resurrection narratives. Matthew has taken the first of these narratives, 28:1–8, from Mark, and has edited it in such a way as to underline the apocalyptic significance of Jesus' resurrection. Mark tells us simply that the three women enter the tomb where they see a "young man" (*neaniskon*) dressed in a "white robe" (*stolēn leukēn*, Mark 16:5), but Matthew tells us, "there was a great earthquake" (*kai idou seismos egeneto megas*, 28:2). Reference to the earthquake recalls the earth shaking in 27:51–53, which links Jesus' resurrection to his death as one more apocalyptic event.

Matthew changes the identity of the messenger as well. He is not simply a "young man" — albeit a mysterious one dressed in the white garment so familiar from apocalyptic texts. Rather, he is "an angel of the Lord" whose descent from heaven is the cause of the earthquake (28:2). Angels, too, are frequently the messengers in apocalyptic visions.[172] Thus Matthew uses an angel to heighten the apocalyptic note of this narrative. Moreover, he emphasizes the angel's appearance. Whereas Mark tells us simply that the young man was dressed in a white robe, Matthew notes, "His appearance was like lightning [*hō astrapē*] and his clothing white as snow" (*kai to enduma autou leukon ōs chiōn*, 28:3). As we observed in the transfiguration narrative, the underscoring of white garments also develops the apocalyptic motif.

In the climax of the scene, Matthew's angel begins his message in typical apocalyptic fashion. Mark has the young man begin, "Do not be amazed" (*mē ekthambeisthe*, 16:6). Matthew, however, has, "Do not be afraid" (*mē phobeisthe hymeis*, 28:5). Matthew's use of the earthquake, his changing of the messenger's identity, emphasizing the radiance of his garments, and altering the opening of the message — all contribute to underscore the apocalyptic significance of Jesus' resurrection and, perforce, his death.

The commissioning at the end of the gospel is significant for our study. There are certain points of reference between 11:25–30 and 28:18–20,[173] and an examination of the similarities illuminates both texts, as well as Matthew's portrait of Jesus as sage. We might structure the similarities in the following way:

11:25–30	28:18–20
kyrie tou ouranou kai tēs gēs	*en ouranō kai epi* [*tēs*] *gēs*
panta moi paredothē	*edothē moi pasa eksousia*
hypo tou patros mou	*edothē* (theological passive)
deute	*poreuthentes*
mathete	*mathēteusate*
arate ton zugon mou	*didaskontes autous . . . panta hosa*
anapausin	*ego meth' hymōn eimi*[174]

Matt. 11:25–30 is composed of two traditional sayings, verses 25–27 (Q) and verses 28–30 (M), both of which bear evidence of redactional activity. Matt. 28:18–20, on the other hand, contains some traditional elements: *en ouranō kai epi gēs*,[175] the liturgical formula in verse 19b,[176] and possibly the promise *egō meth'hymōn eimi*.[177] For the most part, however, the passage is replete with typical Matthean terminology and constructions.[178]

Not only are there similiarities between 11:25–30 and 28:18–20, but there are also parallels between 28:18–20 and Dan 7:14:[179]

Daniel 7:14	Matthew 28:18b–19a
kai edothē autō	*edothē moi*
eksousia	*pasa eksousia*
kai panta ta ethnē	*en ouranō kai*
tēs gēs kata genē	*epi* [*tēs*] *gēs*
kai pasa doksa	*poreuthentes oun mathēteusate*
autō latreuousa	*panta ta ethnē*

The similarities between 28:18–20 to both Dan. 7:14 and 11:25–30 suggest that Matthew was influenced by the Q saying as well as the Daniel text in constructing the great commission.[180]

Attempts to find precedents in a single literary form in the Hebrew Bible or Second Temple literature have eluded scholars.[181] I do not believe that there is any single literary form behind Matt. 28:16–20. However, I believe one can find patterns in earlier traditions helpful in understanding the Matthean passage. Thus, one might view 28:16–20 from the perspective of commissionings by departing scribes which take place on mountain-tops.[182] In at least one instance, Enoch is called "teacher of heaven and earth" (*T. Abr.* [b] 11:3).

These similarities suggest that Matthew wishes to identify the risen Jesus as departing seer who acts in the chain of tradition, receiving authority from God and then commissioning disciples. That is, he hands over authority to them. The similarities with *1 Enoch* 71, where the seer is closely associated, if not identified, with the Son of Man, as well as Dan. 7:14, suggest, however, that Matthew has intensified the significance of the portrayal of Jesus as apocalyptic seer; his scribe and seer is the apocalyptic Son of Man.

And finally, the reference to the mountain, as well as Jesus' charge to teach "all I have commanded you" suggests the presence of Moses/Sinai typology.[183] The content of the teaching that Jesus commissions his disciples to transmit is, of course, his teaching as contained in Matthew's gospel.

In several texts that describe Jesus' identity or the significance of his death and resurrection, Matthew adds to or heightens the apocalyptic tone of these narratives. Through his redactional activity, Matthew suggests that Jesus himself — his death and resurrection — is the focus of apocalyptic revelation and that in those events the final apocalyptic time has begun. Moreover, the echoes of Moses/Sinai typology suggest that, as did the authors behind 4 Ezra and 2 *Apoc. Baruch*, Matthew understands Jesus as standing in continuity with Moses. Jesus, however, surpasses the Sinai law-giver and teacher.

Conclusion

Because of his own function within the community, Matthew is interested in enhancing in a variety of ways the traditional portrait of Jesus
as teacher, both in the context of the Wisdom passages and in the entirety of gospel. For one thing, he uses the verb *didaskō* in such a way
as to suggest the primacy of Jesus' teaching role. He then *shows* Jesus
teaching and engaged in debate as a teacher with other teachers, those
of the opposition.

Jesus functions as teacher in Matthew's gospel much as do teachers
in other texts of this period. That is, he is a prophet, calling people to
repentance and pronouncing judgment on those who do not heed his
words. He is a wonder-worker, healing, exorcising, and raising people
from the dead. He gathers disciples and defines himself as the lowly one,
over against the opposition's teachers. And he is a visionary, who takes
three disciples with him to ascend the mountain.

The content of Jesus' teaching includes what Matthew regards as definitive interpretation of *halachah*. Torah remains for Matthew, but it is
no longer the center of his symbolic system.[184] Rather, it is Torah interpreted by Jesus. For Matthew, Wisdom is not identified with Torah,
but with Jesus who interprets it. And the identification of Jesus with
Wisdom serves to legitimate that interpretation particularly when it is in
opposition to that of the opposing teachers.

Matthew identifies Jesus-Wisdom as the Son of Man, likely drawing
on the inspiration of earlier sources. This makes Jesus the content of
the revelation as well as the teacher who discloses apocalyptic mysteries.
And the evangelist places Jesus-Wisdom, apocalyptic teacher and interpreter of Torah, in the chain of tradition with the Father. In that context,
Jesus will hand on the *paradosis* to the disciples he has gathered.

Jesus, Wisdom and teacher, is the lowly one. In the context of Second
Temple and tannaitic Judaism, this quality defines him as the authentic teacher, particularly in opposition to the "scribes and Pharisees"
who are the "hypocrites." Matthew's Jesus subscribes to certain halachic interpretations that place him in opposition to those teachers,
while remaining within the halachic system. He attacks his opposition
by impugning their moral integrity, as well as arguing from the system's
hermeneutical base. For Matthew, the ultimate justification for Jesus'
teaching is that it is the interpretation of Wisdom and Son of Man.

Matthew's Jesus-Wisdom is indeed a teacher with the features of
prophet, apocalyptic seer, interpreter of Torah, lowly one. Yet in each
instance Matthew seems to say that Jesus is "more than...." More than
prophet and sage, for he is Wisdom itself. More than apocalyptic seer,

for he is Son of Man and subject of visions. More than an ordinary teacher, for he stands in a chain of tradition not descending from a human teacher but from God's own self. All of this serves to give Matthew's Jesus an advantage over his competitors. And it legitimates the teaching given in his name, particularly in the face of criticism regarding observance (e.g., Sabbath, purification, tithes, and so on).

Matthew's Jesus is, of course, rejected. By implication, so is his teaching. The evangelist's identification of Jesus with Wisdom serves to explain that rejection. Since Wisdom is rejected, the rejection of Jesus actually authenticates his "story" and his teaching as that of Wisdom's own self.

Chapter 4

Jesus-Wisdom, Disciples, and Sages

Matthew absorbs the female figure of Lady Wisdom into the male and historical, if exalted, figure of Jesus. In doing so, he legitimates Jesus' teaching over against that of opposing teachers, usually called "scribes" and/or "Pharisees." But what social function does such use of metaphor serve? From which group in the Matthean community does it emerge and which group benefits by it?

The text itself will lead us to believe that Matthew's use of the Wisdom metaphor emerges from the context of a learned class and serves — at least in the attempt — to legitimate the function of that class.[1] Matthew parallels his description of the disciples[2] with his portrait of Jesus. Thus, the disciple is to be ready to suffer (10:17–18, 22–23; 16:24–26), to be poor (6:19, 19:23–26), to be humble (11:25–30, 18:1–4, 23:8–12), and to love (7:12, 22:34–40).[3] The parallel between Jesus and the disciples extends beyond inner attitude to outward mission. For just as Jesus preaches to Israel, so do the disciples (10:7, 18–19). And their message is identical: the nearness of the *basileia tōn ouranōn* (4:17, 10:7). The message is confirmed by mighty deeds; the disciples are commissioned to exorcise and heal, paralleling Jesus' ministry (4:23–24; 9:35; 10:1, 8).[4] They are sages, in the pattern of Jesus' own teaching role, as we will see. Matthew's use of the Wisdom metaphor emerges from that group and legitimates their authority, both within the community and, more significantly, in the face of the opposing teachers.

We will turn once again to the Wisdom passages to see how the disciples are portrayed, to see what they do, what kind of teachers they are, and what we can discern of the content of their teaching.

Matthew 8:18–22

Matt. 8:18–22 has Jesus-Wisdom tell two people something of the nature of discipleship. To follow Jesus means to be homeless. And the demands of following Jesus are of such urgency that one must turn one's back on the most fundamental responsibilities of normal social life.[5]

The seeming folly of such a lifestyle is legitimated, indeed authorized, by the fact that it is Jesus as Wisdom and Son of Man who makes the demand.

Matthew has the logion about the homelessness of the Son of Man addressed to a scribe who approaches Jesus and says, "Teacher, I will follow you wherever you go" (8:19). The designation of Jesus' interlocutor as "scribe" and the latter's address "teacher" are Matthean redactional additions (Luke 9:57–62).[6] Some readers question whether the addressee of verses 18–20 is a disciple, either prospective or actual.[7]

Beyond the limits of this passage, the only instances of a positive use of the term *scribe* in Matthew's gospel are 13:52 and 23:34. And the vocative *didaskale* is used, in Matthew's gospel, by Jesus' opponents (12:38, 22:16, 22:36) or by the half-hearted (19:16).[8] The dubious point out the usual address by believers, "Lord" (*kyrie*), as it is in 8:21.[9] Finally, one scholar contrasts 8:18–22 with call stories such as 4:18–20, 21–22; 9:9, which emphasize Jesus' initiative. He believes that 8:18–19 follows a rabbinic pattern and "constitute[s] . . . an arrogation to oneself of Jesus' peculiar authority."[10]

I believe that, in 8:18–20, Matthew presents a scribe as a disciple responding to the command given in verse 18 to "go over to the other side."[11] Matthean use of titles is not absolutely rigid. The introduction of the designation "scribe" could indeed be positive, given Matthean usage in 13:52 and 23:34. Furthermore, the vocative *didaskale* occurs in 19:16, where the interlocutor inquires about the requirements for eternal life.[12] And in 25:44 the damned as well as the blessed address the Son of Man as "Lord."[13] Moreover, the text itself suggests that the scribe is a disciple by designating the interlocutor of verses 21–22 as "another of the disciples"[14] (*heteros de tōn mathētōn*) instead of "another" (Luke 9:61).[15] And finally, 8:18–22 is not a call story. The phrase "another of the disciples" (*heteros de tōn mathētōn*) in 8:21 suggests that both of the interlocutors are already disciples according to the Matthean text.

Matthew, then, has Jesus-Wisdom address a scribe with a saying about Wisdom's homelessness. This is fitting in several ways. It speaks to the scribe's offer to follow Jesus. If Matthew is here portraying Jesus as Wisdom, it is appropriate that the saying about Wisdom's homelessness be addressed to a scribe, for it was the learned classes that had generated and appropriated the metaphor of Wisdom. Finally, the function of learned groups would require at least some degree of stability and access to resources. This underscores the radicality of Matthew's presentation of the saying about the homelessness of the Son of Man, a plight that Jesus implies the scribe must be willing to share.

Matt. 8:18–22, of course, occurs in the context of chapters 8 and 9, which show Jesus the teacher to be wonder-worker. But in Matt. 9:9–17 that same teacher also calls a tax collector to follow him, and shares table fellowship with tax collectors and sinners, only to receive the criticism of opposing teachers, the Pharisees (9:9–13). And Jesus answers the question posed by John's disciples about why his own disciples do not do so (vv. 14–17). Matt. 11:16–19, in the following section, suggests that Jesus' disciples do not fast because *he* does not do so.

Both passages are traditional (Mark 2:13–17, 18–22). In Matthew, as in Mark, they depict Jesus' followers as hearing a critique of Jesus' behavior on the part of rival teachers and groups. Jesus invites social outcasts, some of whom have done real harm to society, to discipleship and table fellowship — clearly scandalous behavior in some quarters.[16] His disciples do not follow the ascetical practices common in some Jesish groups and in many religio-philosophical circles in late antiquity. Matthew can thus imply that the leaders' inclusion of outcasts and neglect of ascetical practices are justified because that is also the behavior of Jesus who is not only teacher, but Wisdom and Son of Man. This may have been a legitimation for those within his community who found such behavior difficult to follow or accept. And it may also suggest an argument with those who opposed the Matthean community and its leaders.

We learn more about the nature of leadership in the Matthean community in chapter 10. In the previous chapter we indicated that Matthew speaks of Jesus-Wisdom as prophet and that as Wisdom he sends some out as prophets (23:34). We noted that 10:42 supports a view that Matthean leadership included prophets. The chapter, moreover, links the function of prophecy with preaching (10:7) and wonder-working (10:8).

Matt. 10:1–16 represents a commission speech. It is clearly addressed to the community leaders — in Matthew, as in his Markan source, the Twelve are named specifically (10:1–4 ‖ Mark 3:16–19). And the Matthean Jesus sends them to exorcise, heal, preach, and raise the dead (10:1, 7–8).

Matthew's editing of his sources is instructive. Unlike Luke, who keeps separate the Q speech (Luke 10), from the Markan (Luke 9:1–6 ‖ Mark 6:6b–13), Matthew conflates his sources. Thus, Matt. 10:1–4 follows Mark 6:7, 3:13–19. Matt. 10:5–6 represents an M saying, and 10:7–16 conflates Q (Luke 10:3–12) with Mark (6:8–11). The commission concludes with a Q saying (10:16 ‖ Luke 10:3) originally present at the *beginning* of the Q speech. Matthew likely transferred it to the end of his version of the commissioning speech because it provides a nice transition to the warnings about persecution.[17]

Beyond the ordering of materials, Matthew's editorial work highlights the disciples' function as wonder workers. The opening statement follows Mark 6:7. But where Mark tells us that Jesus gave the Twelve "authority over the unclean spirits," Matthew adds immediately "to cast them out" (*hōste ekballein auta*, 10:1). It is likely that Matthew has transferred the phrase from the conclusion of the Markan pericope (6:13) and, in so doing, has emphasized the commissioning of the Twelve to exorcise.

Matthew continues: "and to cure every disease and every sickness" (*kai therapeuein pasan noson kai pasan malakian*, 10:1b). Matthew has transferred another reference to the disciples' wonderworking activity from its place at the end of the Markan narrative, albeit omitting the mention of anointing. He has reworded the Markan *kai etherapeuon*, following the summary statement describing *Jesus'* healing activity in 9:35. Moreover, the evangelist's editing brings healing under the authority granted to the Twelve by Jesus.[18]

Matthew takes the command to preach from Mark (Mark 3:14b), placing it in direct discourse and joining it with the instruction that the content of that preaching is to be "the *basileia tōn ouranōn* has come near" (*ēggiken hē basileia tōn ouranōn*, 10:7). Matthew has taken this from Q, where it is located in another context in the missionary speech (Luke 10:9). In Q it reads *ēggiken eph'hymas hē basileia tou theou*. Matthew has omitted the extraneous *eph' hymas* and substituted *basileia tōn ouranōn* for *basileia tou theou*, as is his usual practice.[19] The disciples' preaching parallels that of Jesus (4:17, 23; 9:35).

There follows immediately the command to heal the sick (*asthenountas therapeuete*, 10:8), adopted from Q and transposed from another context in the missionary speech (Luke 10:9), where the command to heal is also joined to the preaching of the *basileia tou theou*.[20] Matthew, however, has the command to preach the *basileia tōn ouranōn* precede the command to heal. He then expands the latter: "Raise the dead, cleanse lepers, cast out demons" (*nekrous egeirete, leprous katharizete, daimonia ekballete*, 10:8b).[21] Matthew concludes the command: "You received without payment; give without payment" (*dōrean elabete, dōrean dote*, 10:8c).

Matthew's editorial changes specify the content of the disciples' message, and directly relate their wonder-working activity to that message. Moreover, the evangelist tells us that true leadership is exercised gratis — possibly a reflection of abuse in his community.[22] The expansion of the command to heal parallels the disciples' wonderworking activity to that of Jesus described in chapters 8 and 9, and again in 11:2–6. And 10:8b makes the disciples' activity an immediate response to the kingdom they have received.

Matthew then proceeds to the command to "travel light" (Matt. 10:9–10). Here Matthew conflates and edits both Markan and Q materials. Matthew — as does Q — uses direct discourse here, including the Markan references to a bag (*pēra*) and two tunics (Mark 6:9), and the Q injunction against wearing sandals (Luke 10:4).[23]

There are several differences significant for our purposes: Mark has Jesus tell the envoys not to put on (*mē endusēsthe*) two tunics, whereas Matthew has them not *take* two tunics for the journey. Mark has Jesus tell the envoys to take no copper for their belts (*mē eis zōnas chalkon*), and Q has "no purse" (*ballantion*, Luke 10:4). But Matthew has "Take no gold, or silver, or copper in your belts" (*mē ktēsēsthe chruson mēde arguron mēde chalkon eis tas zōnas hymōn*). Why does Matthew, who usually edits and abbreviates extraneous material, expand the reference to money? Expanding that reference makes it both more specific and more emphatic.

Matthew then follows with the remark, "For the laborer deserves his food" (10:10b).[24] Matthew takes this from Q where the latter has it in another context in the missionary speech, following the instruction about entering a house, remaining there, and partaking of what is provided (Luke 10:5–7a). Matthew has eliminated the Markan injunction against carrying bread and then altered the Q reference to "reward" or "wages" (*misthou*, Luke 10:7) to "food" (*trophēs*, Matt. 10:10).

Matthew's version is, in some ways, more emphatic than either Mark or Q.[25] He states that the Twelve are not to take two tunics for the journey, includes the Q injunction against wearing sandals, and specifies the injunction against money. And yet he softens the radicality of the command to "travel light" with the reassurance of the saying about the laborer's food.

Matthew's version of the missionary speech links together preaching and wonder-working in a way that parallels disciples and master. Moreover, Matthew's Jesus commands a radical material detachment while assuring the disciples of provision for their needs.

What makes this section a reflection on the disciples as *teachers*? Certainly the message of the *basileia tōn ouranōn* gives reason. The designation of the disciples as wonder-workers recalls various notions in biblical, Greco-Roman, and Jewish sources regarding the sage that we have seen in a previous chapter. The injunction to travel light echoes descriptions of wandering teachers common in the Mediterranean world, specifically Cynic philosophers,[26] and the reference to begging recalls the Cynic practice of begging for the necessities.[27] The staff (*baktron*), cloak (*tribōna*), and bag (*pēra*) are the standard equipment of the Cynic philosopher[28] and indeed to take up the wallet and staff, to double one's cloak, is the equivalent of becoming a Cynic.[29]

Matthew imposes upon his wandering preachers a lifestyle more radical even than that of the Cynics.[30] They are *not* to take bag or staff, or even sandals and extra tunic, although — like the Cynics — they are to receive the necessities of life from those to whom they preach. Is Matthew intentionally distinguishing the wandering preachers of his community from their Cynic counterparts? Were his sources? Quite possibly. After all, Cynics were known in the eastern Mediterranean.

And finally, did Matthew intend all of his community's leaders to lead such a radical lifestyle? This is unlikely, for, as we shall see, some of those leaders exercised responsibilities that would have required a settled lifestyle. Moreover, the evangelist sometimes mitigates the radicality present in his sources.[31] Matt. 10:1–16 may have been addressed to those leaders who were designated as missionaries.

Emphasis on wonder-working and a visibly radical lifestyle would have a rhetorical function. Our study would suggest that Matthew's presentation of Jesus in conflict with opposing teachers is even more, that it is a portrait of the leaders in his community in conflict with those teachers. Matt. 23:13, 15 suggests that proselytizing efforts by Pharisees were very successful. In fact, the heat of the polemic suggests that the evangelist perceived that success as a threat to the endeavors of his community's missionaries. In the context of the Greco-Roman world, wonder-working as well as a visibly radical lifestyle would have been persuasive means of legitimating those missionaries' endeavors.

The remainder of chapter 10 (Matt 10:17–42) reflects various responses to the missionaries. In 10:17–25, Matthew adds significantly to the material he takes from Q (Luke 12:11–12, 6:40). He exhorts the disciples not to be anxious even when they are brought before civil and religious authorities, both Jewish and gentile. And he warns that families will be torn apart by conflicts concerning Jesus (vv. 21, 34–36). He is explicit in likening the disciples' coming ordeal with that of Jesus the teacher (vv. 24–25). Discipleship bears a demand that exceeds even those of family, and the evangelist tells his audience that bearing the cross is concomitant with following Jesus (vv. 37–39 ‖ Luke 14:25–27). He refers to the accusation of demon possession against Jesus, a charge the evangelist says will be leveled against the disciples as well (v. 25).[32] Matthew closes with a promise about those who receive the prophet and the righteous one. Prophet and righteous one are identified with Jesus, and to those who receive them Matthew's Jesus holds forth the promise of reward (vv. 40–42).[33]

Matt. 8:18–22 would then tell a scribe something of the nature of Wisdom. The Matthean context would suggest that it reflected a demand that some among the community leadership become wandering missionaries, a lifestyle Matthew presents as being like that of Jesus-Wisdom, the Son of Man. That form of leadership would have included preaching, wonder-working, and exorcising, modeled on that of Jesus. It would have also brought with it the probability of rejection, and even delation to civil or religious authorities. Such, after all, was the "story" of Wisdom, homeless because rejected. But for those who received the missionary there would be reward, just as reward was promised to those who persevered in the quest for Wisdom, and accepted her. The Wisdom metaphor, then, serves to explain not only the form of Jesus' teaching, but also the responses to it. It explains as well the continuation of Jesus' teaching in the labor of the missionaries, and the rejection that teaching meets.

Matthew 11:2–13:58

Matt. 11:16–19 does not bear directly on the teaching function in Matthew's community. But it speaks to the rejection of Jesus-Wisdom, and of his work as prophet and wonder-worker, and thus confirms the instruction given in the previous material. If Matthew intends for the teachers in his community to follow the model he perceives in the activity of Jesus-Wisdom, then the context of 11:16–19 suggests that, like Jesus-Wisdom, the leaders in the Matthean community are to address their teaching to the outcast. And it shows that they and their teaching will likewise meet rejection.

Matt. 11:25–30, however, yields more information. Verses 25–30 bless God for having revealed "these things" to "infants" (*nēpioi*). The disciples, both leaders and community members at large, are the "infants" (*nēpioi, pt'im, tinuqôt*).[34] And Jesus is the gentle and lowly one (*praus kai tapeinos*). While the terms are not synonymous, in both cases the language is that of humility and lowliness. And the description of the disciples as *nēpioi* is congruent with that of Jesus as meek and humble of heart.

In chapter 1 we suggested that such language is common to learned circles of this period. In terms of 11:25–30, the invitation recalls that of the sage in the Sirach 51 acrostic. The author of the *hôdāyôt* describes his relationship to the members of his community, his disciples, as that of a wet-nurse (*yônēq*) to a suckling child (*'ulul*, 1QH 7:21–22),[35] while beginners in rabbinical schools are called *tinuqôt* (*Esth. Rab.* on Esth.

3:9; *b. Šabb.* 119b).[36] And meekness is associated with both apocalyptic revelation and the study of Torah.

All of this leads us to believe that, in 11:25–30, the evangelist identifies Jesus as Wisdom and teacher, and refers to the disciples in the language of the schools. The phrase *kopiōntes kai pephortismenoi* confirms this. The presence of the substantive *phortion* ("burden") in 23:4, where it refers to Pharisaic halachic interpretation, leads us to believe that the phrase in verse 28 similarly refers to Pharisaic legal interpretation.[37] And so, verses 28–30 would not be directed to those who were already disciples of Jesus, but to those who were still disciples of opposing teachers, that is, Pharisees.

Matt. 11:25–30 is clearly a polemical text. Verses 25–27 refers to Jesus' disciples — the members of Matthew's community — as "infants" who receive revelation. They form a contrast to the "wise and understanding" to whom "these things" have *not* been revealed. The context suggests that, for Matthew, these are the scribes and Pharisees (12:2, 14, 24, 38).[38] Matthew is not setting the opposition's learned class over against the unlearned of his own community. And, while he is countering a religious and political elite, he is not contrasting that elite with a community whose members "either do not know the traditions of interpreting the Law or who refrain from exploiting their knowledge."[39] Quite the contrary. Matthew presents us with an irony. The wise and understanding are not really wise and understanding. Revelation is given to the "infants" whom Matthew implies are the truly wise and understanding.[40] It is they who receive the revelation of "these things" — the true perception of who Jesus is and the significance of his work and teaching in light of the apocalyptic mysteries.

The invitation, addressed to those who are "weary and are carrying heavy burdens," is directed to the Pharisees' disciples. It reflects a context of competition for disciples between the teachers of Matthew's community and those of the opposition. To be a disciple of the Pharisees means to bear a heavy burden, one in which there is no solidarity between teacher and disciples (23:4). To be a disciple of Jesus — and, a fortiori, of the teachers who continue his work — means solidarity with the master who is Wisdom and who can therefore promise rest.

Matthew's use of the Wisdom metaphor in 11:25–30 implies that those disciples who are teachers in the community will hand on what they have received in the chain of tradition — knowledge about the significance of Jesus-Wisdom, the apocalyptic mysteries, and proper interpretation of Torah. That chain of tradition has its origin in the direct transmission of revelation by God to Jesus. Use of the chain of tradition as a rhetorical strategy would place the Matthean teachers at an advantage over their adversaries — at least in their own estimation.

The teaching role of Jesus-Wisdom and its relationship to the Matthean leadership is also reflected in 12:1–8, 9–14, the two controversy stories that follow. Matthew's editing of these stories, inserting materials that follow rules of early rabbinic exegesis, suggests that Pharisees' objection to traditions concerning Jesus' interpretation of Sabbath observance continued to be a matter of challenge for the Matthean community.[41] Matthew justifies that observance on the grounds of Jesus' halachic interpretation as well as his identity as Son of Man and, the context implies, Wisdom. Such would have authorized the teachers in his community to continue with an interpretation of Sabbath observance that had become tradition.

Understanding

In the broader context of 11:2–13:58, one notes the use of *syniēmi* in chapter 13, where five of Matthew's eight redactional usages of the verb occur.[42] Matthew's use of the word and his editing of traditional material serve to contrast the disciples' understanding with the crowds' lack thereof.[43] In verse 10, the disciples ask Jesus why he speaks in parables. Matthew has reworked Jesus' response, adding "for" (*hoti*) in verse 11b, and replacing "so that" (*hina*) (Mark 4:12) with "for" (*hoti*) (Matt. 13:13), so that the veiling of Jesus' teaching in parables becomes the direct result of the crowd's lack of understanding.[44] For Matthew, Jesus speaks in parables, not so that people's hearts might become dulled (Mark 4:12), but because they are *already* dulled — that is, they do not understand.[45] Their lack of understanding corresponds to the fact and explains why the mysteries of the kingdom have not been revealed to them (v. 10),[46] for understanding is the condition for apocalyptic revelation. Thus the disciples — those who understand and receive the revelation of the mysteries — stand over against the crowds who lack understanding and do not receive that revelation.[47]

Matthew's extension of the Isaiah quotation present in Mark 4:12 (Matt. 13:14–15) emphasizes the crowds' lack of understanding.[48] Matthew edits the citation present in Mark 4:12 so that it ends with *syniēmi*, and he follows this with a full citation of Isa. 6:9–10, which includes the verb in its final clauses. Thus, his editing and expansion of the allusive quotation in verse 13 emphasize the significance of understanding and lack thereof with specific reference to the parables and the revelation of the mysteries of the *basileia*.[49]

Matthew has placed the macarism about seeing and hearing immediately after the Isaiah citation. That saying is in another context in Luke, and comes from Q, where it reads, "Blessed are the eyes which see what you see! For I tell you that many prophets and kings desired to see what you see, and did not see it, and to hear what you hear and did not hear it" (Luke 10:23–24).[50] Matthew, however, has "But blessed are your eyes, for they see, and your ears, for they hear. Truly, I say to you, many prophets and righteous people longed to see what you see, but did not see, and to hear what you hear, but did not hear it" (13:16–17).

Matthew has reworked the macarism to link it to the Isaiah citation and to contrast the crowds' lack of perception and understanding with the disciples' possession of the same.[51] Thus, the particle *de* links the macarism to the preceding citation. And Matthew has "Blessed are your eyes... and your ears" (13:16), thus emphasizing the disciples' understanding through the use of the possessive pronoun *hymōn*.[52] Matthew, furthermore, has "for [*hoti*] they see,... for they hear" rather than "which see" (*hoi blepontes,* Luke 10:23). The use of *hoti*, which is repeated in the extension of the macarism in verse 16b, contrasts with "for seeing they do not see" in verse 13.[53] And the extension of the macarism in verse 16b corresponds to verse 13b as well as to the repeated references to hearing in the Isaiah citation.

Matthew has redacted substantially the question about teaching in parables and Jesus' response. The addition of *hoti* in verse 11 and the change from *hina* to *hoti* in verse 13 join the following statements to the disciples' question in verse 10. Matthew eliminates Mark 4:12c so that the allusive quotation ends with *syniēmi*, thus emphasizing the verb by giving it the ultimate position. That emphasis is developed in the lengthy citation from Isa. 6:9–10, added here by Matthew, as well as by Matthew's version of the macarism in verses 16–17. Thus, the discussion in verses 10–17 is no longer about parabolic teaching; rather, it is about perception and understanding.

Immediately after the macarism begins the interpretation of the parable of the sower. Matthew adopts the interpretation found in Mark 4:13–20 and makes redactional changes. Thus, the seed is "the word of the *basileia*" (*logos tēs basileias,* Matt. 13:19).[54] Mark's version of the interpretation speaks of those along the path from whom Satan takes away the word, and follows with two examples: those who receive the word with joy but are not steadfast (4:16–17), and those who are distracted by pleasure (4:18–19). Matthew, however, modifies the Markan version by stating that the condition under which the "evil one"[55] snatches away the word of the *basileia* is lack of understanding (Matt. 13:19). And the person who hears the word but lacks steadfastness and the one distracted by pleasure become examples of hearing the word without understanding. Conversely, the seed sown on good soil which bears fruit is the one who hears the word and understands it.[56] Finally, the phrase "hears and understands" (*akouon kai synieis*, v. 23) forms an inclusion with the beginning of the interpretation (v. 19). Once again, as in verses 10–17, Matthew has edited his material to emphasize understanding as characteristic of the disciple.[57]

The final instance of *syniēmi* in 11:2–13:58 occurs in 13:51, where — concluding the series of the parables of the *basileia* — Matthew has Jesus ask the disciples, "Have you understood all this?" Thus he introduces the final parable of the series, that of the scribe trained for the *basileia*, which we will discuss more fully below. Anticipating that discussion we will say only that, given the significance of the parable, we may say that in verse 51 the disciples' understanding bears a relation to the transmission of the tradition[58] with particular reference to apocalyptic teaching regarding the *basileia tōn ouranōn*.[59]

Matthew thus shows a redactional preference for presenting the disciples as understanding.[60] Within the context of 11:2–13:58, the referent of understanding is the *basileia tōn ouranōn*, the word of the *basileia*, and the mysteries. The disciples are brought to understanding through Jesus' instruction.

Given the fact that Matthew describes the disciples as "understanding" in chapter 13, one can see that his identification of Jesus as Wisdom and sage does indeed influence the evangelist's consideration of the disciples. From a literary and redactional point of view this is true for two reasons. First, the disciples understand because *Jesus* brings them to understanding. From the perspective of the narrative, it is important that the disciples understand in order to show Jesus as their teacher.[61] Second, it is also important that they understand because of their teaching role in the Matthean community. Thus, the motif of understanding reflects the effectiveness of Jesus' teaching and legitimates their own teaching.[62]

From the point of view of the broader cultural world, one recalls the occurrence of "wise" and "understanding" to refer to those who receive apocalyptic revelation.[63] The disciples understand precisely as the sages who receive and transmit teaching about the *basileia tōn ouranōn* and its apocalyptic fulfillment.[64] "Understanding" corresponds to the irony of the "wise and understanding" of 11:25. It refers to the disciples' receiving revelation of "these things," of the mysteries. And it forms part of the boundary language, which sets them apart from their opponents in formative Judaism, on the one hand, and from the "crowds" who do not understand on the other.

The Scribe Trained for the Kingdom (Matt. 13:52)

Matthew 13 comes to a climax with the parable of the scribe trained for the *basileia*.[65] In Matthew's gospel the only instances of "scribe" (*grammateus*) referring to a function in the Matthean community actually occur here, in 8:18–22 and in 23:34.[66] All three instances occur within contexts that refer to Wisdom, and that in an apocalyptic context. In 13:51, at the conclusion to the parables of the *basileia tōn ouranōn* Jesus says to the disciples:

> "Have you understood all this?" They answered, "Yes." And he said to them, "Therefore every scribe who has been trained for the kingdom of heaven is like the master of a household who brings out of his treasure what is new and what is old." (13:51–52)

The question and answer in verses 51–52 are the redactor's creation, as indicated by the presence of *syniēmi*.[67] "All this" (*tauta panta*) refers to the preceding parables, with the disciples' reply indicating that they have indeed understood the parables of the *basileia*. Moreover, the question and response rejoin the use of *syniēmi* earlier in the chapter. Thus, the implied contrast between the disciples and the crowds in verses 10–17 is made explicit, and gives an illustration of the person who hears the word of the *basileia* and understands it (see vv. 18–23).

The word "therefore" (*dia touto*) links the brief parable to the question and response in verse 51. The link is a difficult one, however.[68] The association is one of ideas, and the reference points are understanding as both condition and result of receiving revelation, understanding as the mark of the disciples, and the office of scribe as the one who both understands and transmits the tradition or *paradosis*. In the context of Second Temple literature, understanding is one of the sage's or scribe's characteristics. In light of that, Matthew's Jesus can speak of some of the disciples as scribes precisely *because* they "understand" parables.[69]

The parable is from special M.[70] However, one can discern redactional traces in "all" (*pas*), "the kingdom of heaven" (*hē basileia tōn ouranōn*), "trained" (*mathēteuestheis*) and possibly "brings out of his treasure" (*ekballei ek tou thesaurou*).[71] The scribe in 13:52 is "trained (*mathēteutheis*) for the *basileia tōn ouranōn*." While the passive voice of *mathēteuo* can mean either "to instruct" or "to make someone a disciple,"[72] in the context of Matthew's gospel either translation is suitable, for the aorist passive participle here corresponds to the use of *talmid* for "disciple."[73]

The scribe of our parable is "like a householder who brings out of his treasure what is new and what is old." On the level of the narrative this scribe is a disciple of Jesus. But Matthew's audience would have understood him as one who holds a particular teaching office within the Matthean community.[74] One best understands the comparison to "householder who brings out of his treasure what is new and what is old" in the framework of the scribe's function in Second Temple and tannaitic Judaism. In that context the scribe's or sage's role was to receive accurately the tradition, to interpret it for a new age,[75] and to transmit it.

The "new and old" has been interpreted in various ways. The "new" is understood to signify the preceding parables,[76] the scribe's own "production of new parables, new wise sayings from the store of divinely granted insight."[77] Or it might suggest the secrets of the end-time.[78] The "old" might be construed to refer to the Hebrew Scriptures,[79] interpreted in the context of the fulfillment motif present in Matthew's gospel.[80] It might suggest prior Jewish tradition. Or it might refer to the secrets hidden since creation,[81] or to the original Jesus tradition, which is interpreted anew and transmitted for the community.[82]

Commentators usually prefer to give priority to one or another interpretation. However, while "scribe" might seem to designate a sapiential function in chapter 13,[83] in 23:34 the context would suggest that it also means an interpreter of Torah. I prefer to understand "new and old" as multivalent, bearing various levels of meaning. Matthew's scribe would interpret the Hebrew Bible, ongoing Jewish tradition, and the Jesus tradition as a continuous whole for the community.[84] The life and teaching of Jesus would provide the focus for that process.

Matt. 11:2–13:58 presents the disciples in the school language of Second Temple and tannaitic Judaism — they are the "infants," the "understanding." They receive revelatory knowledge of Jesus' identity, the significance of his words and deeds, the apocalyptic mysteries of the *basileia tōn ouranōn*. Their implied halachic interpretation is legitimated by the precedent set by the sage who is Wisdom and Son of Man. It is implied that they are to continue that tradition and to carry forward with the ongoing interpretation of the *paradosis*. Matthew suggests that the Jesus tradition will serve as the framework for interpreting Torah and the apocalyptic mysteries.[85] Thus, the scribes of the Matthean community will rival those of the parent community, the "Pharisees," the teachers of formative Judaism.[86]

Matthew 23:34–36, 37–39

An examination of Matthew's description of discipleship in the context of 23:34–36, 37–39 is, of course, simplified by the fact that Wisdom's envoys are actually called "prophets and wise men and scribes" (v. 34). Thus, within the limits of the Wisdom passage itself, we see explicit reference to a didactic function in the Matthean community.[87] Just as Jesus is Wisdom and therefore prophet, so too some of his disciples and envoys are sages, prophets, and scribes.

Wisdom's oracle (23:34–36) and lament (23:37–39) conclude the woes against those whom Matthew calls scribes and Pharisees. The context thus places Wisdom's scribes over and against the scribes addressed by the woes. This is confirmed immediately by the fact that the "scribes and Pharisees" are the "sons of those who murdered the prophets" (v. 31) and will kill and crucify some of the prophets, wise men, and scribes sent by Wisdom, and scourge and persecute others (v. 34).[88]

Matthew's redactional addition of the verb "crucify" (*stauroō*) means that he likens the fate of Wisdom's envoys both to the great prophets of Israel's past, and to that of Jesus-Wisdom.[89] Such would explain the opposition met by the teachers of his community in the face of the success of the teachers of formative Judaism. The teachers of Matthew's community are rejected, persecuted precisely because they are *Wisdom*'s envoys. Thus, they participate in the age-old story of Wisdom's rejection, a story already ongoing in the history of the prophets of old, and ultimately enacted in the life of Jesus-Wisdom and the teachers he continues to send.

The Wisdom saying in verses 34–36 tells us nothing about the nature of the task of the scribe and sage. Furthermore, it links sages and scribes with prophets. Is Matthew using three words to refer to those who bear the scribal function? In other words, do the three terms describe different aspects of the same role? Or do those terms refer to three separate groups of leaders. It is difficult to say.[90]

We can, however, make certain assertions about the role of prophecy in Matthew's community. Matt. 23:34 is the most direct reference to the designation of certain leaders as "prophets."[91] But there are other indications of the presence of prophets among his community: the saying about the reception of the prophet and the righteous one in the missionary speech (10:40–42),[92] the references to false prophets (*pseudoprophētēs*) in 7:15–23 and 24:11, 23. False prophets lead people astray, falsely proclaiming the apocalyptic advent of the Messiah, a moment whose day and hour is unknown (24:36). They prophesy, work wonders, and exorcise — all in Jesus' name — but without doing the

Father's will (7:21–23). We might conclude that for Matthew the true prophet's task is preaching the apocalyptic mysteries, exorcising, and wonder-working — all in Jesus' name and in accord with the Father's will.[93] And this is just what the saying in chapter 10 suggests.[94]

But that, of course, is what Jesus does, as the previous chapter has shown. And that is what sages do in Second Temple literature and some tannaitic traditions. Moreover, we have seen examples of the prophetic commissioning used for the commissioning of scribes in Second Temple literature (e.g.,*1 Enoch* 12; *2 Apoc. Bar.* 4:7; 4 Ezra 2:33; 14:20, 23, 27). The singer of the *hôdāyôt* speaks as a prophet. And, of course, the scribes are wise. It would seem, then, that it is best to conclude that while "prophets and wise men and scribes" refers to three functions, these may be exercised separately or they may converge in the manner suggested by contemporary portrayals of teachers.[95] The literature discloses a point of view according to which the learned were endowed with prophetic qualities and thus foretold the future, interpreted Torah by inspiration of the Holy Spirit, and sometimes stood over against the establishment. It is likely that Matthew associates prophecy with the same activities.[96]

Although Matt. 23:34–36 tells us nothing directly about the sages' task in Matthew's community, the broader context of his gospel suggests that it parallels that of other contemporary sages. Moreover, in the immediate context of chapter 23, we find material that gives further evidence of the didactic aspect of Matthew's understanding of discipleship. Matt. 23:34–39 concludes a section that begins with verses 1–12. In verses 8–10, which is traditional material, the disciples are to call no one "rabbi" because they have one teacher and they are all brothers. The one teacher, of course, is Jesus (v. 10).[97] The disciples are further exhorted to "call no man your father on earth for you have one Father — the one who is in heaven" (v. 9). This is not a reference either to the familial relationship or to the oneness of God.[98] Rather, it is a reference to the title *abba* given to teachers of this period.[99] That title, according to Matthew, belongs only to God.

Matthew's community clearly knows a delineation of functions and a developing hierarchy in its structure. However, as a reform group, it has an egalitarian ideology. Titles of authority and rank would contradict such an ethos. Matthew would therefore have the officials in his community eschew titles.[100]

Matthew joins verses 8–10 to verses 11–12, a saying about service and humility.[101] Joined as it is to verses 8–10, the saying gives the reader Matthew's interpretation of those earlier verses. For Matthew, refusal to bear titles due the teaching function is not simply a consequence of the oneness of Teacher and Father. It is as well the effect of the humility, meekness, and lowliness that is the mark of discipleship and, all the more, the teaching office, so familiar from Second Temple and tannaitic literature. A close look at Matthew's gospel indicates that the evangelist has a certain preference for that language.[102] For example, Matthew introduces the sayings about the meek (*praeis*) into the beatitudes in 5:5 (Luke 6:20b–23). This, of course, pertains to the entire community portrayed in the Sermon on the Mount as listening to a teacher interpret Torah (e.g., 5:21–48). In chapter 18 Matthew, following Mark, uses "little ones" (*mikroi*) to refer to the community (18:6 ‖ Mark 9:42). Matthew uses the word redactionally to introduce and conclude the parable of the Good Shepherd in that same chapter (18:10–14 ‖ Luke 15:3–7). There, however, it refers particularly to erring members of the community.

Finally, Matthew's redaction in chapter 18 of the discussion about true greatness and humility is instructive for the elements of the Markan version adapted by Matthew, and for the additions as well. Matthew abbreviates a rather lengthy Markan introduction, eliminating altogether Jesus' question ("What were you discussing on the way?" Mark 9:33). and transforms the indirect question of the Markan account into a direct question: "Who is the greatest in the *basileia tōn ouranōn?*" (18:1 ‖ Mark 9:34). Next, Matthew eliminates Mark's description of Jesus' gathering the Twelve, and the saying about greatness and servanthood (Mark 9:35). Matthew then abbreviates and alters the description of Jesus' reference to the child (*paidion*, Matt. 18:1 ‖ Mark 9:36). Where Mark tells us that Jesus "took a little child, and put it among them," Matthew has "He called a child, whom he put among them," using the verb *proskaleomai*, which is usually directed at disciples or would-be disciples.[103]

Matthew then introduces the sayings about becoming like children and humbling oneself "like this child" (18:3–4). It is possible that verse 3, the saying about becoming like children, is traditional and originates in special M. Verse 4, regarding the humbling of the disciples, is most likely of Matthean redactional construction: the phrase "like *this* child" (*hōs to paidion touto*) clearly refers to the child of verse 2. And the phrase "the greatest in the *basileia tou theou*" (*ho meizōn en tē basileia tōn ouranōn*) corresponds to the disciples' opening question in verse 1, which is itself part of Matthew's redactional introduction to the pericope.

Matthew resumes following the Markan version with the conclusion of the pericope: "Whoever welcomes one such child in my name welcomes me" (v. 5 ‖ Mark 9:37a). Matthew omits the final clause of

Mark's conclusion (Mark 9:37b). His editing of the pericope makes the child an icon of the believer. And Jesus' words about humility are thus addressed to the community at large and, all the more so, to its leaders.

The designation of community leaders with the vocabulary of lowliness is explicit in Matt. 10:40–42.[104] Matthew takes the saying about receiving the child, which he retained and abbreviated in 18:5, and alters it to "Whoever welcomes you welcomes me, and whoever welcomes me welcomes the one who sent me" (*ho dechomenos hymas eme dechetai, kai ho eme dechomenos dechetai to aposteilanta me*). He follows with a saying about the rewards for receiving a prophet and a righteous man, and closes with a version of the saying found in Mark 9:41 about the cup of water. There, however, Matthew substitutes "one of these little ones" (*hena tōn mikrōn toutōn*) and "in the name of a disciple" (*eis onoma mathētou*) for "because you bear the name of Christ." In the context of chapter 10, the missionary speech, one might argue that "little ones" and "disciple" refer in 10:40–42 to the missionaries among the communities' leaders. Those missionaries are prophets, exorcists, and wonder-workers.

Matthew's preference for *anawim* language allows us to understand more clearly 23:8–12. That vocabulary, the language of status reversal, designates traditionally not simply the community in general, but specifically the teacher, as we noted in chapters 1 and 3. Traditional usage, as well as Matthew's own usage throughout his gospel, gives evidence of the way in which he associates the teaching office with humility. This is not only a commonplace in contemporary Jewish literature, as we observed earlier, but it also echoes Matt. 11:25–30 where revelation is given to the "infants" and Jesus who is Wisdom and sage is also the "meek and lowly."

Matthew's use of *anawim* language presumably indicates ideal attitudes in the framework of status reversal. But it also serves as a boundary marker, in chapter 23, distinguishing Matthew's prophets, wise men, and scribes from the "scribes and Pharisees" who represent the teachers of formative Judaism in Matthew's area. In chapter 23, Matthew characterizes the latter by lack of solidarity with those they instruct (vv. 3–4), ostentation (vv. 5–7),[105] and a neglect of the "weightier matters of the law" (v. 23). The teachers of the Matthean community — it is implied — stand with their community, eschew honors and titles, and attend to the inner significance of religious observance. They are characterized by attitudes of meekness, justice, and mercy.

Matthew's teachers will retain Torah, which includes not only scripture but oral tradition. But, the text implies, Matthew's teachers will interpret it according to the tradition handed down in Jesus' name.

Thus, their halachic interpretation will sometimes be at variance with that of the Pharisees, as in the case of oaths. And, the juxtaposition of the apocalyptic discourse (chaps. 24–25) suggests that Matthew understands the teaching of Wisdom's envoys to include teaching about the end of the age and the coming of the fullness of the *basileia tōn ouranōn*, as well as *halachah*. Their teaching is authorized by the fact that they are the envoys of Jesus-Wisdom. This is particularly true of teaching that contradicts that of the Pharisees. Contrary to the Pharisees, caricatured as "hypocrites," Matthew's teachers will be characterized by solidarity with the community membership, humility, understanding of the true significance of the tradition, and integration of intention, teaching, and practice.

Matthew's portrayal of the teacher's role and his critique of scribes and Pharisees bear several similarities with currents in Second Temple and tannaitic literature: the description of sage and disciples in familial terms;[106] the ideal of humility;[107] and the awareness of the importance of intention or inner concentration (*kavvanah*).[108] Matthew transforms the first of these so that Jesus the teacher and God the Father remain at the center of his egalitarian ideology of community. And he holds up the latter two as ideals for his portrayal of the learned group. He also uses those traditions to ridicule and call into question the very integrity of the opposing teachers — who presumably know and hold those same traditions.

In effect, Matthew addresses chapter 23 to *three* groups. Certainly the force of his invective falls on the scribes and Pharisees. But the inclusive reference to crowds and disciples in verse 1 makes of the chapter a warning to his own learned group as well as the community at large lest they, too, become like their opponents.[109] The presence of verses 8–12 suggests at least the possibility that some among Matthew's teachers have succumbed to the temptation to compete for titles of authority commensurate with their role.

But what does one make of verses 2–3? Why would Matthew describe Jesus as acknowledging the authority of scribes and Pharisees?[110] These verses may indeed have a long history in Matthew's source.[111] However, one need not interpret verses 2–3 as reflecting several layers of tradition or distinctly different historical stages from verses 13–39.[112] Rather, it is most likely that Matt. 23:2–3 simply reflects the evangelist's acknowledgment of the local political status quo: it is possible that the Pharisees either hold official positions in local government or exert power on those who do hold office.[113] But while the evangelist appears to acknowledge their authority, he actually undercuts it through the rhetoric of the woes which calls into question their integrity.[114]

The Pharisees, then, have some kind of official power. Moreover, verses 13 and 15 suggest that their proselytizing efforts are enjoying success. Possibly they are drawing recruits from among the membership of Matthew's community. Certainly they are winning followers from those outside. The invective indicates that Matthew perceives that success as a threat to the efforts of his own learned group, and possibly to the community's survival.

In chapter 23, Matthew engages his opponents from within the system — as he does elsewhere. The Pharisees hold political power and must be obeyed. But Jesus — and the Matthean teachers — are the true interpreters of *halachah*. The Matthean teachers are humble, eschew honors, and stand with their community members. Their teaching is legitimated, authorized by the fact that it is the teaching of Jesus-Wisdom, whose envoys they are, and by the meekness, justice, and mercy that mark them — the characteristics of Jesus-Wisdom's very self. And the rejection of their teaching is explained by the fact that they are the envoys of the rejected Jesus-Wisdom.

The Disciples and Torah

Chapter 23 implies that the learned group in Matthew's community is to interpret *halachah*. This is confirmed by material beyond the limits of this text. One might say by way of speculation that anywhere Matthew shows Jesus as interpreting Torah might imply an example for the leaders in the Matthean community, particularly when that interpretation sets them at variance with the scribes and/or Pharisees (e.g., the Sermon on the Mount, the Sabbath controversies, and so on).

There are also places, however, where the disciples are involved directly or indirectly in discussions about halachic matters.[115] Matthew has edited these materials and has portrayed the disciples as learning proper interpretation of *halachah* from Jesus the sage. For example, in Matt. 15:1–20, the Pharisees and scribes ask Jesus why his disciples violate Pharisaic laws of ritual purity and do not wash their hands before eating. Matthew heightens the note of controversy by having Jesus respond in kind, asking why the Pharisees transgress the "commandment of God for the sake of your tradition." Jesus then cites Exod. 20:12; Deut. 5:16; Exod. 21:17; Lev. 10:9 (v. 4), and caricatures Pharisaic observance of corban. Jesus brings his words to a climax by proclaiming, "You hypocrites!" and citing Isa. 29:13 (v. 7). Matthew's editing of the material heightens the air of conflict between Jesus and the opposing teachers, and makes it clear that the discussion is about more than ritual purity, that it concerns proper understanding of the relationship between God's law and tradition.[116]

Matthew has focused on this material as a halachic controversy by reorganizing the Markan material (Mark 7:1–23). He has eliminated the Markan explanation of Pharisaic rules of ritual purity, and transferred the comment about Pharisees' abandonment of God's commandment. He has transformed the latter into a question that follows immediately the Pharisees' question, and Matthew changes "the tradition" to "your tradition." Thus he emphasizes the conflict between Pharisaic *paradosis* and God's word (vv. 3, 6). Matthew has further reorganized the Markan material by placing together the legal material, which is more diffuse in the Markan arrangement, and following it with the Isaiah citation (Matt. 15:4–9). Matthew's redaction heightens the note of controversy between Jesus and the scribes and Pharisees. It places Jesus' *paradosis* and his disciples' practice on the side of God's commandment over against the Pharisees' tradition.

There follows a statement to the crowd about what truly renders a person ritually impure (vv. 10–11 ‖ Mark 7:14–15). Matthew alters the Markan source, changing the disciples' question about the "parable" (Mark 7:14–15) to a question about the Pharisees taking offense at Jesus' saying about ritual defilement (v. 12). Again Matthew highlights the debate between Jesus and the Pharisees, this time introducing the disciples into the discussion.

Matthew inserts two brief parabolic sayings: the one from special M about the plant not planted by the Father (v. 13) and the one from Q about the blind guides (v. 14 ‖ Luke 6:39). He signals the Pharisees as the blind guides and orders the disciples to "let them alone" (*aphete autous*, v. 14), implying that Jesus is the authentic "guide" who "sees."[117] Matthew then has Peter request an explanation of "the parable" (v. 15). Jesus exclaims at the disciples' lack of understanding (v. 16 ‖ Mark 7:18) and then explains the saying about ritual defilement (vv. 15–20). Matthew sometimes introduces Peter to request, on behalf of the disciples or in their company, instruction on *halachah* or community order.[118] His appearance in this pericope thus underscores the note of legal debate.

Matthew's redaction of Mark 7:1–23 highlights the debate between Jesus and the Pharisees, and emphasizes the halachic issue of ritual purity and defilement. It also emphasizes the disciples' role in the discussion, and, through the introduction of the parables in verses 13–14, focuses on the question of who actually is authorized to lead the community. The introduction of Peter suggests that he and his fellows will carry on Jesus' role as authentic teachers and guides.

Mark's account sweeps aside the issue of the ongoing significance of discussions about ritual purity and food laws with "Thus he declared all foods clean" (7:19). Matthew omits that statement, thus stopping short of abrogating the food laws.[119] He and his community do not follow the opposing teachers in their interpretation of certain purity laws. Clearly his community has been accused of laxity regarding ritual purity. His redaction suggests that the teachers in his community are in conflict with Pharisees about the issue.

Matthew argues from within the Jewish tradition by citing biblical material. He follows the Markan source in citing Isa. 29:13, as well as legal material.[120] However, he reverses the order of the citations, placing the legal first and thus emphasizing it. That citation of verses from biblical legal texts, however, is not to the point of ritual purity, but rather that of honoring mother and father. By accusing the Pharisees of using oaths to avoid familial responsibilities, Matthew calls into question the Pharisees' moral integrity, and, thus, their right to claims of leadership.

In response to Peter's question about the parable, Matthew presents a list of things that defile.[121] It would appear that the Matthean community is not as strict in its observance of customs of ritual purity as the Pharisees would have them be. Matthew and his fellow teachers justify their interpretation, declaring that eating with unwashed hands is not a violation of Torah observance.[122] They do this by calling on Jesus' teaching as precedent, including the parables regarding legitimate leaders and Peter's question for an explanation.

Some among the Matthean teachers, however, may have sought rapprochement with their opponents. Or opposition may have caused them to doubt their position. And Pharisees' opposition and the attractiveness of their position may have caused some in the Matthean community to doubt their own leadership. Thus, Matthew has Jesus warn the disciples, "Let them alone; they are blind guides of the blind" (v. 14).[123] And so, Matthew's redaction of 15:1–20 is addressed both to the community at large and to the leadership.

Matt. 16:17–19 again presents the disciples as teachers, here in the figure of Peter. In this text, acknowledgment of Simon as recipient of revelation is followed by bestowal of a new name and the granting of the "keys of the *basileia tōn ouranōn*" with the authority to bind and loose (vv. 18–19).[124] Matt. 23:13 suggests that the "keys of the kingdom of heaven" refers specifically to the teaching office.[125]

This is verified by the reference to the power to bind and loose. Matthew's gospel gives us two points of reference for understanding verse 19b. The first is 18:18: "Whatever you bind on earth will be bound

in heaven, and whatever you loose on earth will be loosed in heaven."
The verbs *deō* and *lyō* appear in this instance as they do in 16:17–19.
The context of 18:18 speaks of communal correction and forgiveness
and climaxes with excommunication in the event that the offending
community members refuse to heed those who would admonish them.
Thus, we may conclude that the power of binding and loosing in 18:18
refers to forgiveness and the ban of excommunication.[126] It has to do,
in other words, with control over membership, with members ongoing
participation or their expulsion.

The other text that illuminates Matt. 16:19b is 5:19:

> Therefore, whoever breaks (*lysē*) one of the least of these com-
> mandments, and teaches others to do the same, will be called least
> in the kingdom of heaven; but whoever does (*poiēsē*) them and
> teaches them will be called great in the kingdom of heaven.

The context of Matt. 5:17–20 suggests that the object of *lyō* is the whole
of the law and the prophets. One cannot draw firm conclusions from
this text alone, for the verb that stands in antithetical parallel to *lyō* in
5:19 is not *deō* but *poieō*. However, it would appear that the power
of binding and loosing in 16:19 has something to do with halachic
interpretation, teaching about permitted and forbidden actions.[127]

External evidence verifies this. *Lyō* and *deō* represent the Aramaic
šr' and *'sr* (Hebrew *htîr* and *'sr*). In rabbinic usage these terms signify to
"permit" and to "forbid," particularly with regard to halachic decisions.
This pertains in tannaitic usage, as well as in later material.[128]

The word pair *lyō–deō* also refers to the imposing of the absolving
of the ban. Thus, Josephus tells us that under Alexandra, the Pharisees assumed the royal prerogative of banishing or recalling (*Wars*
1:3).[129] There is evidence, then, for a usage of these terms which corresponds to that of Matthew in halachic matters.[130] And it is significant
for our study that the terms refer to decisions that are the function of
the sage.

There is also a possibility that binding and loosing refers to exorcism. In an earlier chapter, we noted that that function was attributed
to Solomon, and that it characterized Jesus the sage. And Jesus speaks
of exorcism as "binding" (*dēsē*, 12:29 ‖ Mark 12:27). Moreover, Matthew ascribes exorcism to the missionaries in chapter 10, as we saw
above. And apocalyptic literature sometimes understood the binding of
the evil spirits as characteristic of the end-time.[131] Given the apocalyptic cast of Matthew's gospel, it is possible that binding and loosing
refer to the authority to exorcise as well as to give halachic interpretation.[132]

Peter is indeed the type of the disciple.[133] But he is also guarantor of *halachah* and represents for Matthew the function of teaching and discipline present in the community.[134] In Matt. 16:17–19 Peter receives a sage's commission on behalf of the teaching function office exercised within the Matthean community.[135]

In 17:24–27, Matthew has given us a narrative from his special tradition (M). The issue is the temple tax, another halachic question.[136] And the interlocutors are the tax collectors, Peter, and Jesus. Matthew's Jesus tells Peter that his followers are to continue to pay the tax in order not to scandalize "them" (v. 27).

Even after the Temple's destruction in 70 C.E., the temple tax continued to be levied, although the Romans diverted it for the upkeep of the temple of Jupiter Capitolinus in Rome.[137] Refusal to pay the *fiscus judaicus* would have severed Matthew's community from the parent group.[138] And, of course, it would have meant reprisals from the Roman administration.[139]

Peter appears in 18:21–22, again in the company of the disciples, asking about the obligation to forgive. This follows the provisions for correction of a straying member (vv. 15–22), and the statement about the Father's granting of the request of two who agree about any case (*pragmatos*)[140] and the saying about Jesus' presence with those gathered in his name, material from Q and M.[141]

Finally, the disciples again ask a question about a halachic matter in 19:10. Matthew has added their question about the expediency of marriage in the face of Jesus' prohibition against divorce except in the case of *porneia* (19:3–9 ‖ Mark 10:2–12). The context is a challenge by the Pharisees, and Jesus responds by citing Gen. 1:27, 2:24, and Deut. 24:1–4. Matthew has inserted the Deuteronomy citation, strengthening the argument by adding a halachic reference.

Matthew edits the Markan source that would prohibit all divorce and remarriage (7:10). He makes an exception in the case of "unchastity" (*porneia*, v. 9). Mark 7:10 has Jesus make the statement to the disciples "in the house" (7:10). Matthew, however, has the statement as the climax of the debate with the Pharisees. Only afterward do the disciples approach Jesus, to remark, "If such is the case of a man with his wife, it is better not to marry" (Matt. 19:10). Their remark acts as an introduction to Jesus' saying about the eunuch for the *basileia tōn ouranōn*.

In several instances, thus, Matthew portrays Jesus' disciples as sages. They receive instruction in Torah and authorization from Jesus the Teacher who is Wisdom and Son of Man. Thus, the learned in Matthew's group can see in those disciples a mirror of their own role.

The Disciples: Apocalyptic Sages

In the context of the Wisdom passages it is clear that Matthew's portrayal of the disciples includes an apocalyptic element. The apocalyptic nature of the disciples' teaching is explicit in chapter 10, where their message of the *basileia tou theou* corresponds to that of Jesus, and the tasks of wonder-working and exorcism are those of apocalyptic sages.

Chapters 13 and 24–25 show the disciples as receiving instruction about apocalyptic matters. This is evident in the content of those chapters — in chapter 13, the apocalyptic *basileia tou theou,* and in chapter 24–25, the time of final cataclysm that will inaugurate the full arrival of that *basileia.*

The nature of that instruction is underscored, in chapter 13, by Matthew's use of *syniēmi,* which has apocalyptic connotations in the context of Second Temple literature. In verse 35 he adds a fulfillment saying from Ps. 78:2: "I will open my mouth to speak in parables, I will proclaim what has been hidden from the foundation of the world."[142]

Moreover, after the first parable (13:1–9), all of the instruction in this chapter is given to the disciples, apart from the crowd.[143] The apocalyptic, indeed esoteric, nature of that instruction is highlighted by the way in which Matthew's Jesus responds to the disciples' question, "Why do you speak to them in parables?" (13:10). Jesus replies, "To you it has been given to know the secrets of the *basileia tōn ouranōn* but to them it has not been given" (*hoti hymin dedotai gnōnai ta mystēria tēs basileias tōn ouranōn,* 13:11). Mark, however, has "To you has been given the secret of the *basileia tou theou,* but for those outside everything comes in parables" (Mark 4:11). Matthew thus sharpens the division between the disciples and the "crowd." Revelation of the secrets of God's reign is in parables because it is about apocalyptic matters and thus the disclosure is esoteric, given only to the inner circle.[144]

Again, in chapter 24, we see the disciples as an esoteric group. They approach Jesus "privately" (*kat'idian,* 24:3 ‖ Mark 13:3) and inquire about matters pertaining to the final coming of the *basileia.* They ask, "Tell us, when will this be, and what will be the sign of your coming and of the end of the age?" (*eipe hēmin pote tauta estai kai ti to sēmeion tēs sēs parousias kai synteleias panta*).

Matthew has adopted the Markan "apocalypse," including the reference to private instruction. However, he enhances Mark's version of the question, "Tell us when will this be and what will be the sign that all these things are about to be accomplished?" (*eipon hēmin pote tauta estai kai ti to sēmeion hotan mellē tauta synteleisthai panta,* Mark 13:4). Mark's version could easily be construed as referring primarily to the destruction of the Temple. Matthew's question, however, focuses attention on the specifics of Jesus' coming and the close of the age. Thus, the evangelist makes it clear to his audience that Jesus' words about the Temple refer in their truest sense to the apocalyptic cataclysm. And, in doing so, the evangelist creates the impression of a group receiving esoteric instruction.

In the context of chapter 23, Matthew implies that the divine presence has abandoned the Temple and its leaders because they have rejected and ultimately killed Wisdom. Authority rests with those leaders in the Matthean community who are Wisdom's envoys. They are themselves the object of persecution precisely because they are Wisdom's envoys.

In chapter 24 Matthew follows the Markan source, warning against those who would lead the community astray (vv. 4–8 ‖ Mark 13:5–8). He speaks of the disciples' being delivered over and executed, inserting the apocalyptic term *thlypsis* (v. 9 ‖ Mark 13:9). Matthew inserts verses 10–12 about false prophets and community division, allowing us to perceive something of the social purpose served by his redaction of chapter 24. Matthew shows the disciples as receiving *proper* apocalyptic instruction, in contrast to the false prophets who lead people astray and proclaim the final advent of the Christ (vv. 23–28, 36). And he warns against the division that already threatens the Matthean community (24:9b–14).

Beyond the framework of the Wisdom texts, one finds other examples of the evangelist's tendency to portray the disciples and their role in apocalyptic terms. That is, Matthew describes them receiving revealed knowledge of matters pertaining to the *basileia tōn ouranōn,* or the end-time. The apocalyptic motif in Matthew's portrayal of the disciples emerges in Matt. 16:17–19.[145] There the bestowal of the keys of the *basileia tōn ouranōn* and the authority to bind and loose are linked with the macarism and acknowledgment of revelation.

In verse 17 Jesus says to Simon, "Blessed are you, Simon son of Jonah! For flesh and blood has not revealed this to you, but my Father in heaven." Verses 17–19 are composed of traditional material, which was inserted into its present context by Matthew.[146] It is impossible to ascertain the referent of "reveal" in the original context of these verses. However, in the present context verse 16 suggests that it is the identity of Jesus as "the Messiah, the Son of the living God."[147] This echoes 11:25–27, in which the most immediate referent of revelation is, likewise, the identity of Jesus as Son.[148] In both texts, Jesus acknowledges his disciples, whether the "infants" or Simon, as the recipients of revelation.

The acknowledgment of the "infants," the prayer of thanksgiving in 11:25–27, is followed by the invitation to discipleship. The acknowledgment of Simon as recipient of revelation, however, is followed by the bestowal of a new name and the granting of the keys of the *basileia tōn ouranōn* with the authority to bind and loose (vv. 18–19). The authority given to Peter is the authorization of the sage to interpret *halachah*, to control membership and excommunication, and to exorcise. All of these occur in reference to sages in apocalyptic literature during the Second Temple era. Here in Matthew that authority is legitimated by Jesus' acknowledgment and, as in Second Temple and tannaitic literature, by claims to revelatory experience.

In the transfiguration narrative we have already seen Jesus as the center of apocalyptic vision, as well as participating in that vision. Peter, James, and John are also cast as apocalyptic visionaries. In the preceding chapter we noted that Matthew's description of the disciples' reaction to the vision — fear, prostration — accords with that of apocalyptic visionaries in Second Temple literature (Matt. 17:6). And the same is true of the reassurance and the command to rise (17:7).

Finally there is the commission in 28:16–20, which represents the Matthean disciples' authorization for leadership by the risen Jesus, and provides the ultimate legitimation for their teaching function. We noted in chapter 1 that apocalyptic visions sometimes serve as commissioning narratives. And we have seen in the preceding chapter that in 28:16–20 Matthew has Jesus describe himself in language remarkably similar to Dan. 7:14. Thus, for the evangelist, Jesus is the apocalyptic Son of Man, and it is in that capacity that the risen Jesus commissions the disciples, thus placing them in the chain of tradition.

Conversely, the disciples for Matthew are apocalyptic visionaries. How else could they see the risen Jesus who is the apocalyptic Son of Man? It is as seers that they receive the commission to make disciples of all nations, to baptize and to teach all Jesus has commanded.

The terminology of that command is instructive. The imperative *mathēteusate* is followed by the participles *baptizontes* and *didaskontes*. The strength of the imperative, compared to the weaker participial form, indicates that the emphasis in verse 19 is on *mathēteusate*.[149] The use of that verb recalls the occurrence of *mathēteutheis* in 13:52, and signals the fact that we are once again confronted by the language of the school. The making of disciples is accomplished through baptism and through the teaching of Jesus' commands.[150] The syntax of the command suggests that learning, for Matthew, is of equal importance with baptism in entering the path of discipleship.

The commission of 28:16–20 functions within the context of a chain of tradition, as does 11:25–30. In 11:25–30, the bestowal of all things on Jesus authorizes him to call people to learn of him. In 28:18–20, the *eksousia* given the risen Jesus by God (indicated by the theological passive) authorizes him to send forth his disciples to make yet further disciples and thus to continue that chain. As Jesus has received authority during his earthly existence, so now in his resurrection existence he bestows it upon his disciples. Thus, the authority to make disciples and to teach, which has belonged only to Jesus during the earthly ministry, is handed on to the disciples in the postresurrection community.

The content of the disciples' teaching is the observance of "all that I have commanded you" (*tērein panta hosa eneteilamēn hymin*). The phrase *panta hosa* summarizes the entire teaching of Jesus as described in Matthew's gospel, a teaching that is often expressed as authoritative interpretation of Torah, as we have demonstrated. Indeed, the verbs "observe" (*tēreō*) and "command" (*entellomai*) emphasize the significance of Jesus' teaching as interpretation of Torah, to be transmitted by the disciples, who represent here the teachers in Matthew's community.[151] And the use of the aorist *eneteilamēn* emphasizes that the disciples are to teach what the earthly Jesus has commanded, thus identifying the message of the risen Jesus and the Matthean teachers with that of his earthly life.[152]

In chapter 2, we acknowledged the allusive nature of much of Matthew's use of the Wisdom construct. That quality meant that only those in the community possessing specialized knowledge of the tradition would have comprehended the fact that Matthew was identifying Jesus with Wisdom. In the context of the Wisdom passages, Matthew's portrayal of the disciples suggests that some in his community do indeed possess such knowledge and exercise a teaching function. The Wisdom passages, and the gospel as a whole, describe the disciple-sages in the categories of Second Temple and tannaitic Judaism. They are prophets, wonder-workers, exorcists, and seers. They interpret and transmit proper understanding of Torah and the apocalyptic mysteries. Matthew's use of the Wisdom construct serves the teaching class in two ways. It legitimates their teaching activity in the face of external opposition and possible internal doubt. After all, despite the success and power of the Pharisees, Matthew's teachers are the disciples authorized by Jesus who is Wisdom's very self.

Matthew's use of the Wisdom construct also serves to explain not only the story of Jesus-Wisdom but the teachers' "story" as well. The rhetoric of Matthew's gospel suggests that the Pharisees were more than just the emerging leadership of formative Judaism, his primary source of opposition, but that they were enjoying such success that they posed a threat to the Matthean community. That threat could have had two forms. The first, or more obvious, would have kept people from acknowledging Jesus as the Christ and Son of God and joining the Matthean group. The second threat may have been doubts occasioned by that success in the minds of members of Matthew's community. Such doubts would have undermined the power of those in positions of leadership as well as (eventually) the existence of the group.

Use of the Wisdom construct helped to explain the rejection experienced by Matthean teachers. After all, Jesus-Wisdom, was rejected. Using the Wisdom story Matthew is able not only to explain the rejection of his teachers, but to make of it a sign of the authenticity of their ministry.

Those teachers may have been an exclusively male group. Some evidence suggests a certain degree of tension in the Matthean community regarding women assuming public roles. Indeed, the redactor himself appears ambivalent about the issue.[153] In the Gospel of Matthew, women most often appear as minors, as is the case in a patriarchal society. Thus they are placed with the children in the redactional additions in Matt. 14:21 and 15:38, distinct from the men as part of the crowds Jesus feeds miraculously.[154] Women do all the things one would expect in a patriarchal social structure — they give birth (24:8), make bread (13:33), go to weddings (25:1–13). In other contexts they intervene on their children's behalf (15:21–28). Only in the genealogy do we see women who puzzle us (1:1–17) — Tamar, Rahab, Ruth, the wife of Uriah (Bathsheba), and Mary the mother of Jesus. The first four are foreigners, outsiders, and there is something irregular about the way in which all five women produced male heirs.[155] Moreover, in addition to their status as women and as foreigners, Rahab and Bathsheba are liminal by fact of being prostitute and adulteress. And Mary is liminal by fact of the way in which she is said to have conceived her son — not by a human father, but "from the holy spirit" (1:18, 20).[156]

"Marginal" is a word that comes to mind in considering the women in Matthew's gospel.[157] That is, these women are not seen in roles of public leadership or decision-making. One might safely assume that such was also the case in the Matthean community. This is not to say that women receive negative evaluation. On the contrary. Matthew's redactional addition in 14:21 and 15:38 suggests that Jesus addresses his message to women and children as well as to men. And the presence of the women at the scene of Jesus' crucifixion, derived from the Markan source (Mark 15:40–41), stands in a stark and positive contrast to the absence of any reference to Jesus' male followers. Jesus praises women along with other marginal persons (tax collectors, harlots, the ritually impure). They make their needs known, sometimes with an audacity that is itself praised (15:21–28). Tax collectors and harlots repent (21:32).[158] Women frequently are in need of help, for themselves or for someone dependent on them. They ask for it and exhibit faith in doing so.[159] Women's status becomes a challenge to Matthew's audience to learn faith from those who are marginal.[160]

But there are indications of another current in the Matthean community, as well as in the redactor's own thinking. The clearest examples emerge from the passion and resurrection narratives. Matthew adopts from Mark the account of the women at the scene of Jesus' crucifixion (Matt. 27:55–56; Mark 15:40–41). He makes several redactional changes, following the introduction of the women's presence with a clause "who had followed Jesus from Galilee, ministering to him"[161] (*haitines ēkolouthēsan tō Iēsou apo tēs Galilaias diakonousai autō*), and then naming the women. He eliminates Mark's clause about "many other women." Mark follows the introductory clause with the names of the women, and then "who when he was in Galilee, followed him, and ministered to him" (15:41). Matthew's changes emphasize the verbs *akoloutheō* and *diakoneō*, the first of which pertains to discipleship, and the second of which suggests ministry — perhaps public ministry — in the community.[162]

In the account of the resurrection, Matthew adopts the narrative from the Markan source (Mark 16:1–8; Matt. 28:1–8). Again, he makes several redactional changes significant for our study. As we noted earlier, Matthew heightens the apocalyptic motif already present in the Markan narrative.[163] The heightening of the apocalyptic motifs suggests that the women who come to the tomb experience an apocalyptic vision in the nature of those ascribed to seers in Second Temple Jewish literature. It is, however, the guards rather than the women who respond by fainting. In view of the commission that immediately follows, the women *cannot* faint.

There are other Matthean redactional changes. The angel commissions the women, "Go quickly and tell his disciples, that he has been raised from the dead, and behold, he is going before you to Galilee" (v. 7).[164] Matthew adds the adverb "quickly" (*tachu*) as well as the announcement of the resurrection, and omits Peter's name (Mark 16:7). He then abbreviates the description of the women's emotions in response to the angel's announcement and commission (v. 8). He adds the closing remark, telling us that they "ran to tell his disciples" (*edramon apaggeilai tois mathētais autou*, v. 8), thereby echoing the angel's command in verse 7.

There is, perhaps most significantly, the insertion where Matthew describes the women who meet the risen Jesus and are told to tell "my brothers" (*adelphous mou*) to go to Galilee where they would see him (Matt. 28:9–10).[165] Jesus thus repeats the angel's commission, and the women receive their commission from Jesus himself. Matthew's redaction of the resurrection narrative thus emphasizes the element of apocalyptic vision as well as the commission to announce the news of Jesus' resurrection. Moreover, it serves as a parallel to the commission of the disciples in verses 16–20. The commissioning of the women in the context of apocalyptic visionary experience recalls the reference to the use of apocalyptic vision as commission in chapter 1. And it suggests the possibility of conversation in the Matthean community regarding women's missionary activity.

Despite Matthew's generally positive valuation of women and the suggestion of openness to women in positions of public community responsibility, he ultimately asserts an official leadership class of males. The title "disciple" is attached to a proper name only in the case of males. And while the women receive the commission to announce the resurrection to Jesus' disciples not only from the angel but from Jesus himself, it is the "eleven" — males — who receive the commission to "make disciples of all nations" (28:19). The "disciples" of verses 16–20 does not include the women, but refers to "my brothers."

Was there a discussion in the Matthean community specifically about women sages, that is, about female scholars with a *technical* role in the preservation, interpretation, and transmission of the Jewish tradition and of the traditions about Jesus? Certainly, as we indicated in chapter 1, evidence from the broader Jewish world, as well as from Greco-Roman culture, suggests the possibility that some women in Matthew's community, particularly those of the upper class, may have been learned as well. If the Matthean community was indeed composed of a number of households, then women may have been heads of those households and in that capacity may have been scholars and teachers. The use of the metaphor of Lady Wisdom, teacher par excellence, could have served to legitimate their study and teaching. But there is no evidence of women playing a public role in the context of the broader Matthean community in their capacity as scholars.[166]

As we saw in the preceding chapter, Matthew has absorbed a female metaphor into the male personage of Jesus. He uses that metaphor to portray Jesus because he is using the tropes of Jewish tradition to understand Jesus' life and teaching. Conversely, he reinterprets that tradition through that same life and teaching.

It is to be expected that Matthew would use the metaphor of Lady Wisdom. After all, that metaphor had emerged from learned circles and legitimated their authority in Second Temple and tannaitic Judaism. Sages were those who were united with Lady Wisdom.

In the face of opposition Matthew is trying to legitimate the work of the teaching class in his own community. And so he subsumes the already-transformed female metaphor into the collective male personage of that class. This process may have so co-opted the metaphor for a male elite that it served not only to subordinate the female to the male, but to actually exclude women from egalitarian participation in the teaching function of the Matthean community.[167]

Matthew uses a metaphor familiar to him and his colleagues from earlier and contemporary Jewish sources. That metaphor allows him to do more than articulate certain fundamental religious questions, as we saw in the previous chapter. Its use allows the evangelist to make sense of his community's teachers' experience of rejection in light of communal tension as well as competition posed by the "scribes and Pharisees."

The content of the Matthean sages' teaching includes *halachah*, with specific reference to purity laws, oaths, Sabbath observance. It includes as well a concern for *kavvanah*, as does that of other Jewish teachers. What distinguishes the Matthean sages' teaching from that of their colleagues is the fact that it also includes the Jesus tradition, and the community's interpretation of that tradition. For Matthew and his fellows, the central symbol is Jesus, his life and ministry, death and resurrection. They interpret even Torah through that symbol.

Matthew describes the "disciples" — the leaders of his community — in many of the same ways as teachers of Second Temple and formative Judaism, using the categories of prophet, seer, scribe, wonder-worker, sage. And, as did his predecessors and contemporaries, he uses the vocabulary of lowliness, of status reversal. This suggests an egalitarian ideology and yet a relatively elevated status.

There is a certain level of tension present. Despite the egalitarian ideal, the community and its leaders must still cope with the fact that some are indeed cast in roles of institutional leadership. Moreover, that tension reaches across gender boundaries. The text suggests at least some tension surrounding women's roles in public leadership. And it indicates that Matthew's use of the Wisdom metaphor ultimately legitimates a male learned class. For just as divine Wisdom is identified with Jesus, and is accessible through his teaching, so, too, Matthew's community has access to that teaching only through the teaching of the "disciples" — the teaching class of his community.

Chapter 5

Conclusions

Metaphor brings together words, phrases, fields of meaning in such a way as to create new meaning. It is a form of symbol, pointing to a reality beyond itself. And yet, because of the metaphorical process, the terms of the metaphor speak of each other in new ways. Matthew's use of the metaphor Lady Wisdom is a fascinating illustration of metaphor used to articulate religious meaning and legitimate a group's authority. By the time the evangelist wrote his gospel at the end of the first century c.e., the metaphor Lady Wisdom had had a long and rich history. In the Second Temple era, Woman and Wisdom appeared together as metaphor so that Woman said something about Wisdom. Wisdom was portrayed as a woman with many roles — God's daughter, source of life and nurturer, sage, prophet and bearer of God's word, wife, lover, and householder. Wisdom says something about Woman — and women. It bespeaks the many roles women played in the Second Temple and early rabbinic periods, as wives and lovers, householders, as mothers and nurses, and royal consorts, in effect, all the domestic roles associated with women. And it refers as well to public roles occasionally assumed: prophet, teacher, sage. Use of the metaphor tells us that the understanding of divine Wisdom is accessible in the observation of Woman in her many roles. And it says that Woman is to be known in looking to divine Wisdom.

The content or tenor of the metaphor is divine, social, and cosmic order. The metaphor Lady Wisdom articulates the sages' experience of the ways in which God creates the world, reveals the divine self and will, and calls people to repentance when they fail to respond appropriately. It reflects the sages' speculation about the mediation of God's presence and activity in the cosmic order and in Israel's history. The metaphor speaks of a divine Wisdom, which is on the one hand immanent, approaching humankind and accepted, and on the other hand transcendent, rejected, and withdrawing in the face of evil and repudiation. Lady Wisdom is usually associated with the sages' teaching, whether that be the proverbs used as learning exercises by scribes-in-training, apocalyptic mysteries, interpretation of Torah, or the school curriculum of the Greco-Roman world. Eventually she is identified with

Torah. Occasionally the metaphor is associated with the Holy Spirit and, in one important instance, with the figure of the apocalyptic Son of Man.

Metaphor belongs to the symbolic order. Thus, it emerges from social groups and legitimates their functions. The metaphor Lady Wisdom originates in learned groups. It expresses the sages' experience of study, the quest for Lady Wisdom, as a passionate engagement and exercise of piety. It tells us that that quest is a matter of relationship — tender, intimate, nurturing, and disciplinary — between God and the sage, between master and disciple.

Lady Wisdom herself is located in the sages' teaching, God's gift though she may be. (Only Philo reflects an ideal in which the maturity concomitant with wisdom demands independence of human teachers and the company of fellow sages.) It is precisely here that the metaphor's social function becomes most visible. The texts suggest that the metaphor does more than emerge in learned circles and articulate various aspects of the members' religious experience. It also serves to legitimate the sages' teaching authority, for if the sages are united with Lady Wisdom, if she is indeed associated most intimately with their teaching, then surely their instruction is authoritative.

The precise locations of many of those groups vary widely: the retainer Ben Sira engaged in the public life of Jerusalem, while the visionaries and scribes of Qumran, the wealthy Philo, and the tannaitic sages stayed with their varying social backgrounds — peasants, artisans, and aristocrats. Many were from priestly families, wealthy or not.

Unfortunately, we know too little about the precise location of many of the communities that produced the texts in which Lady Wisdom occurs. But we can say with certainty that the metaphor occurs in learned circles that draw upon vast resources of earlier traditions. The materials in which Lady Wisdom appears are complex and sophisticated. Thus, the sages must have been sufficiently affluent to have learned to read, and been situated in communities large enough to possess the texts used as resources. They also must have had the time to cultivate such specialized learning.

The texts exhibit a variety of relationships between the sages and their immediate circle — be it school or community — on the one hand, and the broader Jewish community on the other. At one end of the spectrum is the Qumran community, an "introversionist" sect withdrawn from the broader community.[1] On the other end of the spectrum are the retainers such as Ben Sira, the Pharisees, and the rabbis, often engaged in the life of the community and the development of its tradition. And then there are the texts that are more difficult to locate in the typology — for example, *1 Enoch*, 4 Ezra. The variety is interesting, but what is most significant for our purposes is that wherever the metaphor Lady Wisdom occurs, it authenticates the identity and legitimates the authority of the sages behind the text — often over against other sages. This often serves the sages in their attempt to attract and retain disciples.

The metaphor of Lady Wisdom, then, served both theological and social functions. It articulated questions about the mediation of God's presence and activity in the world and in Israel's history. And it expressed the passion and affective engagement required of the sage in the quest for Lady Wisdom. That quest was synonymous, for the sages, with the life of study. Thus, study became an exercise of piety and the search for wisdom identified with discipleship to the sages.

Despite the fact that Second Temple and tannaitic literature bears evidence of at least a few women sages, they were exceptions. Beyond the confines of the household, learned circles — at least those that produced the only literary evidence we have on the question — were all-male social groupings. And the various roles in which Lady Wisdom appears reflect the male sages' perceptions of women's roles in a patriarchal society.

Certainly, the metaphor Lady Wisdom may have served learned women for their own ends, for example, the articulation of their religious experience as women in women's roles, or legitimating their engagement in activities usually perceived as "male," such as scholarly pursuits. We have no direct evidence since, as we have observed, the literary evidence we do possess is the product of male circles. In that context, the female metaphor itself is subverted, absorbed into the male structure, and the process may indeed have served to foster the exclusion of women.

By the time Matthew wrote his gospel at the end of the first century C.E., the metaphor Lady Wisdom had already been identified with Jesus in the Sayings Source. Matthew adopted and enhanced that identification. The association of a highly developed female metaphor with a historical male figure is startling. However, it can be explained from several perspectives. There is, first of all, the tensive nature of metaphor which, for Matthew as well as his sources (earlier Jewish traditions and the Sayings Source) applied to the vehicle as well as the tenor of the metaphor. That is, Matthew might alter the tenor of the metaphor so that it is identified, among other things, with Jesus' interpretation of Torah, rather than with Torah itself. So, too, Matthew might alter the vehicle so that gender shifts; the vehicle becomes a historical male rather than a female metaphor. There is precedent for the shift in gender in Philo's writings, where that author identifies Wisdom as both male and female. And the identification of a female hypostasis with a male human being was quite possible in the context of the cult of virtues prevalent in the broader culture of the Greco-Roman world.

Matthew uses the metaphor Lady Wisdom to describe Jesus' identity, ministry, and story. It allows him to articulate questions of divine immanence and transcendence, of revelation, and of the meaning of historical events such as the fall of Jerusalem and the Second Temple.

As Wisdom, Jesus is Son who mediates divine revelation. That revelation includes knowledge of the Son's identity and the meaning of his works, the mysteries of the *basileia tōn ouranōn*. Jesus-Wisdom is teacher who discloses apocalyptic knowledge and interprets Torah. He invites disciples to follow him and learn from him, and sends them out to teach others. And Jesus-Wisdom is prophet whose actions are associated with God's Spirit, calling people to repentance, threatening retribution if they do not obey. At the same time Jesus-Wisdom is maternal and nurturing; even while threatening judgment and withdrawal he would gather up the people in a motherly fashion.

The prophetic aspects of the identity of Jesus-Wisdom present most visibly the harsh side of the metaphor as identified with Jesus. There is more. While Jesus-Wisdom is accepted, he also meets rejection. And he is homeless even while enjoying table fellowship with the rejected.

The metaphor Lady Wisdom allowed the sages to articulate certain theological concerns, particularly those of revelation, cosmogony, and retribution. While Matthew seems to have left aside cosmogony, he uses the identification of Jesus with Wisdom to articulate similar concerns. Moreover, Matthew uses the metaphor to answer questions of his own. He can explain the rejection of Jesus and the fall of the Temple as the rejection of Wisdom and Wisdom's subsequent withdrawal.

In the process of transforming the metaphor of Lady Wisdom, Matthew shifts the center of the symbol system. The center of that system — at least among the sages — had increasingly become Wisdom identified as Torah. And Torah, of course, was associated with apocalyptic mystery, prophetic judgment, *halachah*. In Matthew's shift, the center of the system becomes Jesus identified, in our instance, as Wisdom. And just as the terms of the metaphor Lady Wisdom speak of one another, so, too, do those of Jesus-Wisdom. Transformation of the metaphor Lady Wisdom implies that if we wish to know who Jesus is, we must look to Wisdom, and if we wish to know Wisdom, we must look to Jesus. Jesus-Wisdom is Teacher. And Matthew's identification of Jesus as Wisdom legitimates his understanding of Jesus' teaching. As the sages described in earlier and contemporary texts, the Matthean Jesus is interpreter of Torah and apocalyptic mysteries, prophet, wonder-worker. He is, moreover, at the center of apocalyptic revelation and is identified with the

Son of Man. Disciples receive proper interpretation of Torah and disclosure of apocalyptic mysteries in the relationship of discipleship to Jesus-Wisdom.

While Matthew's use of the Wisdom metaphor serves a speculative function, as in other Jewish texts it serves a social function as well. Matthew's Jesus-Wisdom invites disciples to share his own homelessness, his ministry of preaching, prophecy, wonder-working, and teaching. They, too, will meet both acceptance and rejection.

These disciples correspond primarily to the leaders in the Matthean community. Matthew's identification of Jesus with Wisdom would have legitimated Jesus' teaching in the community in the face of teaching deemed unacceptable by the evangelist — whether false apocalyptic predictions, "incorrect" interpretation of *halachah*, or the amorphous *anomia*. The teaching presented by the evangelist, it is implied, is authentic because it is the teaching of Jesus-Wisdom.

For Matthew, Jesus' teaching is inseparable from that of the teachers of his community. Indeed, Jesus' teaching continues in that of the Matthean teachers. Like their counterparts in the broader parent group, these teachers attempt to consolidate authority over their community in the wake of the destruction of the Second Temple. They and their community attempt to rethink their identity and define themselves in light of that event and of their understanding of Jesus, his life and ministry, death and resurrection. Like other Jewish teachers, Matthew's functionaries are also wonder-workers, apocalyptic seers, prophets, sages, and scribes. And they constitute an all-male leadership group. Their teaching is legitimate, authentic, because it is the teaching of Jesus-Wisdom who sends them. And they meet opposition, are rejected, because that was the fate of Jesus-Wisdom.

The rhetorical function of Matthew's use of the Wisdom metaphor is directed to those within the evangelist's community who proffer teaching other than that he considers to be correct, or who would be inclined to accept that teaching. Some of Matthew's addressees may have been people who supported the activity of women in roles of public leadership. Matthew locates Wisdom with an ultimately male teaching class. There is nothing to suggest that learned women in Matthew's community could not have used the portrayal of Jesus as Wisdom for their own purposes, understanding the female allusions in the new use of the metaphor to articulate their own religious experience and to legitimate their activities. But there is also nothing to support a conclusion that they actually did so.

The dominant struggle reflected in Matthew's gospel, however, is the debate between the teachers of his community and the local "scribes and Pharisees" for ascendancy as authoritative teachers, and thus for leadership of the Jewish community. The ferocity of Matthew's invective suggests that the leadership of the opposition present a compelling alternative to enough members of his own community that the "scribes and Pharisees" constitute a threat to his and his colleagues' leadership.

Matthew's teachers thus meet opposition, perceived as persecution. His use of the Wisdom metaphor would have explained that opposition, internal as well as external. The prophets, sages, and scribes described by Matthew are rejected because Wisdom is rejected and they are Wisdom's envoys. Using the Wisdom metaphor, Matthew interprets opposition as authenticating the effort of his teaching class. Opposition becomes not a sign of failure but rather a means of legitimation.

Matthew's identification of Jesus with Wisdom constitutes an attempt to understand who Jesus is and the meaning of his life and ministry, death and resurrection. It is also an attempt to establish the superiority of his own teaching class vis-à-vis the opposing teachers. Use of the metaphor, so beloved of the sages, is well suited to an evangelist who is himself not only a follower of Jesus but also a member of the learned class. It is a graceful and compelling metaphor in the earlier and contemporary texts, as in Matthew's gospel. But there is a pernicious element to the metaphor as it occurs in the earlier and contemporary texts, absorbed as it is into a male social structure. In Matthew, it is used to legitimate the authority of an all-male collective leadership while the female identity of the metaphor is absorbed into the male figure of Jesus and disappears.

Abbreviations

AB	Anchor Bible
AJP	*American Journal of Philology*
AnBib	Analecta Biblica
ANRW	*Aufstieg und Niedergang der römischen Welt*
ASTI	*Annual of the Swedish Theological Institute*
ATANT	Abhandlungen zur Theologie des Alten und Neuen Testaments
BA	*Biblical Archaeologist*
BASOR	*Bulletin of the American Schools of Oriental Research*
BENT	Beiträge zur Einleitung in das Neue Testament
BETL	Bibliotheca ephemeridum theologicarum lovaniensium
BHT	Beiträge zur historischen Theologie
BJS	Brown Judaic Studies
BKAT	Biblischer Kommentar: Altes Testament
BZ	*Biblische Zeitschrift*
BZAW	Beihefte zur *ZAW*
BZNW	Beihefte zur *ZNW*
CBQ	*Catholic Biblical Quarterly*
CBQMS	Catholic Biblical Quarterly Monograph Series
CJ	*Classical Journal*
CSJCA	Center for the Study of Judaism and Christianity in Antiquity
EBib	Études Bibliques
EKKNT	Evangelisch-katholischer Kommentar zum Neuen Testament

ETR	*Études théologiques et religieuses*
Exp Tim	*Expository Times*
FRLANT	Forschungen zur Religion und Literature des Alten und Neuen Testaments
HNT	Handbuch zum Neuen Testament
HR	*History of Religions*
HSS	Harvard Semitic Studies
HTR	*Harvard Theological Review*
HUCA	*Hebrew Union College Annual*
ICC	International Critical Commentary
IEJ	*Israel Exploration Journal*
Int	*Interpretation*
IRT	Issues in Religion and Theology
JAAR	*Journal of the American Academy of Religion*
JANESCU	*Journal of the Ancient Near Eastern Society of Columbia University*
JBL	*Journal of Biblical Literature*
JJS	*Journal of Jewish Studies*
JNSL	*Journal of Northwest Semitic Languages*
JQR	*Jewish Quarterly Review*
JRelS	*Journal of Religious Studies*
JRH	*Journal of Religious History*
JSJ	*Journal for the Study of Judaism in the Persian, Hellenistic and Roman Period*
JSNT	*Journal for the Study of the New Testament*
JSNTSS	Journal for the Study of the New Testament Supplement Series
JSOT	*Journal for the Study of the Old Testament*
JSOTSS	Journal for the Study of the Old Testament Supplement Series

JTS	*Journal of Theological Studies*
LCL	Loeb Classical Library
LTP	*Laval théologique et philosophique*
NovT	*Novum Testamentum*
NovTSup	Novum Testament Supplements
NRT	*Nouvelle Revue Théologique*
NTAbh	Neutestamentliche Abhandlungen
NTD	Das Deue Testament Deutsch
NTS	*New Testament Studies*
OBO	Orbis biblicus et orientalis
RB	*Revue biblique*
ResQ	*Restoration Quarterly*
RevQ	*Revue de Qumran*
RGG	*Religion in Geschichte und Gegenwart*
RSR	*Recherches de science religieuse*
SANT	Studien zum Alten und Neuen Testament
SBL	Society of Biblical Literature
SBLDS	SBL Dissertation Series
SBLMS	SBL Monograph Series
SJLA	Studies in Judaism in Late Antiquity
SNTSMS	Society for New Testament Studies Monograph Series
SR	*Studies in Religion/Sciences religieuses*
StJud	Studia Judaica
SUNT	Studien zur Umwelt des Neuen Testaments
TDNT	*Theological Dictionary of the New Testament*
TLZ	*Theologische Literaturzeitung*
TRu	*Theologische Rundschau*
USQR	*Union Seminary Quarterly Review*
VC	*Vigiliae christianae*

VT	*Vetus Testamentum*
WMANT	Wissenschaftliche Monographien zum Alten und Neuen Testament
WUNT	Wissenschaftliche Untersuchungen zum Neuen Testament
ZAW	*Zeitschrift für die alttestamentliche Wissenschaft*
ZNW	*Zeitschrift für die neutestamentliche Wissenschaft*
ZTK	*Zeitschrift für Theologie und Kirche*

Notes

Introduction

1. E. Norden, *Agnostos Theos: Untersuchungen zur Formengeschichte religiöser Reden* (Leipzig: Teubner, 1913), 282–84; J. Weiss, "Das Logion Mt. 11, 25–30," in *Neutestamentliche Studien: Georg Heinrici zu seinem 70. Geburtstag* (Leipzig: Heinrich, 1914), 120–29.

2. On specific passages or units, see Deutsch, *Hidden Wisdom and the Easy Yoke: Wisdom, Torah and Discipleship in Matthew 11.25–30*, JSNTSS 18 (Sheffield, England: Sheffield Academic Press, 1987); F. Burnett, *The Testament of Jesus-Sophia: A Redaction Critical Study of the Eschatological Discourse in Matthew* (Washington, D.C.: University Press of America, 1981); B. R. Doyle, "Matthew's Wisdom: A Redaction-Critical Study of Matthew 11:1–14:3a," Ph.D. diss., University of Melbourne, 1984. On more general surveys of the Matthean Wisdom texts, see my "Wisdom in Matthew: Transformation of a Symbol," *NovT* 32 (1990): 13–47; R. Pregeant, "The Wisdom Passages in Matthew's Story," *SBL Seminar Papers* (1990): 469–93; M. J. Suggs, *Wisdom Christology and Law in Matthew's Gospel* (Cambridge: Harvard University Press, 1970).

3. I discuss the "metaphor" at greater length in chapter 2. At this point it is most helpful to say that I use the word "metaphor" to signify a mode of symbolic language which brings together two words with their fields of meaning, and in that process creates new meaning. See I. A. Richards, *The Philosophy of Rhetoric* (New York: Oxford University Press, 1936), 93.

4. Matthew's status as learned has long been the subject of scholarly discussion; e.g., E. von Dobschütz, "Matthäus als Rabbi und Katechet," *ZNW* 27 (1928): 338–48; K. Stendahl, *The School of St. Matthew and Its Use of the Old Testament*, 2nd. ed. with new introduction by the author (Philadelphia: Fortress, 1968); P. Minear, *Matthew: The Teacher's Gospel* (New York: Pilgrim Press, 1982); D. Orton, *The Understanding Scribe: Matthew and the Apocalyptic Ideal*, JSNTSS 25 (Sheffield, England: Sheffield Academic Press, 1989).

5. One might find such discussion in B. Mack, *Logos und Sophia: Untersuchungen zur Weisheitstheologie im hellenistischen Judentum*, SUNT 10 (Göttingen: Vandenhoeck and Ruprecht, 1973); with reference to New Testament materials, one finds examples in C. H. Dodd, *The Interpretation of the Fourth Gospel* (Cambridge: Cambridge University Press, 1968), 273–85; R. E. Brown, *The Gospel According to John (i-xii)*, AB (Garden City, N.Y.: Doubleday, 1966), 519–24; Ben Witherington, *Wisdom's Gospel: A Sapiential Reading of the Beloved Disciple's Testimony* (Louisville: Westminster/John Knox, forthcoming).

6. G. Lenski, *Power and Privilege: A Theory of Social Stratification* (New York: McGraw-Hill, 1966), 74–75.

7. H. Koester, *Ancient Christian Gospels: Their History and Development* (Philadelphia: Trinity Press International, 1990), 319. Q, or the Sayings Source, is a *hypothetical* source and some scholars have raised serious questions as to the likelihood of its existence. The discussion is reflected in the essays gathered in the volume edited by D. L. Dungan, *The Interrelations of the Gospels: A Symposium Led by M. E. Boismard, W. R. Farmer, F. Neirynck, Jerusalem 1984*, BETL 95 (Macon, Ga.: Mercer University Press, 1990). I believe that the Two-Document theory represents the most plausible way in which to account for the development of the synoptic tradition.

8. Matt. 7:28, 11:1, 13:53, 19:1, 26:1. For a discussion of various theories regarding the structure of Matthew's Gospel, see W. D. Davies and D. C. Allison Jr., *A Critical and Exegetical Commentary on the Gospel According to Saint Matthew*, vol. 1, *Introduction and Commentary on Matthew I–VII*, ICC (Edinburgh: T. and T. Clark, 1988), 58–72.

9. This is the majority opinion. Davies and Allison give a thorough description of the ongoing discussion in ibid., 7–33, 58. See also D. J. Harrington, *The Gospel of Matthew*, Sacra Pagina 1 (Collegeville, Minn.: Michael Glazier/ Liturgical Press, 1991), 10–22. There are significant exceptions to this; e.g., J. P. Meier, *Law and History in Matthew's Gospel*, AnBib 71 (Rome: Pontifical Biblical Institute, 1976), 14–21.

10. J. A. Overman, *Matthew's Gospel and Formative Judaism: The Social World of the Matthaean Community* (Minneapolis: Fortress, 1990), 75.

11. A. J. Saldarini, "The Gospel of Matthew and Jewish-Christian Conflict," in *Social History of the Matthean Community: Cross-Disciplinary Approaches*, ed. D. L. Balch (Minneapolis: Fortress, 1991), 59. Contra Overman, who sees little evidence of gentile presence; *Matthew's Gospel*, 157.

12. A.-J. Levine, *The Social and Ethnic Dimension of Matthean Salvation History: 'Go Nowhere Among the Gentiles...' (Matthew 10:6)* (Lewiston, N.Y.: Edwin Mellen, 1988), 179. Contra Meier, *Law and History*, 29–30. Meier argues from the absence of all reference to circumcision, in the gospel as a whole, and in particular in the Great Commission (28:16–20). It is likely that the gospel is silent about circumcision because community members and leaders simply take for granted continued practice of the ritual.

13. Overman, *Matthew's Gospel*, 127.

14. Ibid., 98.

15. On the significance of *anomia*, see below, chapter 3. Overman notes correctly that the word is part of the sectarian vocabulary of contemporary Judaism: *Matthew's Gospel*, 17–18, 98. However, 5:17–20 may well represent a concern regarding antinomianism, a conflict over the observance of *any* Torah observance, rather than the more generalized term signifying the corruption of God's will and focusing on issues of Torah interpretation or teaching authority. For examples of the occurrence of *anomia* in Second Temple Jewish literature, see *Pss. Sol.* 1:8; 2:3, 12; 4:1, 8, 12; 8:8–9; 9:2; 17:11. Interpretation of Torah, however, was the battleground on which competing factions sought to establish their legitimacy.

16. For a discussion of the identity of the scribes and the Pharisees, see A. J. Saldarini, *Pharisees, Scribes and Sadducees in Palestinian Society: A Sociological Approach* (Wilmington, Del.: Michael Glazier, 1988). On the term "formative Judaism," see Overman, *Matthew's Gospel*, 2–4.

17. I am using Lenski's categories here. Thus, I understand power as "the probability of persons or groups carrying out their will even when opposed by others"; *Power and Privilege*, 44. And authority is "the enforceable right to command others. Influence . . . is the ability to manipulate the social situation of others, or their perception of it, by the exercise of one's resources and rights, thereby increasing the pressures on others to act in accordance with one's wishes" (57).

18. On Matthew's rhetoric in the light of the shift of symbol system, see A. J. Saldarini, "Delegitimation of Leaders in Matthew 23," *CBQ* 54 (1992): 668. For Jesus as true teacher, see 672.

19. Ibid., 659–80; Overman, *Matthew's Gospel*, 156.

20. For description of various positions proposing a decisive separation between Matthew and Judaism, see Meier, *Law and History*, 12–13; Saldarini, "Gospel of Matthew and Jewish-Christian Conflict," 42.

21. A. J. Saldarini, *Matthew's Christian-Jewish Community* (Chicago: University of Chicago Press, 1994), 44–67.

22. Matt. 10:17–18, 23:34; C. Setzer, *Jewish Responses to Early Christians: History and Polemics, 30–150 C.E.* (Minneapolis: Fortress, 1994), 38–40.

23. Matt. 4:23, 9:35, 10:17, 12:9, 13:54; "your synagogues" in Matt. 23:34 where the context requires the second-person-plural pronoun. Matthew takes the personal possessive pronoun from his source only in 4:23 (Mark 1:39). Otherwise his usage is redactional. In 6:2, 5 (M) and 23:6 (Mark 12:39) he has "the synagogues."

24. While Saldarini believes that Matthew's community has separated from Judaism, he acknowledges the complexity of ways in which groups can be characterized: "A tradition and community is always a complex symbolic and social reality including many subcommunities, systems, and groups with shifting boundaries" ("Gospel of Matthew and Jewish-Christian Conflict," 40).

25. L. Johnson, "The New Testament's Anti-Jewish Slander and the Conventions of Ancient Polemic," *JBL* 108 (1989): 419–41.

26. L. Coser, *The Functions of Social Conflict* (Glencoe, Ill.: Free Press, 1956), 67. Luz would have it that there is no indication of conversation between Matthew's community and "the synagogue," and that it is outside the boundaries of Judaism: U. Luz, *Das Evangelium nach Matthäus*, 2 vols., EKK (Neukirchen-Vluyn: Neukirchener Verlag, 1985), 1:70–71, 242. Actually, the polemic suggests an ongoing *debate*.

27. E.g., D. Hill, *The Gospel of Matthew*, New Century Bible (Grand Rapids, Mich.: Eerdmans, 1972), 41, 309; G. D. Kilpatrick, *The Origins of the Gospel According to St. Matthew* (Oxford: Clarendon, 1950), 109. While Luz finds no reference to the *bîrkhat ha-mînîm*, he still holds to such a definitive separation; U. Luz, *Evangelium nach Matthäus, 1–7*, 1:70–71; Doyle also believes that Matthew's community has broken with "the Synagogue" ("Matthew's Wisdom," 336). One may find primary texts at *b. Meg* 17b; *Ber.* 28b; *j. Ber.* 4.3.

See I. Elbogen, *Der jüdische Gottesdienst in seiner geschichtlichen Entwicklung* (Leipzig: Gustav Fock, 1913), 36; L. Finkelstein, "The Development of the Amidah," *JQR*, n.s. 16 (1925–26): 19; J. Heinemann, *Prayer in the Talmud*, StJud 9 (Berlin: de Gruyter, 1977), 22 n. 5; L. Hoffman, *The Canonization of the Synagogue Service*, CSJCA 4 (Notre Dame, Ind.: University of Notre Dame Press, 1979), 50.

28. For a discussion of the debate, see R. Kimelman, "*Birkat ha-Minim* and the Lack of Evidence for an Anti-Christian Jewish Prayer in Late Antiquity," in *Jewish and Christian Self-Definition*, vol. 2, *Aspects of Judaism in the Graeco-Roman Period*, ed. E. P. Sanders, A. I. Baumgarten, and A. Mendelson (Philadelphia: Fortress, 1981). Davies and Allison, while acknowledging the debate, believe the *bîrkhat ha-mînîm* to have had Jewish Christians in mind, and to have "had a significant impact on Jewish-Christian relations": *Commentary on Matthew*, 1:136–37.

29. Saldarini, *Matthew's Christian-Jewish Community*, 18–19.

30. Overman, *Matthew's Gospel*, 8–9, 150–61; Saldarini, "Gospel of Matthew and Jewish-Christian Conflict," 59. For a description of various Second Temple groups as "sects" see J. Blenkinsopp, "Interpretation and Sectarian Tendencies: An Aspect of Second Temple History," in *Jewish and Christian Self-Definition*, ed. Sanders et al., 2:1–26; Saldarini, *Pharisees, Scribes and Sadducees*.

31. J. Gnilka, *Das Matthäusevangelium*, 2 vols. (Freiburg: Herder, 1986, 1988), 2:532–33; Luz, *Evangelium nach Matthäus*, 1:61.

32. 4 Ezra 14:40–42; Overman, *Matthew's Gospel*, 29.

33. On 2 *Apoc. Baruch* and 4 Ezra as providing a context in which to understand the Matthean community's effort to articulate its self-understanding in the wake of the destruction of the Second Temple, see Harrington, *Gospel of Matthew*, 12–14; Overman, *Matthew's Gospel*, 32–33.

34. Coser, *Functions of Social Conflict*, 91–141.

35. Harrington, *Gospel of Matthew*, 9.

36. For a discussion of the various opinions regarding the geographical origin of the Gospel of Matthew, see Davies and Allison, *Commentary on Matthew*, 1:138–47.

37. On scholarly activity in early Christian circles, see W. A. Meeks, *The Moral World of the First Christians*, Library of Early Christianity 6 (Philadelphia: Westminster, 1986), 116–19.

38. Overman, *Matthew's Gospel*, 56–62; L. Hoppe, *The Synagogues and Churches of Ancient Palestine* (Collegeville, Minn.: Michael Glazier/Liturgical Press, 1994), 12–13; the modesty of first-century synagogue structures is suggested by the fact that, while written sources speak of Jews worshiping in synagogues, there are few Palestinian synagogues that can be dated with certainty before the sixth century C.E. (Hoppe, *Synagogues and Churches*, 12). Gamla is the earliest; coins from the excavation date to the rule of Alexander Janneus (103–76 B.C.E.); S. Gutman, "The Synagogue at Gamla," in *Ancient Synagogues Revealed*, ed. L. I. Levine (Jerusalem: Israel Exploration Society, 1981), 30–34.

39. Saldarini, *Matthew's Christian-Jewish Community*, 100. Households

served as meeting places for the *collegia* so prevalent in the Roman world; see W. A. Meeks, *The First Urban Christians*, 31. The *collegia* might also convene in specially intended temples or other buildings.

40. Saldarini, *Matthew's Christian-Jewish Community*, 90–94; E. M. Wainwright, *Towards a Feminist Critical Reading of the Gospel According to Matthew* BZNW 60 (Berlin: de Gruyter, 1991), 340–43; M. H. Crosby, *House of Disciples: Church, Economics, and Justice in Matthew* (Maryknoll, N.Y.: Orbis Books, 1988), 21–48.

41. On the household as center of education in the Roman world, see Saldarini, *Matthew's Christian-Jewish Community*, 91. In the context of Jewish sources, Sir. 51:13–30 suggests that the sage's own house was such a center. And *'Abot* 1:4 suggests that a person with a large house might offer space to sages for their work.

Chapter 1. The Metaphor of Lady Wisdom

1. I have presented a similar discussion under the category of "symbol" in "Wisdom in Matthew," 14–16.

2. C. Camp, *Wisdom and the Feminine in the Book of Proverbs*, Bible and Literature 2 (Decatur, Ga.: Almond Press, 1985), 72.

3. Richards, *Philosophy of Rhetoric*, 93, 97, 99.

4. M. Black, *Models and Metaphors* (Ithaca, N.Y.: Cornell University Press, 1962), 40.

5. Ibid., 38–44; P. Henle, "Metaphor," in *Language, Thought and Culture*, ed. P. Henle (Ann Arbor: University of Michigan Press, 1958), 173–55; P. Ricoeur, *La métaphore vive* (Paris: Éditions du Seuil, 1975), 238–42. Some understand this process as a substitution of one thing for another; e.g., L. Perrine, *Sound and Sense: An Introduction to Poetry*, 6th ed. (San Diego: Harcourt Brace Jovanovich, 1982), 56–57.

6. J. D. Sapir, "The Anatomy of Metaphor," in *The Social Use of Metaphor: Essays on the Anthropology of Rhetoric*, ed. J. D. Sapir and J. C. Crocker (Philadelphia: University of Pennsylvania Press, 1977), 7–12. Sapir speaks of metaphor as tropes, i.e., "those figures of speech that operate on the meaning ('the signified') rather than the form ('the signifier') of words." Moreover, they "define a relationship between terms" (3).

7. I understand symbols as "meaningful equivalents of things meant which belong to another level of reality"; C. Lévi-Strauss, *Structural Anthropology*, trans. C. Jacobson and B. Grundfest Schoepf (New York: Basic Books, 1963), 200.

8. N. Perrin, *Jesus and the Language of the Kingdom: Symbol and Metaphor in New Testament Interpretation* (Philadelphia: Fortress, 1976), 30. Perrin is discussing symbol in this context.

9. Regarding myth and symbol, see Deutsch, "Transformation of Symbols: The New Jerusalem in Rv 21:1–22:5," *ZNW* 78 (1987): 108.

10. S. McFague, *Metaphorical Theology: Models of God in Religious Language* (Philadelphia: Fortress, 1982), 34; Richards, *Philosophy of Rhetoric*, 93;

P. E. Wheelwright, *Metaphor and Reality* (Bloomington: Indiana University Press, 1964), 169–70.

11. McFague, *Metaphorical Theology*.

12. E.g., Wheelwright, *Metaphor and Reality*, 61–64.

13. Perrine, *Sound and Sense*, 56.

14. Camp, *Wisdom and the Feminine*, 213.

15. I use uppercase for the personification and lowercase for the common noun.

16. Regarding the prevalence of the metaphor in biblical and apocryphal sources, see S. Cady, M. Ronan, and H. Taussig, *Sophia: The Future of Feminist Spirituality* (San Francisco: Harper and Row, 1986), 16.

17. On the definition of *ḥokmâh*, see Deutsch, "Wisdom in Matthew," 17.

18. Prov. 3:19; Jer. 10:12, 51:15; Ps. 104:24.

19. Sir. 24:23–29. For other examples of the identification of Wisdom and Torah, see Bar. 3:9–4:4; 11QPsa 18.12–14; 4QBeat 4; *2 Apoc. Bar.* 38:1–4, 48:24; *m. 'Abot* 6:7; *Sifre Deut.* 48; *2 Apoc. Bar.* 38:1–4 does not present an example of personified Wisdom, however. The identification of Wisdom and Torah in 4Q185 is not explicit, but the reference to Wisdom as the inheritance given to the fathers in 4Q185 2.14 suggests that the text identifies her with Torah. While the word *ḥokmâh* does not occur in 4Q185, the pronominal *h* which occurs throughout the fragment suggests Wisdom in II.8–III.1; J. Strugnell, "Notes sur le No. 184 des 'Discoveries in the Judean Desert of Jordan," *RevQ* 7 (1969–71): 272–73; H. Lichtenberger, "Eine weisheitliche Mahnrede in der Qumranfunder (4Q185)," in *Qumran: Sa piété, sa théologie et son milieu*, ed. M. Delcor (Paris: Gembloux, 1978), 152; T. H. Tobin, "4Q 185 and Jewish Wisdom Literature," in *Of Scribes and Scrolls: Studies on the Hebrew Bible, Intertestamental Judaism and Christian Origins*, ed. H. W. Attridge, J. J. Collins, and T. H. Tobin, College Theology Society Resources in Religion 5 (Lanham, Md.: University Press of America, 1990), 148.

20. *1 Enoch* 42. While *2 Apoc. Bar.* 38:1–4, 42:24 and 4 Ezra 8:4, 12 associate Wisdom primarily with Torah, the broader context also associates her with apocalyptic mysteries.

21. B. Mack, "Wisdom Myth and Mytho-logy," *Int* 24 (1970): 46–60.

22. On public and domestic roles, see M. Zimbalist Rosaldo, "Woman, Culture and Society: A Theoretical Overview," in *Woman, Culture and Society*, ed. M. Zimbalist Rosaldo and L. Lamphere (Stanford, Calif.: Stanford University Press, 1974), 17–42.

23. On Wisdom as teacher, see B. Lang, *Frau Weisheit: Deutung einer biblischen Gestalt* (Düsseldorf: Patmos, 1975), 23–53; W. McKane, *Proverbs: A New Approach* (Philadelphia: Westminster, 1970), 276. In this section, McKane speaks of her as preacher, teacher and prophet (272–77). R. N. Whybray, *Wisdom in Proverbs: The Concept of Wisdom in Proverbs 1–9*, Studies in Biblical Theology (Naperville, Ill.: Allenson, 1965), 74–77. We do not intend to imply that Israelite and Jewish women *never* filled public roles, i.e., roles beyond the confines of home and family. While the Book of Proverbs itself suggests that there were women teachers behind the traditions that formed the basis of chapters 1–9, these may have been active primarily in household settings in the

postexilic era: Camp, *Wisdom and the Feminine*, 258–69. In the absence of king and court, the extended household becomes once again the primary social structure and "definitive symbol for Israel's collective identity" (261–62). On women as teachers, see pp. 82, 94, 188. We also have evidence of wise women (e.g., 2 Sam. 14:1–20, 20:14–22) and women prophets in Miriam (Exod. 15:20–21), Deborah (Judges 4–5), and Huldah (2K 22:11–20). These women, while exceptions in surviving literary sources, may actually represent a more widespread phenomenon. On the question of women's presence in androcentric texts, see E. Schüssler-Fiorenza, *In Memory of Her: A Feminist Theological Reconstruction of Christian Origins* (New York: Crossroad, 1983), 41–43.

24. Lang, *Frau Weisheit*, 24–30; Whybray, *Wisdom in Proverbs*, 77. On the gate in ancient Israel, particularly as the place of judgment and prophecy, see G. Evans, " 'Gates' and 'Streets': Urban Institutions in Old Testament Times," *JRH* 2 (1962/63): 1–12.

25. Unless otherwise indicated, biblical and deuterocanonical texts are cited according to the NRSV. In Proverbs there are a number of similarities between Lady Wisdom's message and that of the sage/father, which leads one to believe that the teacher's role is significant for the metaphor. For example, her message is associated with security, life, and longevity, as is the teacher's instruction (1:32–33, 4:13, 8:35; cf 3:22–24; 4:10–12, 22; 7:2). She uses the teacher's address "my child" (8:32; cf. 1:8, 15; 2:1; 3:1, 11; 4:1; 5:7; 7:24). Death and disaster are the consequences of ignoring her message (1:32–33, 8:36; cf. 2:20–22, 4:11–14); Whybray, *Wisdom in Proverbs*, 76–77; McKane, *Proverbs*, 276.

26. With the LXX *hoti diestrammenōs poreusetai met' autou*.

27. LXX has *apaideutois;* the Hebrew has *l'wîl*.

28. For other examples of the association of Lady Wisdom with discipline, see 4QBeat l.4, where the author speaks of the one who "restrains himself by her corrections." E. Puech transliterates this *wyt'pg byswryh;* "Un hymne essénien en partie retrouvé et les béatitudes, 1 QH V 12–VI 18 (= col XIII–XIV 7) et 4QBeat," *RevQ* 13 (1988): 86. He translates the phrase in question "et dans ses corrections toujours se plaît." Brooke translates it "always takes pleasure in her corrections"; G. J. Brooke, "The Wisdom of Matthew's Beatitudes (4QBeat and Mt 5:3–12)," *Scripture Bulletin* 19, no. 2 (1989): 35. Brooke notes that while it is Wisdom who corrects in 4QBeat, "the text is careful to say that the testing and refining is not instigated by her" (38). Von Lips would see only 11QPsa 18 as presenting an example of personification and hypostasis; *Weisheitliche Traditionen in Neuen Testament*, WMANT 64 (Neukirchen-Vluyn: Neukirchener Verlag, 1990), 164. I myself included only 11QPsa 21.11–17, 22.1 in my earlier study, "Wisdom in Matthew." Philo also speaks of Lady Wisdom as disciplinarian, in *Congr.* 123–24, where Leah represents *aretē*, which is synonymous with *sophia*. There he tells us that she can sometimes try her students "to test their zeal and earnestness" (*Congr.* 124).

29. The reference to seven pillars connotes a spacious house; Lang, *Frau Weisheit*, 120–22; Whybray, *Wisdom in Proverbs*, 90–92. McKane, however, believes that the "house" is actually a temple: *Proverbs*, 362–63. N. Habel notes that 8:22–23 suggests that creation is the house Wisdom builds or, more

likely, "that her house, like ancient temples, is the earthly counterpart of the cosmic superstructure": "The Symbolism of Wisdom in Proverbs 1–9," *Int* 26 (1972): 156.

30. Here as elsewhere in chapter 24, Ben Sira is recasting Proverbs 8–9; P. W. Skehan, "Structures in Poems on Wisdom: Proverbs 8 and Sirach 24," *CBQ* 41 (1979): 365–79.

31. On the sage's home as place of instruction, see below.

32. As mentioned above (note 23), there are female prophets in Israelite history, e.g., Miriam (Exod. 15:20), Deborah (Judg. 4:4), and Huldah (2K 22:11–20; 2 Chron. 34:22–28). Nonetheless, the accounts are predominantly of male prophets. On prophetic aspects of Wisdom's role in 1:20–33, see C. Kayatz, *Studien zu Proverbien 1–9: eine form- und motivgeschichtliche Untersuchung unter Einbeziehung zur ägyptischen Vergleichsmaterials*, WMANT 22 (Neukirchen-Vluyn: Neukirchener Verlag, 1966), 122–29; contra McKane, *Proverbs*, 273–74; Whybray, *Wisdom in Proverbs*, 77.

33. The NRSV translates this as "Give heed to my reproof." That Wisdom is here portrayed as a prophet is indicated by the command *tāshûbu* in v. 23; see Hos. 14:2; Isa. 31:6; Jer. 3:12, 14, 22; Jer. 18:11, 25:5, 35:15; Ezek. 14:6, 18:30, 33:11; Joel 2:12; Zech. 1:3, 4. *qr'* (Prov. 1:24) is used with a reference to Israel's refusal to respond in Isa. 50:2, 65:12, 66:4; Jer. 7:13. *'mn* (Prov. 1:24) occurs with *qšb* in Zech. 7:11, and with *šûb* in Jer. 5:3; Hos. 11:5. For other parallels with prophetic literature, see R. E. Murphy, "Wisdom's Song: Proverbs 1:20–33," *CBQ* 48 (1986): 456–60; C. Kayatz, *Studien zu Proverbien 1–9*, 120–29; R. B. Y. Scott, *Proverbs, Ecclesiastes*, AB 18 (Garden City, N.Y.: Doubleday, 1965), 39; Whybray, *Wisdom in Proverbs*, 77.

34. In the context of Qumran, the *maskîl* is a hymnist — a function that occurs elsewhere in early Jewish literature; e.g., *1 Enoch* 39:9–14; *Apoc. Abr.* 17:8–21; *T. Job* 33:3–9. See also Sir. 51:22, where the sage praises God for his gifts to him, as well as 39:6ff., 12ff.; 42:15ff.; 51:1.

35. See also 4Q185 where seeking and finding Wisdom is in the context of the sage's exhortation which refers to God's wonders in Egypt (1.14).

36. This recalls Wisdom's meal in Prov. 9:1–6; Sirach 24.

37. *ḥbq* can be used for "clasp" or "fold the hands"; see Gen. 33:4; Prov. 6:10, 24:33; however, it can have erotic connotations, such as in Prov. 5:20. Cf. Cant. 2:6, 8:3.

38. "Crown" as verb or noun usually signifies literally a royal crown, or figuratively the sign of honor; e.g., Prov. 16:31. However, it can also refer to the crown worn by a bride or groom; e.g., 3:11; Isa. 62:3; Ezek. 16:12. It is used ironically of harlotry in Ezek. 23:42.

39. Cf. Cant. 4:9–12, 5:1; Whybray, *Wisdom in Proverbs*, 89.

40. Prov. 8:17. The qetib reads *'ŏnî 'ōhobāih 'ēhāb*, which yields no satisfactory explanation; see M. Gilbert, "Le discours de la Sagesse en Proverbes, 8," in *La sagesse de l'Ancien Testament*, ed. M. Gilbert (Gembloux: Duculot, 1979), 207. We have preferred to render the text with the *qereh: 'ŏnî 'ōhabî 'ēhāb*. See Kayatz, *Studien zu Proverbien 1–9*, 101; McKane, *Proverbs*, 222; Scott, *Proverbs, Ecclesiastes*, 67.

41. E.g., Sir. 14:20–15:8, 51:13–30; Wis. 6–9; 11QPsa 21.11–17, 22.1. There may also be a trace of erotic imagery in a passage of 4Q Beatitudes, where the text has *'šry 'dm bšyg ḥwkmh* (using Puech's transliteration). The verb *zyg* can signify "couple," "join," or "match." However, it also means "to wed." Given the erotic imagery elsewhere associated with Lady Wisdom, we are assigning that meaning here. Puech translates: "Heureux l'homme qui a atteint la Sagesse" ("Un hymne essénien," 86); Brooke has "Blessed is the man who has obtained Wisdom" ("The Wisdom of Matthew's Beatitudes," 35).

42. See Deutsch, "The Sirach 51 Acrostic: Confession and Exhortation," *ZAW* 94 (1982): 406–7. Both the authorship and the extent of eroticism in the language of the text are the subject of debate.

43. D. Georgi believes that there is no erotic mysticism in either 14:20–15:8 or 51:13–15: "Weisheit Salomos," in *Jüdische Schriften aus hellenistisch-römischer Zeit*, bd. 3, t. 4, ed. W. G. Kümmel et al. (Gütersloh: Gütersloher Verlagshaven Gerd Mohn, 1980), 430. While this may be true of vv. 13–15, it is difficult to understand his assertion in terms of the remainder of the acrostic. Moreover, on p. 421, he admits of at least a limited eroticism in 15:1–8 and 51:18–21.

44. On Proverbs, see P. Skehan, *Studies in Israelite Poetry and Wisdom*, CBQMS 1 (Washington D.C.: Catholic Biblical Association of America, 1971), 173–91; regarding Sirach, see D. Winston, *The Wisdom of Solomon*, AB 43 (Garden City, N.Y.: Doubleday, 1979), 35–36.

45. Winston, *Wisdom of Solomon*, 40. Lady Wisdom appears in Wisdom of Solomon as the desirable bride who is beyond all price and is the sum of all wealth (7:8–9, 11; 8:2).

46. Ibid., 41; R. A. Horsley, "Spiritual Marriage with Sophia," *VC* 33 (1979): 34.

47. The language of this material may allude to a kind of mystical experience, a feature we will explore in a later chapter; see Winston, *Wisdom of Solomon*, 42.

48. E.g., *Fug.* 109; *QG* 4.66. Winston notes that use of sexual imagery for the intellectual life is found already in Plato (*Republic* 490B [LCL 276:29]); D. Winston, "The Sage as Mystic in the Wisdom of Solomon," in *The Sage in Israel and the Ancient Near East*, ed. J. G. Gammie and L. G. Perdue (Winona Lake, Ind.: Eisenbrauns, 1990), 390–91. I have used the Loeb Classical Library edition of the texts of Philo and, unless otherwise noted, I have followed the LCL translations.

49. R. A. Baer Jr. prefers to avoid calling this dual imagery "bi-sexual," noting that Philo does not describe Wisdom as male and female at the same time: *Philo's Use of the Categories of Male and Female* (Leiden: Brill, 1970), 62–63. On the dual nature of the imagery, see E. R. Goodenough, *By Light, Light: The Mystic Gospel of Hellenistic Judaism* (New Haven: Yale University Press, 1935), 248; Horsley, "Spiritual Marriage," 34–35.

50. *Fug.* 51–52; *Somn.* 1.200; *Cont.* 68; Baer, *Philo's Use*, 57. The usage in *Cont.* is less startling; there Philo is describing the Therapeutae, who are actually women.

51. Goodenough, *By Light, Light*, 248.

52. Philo is clearly informed by patriarchal notions regarding gender roles, and assumes that women are secondary in status and passive in sexual relationships; see Horsley, "Spiritual Marriage," 34–37; Baer, *Philo's Use*, 62–63.

53. E.g., *Sifre Deut.* 37; cf. G. F. Moore, *Judaism in the First Centuries of the Christian Era: The Age of the Tannaim*, 3 vols. (Cambridge: Harvard University Press, 1927, 1930; rpt., New York: Shocken, 1971), 1:265. Urbach states categorically that the personification of Wisdom in its specifically feminine roles is absent in the Talmuds and Midrashim; E. Urbach, *The Sages: Their Concepts and Beliefs*, 2 vols., trans. I. Abrahams (Jerusalem: Magnes Press [Hebrew University], 1975), 1:65. Urbach acknowledges, however, that personification of the Shekinah as feminine "play[s] a significant role in the Cabbalah [*sic*] under the influence" of Gnosticism.

54. E. Wolfson, "Female Imaging of the Torah: From Literary Metaphor to Religious Symbol," in *From Ancient Israel to Modern Judaism; Intellect in Quest of Understanding, Essays in Honor of Marvin Fox*, ed. J. Neusner, E. S. Frerichs, N. M. Sarna, BJS 173 (Atlanta: Scholars Press, 1989), 2:274. Later sources also portray Torah as Israel's mother; ibid.

55. *Lev. Rabbah* is admittedly of later composition. However, it contains a significant portion of Palestinian materials, ascribed to Tannaim and Amoraim. Since the *mashal* cited coincides with other references to the personification of Torah in the tannaitic period, we have included it here. For later examples of the personification of Torah as God's daughter, cf. *Exod. Rab.* 30:5, 33:1; *Deut. Rab.* 8:7.

56. *Fug.* 109; *Conf.* 49.

57. Commenting on Deut. 32:13. Cf. *QG* 4.143–46, where Wisdom is both mother and wife.

58. F. Christ, *Jesus Sophia: Die Sophia-Christologie bei den Synoptikern*, ATANT 57 (Zurich: Zwingli, 1970), 139; O. Steck, *Israel und das gewaltsame Geschick der Propheten: Untersuchungen zur Überlieferung des deuteronomistischen Geschichtsbildes im Alten Testament, Spätjudentum und Urchristentum*, WMANT 320 (Neukirchen-Vluyn: Neukirchener Verlag, 1967), 234.

59. *Nossiai sophias hairetōterai chrysiou, nossiai de phronēseōs hairetōterai hyper argyrion.*

60. *Meta anthrōpōn themelion aiōnos enosseusen.*

61. *Kai meta tou spermatos autōn empisteuthēsetai.*

62. *qnh* can also signify "acquire" (Gen. 25:10; Deut. 32:6; Lev. 27:24; 2S 24:24; etc.); it is so translated by B. Vawter ("Prov. 8:22: Wisdom and Creation," *JBL* 99 [1980]: 213). R. B. Y. Scott translates it "possess": *Proverbs, Ecclesiastes*, 68, 71–72. However, the context, which describes God's activity in creation, indicates "create" or "beget" as the better choices; e.g., Whybray, *Wisdom in Proverbs*, 101; B. Lang, *Wisdom and the Book of Proverbs: A Hebrew Goddess Redefined* (New York: Pilgrim, 1986), 54; G. A. Yee, "An Analysis of Prov 8:22–31 According to Style and Structure," *ZAW* 94 (1982): 61. McKane discusses the alternatives in *Proverbs*, 352–53.

63. *Nîsak^etî* and *ḥôlāl^etî* are both theological passives; cf. Gilbert, "Le discours," 210. The language of these verses indicates that Sophia is not to be identified with God, on the one hand (e.g., Schüssler-Fiorenza, *In Memory of Her*, 130–36), nor to be seen as independent of God (e.g., Lang, *Frau Weisheit*, 168–71). The language of vv. 22–23 is both masculine and feminine. Camp calls attention to the maternal imagery in vv. 22–31: *Wisdom and the Feminine*, 262–63.

64. We depart from the NRSV here. Syntactically and etymologically *'āmôn* can be translated as darling or infant, confidant, master builder or architect, counselor: Whybray, *Wisdom in Proverbs*, 101–3. However, the context, with the presence of *ša'ăšū'im* and *m^eśaḥeqeth* supports our translation (66); Gilbert, "Le discours," 214; Kayatz, *Studien zu Proverbien 1–9*, 96; Yee, "Analysis of Prov 8:22–31," 65.

65. Whybray, *Wisdom in Proverbs*, 103. Philo takes up this motif and tells us that Lady Wisdom is God's daughter, "begotten of her father alone, even God the father of all" (*Her.* 62). He tells us that she has no mother because she is herself the ruling principle *archē*.

66. *'Abot R. Nat. a* 31 may be speaking of Torah as daughter as well as lover when it tells us that R. Eliezer, the son of R. Yose the Galilean, taught that before the creation of the world the Torah "lay in the bosom of the Holy One, blessed be He, and recited the Song along with the ministering angels" (*'Abot R. Nat. a* 31). The "Song" refers to Ezek. 3:12: "Blessed be the glory of the Lord from his place": *The Fathers According to Rabbi Nathan*, ed. and trans. J. Goldin (New Haven: Yale University Press, 1955; rpt., New York: Shocken, 1974), 204 n. 12, and 189 n. 21. The passage cites Prov. 8:22 as a proof-text although nothing explicitly identifies Wisdom and Torah. In this passage, Torah is personified as an intimate of God, whether as daughter or lover. The personification makes clear that Torah is cherished by God, pays honor to the divine, and pre-exists the world.

67. E.g., Job 28:27; Sir. 1:4; Wis. 7:22, 8:6; Philo, *Det.* 225–26; *Conf.* 49. Lady Wisdom's role as mother and nurse to the universe in Philo implies that she is pre-existent (*Conf.* 49; *Det.* 115–16). And, he says, Wisdom's years, "are from of old, ere not only I, but the whole universe was born" (*Virt* 62). Here he alludes to Prov. 8:22.

68. One finds similar lists in *Mek. Shirata* 9:118–26; *Sifre Deut.* 37 and 309, and *b. Pesaḥ.* 54a (bar.). The lists vary. All, however, include Torah as one of the pre-existent "possessions"; and all cite Prov. 8:22 to support that assertion. For later usages, see *b. Pesaḥ.* 54a; *Ned.* 39b. Although the proem of *Gen. Rab.* 1:1, attributed to R. Hoshaia, does not have a list, he does speak of Torah-Wisdom as the pre-existent instrument of creation, citing Prov. 8:22.

69. The LXX has *hodon autēs*. *Dar^ekâh* is more coherent with the immediate context and with the usage in v. 23 than is *'er^ekâh;* the latter may easily be the result of scribal error.

70. For this author Wisdom is utterly transcendent. Indeed, it is not even clear that Wisdom is God's creation for this poet. While v. 27 indicates that Wisdom is subordinate to God, it does not say that God created it, but rather, at the moment of creation, God *saw* it (*râ'âh*).

71. Concerning light imagery, see Mack, *Logos und Sophia*, 169–71.

72. Elsewhere Philo speaks of illumination, vision, and apprehension of the divine without mentioning wisdom; e.g., *Praem.* 45–46; *Cher.* 27. In *Mig.* 34–37, he speaks of it in relation to *aretē*, a synonym for *sophia*. On Philo's mysticism, see D. Winston, ed., *Philo of Alexandria: The Contemplative Life, the Giants, and Selections*, Classics of Western Spirituality (New York: Paulist, 1981), 21–35.

73. E.g., Prov. 8:22–30; Sir. 1:10; 24:3, 6; Wis. 7:22; 8:1, 6; Philo, *Ebr.* 30–31; *Fug.* 109; *Gen. Rab.* 1:1, proem.

74. Sir. 24:3, 9. The Wisdom of Solomon uses Stoic categories, identifying Wisdom with the *pneuma* and *logos* (7:22, 24). On the relationship of Wisdom to *pneuma* and *logos* see Deutsch, *Hidden Wisdom*, 58; C. Larcher, *Études sur le livre de la Sagesse*, EBib (Paris: J. Gabalda, 1969), 367–70; J. Reider, *The Book of Wisdom* (New York: Harper and Brothers, 1957), 144ff. Mack, *Logos und Sophia*, 64, 71, 96–103.

75. See *Gen. Rab.* 1:1, proem, where the tradent constructs a play on the word *rē'šît* and alludes to the beginning of the Hebrew Bible, the creation story, to tell us that Wisdom-Torah is the blueprint that God consulted in creating the world. Moore, Schubert, and Hengel have all noted the similarity between this passage and Philo's *Ap.* 16ff. Cf. Moore, *Judaism in the First Centuries*, 1:267; K. Schubert, "Einige Beobachtungen zum Verständnis des Logosbegriffs im frührabbinischen Schrifttum," *Judaica* 9 (1953): 71ff.; M. Hengel, *Judaism and Hellenism: Studies in Their Encounter in Palestine during the Early Hellenistic Period*, 2 vols., trans. J. Bowden (Philadelphia: Fortress, 1974), 1:171. This passage is slightly later than our period; R. Hoshaia is a first-generation Amora.

76. Whybray, *Wisdom in Proverbs*, 104; Camp, *Wisdom and the Feminine*, 222. One must note that there is a concrete quality about Wisdom, which implies loyalty, proper action — everything from God's righteousness and truthfulness (3:28) to proper appreciation for one's wife (5:15–23), to fiscal prudence (6:6–11). And, of course, it is associated with fear of the Lord (1:7, 29; 2:5) and knowledge (1:22, 29).

77. E.g., 2:4, 8:17.

78. Winston, *Wisdom of Solomon*, 43, 172.

79. Georgi considers Wisdom of Solomon to be the oldest gnostic writing, concerned with consciousness as are texts from Nag Hammadi and the Corpus Hermeticum: "Weisheit Salomos," 394–95. Georgi seems to concentrate solely on the nature of gnosis as concern with consciousness. He does not address issues of good and evil, matter and spirit, creation and salvation, dualism.

80. Ibid., 332. It is likely that 24:4 recalls not only the pillar of cloud of Exod. 13:21–22, 14:19–20, 33:9–11, and 40:38, but also the references to God's throne in texts such as Isa. 66:1; Ps. 103:19; Ezek. 43:6, 7; G. Sheppard, *Wisdom as Hermeneutical Construct: A Study in the Sapientializing of the Old Testament*, BZAW 151 (Berlin: de Gruyter, 1980), 31–32. As Sheppard notes, Sirach 24 tends to "assign to Wisdom a share in the Old Testament [*sic*] depictions of God's presence within Israel's sacred traditions" (32).

81. The Wisdom of Solomon also describes Lady Wisdom as immanent

in history, beginning with the first parents and continuing with the events of Exodus and desert wandering (Wis. 10:1–11:1).

82. See also 1:26–27, 15:1, 21:11, 34:8; P. W. Skehan and A. A. Di Lella, *The Wisdom of Ben Sira*, AB 39 (New York: Doubleday, 1987), 336; J. Marbock, "Gesetz und Weisheit: Zum Verständnis des Gesetzes bei Jesus Ben Sira," *BZ*, n.f. 20 (1976): 1–21.

83. In 17:1–14 Ben Sira juxtaposes the events of Creation and Sinai. He does not, however, refer to Wisdom.

84. W. Harrelson, "Wisdom Hidden and Revealed According to Baruch (Baruch 3.9–4.4)," in *Priests, Prophets and Scribes: Essays on the Formation and Heritage of Second Temple Judaism in Honour of Joseph Blenkinsopp*, ed. E. Ulrich et al., JSOTSS 149 (Sheffield, England: JSOT, 1992), 158–71.

85. E.g., *Sifre Deut.* 37; Moore, *Judaism in the First Centuries*, 1:265.

86. Unless otherwise noted, I have used Reuven Hammer's translation, *Sifre: A Tannaitic Commentary on the Book of Deuteronomy*, Yale Judaica Series 24 (New Haven: Yale University Press, 1986). Toward the close of the chapter, the author cites Prov. 3:16, 18 and Prov. 4:22 and 9 to support the exhortation, "Study it [Torah] for its own sake, and honor will come eventually." See *'Abot* 6:7 which cites Prov. 4:22; 3:8, 18; 1:9; 4:11; 9:11; 3:16, 2. Cf. *baraita* in *b. Ta'an.* 7a in which Prov. 3:18 is used to describe Torah as life. Cf. also *Mek. Vayassa* 1:13–15, which cites Prov. 3:18 to liken Torah to a tree; *Sifre Deut.* 306 (Prov. 4:8).

87. On Wisdom as representing cosmic order, see G. Von Rad, *Wisdom in Israel*, trans. J. D. Martin (Nashville: Abingdon, 1981), 174; on Wisdom as representing the human wisdom traditions, see Camp, *Wisdom and the Feminine*, 217–22.

88. U. Wilckens, *Weisheit und Torheit: Eine exegetisch-religionsgeschichtliche Untersuchung zu 1.Kor.1 und 2*, BHTh 26 (Tübingen: J. C. B. Mohr [Paul Siebeck], 1959), 160–61. See also *2 Apoc. Bar.* 48:36 and 4 Ezra 5:9–11. In *2 Apoc. Baruch*, the withdrawal of Wisdom corresponds to the people's abandonment of the ways of Torah, and the lack of proper teachers (cf. 48:33, 36). And in 4 Ezra Wisdom's withdrawal corresponds to the author's inability to make sense of the nation's catastrophe.

89. G. W. E. Nickelsburg, *Jewish Literature between the Bible and the Mishnah: A Historical and Literary Introduction* (Philadelphia: Fortress, 1981), 216. In earlier work I have taken *1 Enoch* 84:3 and 94:5 to represent examples of the metaphor Lady Wisdom. I am revising that reading in light of the evidence presented by E. Isaac in *The Old Testament Pseudepigrapha*, gen. ed. J. H. Charlesworth, 2 vols. (Garden City, N.Y.: Doubleday, 1983, 1985), 1:62, 75.

90. For a discussion of the structure of the Parables of Enoch, see D. Suter, *Tradition and Composition in the Parables of Enoch*, SBLDS 47 (Missoula, Mont.: Scholars Press, 1979), 140–43.

91. I have left "Son of Man" in its specifically gendered form, rather than using an inclusive alternative such as "Human One." I have done so because of the traditionally male roles usually assigned to the figure (e.g., military and royal rule), as well as its history of transmission.

92. See J. J. Collins, "The Son of Man in First-Century Judaism," *NTS* 38

(1992): 458. Collins observes that the portrait of the Son of Man presented in Daniel 7 "was filled out with reminiscences of pre-existent Wisdom (Proverbs 8), which was also a revealer, and of the hidden servant of the Lord (Isa. 49.2: 'in his quiver he hid me away')."

93. H. L. Jansen, *Die Henochgestalt: Eine vergleichende religionsgeschicht-liche Untersuchung* (Oslo: Kommisjon Hos Jacob Dybwad, 1939), 90–91.

94. *1 Enoch* 38:1–3, 45:3, 46:4–8, 48:8, 50:1–5, 55:4, 61:8–9.

95. E.g., the Son of Man is the judge who reveals God's wisdom (48:7), the wisdom figure who judges the secret things (49:3), and the judge who sits on God's throne from whose mouth comes the secrets of wisdom (51:3).

96. G. W. E. Nickelsburg, "The Epistle of Enoch and the Qumran Litera-ture," *JJS* 33 (1982): 334–39; cf. 92:1, 93:8, 98:9, 100:6, 104:9–12.

97. On the sages' sectarian language, see Overman, *Matthew's Gospel*, 16–19.

98. E.g., Hengel, *Judaism and Hellenism*, 1:153–56. As Koester describes, the term *hypostasis* has a variety of usages in ancient texts. For example, the Stoics used it to designate being which has come into existence (*TDNT*, s.v. "ὑπόστασις," 575). It acquired a general meaning of plan, purpose, concern (578), and, in early Christian thought it signified plan project, reality (585–89). Thus, as it is used in modern scholarship it has acquired a somewhat different meaning, to describe an independent entity.

99. Ringgren first gave the term "hypostasis" a prominent place in the in-terpretation of personified Wisdom. He defines it as a "quasi-personification of certain attributes proper to God, occupying an intermediate position between personalities and abstract beings": *Word and Wisdom: Studies in the Hyposta-tization of Divine Qualities and Functions in the ANE* (Lund: Hakan Ohlssons Bokmyekeri, 1947), 8. He cites W. O. E. Oesterly and G. H. Box, *The Reli-gion and Worship of the Synagogue: An Introduction to the Study of Judaism from the New Testament Period* (New York: Scribner's 1907), 169. Later Ring-gren defines the term as "quasi-independent divine essence, which represents a more or less thorough-going personification of a property, efficacy, of any at-tributed of a higher divinity" ("Es bezeichnet eine oft nur halb selbständige göttliche Wesenheit, die eine mehr oder weniger durchgeführte Personifizierung einer Eigenschaft, einer Wirksamkeit, oder irgendeines Attribut einer höher Got-theit, darstellt": *RGG*, 4th ed. (1959), s.v. "Hypostasen," col. 504). Some would reject application of the term to the earlier literature, reserving it for later ma-terials such as the Wisdom of Solomon; e.g., Von Rad, *Wisdom in Israel*, 170; Lang, *Wisdom and the Book of Proverbs*, 139. Others would see its presence already in the Book of Proverbs; e.g., Whybray, *Wisdom in Proverbs*, 13.

100. Ringgren, "Hypostasen."

101. Contra E. A. Johnson, *She Who Is: The Mystery of God in Feminist Theological Discourse* (New York: Crossroad, 1992), 91; E. Schüssler-Fiorenza, *Jesus: Miriam's Child, Sophia's Prophet: Critical Issues in Feminist Christology* (New York: Continuum, 1994), 140.

102. Lang, *Frau Weisheit*, 168–71; regarding Prov. 9:1–6, see McKane, *Prov-erbs*, 363–64. The possibility of such a development is enhanced by the fact that in the Greco-Roman world virtues and abstracts were often deified; see

J. R. Fears, "The Cult of Virtues and Roman Imperial Ideology," *ANRW* II.17.2 (1981): 827–948.

103. E.g., Job 28:23–27; Bar. 3:32.

104. B. Witherington, *Jesus the Sage: The Pilgrimage of Wisdom* (Minneapolis: Fortress, 1994), 39 n. 103.

105. Bultmann was the first to speak of such a Wisdom myth: "Der religionsgeschichte Hintergrund des Prologs zum Johannes-Evangelium," in *Eucharisterion: Studien zur Religion und Literatur des Alten und Neuen Testaments*, ed. H. Schmidt (Göttingen: Vandenhoeck and Ruprecht, 1923), 1–26. For the background of the Wisdom myth in Egyptian and Greco-Roman religion, see H. Conzelmann, "The Mother of Wisdom," in *The Future of Our Religious Past*, ed. J. M. Robinson, trans. C. E. Carlston and R. P. Scharlemann (London: SCM, 1971), 230–43; Mack, *Logos und Sophia*, passim, esp. 34–42, and "Wisdom Myth and Mytho-logy"; U. Wilckens, *TDNT*, s.v. "σοφία."

106. Mack speaks of "mytho-logy," defining it as a kind of theological reflection in which "the theologian has little interest in reproducing the mythos itself, but works its patterns, motifs, and mythologumena into new configurations in the service of his central theological concern" ("Wisdom Myth," 53).

107. Ibid., 52; Conzelmann, "Mother of Wisdom," 232.

108. Mack, "Wisdom Myth," 58–60.

109. Ibid., 59.

110. There is evidence, both papyrological and archeological, for widespread presence of the cult of Isis in Palestine during the Hellenistic period. Indeed, a bas relief depicting the goddess has been found in Jerusalem itself; see Hengel, *Judaism and Hellenism*, 1:158ff. On Isis and Jewish Wisdom speculation, see Mack, *Logos und Sophia*, 38–49. On the Isis myth and Ben Sira, W. L. Knox, "The Divine Wisdom," *JTS* 38 (1937): 230–37; Conzelmann, "Mother of Wisdom," 234–43. On Wisdom of Solomon, see J. Reese, *Hellenistic Influence on the Book of Wisdom and Its Consequences*, AnBib 41 (Rome: Pontifical Biblical Institute, 1970), 42–50; J. Kloppenborg, "Isis and Sophia in the Book of Wisdom," *HTR* 75 (1982): 57–84; on Philo and the figure of Isis, see Mack, *Logos und Sophia*, 165.

111. For the title "mother of all," see SIG III 1138; on Isis's role in creation, e.g., Cyme stele, 1.2; Plutarch, *De Isis* 64; Knox, "Divine Wisdom," 230.

112. Hengel, *Judaism and Hellenism*, 1:158. Worship of Astarte had long been popular in Egypt: S. Morenz, *Egyptian Religion*, trans. Ann E. Keep (London: Methuen, 1973), 237–41; R. Stadelmann, *Syrisch-Palästinensische Gottheitenin Ägypten* (Leiden: Brill, 1967), 12.

113. Cyme, 1.4; Diodorus 1.27; Knox, "Divine Wisdom," 231.

114. Plutarch, *De Isis* 2. On the cult of Isis in this period, see the texts in Werner Peek, *Der Isishymnus von Andros: und verwandte Texte* (Berlin: Wiedmannsche Buchhandlung, 1930), 122–59; also A. D. Nock, *Conversion: The Old and the New in Religion from Alexander the Great to Augustine of Hippo* (Oxford: Oxford University Press, 1963), 48ff.; Morenz, *Egyptian Religion*, 248–50.

115. Plutarch, *De Isis* 3; *POxy.* 1380, l. 117.

116. M. Douglas, *Natural Symbols: Explorations in Cosmology*, 2nd ed.

(London: Barrie and Jenkins, 1973), 68; P. L. Berger and T. Luckmann, *The Social Construction of Reality: A Treatise in the Sociology of Knowledge* (New York: Anchor Books, 1967), 97.

117. C. Geertz, *The Interpretation of Cultures: Selected Essays by Clifford Geertz* (New York: Basic Books, 1973), 131.

118. Ibid., 89–90.

119. Douglas, *Natural Symbols*, 41; Geertz, *Interpretation of Cultures*, 119, 124.

120. Geertz, *Interpretation of Cultures*, 131.

121. N. Frye, *The Great Code: The Bible and Literature* (San Diego: Harvest/HBJ, 1983), 49; J. C. Crocker, "The Social Functions of Rhetorical Forms," in *Social Use of Metaphor*, ed. Sapir and Crocker, 37.

122. Frye, *Great Code*, 33.

123. P. L. Berger, *The Sacred Canopy: Elements of a Sociological Theory of Religion* (Garden City, N.Y.: Anchor/Doubleday, 1969), 34–35, 42. Berger speaks here of religion, which belongs to the order of symbol and myth.

124. Berger and Luckmann, *Social Construction of Reality*, 85.

125. Ibid., 85, 117. Smith refers to the relationship between the scribal class and the development of the symbol of Wisdom: "They projected their scribal activities on high, on a god who created by law according to a written plan, on a god who was a teacher in his heavenly court. They hypostatized the scribe and scribal activities in the figure of Divine Wisdom. They speculated about hidden heavenly tablets, about creation by divine word, about the beginning and the end and thereby claimed to possess the secrets of creation"; J. Z. Smith, "Wisdom and Apocalyptic," in *Visionaries and Their Apocalypses*, ed. P. D. Hanson (Philadelphia: Fortress, 1983), 103.

126. Berger and Luckmann, *Social Construction of Reality*, 81. It also requires the presence of economic surplus, for the development of specialized knowledge means that experts are engaged in activities not immediately related to subsistence (117).

127. E.g., Gammie and Perdue, eds., *The Sage*; H. Z. Dimitrovsky, ed., *Exploring the Talmud*, vol. 1, *Education* (New York: KTAV, 1976).

128. E.g., Prov. 1:8, 2:1, 3:1, 4:1, 5:1, 7:1; cf. 8:32–33.

129. E.g., Prov. 1:20–33, 8:1–36, 9:1–6; Sir. 24:19–22.

130. For example, Lady Wisdom's speech in 1:20–33 follows the sage's exhortation in 1:8–19 and precedes those of the following chapters. Prov. 4:1–27 and 5:1–14 identify wisdom with the sage's instruction and contrast Lady Wisdom with the adulterous woman. See C. Newsom, "Woman and the Discourse of Patriarchal Wisdom: A Study of Proverbs 1–9," in *Gender and Difference in Ancient Israel*, ed. Peggy L. Day (Minneapolis: Fortress, 1989), 142–59.

131. Prov. 1:32–33, 4:13, 8:35, 9:6; cf. 3:22–24; 4:10–12, 22; 7:2.

132. Prov. 1:22; cf 1:4, 7:7.

133. Prov. 8:32, in the plural; for the teacher's use, in the singular, see Prov. 1:8, 15; 2:1; 3:1, 11, 21; 4:10, 20; 5:1; 6:1, 3, 20; 7:1; in the plural, 4:1; 5:7; 7:24. While the Hebrew reads literally "my son," "my sons," the role of women in instruction in the Book of Proverbs, discussed later in this chapter, suggests the inclusive reading of the NRSV to be more appropriate.

134. Prov. 8:6–9, 20; cf. 2:9; 4:11.

135. Prov. 3:13–15, 8:10–11; cf. 1:8–9.

136. Prov. 2:10; cf. 3:1, 3; 4:21; 6:21; 7:3.

137. F. Brown, S. R. Driver, and C. A. Briggs, eds., *A Hebrew and English Lexicon of the Old Testament with an Appendix Containing the Biblical Aramaic* (Oxford: Clarendon, 1907, 1976), 523.

138. Prov. 3:16–18; 8:18, 21; cf. 3:2, 4; 4:10.

139. Prov. 4:9; cf. 1:9, 3:22.

140. Prov. 1:32–33; 8:36; cf. 2:20–22, 4:11–14; McKane, *Proverbs*, 276–77.

141. See also Sir. 15:3; Prov. 9:5.

142. This is an allusion to Isa. 55:1–2. The presence of the acrostic in the Qumran Psalms Scroll (11QPsa 21.11–17, 22.1) suggests that the same association pertained for the compiler(s) of the Scroll.

143. Sir. 6:18–31, 32–27; 14:20–15:10; 24:1–29, 30–34; 51:13–30.

144. 4 Ezra 8:4; cf. 4:2, 10, 21–22; 5:22, 34, 39; 8:3; 13:53–55; 14:40–42.

145. E.g., *2 Apoc. Bar.* 38:1–4, 48:24, 51:3, 77:16. The fact that in each of these instances Torah and Wisdom occur in a parallelism makes it difficult to determine whether the author(s) indeed were making an actual identification.

146. F. J. Murphy, *The Structure and Meaning of Second Baruch*, SBLDS 78 (Atlanta: Scholars Press, 1985), 141–42.

147. Regarding *1 Enoch* see J. J. Collins, "The Sage in the Apocalyptic and Pseudepigraphic Literature," in *The Sage*, ed. Gammie and Perdue, 353.

148. Regarding *1 Enoch* see J. J. Collins, "The Apocalyptic Technique: Setting and Function in the Book of Watchers," *CBQ* 44 (1982): 103–8.

149. The hymnist's understanding of his role, moreover, appears to derive from and contribute to his understanding of the way God relates to the faithful: "For Thou art a father to all [the sons] of Thy truth, and as a woman who tenderly loves her babe, so dost Thou rejoice in them; and as a foster-father bearing a child in his lap, so carest Thou for all Thy creatures" (9.35–36).

150. In another context, we read that the *maskîl* guides members individually "according to the spirit of each and according to the rule of the age" (1QS 9.18).

151. *Sifre Deut.* 34, 305, 335; *Mek. Vayassa* 1:130–31; cf. *b. 'Erub.* 73a; *'Abot R. Nat. a* 14, 18. See J. Neusner, *First-Century Judaism in Crisis: Johanan ben Zakkai and the Renaissance of Torah* (Nashville: Abingdon, 1975), 95.

152. E.g., *Sifre Deut.* 32; *m. B. Mes.* 2:11; see J. Goldin, "Several Sidelights of a Torah Education in Tannaitic and Early Amoraic Times," in *Exploring the Talmud*, ed. Dimitrovsky, 1:5.

153. See Goldin, "Several Sidelights," 5.

154. E.g., Prov. 3:22–24; 4:10–12, 22; 7:2.

155. Prov. 10:13; 23:13; 29:15, 17; Cf. Lemaire, "The Sage in School and Temple," in *The Sage*, ed. Gammie and Perdue, 175.

156. Philo describes the good teacher as encouraging the student to think independently; *Mut.* 270. He describes the bad teacher in eloquent terms; e.g., *Cher.* 9; *Post.* 141; *Congr.* 127–28.

157. E.g., *'Abot R. Nat. a* 36; L. I. Levine, *The Rabbinic Class of Ro-*

man Palestine in Late Antiquity (New York: Jewish Theological Seminary of America, 1989), 59–60.

158. E.g., *m. Sukk.* 2:1, 5, 7, 8; 3:9; *m. Yebam.* 6:4; *m. Betzah* 3:8; *m. 'Erub.* 4:4; S. D. Fraade, *From Tradition to Commentary: Torah and Its Interpretation in the Midrash Sifre to Deuteronomy* (Albany: State University of New York, 1991), 103; J. Jeremias, *Jerusalem in the Time of Jesus: An Investigation into Economic and Social Conditions during the New Testament Period,* trans. F. H. Cave and C. H. Cave (London: SCM, 1969), 242–43; E. Bickerman, "La chaîne de la tradition pharisienne," *RB* 59 (1952): 49–50. As was true of the study of philosophy in the Greco-Roman world at large, so too the study of Torah was considered to be a way of life, taught not only by oral instruction, but through the example of the sage's life; S. Safrai and M. Stern, *The Jewish People in the First Century: Historical Geography, Political History, Social, Cultural and Religious Life and Institutions,* vol. 1, Compendia Rerum Iudaicarum ad Novum Testamentum (Philadelphia: Fortress, 1974), 963; M. Smith, "Palestinian Judaism in the First Century," in *Israel: Its Role in Civilization,* ed. M. Davis (New York: Jewish Theological Seminary of America, 1956), 79–80; P. Lénhardt, "Voies de la continuité juive: Aspects de la relation maître-disciple d'après la littérature rabbinique ancienne" *RSR* 66 (1978): 500–501. In Greco-Roman terms, Judaism was a philosophy — a synthesis of ritual, beliefs, legal code and national customs; Smith, "Palestinian Judaism," 79.

159. Horsley appears to contrast literate groups with prophets and other kinds of popular leaders" " 'Like One of the Prophets of Old': Two Types of Popular Prophets at the Time of Jesus," *CBQ* 47 (1985): 435–63. He does not take into account the ways in which scribes described themselves as prophets.

160. The wisdom poem of Baruch possesses a prophetic quality in its call to conversion (3:9–14, 4:1–2). Indeed, the whole book is "prophetic" in its acknowledgment of Israel's sins, its plea for divine help and for the consolation of Jerusalem. As the prophet "reads" the meaning of historical events, so too does Baruch the scribe "read" the events of the redactor's day. There is as well a prophetic element in the sage's address in the Wisdom of Solomon, with its threat of divine judgment and its exhortation to "Listen" and "Give ear" (6:5–8). The prophetic element is further illustrated by the identification of the sage-righteous one with the servant-child in 2:12–5:14; M. J. Suggs, "Wisdom of Solomon 2.10–15: A Homily on the Fourth Servant Song," *JBL* 76 (1957): 26–33; Mack, *Logos und Sophia,* 85–86; Nickelsburg, *Jewish Literature,* 178–79; Winston, *Wisdom of Solomon,* 119–20.

161. Blenkinsopp, "Interpretation and Sectarian Tendencies," 15.

162. Josephus says that some of the Essenes have "foreknowledge" of future events (*kai prognōsin ek theou tōn mellontōn: Ant.* 15:373) or "profess to foretell the future (*ta mellonta proginōskein hypischnountai: War* 2.159). He relates their foreknowledge to their learning (*War* 2.159). The Essenes are also skilled in interpreting dreams (*War* 2.112–13). I have used the Loeb Classical Library edition of Josephus's works. Unless otherwise noted, I have used the LCL translations.

163. With G. Vermes, *The Dead Sea Scrolls in English,* 4th ed., rev. and extended (London: Penguin, 1995), 218. Unless otherwise noted, I have used

Vermes's translation of the Qumran material when available. Cf. Jeremiah 1:5; also 1QH 15.14–16.

164. Cf Isa. 61:1–3.

165. The allusion is to Isa. 40:11. In the canonical text, however, it refers to God.

166. Nickelsburg, *Jewish Literature*, 53, and "Enoch, Levi, and Peter: Recipients of Revelation in Upper Galilee," *JBL* 100 (1981): 576–82.

167. Woe, exhortation, description of judgment or events leading up to it: Nickelsburg, *Jewish Literature*, 148, and "The Apocalyptic Message of Enoch 92–105," *CBQ* 39 (1977): 310–11.

168. Nickelsburg, "Apocalyptic Message," 326–27. Other apocalyptic texts associate the seer with prophecy. For example, Ezra is called the last of the prophets (4 Ezra 12:42). And the opening of *2 Apoc. Baruch* with the usual format of a prophetic book, giving the date by the king's reign, name of the prophet, and the statement that the "word of the Lord came to Baruch the son of Neriah" (1:1), suggests that the author considers Baruch to be a prophet; cf. Hos. 1:1; Amos 1:1; Mic. 1:1; Zech. 1:1; Isa. 1:1; Jer. 1:1–3; Ezek. 1:1–3. Neither Amos 1:1 nor Isa. 1:1 speaks of God's word coming to the prophet. See G. Sayler, *Have the Promises Failed? A Literary Analysis of 2 Baruch*, SBLDS 72 (Chico, Calif.: Scholars Press, 1984), 113.

169. Certain biblical traditions describe Moses as a prophet; e.g., Num. 11:16–22, 23–29; Deut. 18:15–22, 34:10. Num. 12:6–8, however, contrasts Moses with the prophets, implying that he is greater, for while God speaks to the prophet in dreams and visions he communicates directly (*peh 'el peh*) — literally "mouth to mouth" — with Moses. For other Tannaitic references to Moses as prophet, see *Sifre Deut.* 2 and 9. The appraisal of some of the sages, tannaim and amoraim, was that prophecy had already ceased with Haggai, Zechariah and Malachi; e.g., *t. Sota* 13:2; *b. Sanh.* 11a; *Yoma* 9b; *Sota* 48b; I. Gruenwald, *From Apocalypticism to Gnosticism* (Frankfurt: Peter Lang, 1988), 33. The texts speak to the departure of the Holy Spirit (e.g., *b. Sanh.* 11a; *Yoma* 9b; *Sota* 48b) or to the Holy Spirit ceasing in Israel (*t. Sota* 13:2). This refers, perhaps, not to prophecy as an activity, but to *canonical* prophecy; Urbach, *The Sages*, 1:564–65. The words attributed to the Amora R. Avdimi of Haifa would suggest continuity between prophets and sages: "Since the destruction of the Temple prophecy was taken away from the prophets and given to the sages and it has not been taken away" (*B. B. Bat.* 12a). Regarding the sages as successors to the prophets, see Jeremias, *Jerusalem in the Time of Jesus*, 241–42; Safrai and Stern, *Jewish People*, 1:360; Urbach, *The Sages*, 1:564–67, 577–79.

170. E. Urbach, "The Talmudic Sage — Character and Authority," *Cahiers d'Histoire Mondiale* 11 (1968): 122. The Pharisees, while often acting as retainers, sometimes oppose the ruling class; Saldarini, *Pharisees, Scribes and Sadducees*, 107–33 passim.

171. Moreover, the Amoraim speak of certain Tannaim as divining by the Holy Spirit; e.g., Hillel and Shmuel the Small (*j. Sota* 9.17 [24c, 29ff.]); R. Akiba (*Lev. Rab.* 21:8 on 16:3); R. Meir (*j. Sota* 1.4 [16d, 45ff.]); R. Simon b. Jochai (*j. Seb.* 9.1). The sages were aware of the possibility of abuse regarding the belief in and use of prophecy. In one text, prophecy is preceded by a long list of

qualities — among them humility — and it leads to the resurrection of the dead (*m. Sota* 9:15). The false prophet was liable to death by strangling (*m. Sanh.* 11:1). The criterion of true and false prophecy is the Torah itself (*Sifre Deut.* 83–86). A false prophet might be discerned by his instruction to abandon some of the commandments (*Sifre Deut.* 86).

172. *Songs of the Sabbath Sacrifice: A Critical Edition*, ed. and trans. C. A. Newsom, HSS 27 (Atlanta: Scholars Press, 1985). Despite the reference to the Throne in 4Q 405, the Throne-Chariot is not the focus of the *Sabbath Songs*, but rather the celestial worship of the angelic priesthood (72).

173. For other descriptions of heavenly worship, see *T. Levi* 3:8; *1 Enoch* 39–40; *2 Enoch* 20–21; *Apoc. Abr.* 17–18; Rev. 4–5; *Asc. Isa.* 7–9.

174. E.g., 1QH 3:19–23, 6:12–13, 11:10–14; 1QSb 3:26–27, 4:23–26; 1QS 11:5–10; see Halperin, *Faces of the Chariot: Early Jewish Responses to Ezekiel's Vision*, Texte und Studien zum Antiken Judentum 16 (Tübingen: Mohr/Siebeck, 1988), 50; M. Smith, "Ascent to the Heavens and the Beginnings of Christianity," *Eranosjahrbuch* 50 (1981): 411. These texts evoke faint echoes of Josephus's statement that the Essenes "immortalize" (*athanatizousin*) the souls, which may refer to a rite of ascents: *Ant.* 18.18; Smith, "Ascent to the Heavens"; A. F. Segal, *Rebecca's Children: Judaism and Christianity in the Roman World* (Cambridge: Harvard University Press, 1986), 77.

175. Cf. Winston, ed., *Philo of Alexandria*, 21–35; C. R. Holladay, *THEIOS ANER in Hellenistic Judaism: A Critique of the Use of This Category in New Testament Christology*, SBLDS 40 (Missoula, Mont.: Scholars Press, 1977), 163–67. Ecstasy and prophecy are interrelated in Philo's thought.

176. For other autobiographical passages regarding Philo's mystical experience, see *Spec.* 3.1–6; *Migr.* 34–35; *Somn.* 2.252.

177. *QG* 3.9; *Her.* 69, 74; *LA* 1.82; 3.29, 41, 43; *Somn.* 2.232; *Spec.* 4:49; cf. Baer, *Philo's Use*, 56.

178. A. F. Segal, "Heavenly Ascent in Hellenistic Judaism, Early Christianity and Their Environment," *ANRW* II.2 (1980): 1355–56. Philo describes Moses as a mystic, telling us that Moses "entered ... into the darkness where God was, that is into the unseen, invisible, incorporeal and archetypal essence of existing things. Thus he beheld what is hidden from the sight of mortal nature, and, in himself and his life displayed for all to see, he has set before us ... a model for those who are willing to copy it" (*Mos.* 1.158). He describes Moses' very death as a supernatural ascent, exaltation, and upward flight (2.288–91); see P. L. Shuler, "Philo's Moses and Matthew's Jesus: A Comparative Study in Ancient Literature," *Studia Philonica Annual* 2 (1990): 97. Holladay notes that this description of Moses as visionary may be related to the motif of Moses' kingship, and that Philo is influenced by Plato's description of the philosopher-king who perceives the "eternal and unchanging realities" (*Phaedr.* 249c-e; *Symp.* 211): *THEIOS ANER*, 126–27.

179. On the heavenly ascent in *1 Enoch* 37–71, see Segal, "Heavenly Ascent," 1377–78.

180. Nickelsburg, *Jewish Literature*, 214–17.

181. Regarding the divine glory, *1 Enoch* 14:16, 20; 60:2; Exod. 24:16, 17;

fire, *1 Enoch* 14:10, 17; 71:1–2; Exod. 3:2–3, 19:18, 24:17; cloud, *1 Enoch* 14:20; Exod. 19:9, 16; 24:15, 18; radiant face or altered appearance, *1 Enoch* 39:14, 71:11; Exod. 34:30–35; angelic or divine voice, *1 Enoch* 14:24–16:3; 60:5ff., 71:14; Exod. 3:1–4:23; 19:7–25; 24:12; 25:1–34:27; commissioning, *1 Enoch* 15:1–16:3, 72:14–17; Exod. 3:10–12, 24:12, 34:27–28.

182. On the use of the title "Son of Man" in chapter 71, see B. Halperin, *The Faces of the Chariot,* 86; Segal, "Heavenly Ascent," 1378. On the way the Son of Man and Enoch are paralleled, see Collins, "Son of Man in First-Century Judaism," 453–57.

183. Collins, "The Sage," 346–47. Collins qualifies his remarks by saying, "We do not know whether they induced dreams or practiced heavenly ascents, but it is at least clear that they thought about these things" (346). See also I. Gruenwald, *Apocalyptic and Merkavah Mysticism* (Leiden: Brill, 1980), 32; Hengel, *Judaism and Hellenism,* 1:207; M. E. Stone, "The Book of Enoch and Judaism in the Third Century B.C.E.," *CBQ* 40 (1978): 488. Halperin, *The Faces of the Chariot,* 64–71. M. Himmelfarb is more skeptical: *Ascent to Heaven in Jewish and Christian Apocalypses* (New York: Oxford University Press, 1993), 98, 104–6.

184. See Collins, "The Sage," 345. While 4 Ezra and 2 *Apoc. Baruch* do not have accounts of heavenly ascents, they portray the sages as seers. Moreover, they provide evidence of various practices to induce or prepare for visionary experience: weeping, fasting, eating special foods, special posture. After a vision the seer is weak or faints. Regarding weeping, 4 Ezra 5:20, 6:35; 2 *Apoc. Bar.* 5:6, 6:2, 9:2, 35:11; fasting, 4 Ezra 5:20; 6:31, 35; 2 *Apoc. Bar.* 5:7, 9:2, 20:5–21:1, 47:2; special foods, 4 Ezra 9:23–26, 12:51; special posture, 3:1, 9:27, 13:1, 14:1. There is biblical precedent, both for the descriptions of ascetical practices and for the description of visionary experiences. For references to ascetical practices, see Exod. 34:28; 2K 6:30; 1 Chron. 21:16; Neh. 9:1; Isa. 58:5; Dan. 9:3, 10:2–3; for visionary experience, see Ezek. 1:28–2:2; Dan. 7:1, 9:17–18. See J. C. H. Lebram, "The Piety of the Jewish Apocalyptists," in *Apocalypticism in the Mediterranean World and the Near East,* ed. D. Hellholm (Tübingen: J. C. B. Mohr [Paul Siebeck], 1983), 184–87; L. F. Hartmann and A. A. Di Lella, *The Book of Daniel* (Garden City, N.Y.: Doubleday, 1978): 248. Concerning preparations for visionary experience, see D. S. Russell, *The Method and Message of Jewish Apocalyptic,* The Old Testament Library (Philadelphia: Westminster, 1976), 169–73. See also M. Idel, *Kabbalah: New Perspectives* (New Haven: Yale University Press, 1988), 77; Gruenwald, *Apocalyptic and Merkavah Mysticism,* 99–102.

185. *Mek. R. Simeon* I.ii.2; *t. Ḥag* 2:1–2; *j. Ḥag* 2.1; *b. Ḥag* 14b; see J. Neusner, *Development of a Legend: Studies on the Traditions Concerning Yohanan ben Zakkai* (Leiden: Brill, 1970), 247–52; Urbach, *The Sages,* 1:577. One uses rabbinic sources in relation to first-century material only with the greatest caution since even the tannaitic sources are subject to much later editing. I use them here to suggest a framework that is bounded by Second Temple sources as well.

186. See J. Goldin, "A Philosophical Session in a Tannaitic Academy," in *Exploring the Talmud,* ed. Dimitrovsky, 357–63; Gruenwald, *Apocalyptic and Merkavah Mysticism,* 75–84; Halperin, *Faces of the Chariot,* 13–16.

187. This material is found in *m. Ḥag* 2:1; *t. Ḥag* 2:1–7; *b. Ḥag* 11b–16a; *j. Ḥag* 2:1 (77b); see also *b. Šabb.* 80b, *b. Ber.* 7a; *Ḥul.* 91b; *Meg.* 24b; *Gen. Rab.* 2:4; A. J. Saldarini, "Apocalypses and 'Apocalyptic' in Rabbinic Literature," *Semeia* 14 (1979): 188. Halperin calls the material in *t. Ḥag* 2:1–7, *j. Ḥag* 2:1, and *b. Ḥag* 11b, 15b–16a the "mystical collection" and presents a fuller list of parallels in *Gen. Rab.* (*Faces of the Chariot*, 69 n. 11). He believes it represents a collection redacted prior to these sources and used by all three: *The Merkabah in Rabbinic Literature*, American Oriental Series 62 (New Haven: American Oriental Society, 1980), 65–105.

188. There is also a version of this story in *Mek. R. Simeon* I.ii.2. The Tosefta does not include the miraculous phenomena. Gruenwald and Halperin both believe that the miracles were actually part of the earliest versions, and that the Tosefta surpressed them; Gruenwald, *Apocalyptic and Merkavah Mysticism*, 84–86; Halperin, *Faces of the Chariot*, 15. Neusner believes that the miracles represent additions at the latest stages of the development of the tradition: *Development of a Legend*, 249–51.

189. Two other of Johanan ben Zakkai's disciples, R. Joshua and R. Jose ha-Cohen (R. Simeon b. Nethaneel in the Palestinian Talmud), are then described as engaging in a similar exposition. This too is accompanied by miraculous signs (clouds in a Mediterranean summer sky, a "kind of" rainbow, and ministering angels), and is followed by Johanan ben Zakkai's acknowledgment, "Happy are ye, and happy is she that bore you." The angels are not present in the Palestinian Talmud parallel, though they are present there in the account of Eleazar ben Arak's discourse. For an examination of the ways in which this and other details " 'migrate from one episode to another" see Halperin, *The Merkabah in Rabbinic Literature*, 117–40.

190. The Palestinian Talmud attributes this to Jose ha-Cohen and Shimeon ben Nathanael. It follows directly their *merkabah* exposition; Halperin considers the account in the Babylonian Talmud to resemble more closely the original, since it resembles the account of Levi's ascent in *T. Levi* 2:5–6 (ibid., 130–31).

191. Halperin, *Merkabah in Rabbinic Literature*, 138. Halperin conjectures that "this was the rabbis' retort to the parallel claims of the apocalyptists (IV Ezra 14:1ff.)." Use of Sinai typology also legitimizes the sages' involvement in mystical speculation. One must note that texts such as the account of the four who entered Pardes (*t. Ḥag* 2:3–4) exhibit a cautionary note that reflects the sages' awareness of the potential in such activity for destabilization on religious, psychological and social levels; see Deutsch, *Hidden Wisdom*, 95; S. Niditch, "The Visionary," in *Ideal Figures in Ancient Judaism: Profiles and Paradigms*, ed. J. J. Collins and G. W. E. Nickelsburg (Chico, Calif.: Society of Biblical Literature, 1980), 170; Moore, *Judaism in the First Centuries*, 1:413. See also Gruenwald, *Apocalyptic and Merkavah Mysticism*, 85–86; G. E. Scholem, *Jewish Gnosticism, Merkabah Mysticism and Talmudic Tradition* (New York: Jewish Theological Seminary, 1965), 14–17. Halperin believes that these texts are literally about the exegesis of Ezekiel 1, with its possible reminders in vv. 7 and 10 of the molten calf of Exod. 32:24; *Faces of the Chariot*, 447–49. He believes that the tannaitic texts do not have to do with mystical experience, but with exegesis (12–13). While I would not rule out the exegetical component

to the rabbis' caution, I believe that these materials may also concern mystical speculation.

192. Gruenwald, *From Apocalypticism to Gnosticism*, 11.

193. See Deutsch, "The Sirach 51 Acrostic," 408.

194. *T. Levi* 3:8 refers to heavenly choirs, and *Apoc. Abr.* 17:8–21 is a long hymn recited by the visionary. On the occurrence of hymns in the Merkabah literature which is somewhat later than our period, see Scholem, *Jewish Gnosticism*, 20–30; K. F. Grözinger, "Singen und ekstatische Sprache in der früher jüdischen Mystik," *JSJ* 11 (1980): 66–77.

195. *Dead Sea Scrolls*, 4th ed., Vermes, 189.

196. C. Newsom, "The Sage in the Literature of Qumran," in *The Sage*, ed. Gammie and Perdue, 380–81.

197. This element in the understanding of the sage's function likely reflects tendencies already present in biblical traditions, e.g., Moses, Elijah and Elishah, Daniel.

198. Also 4Q511.I.8.

199. Newsom, "Sage in the Literature of Qumran," 381. Josephus tells us that the Essenes make use of the writings of the ancients to discern the medicinal qualities of roots and stones (*War* 2.136).

200. J. N. Lightstone, *The Commerce of the Sacred: Mediation of the Divine among Jews in the Graeco-Roman Diaspora*, BJS 59 (Chico, Calif.: Scholars Press, 1984), 17–56. Lightstone believes that presence of holy men, theurgy and concerns about the demonic suggest contexts in which the Temple — the normal means of access to the Holy — seems or is remote (56).

201. In 4QprNab a *gazer* pardons Nabonidus's sins and heals him. While the text does not mention exorcism explicitly, the term *gazer* implies it; G. Vermes, *Jesus the Jew: A Historian's Reading of the Gospels* (Philadelphia: Fortress, 1973), 67–68.

202. See D. L. Tiede, *The Charismatic Figure as Miracle Worker*, SBLDS 1 (Missoula, Mont.: Society of Biblical Literature, 1972), 130–37; Holladay, *THEIOS ANER*, 107–8.

203. Holladay, *THEIOS ANER*, 121; *V. Mos.* 1.156.

204. Lightstone, *Commerce of the Sacred*, 51. During the Amoraic period, such concern was widespread both in Palestine and Babylonia: J. Neusner, *There We Sat Down: Talmudic Judaism in the Making* (Nashville: Abingdon, 1972), 79–86.

205. A. Guttmann, "The Significance of Miracles for Talmudic Judaism," *HUCA* 20 (1947): 363–406; Levine, *Rabbinic Class*, 105–8.

206. *m. Ta'an.* 3:8; Josephus, *Ant.* 14:22–24; see Urbach, *The Sages*, 1:125; W. S. Green, "Palestinian Holy Men: Charismatic Leadership and Rabbinic Tradition," *ANRW* II.19.2 (1979): 619–47; Vermes, *Jesus the Jew*, 69–72.

207. *b. Ber.* 34b; *j. Ber.* 9d. See B. M. Bokser, "Wonder-Working and the Rabbinic Tradition: The Case of Hanina Ben Dosa," *JSJ* 16 (1985): 42–92.

208. See 1K 18:42. Hanina, of course, intercedes from a distance, whereas Elijah and Elisha heal in immediate proximity (1K 17:17–24; 2K 4:18–37); see Vermes, *Jesus the Jew*, 74–77; Urbach, *The Sages*, 1:574.

209. Regarding the tannaim, see Gruenwald, *From Apocalypticism to Gnosticism*, 11.

210. Ibid., 44–45; Lightstone, *Commerce of the Sacred*, 56.

211. Collins, "The Sage," 352; M. Knibb, "Apocalyptic and Wisdom in Fourth Ezra," *JSJ* 13 (1982): 62–63; J. M. Myers, *I and II Esdras*, AB (Garden City, N.Y.: Doubleday, 1974), 327–29. For a study of the parallels between Baruch and Moses in 2 *Apoc. Baruch*, see Murphy, *Structure and Meaning of Second Baruch*, 129–30. Ezra is already paralleled with Moses in his roles of teacher of the law and leader in covenant renewal; Neh. 8:19, 38.

212. God recalls to Baruch the precedent of Moses, and his work in mediating law and covenant (17:4–18:1, 19:1–2). It is Baruch's role to help the people "investigate the Law" (46:3). The angel Ramael [?] tells him that he is like Moses, who also received apocalyptic warnings, and revelations concerning the end of time, cosmic and heavenly mysteries, and the meaning of Torah (59:4–12).

213. On the echoes of Deuteronomy in 2 *Apoc. Baruch*, see Murphy, *Structure and Meaning of Second Baruch*, 120–30; M. Desjardins, "Law in II Baruch and IV Ezra," *SR* 14 (1985): 28. The translation is that of A. F. J. Klijn in *The Old Testament Pseudepigrapha*, vol. 1, *Apocalyptic Literature and Testaments*, ed. J. H. Charlesworth (Garden City, N.Y.: Doubleday, 1983).

214. E. Bickerman, "La chaîne de la tradition pharisienne," 44–54; Deutsch, *Hidden Wisdom*, 92–94; B. T. Viviano, *Study as Worship: Aboth and the New Testament*, SJLA 26 (Leiden: Brill, 1978), 5; Smith, "Palestinian Judaism," 79–80; A. J. Saldarini, *Scholastic Rabbinism: A Literary Study of the Fathers According to Rabbi Nathan*, BJS 14 (Chico, Calif.: Scholars Press, 1982), 9–10, 67–78. All of these scholars point out that the chain of tradition has analogues in Greek philosophical schools.

215. E.g., *m. 'Ed.* 8:7; *Yad* 4:3; *Pe'a.* 2:6; *t. Ḥal.* 1:6; *j. Pesaḥ.* 6.1; *b. Pesaḥ.* 66a. That chain omits the priesthood which had been responsible for the guardianship, interpretation, and transmission of Jewish tradition. It reflects a period in which nonpriestly sages had either assumed that role or were attempting to do so; see Fraade, *From Tradition to Commentary*, 70–75.

216. R. Akiba and R. Eliezer ben Hyrcanus had been impoverished; see *'Abot R. Nat. a* 6.

217. W. V. Harris, *Ancient Literacy* (Cambridge: Harvard University Press, 1989).

218. In this interest in the breadth of human experience we see traces of older, international wisdom traditions, as well as the influences of Hellenistic universalism. And Ben Sira's own writing bears ample witness to his own absorption of classical and Hellenistic culture. R. Pautrel, "Ben Sira et le stoïcisme," *RSR* 51 (1963): 535–49; T. Middendorp, *Die Stellung Jesu Ben Siras zwischen Judentum und Hellenismus* (Leiden: Brill, 1973). Nonetheless, one must also note the strong conservative tendency in Ben Sira; see A. A. Di Lella, "Conservative and Progressive Theology: Sirach and Wisdom," *CBQ* 38 (1966): 139–54; Camp, "The Female Sage in Ancient Israel and in the Biblical Wisdom Literature," in *The Sage*, ed. Gammie and Perdue, 195.

219. Such a background is also manifest in the references to wisdom and the court; e.g., 7:5, 8:8, 39:4.

220. Winston, *Wisdom of Solomon*, 172.

221. Higher education was the prerogative of the affluent who were able to procure it through the gymnasium, or who were able to obtain the services of a tutor, whether slave or free; R. Bagnall, *Egypt in Late Antiquity* (Princeton: Princeton University Press, 1993), 99–100; E. Rawson, *Intellectual Life in the Late Roman Republic* (Baltimore: Johns Hopkins University Press, 1985), 117–281. Some slaves were educated by their masters; see Harris, *Ancient Literacy*, 247–48.

222. On education in letters in Greco-Roman Egypt, see Bagnall, *Egypt in Late Antiquity*, 99–100.

223. Lenski, *Power and Privilege*, 243.

224. Cf. J. G. Gammie, "The Sage in Sirach," in *The Sage*, ed. Gammie and Perdue, 364–68.

225. E.g., 7:29–31; 45:6–22, 23–25; 50:1–21. Ben Sira also uses cultic language to describe the disciple's labor (4:14), as well as Lady Wisdom herself (24:10); H. Stadelmann, *Ben Sira als Schriftgelehrter: eine Untersuchung zum Berufsbild des vor-makkabäischen Söfer unter Berüchsichtigung seines Verhältnisses zu Priester-Propheten-und Weisheitlehrtum*, WUNT, 2nd ser., 6 (Tübingen: J. C. B. Mohr/Paul Siebeck, 1980), 48ff.; Gammie, "The Sage in Sirach," 363, 365–66.

226. J. Blenkinsopp, "The Sage, the Scribe and Scribalism in the Chronicler's Work," in *The Sage*, ed. Gammie and Perdue, 312–14. This would accord with tendencies in the Persian, Ptolemaic, and Seleucid administrations to make use of priestly scribes for such functions, especially for judicial affairs. Lady Wisdom appears in other texts associated with priestly groups. For Qumran, see CD 4.1–4; 1QS 5.7–11, 6.9; 1QSb 3.23, 24. The interest in the calendar reflected in *1 Enoch* suggests priestly concerns: Stone, "The Book of Enoch and Judaism," 490; contra C. Rowland, "The Visions of God in Apocalyptic Literature," *JSJ* 10 (1979): 153. And some of the tannaim were priests; e.g., R. Hanina (*m. Pesah.* 1:6); R. Simeon (*m. Ketub.* 2:8); R. Ishmael b. Piabi (*m. Sota* 9:15). The priesthood had been the class which had traditionally been the guardians and interpreters of the community's legal traditions, a role that continued through the Second Temple period; see Fraade, *From Tradition to Commentary*, 70–71.

227. See Josephus, *War* 1.107–14, 2.162–66; *Ant.* 13.5–6, 372–73, 379–83, 404–15; 18.12–17; Saldarini, *Pharisees, Scribes and Sadducees*, 85–105, 114–20. Some appear to have been members of the governing class; *Ant.* 14.163–84.

228. Fraade, *From Tradition to Commentary*, 98.

229. Urbach, "The Talmudic Sage," 131–32.

230. E.g., R. Hanina (*m. Pesah.* 1:6); R. Simeon (*m. Ketub.* 2:8); R. Ishmael b. Piabi (*m. Sota* 9:15).

231. *'Abot R. Nat. a* 38.

232. *'Abot R. Nat. a* 6. Such traditions suggest that the rabbis actually wanted students from all social strata; Saldarini, *Scholastic Rabbinism*, 136.

233. E. P. Sanders, *Judaism: Practice and Belief, 63 B.C.E.–66 C.E.* (London: SCM, 1992), 146–69.

234. E.g., *t. Yom Tob* 3:8; *Sifre Num.* 48; *b. Yom Tob* 15b; Safrai and Stern, *Jewish People*, 964–65.

235. E.g., *Sifre Deut.* 306. Hammer cites Alon (*Jews*, 413 n. 113) to say that the administrator's role was one of spiritual leadership and did not place the sage as head of community or city: *Sifre: A Tannaitic Commentary on the Book of Deuteronomy*, ed. and trans. R. Hammer, Yale Judaica Series 24 (New Haven: Yale University Press, 1986), 492. The word *parnassah*, however, implies temporal leadership.

236. Safrai and Stern, *Jewish People*, 1:966.

237. Saldarini, *Scholastic Rabbinism*, 82. In a traditional society such as that of the Eastern Mediterranean at this period, it is likely that inherited job and class stability were more usual than change; see R. MacMullen, *Roman Social Relations, 50 B.C. to A.D. 284* (New Haven: Yale University Press, 1974), 98.

238. J. L. Crenshaw, "Education in Ancient Israel," *JBL* 104 (1985): 601–15; A. Lemaire, "Sagesse et écoles," *VT* 34 (1984): 270–81.

239. Some of the synagogue excavations in the Galilee give evidence of the existence of meeting halls which were used for various purposes, among them instruction, e.g., Capernaum, Beth Shearim.

240. There is some literary evidence in Prov. 1:8–9, 9:1–6; Sir. 51:23; 'Abot 1:4. Regarding rabbinic sages it is only in the third century of the common era that we can speak of permanent institutions, outside the sages' homes: Levine, *Rabbinic Class*, 25–26.

241. M. I. Finley, *The Ancient Greeks* (New York: Penguin, 1991), 94; Bagnall, *Egypt in Late Antiquity*, 100, 106.

242. Camp, "Female Sage in Ancient Israel," 190–94.

243. *Cont.* 12, 32–33, 68–69, 83–88. R. S. Kraemer, "Monastic Jewish Women in Greco-Roman Egypt: Philo of Alexandia on the *Therapeutrides*," *Signs* 14 (1989): 349–50. There is external evidence which attests to such a level of education among at least some women in Alexandria and other cities with large Jewish communities; S. B. Pomeroy, *Women in Hellenistic Egypt: From Alexander to Cleopatra* (New York: Schocken, 1984), 59–72.

244. *tBQ* 1:6; *BQ* 4:17; *Sifre Deut.* 307; *b. Ber.* 10a; 'Erub. 53b–54a; *Pesaḥ.* 62b; *AZ* 18a-b; *Lam. Rab.* 3:6; D. Goodblatt, "The Beruriah Traditions," *JJS* 26 (1975): 68–85. As Goodblatt notes, the traditions that give her name as "Beruriah" and describe her as possessing an advanced education are all later, dating from the fourth or fifth century. In the earlier materials she is simply the wife of R. Meir.

245. L. Elder, "The Woman Question and Female Ascetics among Essenes," *BA* 57 (1994): 226–30. E. Schuller argues that women were full members of the Qumran community: "Women and the Dead Sea Scrolls," in *Methods of Investigation of the Dead Sea Scrolls and Khirbet Qumran Site: Present Realities and Future Prospects*, ed. M. O. Wise et al., Annals of the New York Academy of Sciences 722 (New York: New York Academy of Sciences, 1994), 122.

246. E.g., *Jos. Asen.* 14–17; *T. Job* 46–53; *Jub.* 25:14, 35:6; *Bib. Ant.* 30:2, 31:1, 33:1; R. D. Chesnutt, "Revelatory Experience Attributed to Biblical Women in Early Jewish Literature," in *"Women Like This": New Perspectives on Jewish Women in the Greco-Roman World*, ed. A.-J. Levine, SBL Early Judaism and Its Literature 1 (Atlanta: Scholars Press, 1991), 107–25.

247. Horsley, "Spiritual Marriage," 30–54.

248. Regarding such appropriation in other contexts, see E. R. Wolfson, "Woman — The Feminine as Other in Theosophic Kabbalah: Some Philosophical Observations on the Divine Androgyne," in *The Other in Jewish Thought and History*, ed. L. Silberstein and R. Cohn (New York: New York University Press, 1994), and "Female Imaging of the Torah," 271–307. I am very grateful to Professors Wolfson (New York University) and Angela Zito (Barnard College/New York) for sharing with me their insights on the symbolization of the feminine.

249. T. Frymer-Kensky, *In the Wake of the Goddesses: Women, Culture and the Biblical Transformation of Pagan Myth* (New York: Free Press, 1992), 183.

250. Asceticism and relativization of material possessions were common in hellenistic philosophical schools; e.g., Cicero, *Tusc. Disp.* 5.15.45, 31.89–32.92; Epictetus, *Discourses* 2.22; the description of Diogenes in *Diogenes Laertius: Lives of Eminent Philosophers*, trans. R. D. Hicks, LCL (Cambridge: Harvard University Press, 1925; rpt., 1980) (hereafter DL) 6; *Enchiridion* 33.7–8, 11ff.; *Cynic Epistles*, 63, 69, 137, 139; Philostratus, *Life of Apollonius* 1.13.

251. The governing class in agrarian societies is a very small group with rather fluid boundaries, which shares the task of government with the king or emperor; Lenski, *Power and Privilege*, 219–42; S. N. Eisenstadt, *The Political Systems of Empires* (New Brunswick, N.J.: Transaction, 1993), 83–84. Philo's brother, Alexander, was alabarch of Alexandria; Josephus, *Ant.* 18.159–60, 259. Philo himself led a delegation to Gaius in the late 30s to mediate a solution of the conflict between Alexandrian Jews and the emperor; *Ant.* 18.257–60; Philo, *Legat.* His nephew, Tiberius Julius Alexander, served as procurator of Judea (46–48 C.E.), and then governed Egypt under Nero, Titus, and Vespasian. He accompanied Titus during the siege of Jerusalem; Josephus, *War* 2.220, 309, 492–93, 497; 4:606; 5:45, 205, 510; 6.237, 242.

252. *Mos.* 1.153, 60ff.; Holladay, *THEIOS ANER*, 114. Elsewhere, he describes Moses' control of his passions; *Mos.* 1.29, 48.

253. T. E. Schmidt, "Hostility to Wealth in Philo of Alexandria," *JSNT* 19 (1983): 85–97.

254. For the Essenes, see *Prob.* 76 and *Hypoth.* 11.4; for the Therapeutae, see *Cont.* 16–18.

255. Philo's description recalls other comparisons of wisdom and material goods; Prov. 3:13–15; 8:10, 19; Wis. 7:8–9.

256. E.g., *b. Sota* 21a; N. Glatzer, *Hillel the Elder: The Emergence of Classical Judaism* (New York: Schocken, 1970), 40–46.

257. Cf. *b. Ta'an.* 24b–25a; Vermes, *Jesus the Jew*, 77. The idealization of poverty and asceticism accords well not only with Josephus' description of the Pharisees, but the portrait of the sage, particularly the Cynic and Stoic sages, but also the Pythagoreans and Epicureans, in the Greco-Roman world. See Smith, "Palestinian Judaism," 79–81.

258. E.g., *'Abot* 5:10.

259. *'Abot* 1:17; 3:11, 14 [6:4].

260. On tannaitic practice of a common fund, see Safrai and Stern, *Jewish People in the First Century*, 1:963.

261. 1QS 6.13–23; regarding sharing of goods among the Essenes, see Philo, *Hypoth.* 11.3–13; Josephus, *War* 2.122.

262. E.g., CD 6.16, 21; 1QM 14.7; 1QH 5.21–22; 1QSb 5.22; 4Q 171.ii.8–11.

263. E.g., *1 Enoch* 97:6–8, 99:11–15, 100:8, 102:9, 103:9–15; G. W. E. Nickelsburg, "Riches, the Rich, and God's Judgment in 1 Enoch 92–105 and the Gospel According to Luke," *NTS* 25 (1978–79): 327.

264. On the question of perceived deprivation with relationship to early Christianity, see J. G. Gager, *Kingdom and Community: The Social World of Early Christianity* (Englewood Cliffs, N.J.: Prentice-Hall, 1975), 27.

265. Similar vocabulary refers to the leaders of Israel's past. Thus the angel asks that God grant Jacob knowledge (*d't*) and understanding (*bînâh*) in the paraphrase of Gen. 32:25–32 (4Q 158.1–2.8). And David is called wise (*ḥkm*) and literate (*sôpr*) and discerning (*nbôn*, 11QPsa 27.2–3). In the latter case, the wisdom language combines with the attribution of prophecy — we read that David composed his psalms "through prophecy" (*bnbu'h*, 11QPsa 27.11).

266. See K. Wengst, *Humility: Solidarity of the Humiliated: The Transformation of an Attitude and Its Social Relevance in Graeco-Roman, Old Testament-Jewish and Early Christian Tradition*, trans. J. Bowden (Philadelphia: Fortress, 1988), 33–35.

267. The collection represented in *1 Enoch* does not present a community's self-definition in terms of *anawim* language. Rather, wisdom and righteousness are associated (e.g., 14:1, 3; 91:10; 99:10; 104:13). And the scribes behind *1 Enoch* stand in opposition to rival groups of teachers, the "foolish" who give false interpretations of Torah (e.g., 98:9, 13, 14; 99:2): Nickelsburg, "Epistle of Enoch and the Qumran Literature," 333–48. At this point wisdom terminology joins with the critique of material wealth to become part of the boundary language by which the community defines its leaders in distinction to those of the opposition.

268. E.g., *'Abot* 4:4, 10; *'Abot R. Nat. a* 9, 11, 23; *Mek. ba-Hodesh* 9:99–116; *Sifre Deut.* 48; *t. Sota* 13:3–4; *Lev. Rab.* 1.5. I am grateful to Prof. David Weiss Halivni (Religion Department, Columbia University, New York) for his comments on the relationship of the temptation to intellectual pride and the frequency with which one meets exhortations to humility and meekness in rabbinic literature, including tannaitic literature.

269. See also *'Abot* 4:4, 15; *m. Sota* 9:15 (end); *'Abot* 5:19; *'Abot R. Nat. a* 9, 11, 16, 23, 26; *'Abot R. Nat. b* 22, 45; *Mek. ba-Hodesh* 9:99–116; D. Flusser and S. Safrai, "The Essene Doctrine of Hypostasis and Rabbi Meir," *Immanuel* 14 (1982): 48 n. 4.

270. My translation.

271. C. W. Bynum, "Women's Stories, Women's Symbols: A Critique of Victor Turner's Theory of Liminality," in *Anthropology and the Study of Religion*, ed. R. L. Moore and F. E. Reynolds (Chicago: Center for the Scientific Study of Religion, 1984), 118.

272. V. W. Turner, *The Ritual Process: Structure and Anti-Structure* (Chicago: Cornell, 1969), 195.

273. With regard to *actual* power, the Qumran community appears to have had little or none.

274. V. W. Turner, "Metaphors of Anti-Structure in Religious Culture," *Changing Perspectives in the Scientific Study of Religion*, ed. A. W. Eister (New York: John Wiley and Sons, 1974), 65.

275. For a definition of sect in the context of Second Temple and tannaitic Judaism, see S. Cohen, "The Significance of Yavneh: Pharisees, Rabbis, and the End of Jewish Sectarianism," *HUCA* 55 (1984): 29–30; Blenkinsopp, "Interpretation and Sectarian Tendencies," 1.

Chapter 2. Jesus as Wisdom

1. Some scholars believe that the historical Jesus thought of himself as the embodiment of divine wisdom: e.g., M. Hengel, "Jesus als messianischer Lehrer der Weisheit und die Anfänge der Christologie," in *Sagesse et Religion, Colloque de Strasbourg, 1976*, Travaux de Centre d'Études Supérieures spécialisé d'Histoire des Religions de Strasbourg (Paris: Presses Universitaires de France, 1979), 147–90; Schüssler-Fiorenza, *Jesus*, 139–41; Witherington, *Jesus the Sage*, 202–8. Witherington would find analogues and precedence for this in prophets such as Ezekiel and Hosea whose lives embodied the divine message (203).

2. E.g., Wilckens, *Weisheit und Torheit*; H. Conzelmann, *1 Corinthians: A Commentary on the First Epistle to the Corinthians*, trans. J. W. Leitch (Philadelphia: Fortress, 1975), 45–46.

3. J. Kloppenborg, "Wisdom Christology in Q," *LTP* 34 (1978): 129–47. J. Robinson, "Basic Shifts in German Theology," *Int* 16 (1962): 82–85; "Jesus as Sophos and Sophia," in *Aspects of Wisdom in Judaism and Early Christianity*, ed. R. L. Wilken, CSJCA 1 (Notre Dame, Ind.: University of Notre Dame Press, 1975), 1–16; and "Very Goddess and Very Man: Jesus' Better Self," in *Images of the Feminine in Gnosticism*, ed. K. King, Studies in Antiquity and Christianity (Philadelphia: Fortress, 1988), 113–27.

4. Bultmann, "Der religionsgeschichtliche," 1–26; Brown, *Gospel According to John*, cxxii-cxxv; Dodd, *Interpretation of the Fourth Gospel*, 275–82; B. Witherington, *Wisdom's Gospel: A Sapiential Reading of the Beloved Disciple's Testimony* (Louisville, Ky.: Westminster/John Knox, forthcoming).

5. S. Davies, *The Gospel of Thomas and Christian Wisdom* (New York: Seabury, 1983), passim, especially 81–99; Davies qualifies his position in a recent article, "The Christology and Protology of the *Gospel of Thomas*," *JBL* 111 (1992): 663–82; Koester, *Ancient Christian Gospels*, 124.

6. A minority has raised serious questions to the position that Matthew portrays Jesus as Wisdom, e.g., Orton, *Understanding Scribe*, 154. See also Hill, *The Gospel of Matthew*, 207–8; D. Verseput, *The Rejection of the Humble Messianic King* (Frankfurt: Peter Lang, 1986), 139, 145; most lengthily, M. D. Johnson, "Reflections on a Wisdom Approach to Matthew's Christology," *CBQ* 36 (1974): 44–64. The majority view is reflected in the literature cited in chapter 1, nn. 1 and 2.

7. Harrington, *The Gospel of Matthew*, 115–16. Throughout this section Matthew retains the word *pistis* (8:10 ‖ Q 7:9; 9:2 ‖ Mark 2:5; 8:22 ‖ Mark

5:34; 8:29 ‖ Mark 19:52. Regarding Matthew's redaction of miracle stories, see H. J. Held, "Matthew as Interpreter of the Miracle Stories," in G. Bornkamm, G. Barth, and H. J. Held, *Tradition and Interpretation in Matthew*, trans. P. Scott (London: SCM, 1963), 165–299.

8. This is actually part of a longer section, Luke 9:57–62. Cf. J. S. Kloppenborg, *The Formation of Q: Trajectories in Ancient Wisdom Collections*, Studies in Antiquity and Christianity (Philadelphia: Fortress Press, 1987), 191.

9. Hengel, "Jesus als messianischer Lehrer," 165; Gnilka, *Das Matthäusevangelium*, 1:311; R. Hamerton-Kelly, *Pre-existence, Wisdom and the Son of Man: A Study of the Idea of Pre-Existence in the New Testament*, SNTMS 21 (Cambridge: Cambridge University Press, 1973), 29.

10. Lips, *Weisheitliche Traditionen*, 269–70.

11. On Matthew's use of the title "Son of Man," see M. Pamment, "The Son of Man in the First Gospel," *NTS* 29 (1983): 116–29; Luz, *Evangelium nach Matthäus*, 2:497–503. Neither author notes the association of Wisdom and the title, either here or in the rest of the gospel. Davies and Allison state simply, "There is no reason to postulate an original 'I' or 'Wisdom' in place of 'the Son of Man'" (*Commentary on Matthew*, 2:52 n. 156).

12. In another context, Doyle notes that the titles "Wisdom" and "Son of Man" are already linked in Q: *Matthew's Wisdom*, 121.

13. Some would place 13:53–58 with the following unit (13:53–19:1); e.g., Davies and Allison, *Commentary on Matthew*, 2:451; J. P. Meier, *The Vision of Matthew: Christ, Church and Morality in the First Gospel* (New York: Paulist Press, 1979), 94. The phrase *hote etelesen ho Iēsous* usually marks a transition between sections in Matthew (7:28, 11:1, 13:53, 19:1, 16:1). In 7:28, 11:1, and 13:53, the phrase seems to go with the preceding material; in 19:1 and 16:1 it appears to go with what follows. Matt. 13:53–58 with its use of *sophia* and *dynameis* is best understood as belonging with the preceding material. For, while *sophia* might signify the synagogue teaching of 13:53–58, *dynameis* can only be understood in reference to 11:2–6, 19, 20–24; 12:9–14, 15, 22–30.

14. E.g., Verseput, *Rejection of the Humble Messianic King;* J. D. Kingsbury, *Matthew: Structure, Christology, Kingdom* (Philadelphia: Fortress, 1975), 20.

15. The RSV, cited here, conveys better than the NRSV, the correspondence of *erga* here and in v. 19.

16. I leave this expression and its equivalents *basileia* or *basileia tou theou*, so central to Matthew's Gospel, in the more inclusive Greek.

17. On *qal ve-homer*, see M. Mielziner, *Introduction to the Talmud*, 5th ed. (New York: Bloch, 1968), 130–34.

18. Matthew adds this question to the Markan narrative; cf. Mark 3:22–27.

19. Matt. 12:14; Mark 3:6.

20. Later, in the passion narrative, however, he does not have the Pharisees involved in the death of Jesus. On the level of the historical Jesus, moreover, halachic dispute would never have been the cause of execution.

21. The NRSV translates the substantive *synetoi* in 11:25 as "intelligent" and the verb *syniēmi* in chapter 13 as "understand." With regard to 11:25, I am in accord with the RSV.

22. P. Hoffmann, *Studien zur Theologie der Logienquelle*, NTAbh 8 (Münster: Aschendorff, 1972), 229; Suggs, *Wisdom Christology*, 39; Wilckens, *Weisheit und Torheit*, 198.

23. On the relationship of personified Wisdom and eschatology in Q, see C. E. Carlston, "Wisdom and Eschatology in Q," in *Logia: Les paroles de Jésus [The Sayings of Jesus]: Mémorial Joseph Coppens*, ed. Joël Delobel, BETL 59 (Leuven: Uitgeverij Peeters and Leuven University, 1982), 101–19.

24. Deutsch, "Wisdom in Matthew," 34; contra D. Lührmann, *Die Redaktion der Logienquelle*, WMANT 33 (Neukirchen-Vluyn: Neukirchener Verlag, 1969), 28. Lührmann believes the original Q unit to have ended in vv. 12ff. and the Matthean unit to end with v. 15.

25. So Suggs, *Wisdom Christology*, 36–38. Bultmann suggests that the original unit in Q was Matt. 11:7–19 ‖ Luke 7:24–35: R. Bultmann, *History of the Synoptic Tradition*, trans. J. Marsh (New York: Harper and Row, 1963), 164. Subunits may also be detected in the material: Matt. 11:2–6 ‖ Luke 7:18–23; Matt. 11:7–11 ‖ Luke 7:24–28; Matt. 11:16–19 ‖ Luke 7:31–35. Luke 7:29–30 is a redactional insert: T. W. Manson, *The Sayings of Jesus* (London: SCM, 1949), 70; Suggs, *Wisdom Christology*, 36. Similarly, Matt. 11:12–15 represents materials that have been removed from their context in Q (Luke 16:16), redacted by Matthew, and placed in their present setting because of the reference to John the Baptist; cf. Manson, *Sayings of Jesus*, 68, by implication; contra Lührmann, who believes that Matt. 11:12ff. represents the end of the original Q unit; *Redaktion*, 28. Those who believe the saying originally to have been in another context include A. H. McNeile, *The Gospel According to St. Matthew* (1915; rpt., Grand Rapids, Mich.: Baker, 1980), 155; M. J. Lagrange, *L'évangile selon s. Matthieu*, 4th ed. (Paris: J. Gabalda, 1927), 221.

26. Other differences between the Matthean and Lukan versions of the parable and its interpretation, however, are merely stylistic. For example, Matthew has omitted John's title in v. 18 and has condensed "eating no bread and drinking no wine" (*mē esthiōn arton mēte pinōn oinon*) to "neither eating nor drinking" (*mēte esthiōn mēte pinōn*), as per his usual practice of eliminating extraneous materials.

27. Bultmann, *History of the Synoptic Tradition*, 172; Lührmann, *Redaktion*, 29; Hoffmann, *Studien zur Theologie*, 225–31. For a discussion of Wisdom's envoys in Q, see Suggs, *Wisdom Christology*, 38–48; Robinson, "Jesus as Sophos and Sophia," 5.

28. Deutsch, "Wisdom in Matthew," 34; Kloppenborg, *Formation of Q*, 110–12; Lührmann, *Redaktion*, 29; Wilckens, *Weisheit und Torheit*, 198. Kloppenborg believes the parable identifies John and Jesus with the children who do the calling and "this generation" with those who do not respond.

29. On the composition of Luke 7:18–23, see Kloppenborg, *Formation of Q*, 115–17.

30. Contrast Luke 7:18: "The disciples of John told him of all these things" (*peri pantōn toutōn*).

31. Those who consider the Lukan form of the pericope likely to be more original include Manson (*Sayings of Jesus*, 66) and Lührmann (*Redaktion*, 26).

32. Cf. 11:15; 13:14–17, 19, 23, 51; also 11:20–24.

33. Earlier commentators believed *ho erchomenos* itself to be a messianic title; e.g., W. D. Allen, *A Critical and Exegetical Commentary on the Gospel According to St. Matthew*, ICC (New York: Scribner's, 1913), 114; A. Plummer, *An Exegetical Commentary on the Gospel According to S. Matthew* (London: Elliott Stock, 1909), 159; T. Zahn, *Evangelium des Matthäus*, KNT 1 (Leipzig: A. Deichert, 1903), 417; contra Lagrange, *L'évangile selon s. Matthieu*, 219; W. Michaelis, *Evangelium nach Matthäus*, 2 vols. (Zürich: Zwingli, 1949), 1:114. Luz believes it to refer back to 3:11 and to the Son of Man; *Evangelium nach Matthäus*, 2: 167. It is unlikely that the title was messianic in the Sayings Source: Kloppenborg, *Formation of Q*, 108. However, Matthew's redactional introduction ("Now when John heard in prison about the deeds of the Christ . . . ") implies that the redactor infused the expression with messianic significance. This is confirmed by usage in 23:39.

34. Hoffmann, *Studien zur Theologie*, 216–24; Lührmann, *Redaktion*, 27.

35. "At whatever point the quotation from Mal. 3:1 entered the tradition, it is a proof text appended to the description of John as 'more than a prophet'": Suggs, *Wisdom Christology*, 45. It is well to point out, however, that there is in pre-Christian Judaism no reference to an Elijah *redivivus* as the Messiah's precursor. In Mal. 3:1, 23 (4:6) and Sir. 48:1–11, Elijah is the forerunner of God himself and comes before the day of the Lord. See Manson, *Sayings of Jesus*, 69.

36. Hoffmann, *Studien zur Theologie*, 222ff.; Suggs, *Wisdom Christology*, 47–48. Contra Luz, who believes that *mikroteros* refers to the community (*Evangelium nach Matthäus*, 2:176); for a discussion of the possible meanings see 175–76; Doyle, "Matthew's Wisdom," 97ff.

37. Robinson, "Jesus as Sophos and Sophia," 10.

38. J. Schniewind, *Evangelium nach Matthäus*, NTD 2 (Göttingen: Vandenhoeck und Ruprecht, 1960), 146; Wilckens, *Weisheit und Torheit*, 198; Doyle, "Matthew's Wisdom," 129. On the significance of this material in Q, see Christ, *Jesus Sophia*, 65–71.

39. Christ, *Jesus Sophia*, 76; Gnilka, *Matthäusevangelium*, 1:422; Hengel, "Jesus als messianischer Lehrer," 154; Luz, *Evangelium nach Matthäus*, 2:189; Pregeant, "Wisdom Passages," 482; Doyle, "Matthew's Wisdom," 65, 124. Contra Hill, *Gospel of Matthew*, 202; Verseput, *Rejection of the Humble Messianic King*, 116.

40. Plummer, *Commentary on Matthew*, 164, and Suggs, *Wisdom Christology*, 56; Doyle, "Matthew's Wisdom," 42.

41. Gnilka, *Matthäusevangelium*, 1:467.

42. For examples of the use of the woe in prophetic texts, see Amos 5:18–20, 6:1–7; Isa. 5:8–10, 11–14, 18–19, 20, 21, 22–24; 10:1–3; 28:1–4, 15, 30:1–3; 31:1–4; Mic. 2:1–4; Harrington, *Gospel of Matthew*, 326–27.

43. Cf. 9:11.

44. Hengel, "Jesus als messianischer Lehrer," 154.

45. Prov. 1:20–33, 8:5, 9:4–6; Schüssler-Fiorenza, *Jesus*, 140.

46. Ibid.

47. *1 Enoch* 37–71, especially chapters 48–51; Hengel, "Jesus als messianischer Lehrer," 177–80. Q identifies Jesus as Wisdom's final envoy through the title "Son of Man" whereas Matthew has identified Jesus as Son of Man with Jesus as Wisdom: Hamerton-Kelly, *Pre-existence Wisdom*, 46. Davies and Allison are more cautious. They note that whether or not "Matthew saw any link between Jesus as the Son of Man and Jesus as Wisdom is hard to determine" (*Commentary on Matthew*, 2:264 n. 127).

48. Deutsch, *Hidden Wisdom*, 64–65.

49. Davies and Allison, *Commentary on Matthew*, 1:419–20.

50. Doyle believes that "this generation" suggests "the ruling classes and positions, any class or person that exercised influence on the people" ("Matthew's Wisdom," 109). Matthew's use is much more varied, however. He uses the phrase to address the scribes and Pharisees in 23:36. He uses *genea ponēra kai moichalis* in relationship to leadership groups in 12:39, 41, 42, 45. However, he also uses *hē genea autē* in a general sense in 24:34, and *genea apistos kai diestrammenē* in relationship to a petitioner and Jesus' disciples, in addressing the crowds in 17:17. Luz believes it to be a general term referring to the chronological generation of John and Jesus: *Evangelium nach Matthäus*, 2:187.

51. See Luke 7:32. The sitting position denotes the teaching function in 5:1, 23:2. However, the verb there is active, *kathizō;* in the Q logion it is in the middle voice, *kathēmai.* In Matt. 19:28; 20:21, 23; 25:31 *kathizō* implies authority, but elsewhere it is neutral; 13:48, 26:36. Similarly, *kathēmai* sometimes refers to the teaching function (e.g., 13:1, 24:3), or to authority (19:28, 22:44, 23:22, 27:19). Usually it is neutral (9:9; 13:2; 20:30; 26:58, 69; 27:36, 61). Doyle does not appear to be aware of the distinction between the active and middle verb forms, or the broader usage: "Matthew's Wisdom," 114–16.

52. Matthew uses *telōnai* in a polemic against opposing teachers in 5:46. And in 21:31–32 he has Jesus respond to the chief priests and elders, contrasting their attitude with that of the tax collectors and prostitutes who believed in John the Baptist.

53. Doyle notes that in Matthew *sophia* always occurs in a situation of conflict (11:19, 12:42, 13:54): "Matthew's Wisdom," 5.

54. "Understanding" with the RSV.

55. On the question of source and unity, see Deutsch, *Hidden Wisdom*, 47–49. Most scholars believe that 11:25–30 is composed of sayings from two sources, rather than being a unit in Q from which Luke would have omitted vv. 28–30. Moreover, with the presence of two literary forms in vv. 25–26, 27 (thanksgiving prayer and revelation saying), it is likely that this material originally represented two sayings that were brought together in Q or in the *Vorlage* of Q; e.g., Bultmann, *History of the Synoptic Tradition*, 159–60; Lührmann, *Redaktion*, 65. I discuss this more fully in *Hidden Wisdom*, 47–49.

56. Matt. 9:37–38, 10:7–16.

57. Matt. 11:20–24.

58. Matt. 10:40.

59. Matt. 13:16–17.

60. Kloppenborg, *Formation of Q*, 197.

61. Matt. 15:28; 16:17; 20:22; 21:21, 24; 22:1, 29; 24:4. *Apokritheis*...

eipen occurs in Q at Matt. 11:4 ‖ Luke 7:22. The phrase in Matt. 11:25 *may* be of Q provenance; however, the frequency with which it occurs with *ho Iēsous* in Matthean redaction indicates probability for its being redactional in our passage.

62. Justin, Irenaeus, Clement, and Origen all have the aorist *egnon* in the Matthean passage. Justin likewise has it in the Lukan parallel. Patristic citations are often unreliable, particularly when unsupported by other textual evidence. Here, none of the uncials has *egnon* for either Matthew or Luke.

63. There is a textual problem regarding the ordering of the clause since most patristic witnesses and two manuscripts have a reversed form of the saying. ("No one knows the Father except the Son, and no one knows the Son except the Father." Cf. Justin, Irenaeus, Eusebius, Ephraim, N.) Despite the patristic evidence, X, and N, the overwhelming manuscript evidence favors the generally accepted reading. Contra A. Harnack, *Sprüche und Reden Jesu: die zweite Quelle des Matthäus und Lukas*, BENT 2 (Leipzig: Hinrichs, 1907), 204; P. Winter, "Matthew xi:27 and Lk x.22 from the First to the Fifth Century: Reflections on the Development of the Text," *NovT* 1 (1956): 130.

64. Cf. Lukan redactional usage in 5:21, 9:9, 10:29, 20:2. Cf. also Luke 7:49, 19:3; Acts 19:35, 21:22. Cf. N. P. Williams, "Great Texts Reconsidered: Matthew xi 25–27 = Luke x 21–22," *Exp Tim* 51 (1939–40): 182.

65. Robinson, "Jesus as Sophos and Sophia," 9ff.

66. S. Légasse, *Jésus et l'Enfant: "Enfants," "Petits," et "Simples" dans la tradition synoptique*, EBib (Paris: J. Gabalda, 1969), 132.

67. Compare the occurrence of v. 28 in the later *Acts of Thomas*, par. 82, in E. Hennecke, *New Testament Apocrypha*, vol. 2, *Writings Related to the Apostles, Apocalypses, and Other Related Subjects*, ed. W. Schneemelcher, English trans. ed. R. McL. Wilson (Philadelphia: Westminster, 1976).

68. H. Koester, *Introduction to the New Testament*, vol. 2, *History and Literature of Early Christianity*, Hermeneia Foundations and Facets (Philadelphia: Fortress; Berlin: Walter de Gruyter, 1992), 152.

69. Deutsch, *Hidden Wisdom*, 48.

70. For examples of Matthew's preference for adding *pas* to traditional material, see 4:4, 9, 24; 5:11; 7:12, 19; 10:22; 12:23, and so on.

71. In the synoptic tradition, *praus* occurs only in our passage, and in Matt. 5:5 and 21:5. In both the latter cases it is redactional, an indication that it is probably redactional in 11:29 as well.

72. Deutsch, *Hidden Wisdom*, 49.

73. Luz, *Evangelium nach Matthäus*, 2:217–19.

74. Christ, *Jesus Sophia*, 102, 112; Luz, *Evangelium nach Matthäus*, 2:217.

75. Prov. 8:4–11, 32–36; 9:5ff.; Sir. 24:19–22.

76. Elsewhere the references to Wisdom's invitation may actually be modeled on the sage's invitation; Robinson, "Jesus as Sophos and Sophia," 2.

77. Cf. also chap. 24.

78. Wisdom is Torah in Sirach 24. Yoke refers to Torah in *2 Enoch* 34:1–2; *2 Apoc. Bar.* 41:3–5; *'Abot* 3:6; *t. Soṭa* 14:4; *m. Ber.* 2:5; *Mek. Pisha* 5:49; *t. Sanh.* 12:9.

79. Pregeant, "Wisdom Passages," 483; Suggs, *Wisdom Christology*, 106–7.

80. I am grateful to my colleague, Prof. Sara Winter of the New School for Social Research (New York City), for pointing out this distinction.

81. Deutsch, *Hidden Wisdom*, 134.

82. Christ and Hengel have misunderstood the text. Christ would describe Jesus Sophia as embodying a new, pure Law, one without *halachah* ("das neue reine Gesetz: das Gesetz ohne Halacha"): *Jesus Sophia*, 117. Hengel would place learning over against an existential imitation of Jesus' behavior: "Jesus als messianischer Lehrer," 162.

83. See Davies and Allison, *Commentary on Matthew*, 2:275.

84. Surprisingly, some commentators do not recognize the Wisdom motif in these verses; e.g., E. Klostermann, *Das Matthäusevangelium*, 4th ed., HNT 4 (Tübingen: J. C. B. Mohr, 1971), 112, and E. Schweizer, *Das Evangelium nach Matthäus*, NTD 2 (Göttingen: Vandenhoeck und Ruprecht, 1973), 190ff.

85. For a discussion of the relationsip of this material to personified Wisdom in Q see Lips, *Weisheitliche Traditionen*, 273.

86. Following his redactional interest, Matthew adds *tou prophētou*. For similar usages elsewhere, note the fulfillment sayings in 1:22; 2:5, 15, 17, 23; 3:3; 4:14; 8:17; 12:17; 13:35; 21:4; 24:15; 26:56; 27:9.

87. Kloppenborg, *Formation of Q*, 132–34.

88. Note the inexactitude with regard to time; the passion predictions in Mark have "after three days" (*meta treis hēmeras*, Mark 8:31, 9:31, 10:34; cf. Matt. 27:63). The parallels to Mark's passion predictions have "on the third day" (*tē tritē hēmera*, Matt. 16:21, 17:23, 20:19). There is no mention of three nights; McNeile, *Gospel According to Matthew*, 182. The latter observes, "In regarding Jonah as a type, Matthew did not weigh details."

89. Bultmann, *History of the Synoptic Tradition*, 112; Klostermann, *Matthäusevangelium*, 112; Manson, *Sayings of Jesus*, 91; Harrington, *Gospel of Matthew*, 188–89. Lührmann finds it difficult to know which was the original order, that of Matthew of that of Luke: *Redaktion*, 38. It would, however, be difficult to understand why Luke would disturb the more logical order of Matthew if, indeed, the latter was more original.

90. Gnilka, *Matthäusevangelium*, 1:467; Witherington, *Jesus the Sage*, 352.

91. Robinson, "Jesus as Sophos and Sophia," 5.

92. The phrase *apo . . . heōs* indicates this: Lührmann, *Redaktion*, 98.

93. A. D. Jacobson, "The Literary Unity of Q," *JBL* 101 (1982): 384ff.

94. Ibid., 387.

95. Ibid.

96. Hoffmann, *Studien zur Theologie*, 181. O. Glombitza focuses on Solomon as Davidic king as the point of reference in Jesus' messianic identity; cf. "Das Zeichen des Jona (zum Verständnis von Matth. xii. 38–42)," *NTS* 8 (1961–62): 364. But he misses the point, for the text specifies the reference point as Solomon's *wisdom*, not his identity as Davidic king.

97. Compare Mark 3:22–27.

98. Witherington, *Jesus the Sage*, 357.

99. 1K 3:1–14, 16–28; 4:29–34; 10:1–10; 2 Chron. 9:1–9.

100. Sir. 47:14–17; Wis. 6–9; Josephus, *Ant.* 8:45–47; *T. Sol.* Cf D. Duling, "Solomon, Exorcism, and the Son of David," *HTR* 68 (1975): 235–52; "The

Therapeutic Son of David: An Element in Matthew's Christological Apologetic,"
NTS 24 (1978): 392–410.

101. E.g., *Bib. Ant.* 60; Josephus, *Ant.* 8:45–49. 11QPsa 27 says that David
sang songs on behalf of the demon-possessed, likely an allusion to 1 Sam.
18:10, 19:9.

102. Isa. 42:1–4; Doyle, "Matthew's Wisdom," 49.

103. Kloppenborg, *Formation of Q*, 122–25.

104. Wis. 1:7, 7:24, 9:17, 12:1; *1 Enoch* 48:1–4; as well, Sir. 24:3, with its
description of Wisdom as covering the earth like a mist, may allude to the Spirit
(or breath) of God hovering over the waters in Gen. 1:2. See Hengel, "Jesus als
messianischer Lehrer," 166–76; Witherington, *Jesus the Sage*, 361.

105. Hengel, "Jesus als messianischer Lehrer," 151–52.

106. Robinson, "Basic Shifts in German Theology," 84; Robinson, "Jesus as
Sophos and Sophia," 1–4.

107. In the original Q context, "this generation" referred to "impenitent
Israel": Kloppenborg, *Formation of Q*, 238.

108. D. E. Aune, "Magic in Early Christianity," *ANRW* II.16.2 (1978): 1522.

109. We recall from 11:25 that "these things" are not revealed to the "wise
and understanding," so that presumably those who do not understand them are
not wise at all.

110. Oddly, many commentators do not observe the significance of Wisdom
and mighty works at the conclusion of 11:2–13:58; so Klostermann, *Matthäusevangelium*, 125ff.; E. Lohmeyer, *Das Evangelium des Matthäus* (Göttingen:
Vandenhoeck and Ruprecht, 1956), 230ff.; McNeile, *Gospel According to Matthew*, 206; E. Schweizer, *Matthäus und seine Gemeinde* (Stuttgart: KBW, 1974),
205. Klostermann, Lohmeyer, and Schweizer simply note that Matthew is dependent on Mark 6:1–6 for this material. Luz refers "wisdom" to Jesus'
preaching but does not appear to associate it with the presentation of Jesus as
Wisdom: *Evangelium nach Matthäus*, 2:384.

111. Cf. F. van Segbroeck, "Jésus rejeté par sa patrie (Matt. 13:54–58),"
Biblica 49 (1968): 173. According to van Segbroeck, the polemic is between
Matthew's community and the synagogue. For other examples of Matthew's use
of the phrase, see 4:23, 9:35, 10:17, and 12:9.

112. Ibid., 184. Van Segbroeck notes the chiasm, with the outer limits being
marked as *pothen toutō hē sophia hautē kai hai dynameis* (v. 54) and *pothen
oun toutō tauta panta* (v. 56).

113. Van Segbroeck understands 13:53–58 as the beginning of a new section
(13:53–18:35). However, the phrase (*kai egeneto hote etelesen ho Iēsous....*)
acts as a transition from one section to another in Matthew's Gospel (7:28,
11:1, 19:1, 26:1). Thus, we can examine 13:53–58 from the perspective of
11:2–13:52.

114. Luke 10:12–15.

115. *Hypokritai* — vv. 13, 15, 23, 25, 27, 29. In each case, the word is
redactional.

116. Matthean redaction; cf. Mark 11:15–17.

117. On the various meanings of *ethnos/ethnē* see Saldarini, *Matthew's*

Christian-Jewish Community, 78–81. In 21:43, *ethnē* most likely refers to leaders of the Matthean community: Harrington, *Gospel of Matthew*, 304.

118. The RSV "slave" is more appropriate in the socioeconomic context of the Greco-Roman world than is the NRSV "servant."

119. 20:29–34. Matthew follows the Markan order here with respect to context. On Matthew's redaction of this pericope, see Held, "Matthew as Interpreter of Miracle Stories," 219–24.

120. Saldarini, *Matthew's Christian-Jewish Community*, 86–88. On the relationship between faith and miracles in Matthew, see Held, "Matthew as Interpreter of Miracle Stories," 275–84.

121. Cf. Mark 10:49–52.

122. *Blepō* — 24:2,4; *horaō* — 24:6, 15, 30. *Blepō* is taken from Mark (cf. Mark 13:2, 5); *horaō* is Matthean in vv. 6 and 30, and Markan in v. 15.

123. Matt. 24:3, 4, 30. In vv. 3 and 24, *sēmeion* is Markan (cf. Mark 13:4, 22); in v. 30, it is redactional.

124. *Typhlos* is redactional in chap. 23.

125. *Typhlos* is synonymous with *hypokritēs* in chap. 23 — cf. vv. 13, 15, 23, 25, 27, 29.

126. Mark, too, warns against false Messiahs (13:6). Matthew, however, sharpens this by changing the Markan *egō eimi* to *egō eimi ho christos*.

127. Matthean redaction.

128. Mark 13:13 has *pantōn*.

129. In the synoptic tradition *anomia* occurs only in Matthew's Gospel at 7:23, 13:41, 23:28, and 24:12. In 7:23 and 24:12, it is associated with false prophecy; see D. Hill, "False Prophets and Charismatics: Structure and Interpretation in Matthew 7, 15–23," *Biblica* 57 (1976): 336–38. The term belongs with "sinners" and "righteous" as part of the vocabulary of the sectarianism of the period: Overman, *Matthew's Gospel*, 17–18, 98; J. E. Davison, "*Anomia* and the Question of an Antinomian Polemic in Matthew," *JBL* 104 (1985): 617–35.

130. For a discussion of this saying in the Q context, see Robinson, "Basic Shifts in German Theology," 84; Robinson, "Jesus as Sophos and Sophia," 2–3, 11; Suggs, *Wisdom Christology*, 24–29; Steck, *Israel*, 28–33.

131. Regarding reconstruction of the woes in Q, see Kloppenborg, *Formation of Q*, 139–47.

132. The Lukan form of the saying is generally regarded as more faithful in reproducing Q with respect to the reference to "the Wisdom of God" and the use of the third-person plural; cf. E. Haenchen, "Matthäus 23," *ZTK* 48 (1951): 53ff.; Suggs, *Wisdom Christology*, 15ff.; Hoffmann, *Studien zur Theologie*, 164; Robinson, "Jesus as Sophos and Sophia," 11. With respect to the original form regarding the sender of envoys, Haenchen asks, "Why would Luke change the identity of the speaker?": "Matthäus 23," 53.

133. So Robinson, "Jesus as Sophos and Sophia," 11; Schweizer, *Matthäus und seine Gemeinde*, 284; Suggs, *Wisdom Christology*, 59ff.; Wilckens, *Weisheit und Torheit*, 197; Hengel, "Jesus als messianischer Lehrer," 156. Several scholars believe that Matthew here presents *Jesus* rather than Wisdom, as sending envoys; e.g., Haenchen, "Matthäus 23," 53; Gnilka, *Matthäusevangelium*, 2:298; Orton, *Understanding Scribe*, 154. All of these state the fact that here

it is Jesus speaking, not Wisdom. They do not mention the possibility, much less the conclusion, that because Jesus is speaking he has therefore taken the place of Wisdom, and is therefore to be seen as personified Wisdom. Pregeant believes that identification of Jesus with Wisdom is possible but not *necessary* at 23:34–36: "Wisdom Passages," 487.

134. Schweizer, *Matthäus und seine Gemeinde*, 284; Suggs, *Wisdom Christology*, 60; J. Zumstein, *La condition du croyant dans l'évangile selon Matthieu*, OBO 16 (Fribourg: Éditions Universitaires, 1977), 155.

135. Steck, *Israel*, 30; Suggs, *Wisdom Christology*, 14; Robinson, "Jesus as Sophos and Sophia," 11. For Luke's redactional addition of *apostolos*, see 6:13, 17:5, 22:14, and 24:10. Mark has *apostolos* only in 3:14 and 6:30; Matthew only in 10:2.

136. Contra Hoffmann, *Studien zur Theologie*, 164; Steck, *Israel*, 29; Suggs, *Wisdom Christology*, 14. These scholars believe that *sophos* is redactional.

137. Steck, *Israel*, 29.

138. See 8:18–22 and 13:52. Cf. G. Strecker, "The Concept of History in Matthew," *JAAR* 25 (1967): 229.

139. Deutsch, "Wisdom in Matthew," 42; Haenchen, "Matthäus 23," 53; Strecker, "Concept of History," 229. Haenchen and Strecker suggest three separate offices, and I shared that opinion in "Wisdom in Matthew." Further examination of the evidence, however, has led me to doubt whether Matthew means three specific groups with distinct functions; Orton, *Understanding Scribe*, 155. I discuss the question below in chapter 4.

140. Haenchen, "Matthäus 23," 53ff.; Steck, *Israel*, 31; Suggs, *Wisdom Christology*, 14ff.

141. R. E. Brown, *A Commentary on the Passion Narratives in the Four Gospels*, vol. 1, *The Death of the Messiah: From Gethsemane to the Grave*, AB Reference Library (New York: Doubleday, 1994), 371; see also 364–72.

142. Ibid., 2:946–47.

143. Haenchen, "Matthäus 23," 53ff.; D. R. A. Hare, *The Theme of Jewish Persecution of Christians in the Gospel According to St. Matthew*, SNTSMS 6 (Cambridge: Cambridge University Press, 1967), 90.

144. Matthew has *mastigōsai kai staurōsai*. Mark has *mastigōsousin auton kai apoktenousin* (10:34). Luke has *mastigōsantes apoktenousin auton* (18:33).

145. H. van der Kwaak, "Die Klage über Jerusalem (Matth. xxiii 37–39)," *NovT* 8 (1966): 159; Manson, *Sayings of Jesus*, 239; Schweizer, *Matthäus und seine Gemeinde*, 284; Suggs, *Wisdom Christology*, 26. Suggs speaks of "persecution." It is difficult to say what this means. It is possible that "conflict" was interpreted by the community to be "persecution." C. Setzer would not rule out physical punishment, understanding the term *mastigoō* to signify "judicial flogging": *Jewish Responses to Early Christians*, 38–39. Hare understands "crucifixion" here to indicate self-denial, similar to "hating one's life" (Luke 14:26): *Jewish Persecution*, 90. This, however, is to miss the point altogether, for the context indicates, at the very least, harsh conflict.

146. Steck, *Israel*, 39.

147. Cf. Matt. 27:4, 24.

148. Cf. also 10:41 and 13:17 where the two terms are also used in parallel fashion.

149. Cf. 6:10, 19; 16:19; 18:18, 19; 23:9; 28:18.

150. Cf. 1:10 ("Joseph, son of David"); 16:17 ("Simon bar Jona"); 20:20 and 26:37 ("the sons of Zebedee").

151. There is no reference in the Hebrew Scriptures to the murder of Zechariah ben Berachiah. The reference to the murder of Zechariah both in Q and in Matthew is due to the confusion of Zechariah ben Berachiah with Zechariah, the son of Jehoiada the priest, who was slain in the Temple by an angry crowd (2 Chron. 24:17–23). In that incident, Zechariah, son of Jehoiada, is actually described as speaking prophetically: "The Spirit of the Lord took possession of Zechariah, the son of Jehoiada the priest" (*rûaḥ 'ĕlōhîm lābᵉšâh 'et-zᵉkarᵉyâh ben yᵉhôyādā' hakōhēn*); cf. Judg. 6:34; 1 Chron. 12:18 (19). That such confusion is actually the case is confirmed by two rabbinic texts, albeit much later, in which the Zechariah of 2 Chronicles is confused with the prophet Zechariah, son of Berachiah (*Tg. Lam.* 2:20; *Lam. Rab.* Proem 28:5). For a discussion of rabbinic traditions regarding the murder of the prophets, see B. Halpern-Amaru, "The Killing of the Prophets: Unraveling a Midrash," *HUCA* 54 (1983): 153–80.

152. Q has *apolomenou*.

153. Lührmann, *Redaktion*, 47.

154. Abel in Gen. 4:1–16; Zechariah in 2 Chron. 24:20–22; Klostermann, *Matthäusevangelium*, 189.

155. Steck, *Israel*, 291.

156. Matthew retains it from traditional material in 19:18; cf. Mark 10:19 and Luke 18:20. He uses it redactionally in 5:21 and 23:31 as well as in the present verse. Beyond the occurrences in Matthew, one finds *phoneuō* in the Synoptics only in Mark 10:19 and Luke 18:20. Matthew's preference for the word probably reflects its use in Exod. 20:13, 14 (LXX).

157. Cf., however, Q (Matt. 25:12 ‖ Luke 12:37); for Matthean redactional use, see 8:10, 10:15, 10:42, 11:11, and 17:20.

158. Cf. Acts 15:17, where the verb occurs in a quotation of Amos 9:12.

159. For examples of Matthean redactional insertion of *pas*, see 5:11, 15; 6:33; 8:16, 32, 33; 13:19, 34, 56; 19:3, 11, 29.

160. Suggs seems to generalize a tradition about Wisdom's envoys, which, to my knowledge, exists only in the Wisdom of Solomon and Proverbs 8 and 9. He implies that it is common in Jewish Wisdom speculation: *Wisdom Christology*, 20–22.

161. Regarding continuity between history and the generation immediately preceding the end-time, see Hoffmann, *Studien zur Theologie*, 168ff.

162. Steck, *Israel*, 305.

163. So called by Suggs, *Wisdom Christology*, 64.

164. Bultmann, *History of the Synoptic Tradition*, 114ff.; Robinson, "Basic Shifts in German Theology," 84.

165. Suggs, *Wisdom Christology*, 64–66.

166. Hoffmann, *Studien zur Theologie*, 172; Hare implies this in *Jewish Persecution*, 94.

167. For a summary of opinion, see Kloppenborg, *Formation of Q*, 227–28.

168. Deutsch, "Wisdom in Matthew," 44.

169. Haenchen, "Matthäus 23," 56.

170. Suggs, *Wisdom Christology*, 65.

171. Steck, *Israel*, 47.

172. Deutsch, "Wisdom in Matthew," 44; Hoffmann refers to this as a Jesus-saying rather than a Wisdom saying: *Studien zur Theologie*, 172. Also D. Garland, *The Intention of Matthew 23*, NovTSup 52 (Leiden: Brill, 1979), 195–96; Gnilka, *Matthäusevangelium*, 2:306. Contra Bultmann, *History of the Synoptic Tradition*, 115; Suggs, *Wisdom Christology*, 64–66; Kloppenborg, *Formation of Q*, 228–29; by implication, Robinson, "Basic Shifts in German Theology," 84.

173. J. Schmid, *Das Evangelium nach Matthäus* (Regensburg: F. Pustet, 1952), 256.

174. Such stylistic variations include the second aorist infinitive *episynagagein* rather than *episynaksai* (Luke 13:34); *ta nossia* instead of *hē nossia; autēs* instead of *heautēs; gar* instead of *de*, the position of the first-person pronoun and the use of *ap'arti* in Matthew, instead of *heōs hēksei hote* as in Luke.

175. Hengel, "Jesus als messianischer Lehrer," 158. Hengel also cites Prov. 16:16 (LXX).

176. For comparison of God to a bird protecting its young, see Deut. 32:11, where the bird is an eagle *(aetos)*; cf. also Exod. 19:4; Isa. 31:5; Pss. 17 (16):8; 36 (35):7; 57 (56):2; 61 (60):5; 62:8 (LXX only); 91 (90):4; Ruth 2:12.

177. E.g., Christ, *Jesus Sophia*, 145; van der Kwaak, "Klage über Jerusalem," 162; T. Preiss, "Jésus et la Sagesse," *ETR* 28 (1953): 71ff.; Schweizer, *Matthäus und seine Gemeinde*, 290; G. Strecker, *Der Weg der Gerechtigkeit*, FRLANT 82 (Göttingen: Vandenhoeck und Ruprecht, 1962), 113; Suggs, *Wisdom Christology*, 66.

178. Thus one finds the expression "under the wings of their heavenly Father" (*tḥt knpî 'bêhm šbšmîm, Mek. Amalek*, 2:146–47).

179. E. Urbach makes this equation in *The Sages*, 1:47.

180. Ibid., 1:64ff. A. M. Goldberg, in his exhaustive study, does not even refer to Wisdom in relation to the Shekinah: *Untersuchungen über die Vorstellung von der Schekinah in der frühen rabbinischen Literatur*, StJud 5 (Berlin: de Gruyter, 1969). Contra Preiss, "Jesus et la Sagesse," 71ff.; Suggs, *Wisdom Christology*, 66.

181. Christ, *Jesus Sophia*, 124.

182. Mark 13:26–27; Christ, *Jesus Sophia*, 68–69, 146–47.

183. Christ, *Jesus Sophia*, 154–55; Doyle, "Matthew's Wisdom," 485.

184. Use of the aorist and future tenses in Luke 11:49–51 suggests that, for Q, Wisdom is pre-existent; Christ, *Jesus Sophia*, 130. Kloppenborg implies that pre-existence is a matter of standing at the beginning of history: *Formation of Q*, 144.

185. E.g., Preiss, "Jésus et la Sagesse," 71; Suggs, *Wisdom Christology*, 106, 114.

186. One recalls Philo's bisexual imagery for Wisdom (e.g., *Congr.* 9; *Fug.* 52). He consciously distinguishes between gender and function in *Fug.* 52.

187. On the shift of the center of Matthew's symbol system, see Saldarini, "Delegitimation," 668.

188. Collins, however, does argue for such influence, recognizable in Matt. 19:28 and 25:31: "Son of Man in First-Century Judaism," 452.

189. I am grateful to Dr. Holland Hendrix for drawing my attention to the potential significance of the Greco-Roman cults of virtues for the study of the metaphor of Woman Wisdom in Second Temple and tannaitic literature and the New Testament. And I am indebted to Prof. Dirk Obbink for his help with this material. See Fears, "Cult of Virtues and Roman Imperial Ideology," 830ff.; Fears' remarks concern Roman religion, but I believe that they apply to Greek religion as well. On the personification and deification of virtues, sometimes referred to as "abstract ideas," see L. Deubner, "Personifikation abstrakter Begriffe," in *Ausführliches Lexikon der griechischen und römischen Mythologie* III, 2 (Leipzig: B. G. Teubner, 1897–1907), 2127–45; L. R. Lind, "Roman Religion and Ethical Thought: Abstraction and Personification," *CJ* 69 (1972): 108–19; K. Reinhardt, "Personifikation und Allegorie," in *Vermächtnis der Antike: Gesammelte Essays zum Philosophie und Geschichtschreibung*, ed. C. Becker (Göttingen: Vandenhoeck und Ruprecht, 1966), 7–40; T. B. L. Webster, "Personification as a Mode of Greek Thought," *Journal of the Warburg and Courtauld Institutes* 17 (1954): 10–21. Christ refers to the possibility of influence of Isis language in the association of Jesus with Wisdom, and the use of "Sophia" as a christological title: *Jesus Sophia*, 154.

190. Cicero, *De natura deorum*, 2.61.

191. Ibid., 3.88.

192. Fears, "Cult of Virtues and Roman Imperial Ideology," 849, 868–69.

193. Robinson thus understands Q's Wisdom christology: "Very Goddess and Very Man," 115–23.

194. Suggs believes this kind of polemic to be present; *Wisdom Christology*, 60. Contra Doyle, *Matthew's Wisdom*, 128.

195. See chapter 1 above.

Chapter 3. Jesus-Wisdom the Teacher

1. Doyle, "Matthew's Wisdom," 436–38.

2. Luke 9:57. We will discuss the nature of the vocative in chapter 4, when we look at the nature of the disciple as sage.

3. Cf. Mark 2:16.

4. Luke 6:40.

5. Cf. Mark 8:11–12.

6. Matt. 22:24 (Mark 12:19); 22:36 (Mtn red; cf. Mark 12:28). Elsewhere, see 17:24 (M); 19:16 (Mark 10:17); 26:18 (Mark 14:14).

7. Mark 1:21–22. Besides the summary in 9:35–38, Matthew also has a similar statement in 4:23, which he may have taken from Mark 2:39.

8. With RSV instead of NRSV.

9. Matthew derives the verb from his sources in 5:19, 9:35, 13:54, 15:9, 22:16, 26:55, and 18:15. He uses it redactionally in 4:23, 5:2, 11:1, 21:23,

and 28:28. "The fact that Matthew uses the verb less frequently than Mark is a healthy warning not to build a theology of a gospel merely on word statistics": Meier, *Law and History*, 95.

10. See also 4:23 ‖ Mark 1:39.

11. The use of the fulfillment text reflects, of course, Matthew's redactional practice of using such texts throughout his gospel. However, in this context, it also reflects an apologetic attempt to demonstrate that Jesus' miracles "were not due to chance or magic, but were predicted by the Old Testament prophets," as Aune observes more generally of early Christian writings: Aune, "Magic in Early Christianity," 1542.

12. E.g., 1QS 4:19–21; 1QM 14:10; 1QH 3:18; Aune, "Magic in Early Christianity," 1533. Josephus speaks of the Essenes as healers (*War* 2.136).

13. See chapter 1 above. E.g., Honi (*m. Ta'an.* 3:8; *t. Ta'an.* 2:13; *b. Ta'an.* 23a; Josephus *Ant.* 14.22–25.

14. The texts appear to expand on 1K 4:29–34 (5:9–14, MT); *T. Sol.*; *Bib. Ant.* 60:3; Josephus, *Ant.* 8.141–49, etc. See Duling in *Old Testament Pseudepigrapha*, ed. Charlesworth, 1:944–51.

15. Cf. Mark 2:14.

16. Mark 2:15–17. Mark calls the challengers "the scribes of the Pharisees" (v. 16).

17. Mark 2:18–22.

18. See Mark 3:22–27; Luke 11:14–23.

19. See Aune, "Magic in Early Christianity," 1523.

20. *Pothen touto tauta; kai tis he sophia he dotheisa toutō kai hai dynameis toiautai dia tōn cheirōn autou ginomenai.*

21. Matt. 13:1–9 ‖ Mark 4:1–9; Matt. 13:10–17 ‖ Mark 4:13–20; Matt. 13:31–32 ‖ Mark 14:30–32. Matthew does not have Mark 4:26–29, the parable of the "seed growing secretly." He has included the material in Mark 4:21–25 in Matt. 5:15, 7:2, 10:26, and 13:12.

22. Cf. Mark 3:1–6.

23. Mark 3:22–27 has only the accusation of possession. Luke 11:14–23 has the account of the miracle, although here the sufferer is simply dumb, as well as the longer version of the accusation and Jesus' response found also in the Markan version. The Markan and Lukan versions probably follow Q.

24. Cf. Mark 6:3.

25. In 16:14, the word is traditional (Mark 8:28); in 21:11 and 46 it is redactional.

26. Matthew takes the verb from Mark in 3:1; 4:17, 23; 9:35; see Mark 1:4, 14–15, 39; 6:6. He takes the verb from Q in 10:7, 27; see Luke 9:2 and 12:3. He uses it redactionally in 9:35 and 11:1. In 10:7, 24:14, and 26:13 it implies the activity of the disciples.

27. Cf. Mark 1:4.

28. E.g., Gen. 41:43; Exod. 32:5, 36:6; 2K 10:20; 2 Chron. 20:3, 24:9, 36:22; Dan. 3:4 (LXX and TH); 5:29 (TH).

29. Jonah 1:2; 3:4, 5, 7; Micah 3:5; Zech. 9:9; Isa. 61:1.

30. See M. Hengel, *The Charismatic Leader and His Followers*, trans. J. Greig (New York: Crossroad, 1981), 16–18. Hengel says that, ultimately,

the one who calls Elishah is God, whereas in the synoptic account, "the call is empowered by Jesus' own *messianic authority*" (17). The text does not refer to messianic authority. Rather, if — as we believe — the text is indeed about Jesus-Wisdom, he calls by virtue of his authority as Wisdom and Son of Man.

31. Cleansing the leper, see 2K 5:1–14; raising the dead, see 1K 17:17–24; 2K 4:18–37.

32. Harrington, *Gospel of Matthew*, 326–27; Saldarini, "Delegitimation," 672 n. 37.

33. See Luke 10:12–15.

34. Kloppenborg, *Formation of Q*, 229.

35. Contrast Luke 13:34–35.

36. In Q, the sign of Jonah is the prophet's preaching, which resulted in Nineveh's repentance (Luke 11:29–30, 32).

37. Jacobson, "Q," 382.

38. The translation is my own.

39. In both traditional and redactional material, Matthew is ambivalent in his use of the title "prophet" for Jesus. In this passage, he implies that Jesus is a prophet. This may also be the case in 5:12 (Luke 6:23) and 23:29–31 (Luke 11:47) as well as 23:37–39 (Luke 13:34–35) if it is in fact true that Jesus is one of the persecuted prophets. Matt. 16:14–16 (Mark 8:28) discounts prophetic identity in favor of Jesus' designation as "the Christ, the Son of the living God." Hence Matthew has enhanced Mark's "the Christ of God." Cf. Mark 8:29.

40. Deutsch, *Hidden Wisdom*, 448.

41. For Jesus: *mikroteros* — Matt. 11:11; Luke 7:28. *Praus* — Matt. 11:29, 21:5; *tapeinos* — Matt. 11:29. *Tapeinōsis* — Acts 8:33; *tapeinoō* — Phil. 2:8. For the community: *mikros* — Matt. 18:6, 10, 14. *Praus* — Matt. 5:5; 1 Pet. 3:4. *Tapeinōsis* — James 4:6; 1 Pet. 5:5 (both cite Prov. 3:34). *Tapeinoō* — Matt. 18:4; Luke 14:11, 18:14. For leaders: *Mikros* — Matt. 10:42. *Tapeinos* — Matt. 23:12. In Paul: *Tapeinos* — 2 Cor. 10:1. *Tapeinoō* — Phil. 4:12.

42. E.g., Mark 9:42 ‖ Matt. 18:6; Luke 7:28 ‖ Matt. 11:11. See also Luke 14:11 and 18:14 (special L). See also James 4:10 and 1 Pet. 5:6. Like Matt. 13:9, Matt. 23:12 seems to have been a floating saying (cf. Rev. 2:7, 3:13).

43. See, for instance, 5:5 regarding the community; 10:42; 18:4, 10, 14.

44. On this passage, see N. Lohfink, "Der Messiaskönig und seine Armen hommen zum Zion: Beo-bachtungen zu Mt 21,1–17," in *Studien zum Mattäusevangelium: Festschrift für Wilhelm Pesch*, ed. Ludger Schenke (Stuttgart: Katholisches Bibelwerk, 1988), 177–200.

45. Christ, *Jesus Sophia*, 115–16.

46. Held, "Matthew as Interpreter," 125–28.

47. Deutsch, *Hidden Wisdom*, 107.

48. Doyle, "Matthew's Wisdom," 261.

49. Davies and Allison, *Commentary on Matthew*, 2:290.

50. Luz, *Evangelium nach Matthäus*, 2:219.

51. H. D. Betz, "The Logion of the Easy Yoke and of Rest (Mt. 11:28–30)," *JBL* 86 (1967): 23–24.

52. E. P. Sanders, *Jesus and Judaism* (Philadelphia: Fortress, 1985), 177–79.

53. E.g., ibid., 174–211; N. Perrin, *Rediscovering the Teaching of Jesus* (New York: Harper and Row, 1976), 102–6.

54. On the relationship of 11:19 and 9:11, see Gnilka, *Matthäusevangelium*, 1:424.

55. Matthew inserts *ho didaskolos hymōn* into the source (Mark 2:16).

56. Matthew, as does Q, alludes to Isa. 29:18–19, 35:5–6, 61:1; Luz, *Das Evangelium nach Matthäus*, 2:169.

57. See Levine, *Social and Ethnic Dimension*, 255.

58. R. Scroggs, "Eschatological Existence in Matthew and Paul: *Coincidentia Oppositorum*," in *The Text and the Times: New Testament Essays for Today*, ed. Scroggs (Minneapolis: Fortress, 1993), 247. As Luz notes, the transmission usually implied by the use of the verb is human, from one generation to another, rather than heavenly revelation. Matthew's usage — and that of the Sayings Source — is metaphorical ("metaphorisch"); *Evangelium nach Matthäus*, 2:211 n. 99.

59. Bickerman, "La chaîne de la tradition pharisienne," 44–54. See the evidence gathered in my *Hidden Wisdom*, 92–94.

60. Gnilka, *Matthäusevangelium*, 1:440.

61. Ibid., 1:439. While the image of the yoke does not occur in the context of a sage's invitation in Second Temple and tannaitic literature, the image of the yoke is related to a teacher's instruction in some texts, e.g., *2 Enoch* 48:9; 1QH 6:19; Sir. 51:26.

62. See Davies and Allison, *Commentary on Matthew*, 2:279 n. 200.

63. Cf. Lev. 24:9.

64. W. D. Davies, *Setting of the Sermon on the Mount* (Cambridge: Cambridge University Press, 1966), 103–4, 456–57. A *qal ve-homer* argument proceeds *a fortiori*. Levine argues that v. 5 refers not to Num. 28:9–10 but to "the widely contested and rigorously defended Pharisaic practice of reaping the first sheaves (i.e., omer) offering" and states that Jesus opposes it (*Social and Ethnical Dimension*, 481). She does not establish her position.

65. Davies, *Sermon on the Mount*, 103; contra D. M. Cohn-Sherbok, "An Analysis of Jesus' Arguments Concerning the Plucking of Grain on the Sabbath," *JSNT* 2 (1979): 31–41.

66. Davies, *Sermon on the Mount*, 104. The reference is to the practice reflected in *m. Yoma* 8:6; *Šabb.* 18:3.

67. Overman, *Matthew's Gospel*, 23–30.

68. Cf. Luke 11:42 for the Q saying on tithes, and Luke 11:39–41 for the Q saying on ritual purity.

69. Saldarini, "Delegitimation," 674–75; contra Haenchen, "Matthäus 23," 48. Haenchen thinks that 23:16–22 indicates that Matthew believes that *all* oaths are to be kept.

70. On the significance of oaths, tithes, and ritual purity in first-century Jewish life, see Saldarini, "Delegitimation," 674–76; J. Neusner, " 'First Cleanse the Inside': The 'Halakhic' Background of a Controversy-Saying," *NTS* 22 (1976): 486–95; E. P. Sanders, *Jewish Law from Jesus to the Mishnah: Five Studies* (Philadelphia: Trinity Press International, 1990), 29–42, 43–57; Sanders, *Judaism*, 146–69.

71. Overman, *Matthew's Gospel*, 118; Gnilka, *Matthäusevangelium*, 2:285. *Hypokritai* occurs in 23:13, 15, 23, 25, 27, 29, and *hypokrisis* in 23:28.

72. Saldarini, "Delegitimation," 677.

73. Ibid., 678.

74. Haenchen, "Matthäus 23," 39ff.; I. Renov, "The Seat of Moses," *IEJ* 5 (1955): 262–67. There is no necessity to see the recognition of scribes' and Pharisees' authority as being in contradiction with the rest of the chapter; as S. H. Brooks, *Matthew's Community: The Evidence of His Special Sayings Material*, JSNTSS 16 (Sheffield, England: JSOT Press, 1987), 117. As Saldarini points out, Matthew is simply acknowledging rival leaders' power in his geographical area: "Delegitimation," 670.

75. See Saldarini, "Delegitimation," 659–80; contra Garland, *Intention of Matthew 23*, 214–15; P. S. Minear, "False Prophecy and Hypocrisy in the Gospel of Matthew," in *Neues Testament und Kirche: für Rudolf Schnackenburg*, ed. J. Gnilka (Freiburg: Herder, 1974), 87.

76. This is a Matthean redactional insertion; cf. Mark 11:1–11.

77. Cf. Jacobson, "Literary Unity of Q," 387.

78. Ibid.

79. For a more complete discussion, see Saldarini, *Matthew's Christian-Jewish Community*, 124–64.

80. Davies, *Sermon on the Mount*, 291–92; Gnilka, *Matthäusevangelium*, 1:115; Saldarini, "Delegitimation," 660, 679.

81. W. Trilling, *Das Wahre Israel: Studien zur Theologie des Matthäus-Evangeliums*, 3rd ed., SANT 10 (Munich: Kösel, 1964), 186. Trilling considers specifically v. 20 as the heading for the antitheses. See also Gnilka, *Matthäusevangelium*, 1:141; Luz, *Evangelium nach Matthäus*, 1:228–44.

82. The redactional character of the formula *me nomisēte hoti ēlthon... ouk ēlthon... alla* is particular to Matthew, occurring elsewhere only in 10:34. The less-developed form in Luke 12:51 is more likely to be original; cf. Zumstein, *La condition du croyant*, 108; and R. G. Hamerton-Kelly, "Attitudes to the Law in Matthew's Gospel: A Discussion of Matthew 5:18," *BR* 17 (1972): 23. Meier states only that the form in Matt. 5:17 is probably redactional: *Law and History*, 68. Contra G. Strecker, *Die Bergpredigt: ein exegetischer Kommentar* (Göttingen: Vandenhoeck and Ruprecht, 1984), 56.

83. See G. Barth, "Matthew's Understanding of the Law," in Bornkamm et al., *Tradition and Interpretation in Matthew*, 67; contra Trilling, *Das Wahre Israel*, 172. Trilling holds that *elthon* indicates an "I-saying" about Jesus' messianic consciousness rather than a saying about Law and Prophets; thus, it is not addressed to a concrete church situation. Hengel believes that v. 17 reflects a reproach directed from outside the Matthean community: "Zur matthäische Bergpredigt und ihrem jüdische Hintergrund," *TRu* 52 (1987): 373.

84. One may find the variety of interpretations of the word discussed in Meier, *Law and History*, 65–89; Luz, *Evangelium nach Matthäus*, 2:232–36; Davies and Allison, *Commentary on Matthew*, 1:485–86.

85. Overman, *Matthew's Gospel*, 88.

86. Matt. 7:12; 11:13; 22:40; also Sirach, Prologue, vs. 1 (LXX); see Harrington, *Gospel of Matthew*, 81.

87. Meier, *Law and Prophecy*, 80; Davies and Allison, *Commentary on Matthew*, 1:486; Saldarini, *Matthew's Christian-Jewish Community*, 161.

88. Only Matthew uses *gar* after *amēn* (10:23, 17:20); see Meier, *Law and History*, 58; Trilling, *Das Wahre Israel*, 169ff. *Heōs an panta genētai* is most likely influenced by Matt. 24:36 (Mark 13:30). On the redactional nature of this clause, see E. Käsemann, "The Beginning of Christian Theology," in *New Testament Questions of Today*, trans. W. J. Montague (Philadelphia: Fortress, 1969), 85; Strecker, *Der Weg der Gerechtigkeit*, 143; Trilling, *Das Wahre Israel*, 169.

89. Luz reflects the difficulty of interpreting this clause; *Matthew 1–7*, 266.

90. See Strecker, *Der Weg der Gerechtigkeit*, 144.

91. E.g., Matt. 24:34; Meier, *Law and History*, 53; Trilling, *Das Wahre Israel*, 169.

92. Cf. Mark 13:30. Luke makes the same substitution in 21:32.

93. Meier, *Law and History*, 30–35.

94. Contra Hamerton-Kelly, "Attitudes to the Law," 30; Meier, *Law and History*, 65.

95. Matt. 28:20; also 13:39, 40, 49.

96. The saying in v. 19 was found in a pre-Matthean tradition, perhaps Q; Bultmann, *History of the Synoptic Tradition*, 138; H. Schürmann, "Wer daher eines dieser geringsten Gebote auflöst... Wo fand Matthäus das Logion Mt 5:19?" *BZ* 4 (1960): 246. *Didaskō* and *houtos* may indicate Matthean redactional traces: R. Banks, "Matthew's Understanding of the Law: Authenticity and Interpretation in Matthew 5:17–20," *JBL* 93 (1974): 240. Strecker believes the saying to have come from M: *Die Bergpredigt*, 59. The saying reflects a discussion between two groups of Jewish-Christians, one with a stricter, the other with a freer view with regard to Torah observance: Schürmann, "Wer daher," 249; Strecker, *Der Weg der Gerechtigkeit*, 145; Zumstein, *La condition du croyant*, 114ff. Far from indicating a provisional validity of Torah, the verse, as well as 5:17, gives evidence that for Matthew "le Christ est le garant eschatologique de la pratique de la Loi dans l'Eglise. Toute critique de la Tora, toute abrogation... entrainera un 'declassement dans le Royaume' ": Zumstein, *La condition du croyant*, 125.

97. Cf. 'Abot 2:1, 4:2; 'Abot R. Nat. a 2; see Luz, *Matthew*, 267.

98. As Lohmeyer, *Evangelium des Matthäus*, 111.

99. Gnilka, *Matthäusevangelium*, 1:141–42; Luz, *Evangelium nach Matthäus*, 1:238. Meier considers the implication that a person who failed to observe a small command might yet be admitted to the Kingdom as foreign to Jewish thought: *Law and History*, 90. Schweizer points out that v. 19 should simply as a parallel to v. 18, not as approving breaking commandments: *Matthäus und seine Gemeinde*, 62; Trilling, *Das Wahre Israel*, 180.

100. Luz, *Evangelium nach Matthäus*, 1:238.

101. Contra Lohmeyer, *Evangelium des Matthäus*, 110.

102. Its redactional quality is indicated by the typically Matthean vocabulary: *legō gar hymin, dikaiosynē, grammateis kai pharisaioi, basileia tōn ouranōn*; see Zumstein, *La condition du croyant*, 109; Gnilka, *Matthäusevangelium*, 1:142; Luz, *Evangelium nach Matthäus*, 1:240–41; Strecker, *Die Bergpredigt*, 59.

103. Trilling, *Das Wahre Israel*, 184; Hengel, "Mattäische Bergpredigt," 359.

104. G. Bornkamm, "End-Expectation and Church in Matthew," in Bornkamm et al., *Tradition and Interpretation in Matthew*, 24–32; Davies and Allison, *Commentary on Matthew*, 1:508.

105. Barth, "Matthew's Understanding of the Law," 75–76. Commenting on v. 20, Strecker notes that the scribes and Pharisees act as anti-types in Matthew's Gospel. The evangelist is not representing them in a manner we may regard as historically true: *Die Bergpredigt*, 62. What I interpret as Strecker's attempt to avoid anti-Jewish stereotyping is well worth noting. However, his effort leaves the reader with the question, "Why does Matthew use the *scribes and Pharisees* as anti-types?" That question can only be answered by a sociohistorical analysis.

106. Cf. Luke 16:18 regarding divorce; 6:29–30 on talion; and 6:27–28, 32–36 on love of enemies.

107. On source and redaction, see Meier, *Law and History*, 126–28. Meier notes that the material in the antitheses on talion and love of enemies may have already stood together in Q.

108. Ibid., 127.

109. Regarding murder, see Exod. 20:13, 21:12; Lev. 24:17; Num. 35:16ff.; Deut. 5:17. Regarding adultery, see Exod. 20:14; Deut. 5:18. Regarding divorce, see Deut. 24:1–4. Regarding oaths, see Exod. 20:7; Lev. 19:12; Deut. 23:22–24.

110. Bornkamm, "End-Expectation," 25; Meier, *Law and History*, 140–61. For a thorough survey of the literature on the antitheses, see the citations in *Law and History*, 135–61; Strecker, *Die Bergpredigt*, 98.

111. E. Lohse, "Ich aber sage euch," in *Der Ruf Jesu und die Antwort der Germeinde; exegetische Untersuchungen Joachim Jeremias* (Göttingen: Vandenhoeck und Ruprecht, 1979), 189.

112. As does Bornkamm, "End-Expectation," 25.

113. Suggs, *Wisdom Christology*, 114; emphasis in Suggs.

114. Meier, *Law and History*, 161.

115. D. Daube, *The New Testament and Rabbinic Judaism* (London: Athlone, 1956), 55–66.

116. M. Smith, *Tannaitic Parallels to the Gospels*, SBLMS 6 (Philadelphia: SBL, 1968), 27–30.

117. As far as I know, only W. D. Davies and D. Hill have accepted Daube's interpretation of the expression as "to understand literally"; see Davies, *Sermon on the Mount*, 101–2; Hill, *Gospel of Matthew*, 120. Others interpret it as "understand" or "misunderstand"; e.g., Lohse, "Ich aber sage euch," 191 and 193; Luz, *Evangelium nach Matthäus*, 1:247.

118. Daube, *New Testament and Rabbinic Judaism*, 56. Daube claims to have isolated a form in which *šmʿ* and *ʾmr* occur together, although it is an I-you form (57). The example he gives is an interpretation attributed to Yehuda ha-Nasi in *Mek.* on Exod. 19:20. I was unable to locate that text in the passage indicated.

119. Smith, *Tannaitic Parallels*, 27–30.

120. E.g., *m. Soṭa* 9:9, which revokes the ruling on the heifer slain in the case of murder (Deut. 21:1–9); the ruling about the bitter water in the case of adultery (Num. 5:11ff.); *m. Soṭa* 9:10, which revokes a tithe law (Deut. 26:12–15); and the prozbul of Hillel, which suspends Deut. 15:2 on the cancellation of loans in the seventh year (*m. Šeb.* 10:3–6).

121. Contra Meier, *Law and History*, 152. Meier appears to misunderstand the significance of this because of lack of awareness of such "revocation" in contemporary Jewish literature. In that context it is not a matter of "revocation" but of proper interpretation.

122. Contra Gnilka, *Matthäusevangelium*, 1:151.

123. Matt. 5:27 ‖ Exod. 20:14; Matt. 5:38 ‖ Exod. 21:24.

124. Matt. 5:21a refers to Exod. 20:13. See also Exod. 21:12 and Lev. 24:17, which speak of punishment consequent upon murder. Matt. 5:31 refers to Deut. 24:1–4 but takes the latter passage out of context (Deut. 24:1–4 refers to the condition under which a man gives his wife a writ of divorce and consequences of the divorce). Matt. 5:33 refers to Exod. 20:7. Verse 33a resembles more closely Lev. 19:12, while v. 33b resembles Deut. 23:22. The latter text, however, refers to a vow (*neder*) not an oath (*šᵉbûʿâ*).

125. N. J. McEleney, "The Principles of the Sermon on the Mount," *CBQ* 41 (1979): 559.

126. E.g., Zumstein, *La condition du croyant*, 119–20; also Hengel, "Matthäische Bergpredigt," 377, 390–95.

127. On the legitimating function of the antitheses, see Strecker, *Die Bergpredigt*, 65.

128. "Hypocrite" is a favorite Matthean designation. He uses it in M material in 6:2, 5, 16, and takes it from Q in 7:5 (Luke 6:42) and Mark in 15:7 (Mark 7:6). He uses it redactionally in 22:18; 23:13, 15, 23, 25, 27, 19. Beyond the context of the Sermon on the Mount it always refers to the Pharisees, with the scribes (15:7; 23:13, 15, 23, 25, 27, 29), or with the Herodians (22:18). It is therefore likely that the word in 6:2, 5, 16 also refers to the Pharisees or the "scribes and Pharisees." In 7:5 it may refer to those groups who would judge negatively the halachic practice of members of the Matthean community, or it may imply that those who judge fellow community members become like the "scribes and Pharisees." Minear believes that "hypocrite" in the Sermon on the Mount refers to officials in the Matthean community: "False Prophecy and Hypocrisy in the Gospel of Matthew," 87.

129. Matthew has indeed heightened the polemical note present in his Markan source (Mark 1:22) by adding the possessive pronoun.

130. Smith, *Tannaitic Parallels*, 29–30. Suggs has not given this text sufficient evaluation: *Wisdom Christology*, 112.

131. Matt. 7:29; 8:9; 9:6; 21:23, 24, 27. He uses it redactionally only in 9:8 and 28:18.

132. Davies, *Sermon on the Mount*, 85; T. L. Donaldson, *Jesus on the Mountain: A Study in Matthean Theology*, JSNTSS 8 (Sheffield, England: JSOT Press, 1985), 105–21; R. H. Gundry, *Matthew: A Commentary on His Literary and Theological Art* (Grand Rapids, Mich.: Eerdmans, 1982), 66, 78; Hengel, "Matthäische Bergpredigt," 347.

133. R. E. Brown, *The Birth of the Messiah: A Commentary on the Infancy Narratives in the Gospels of Matthew and Luke*, 2nd ed., AB Reference Library (New York: Doubleday, 1993), 112–16.

134. There Matthew adds "a very high mountain" (*oros hypsēlon lian*) to Q (Luke 4:5); on the allusion to the Moses story, see Donaldson, *Jesus on the*

Mountain, 92–94; R. E. Morosco, "Matthew's Formation of a Commissioning Type-Scene," *JBL* 103 (1984): 554. Here and elsewhere, Donaldson's analysis on the allusions to Moses is carefully nuanced and notes the presence — even dominance — of other motifs.

135. "And when Jesus finished these sayings" (*kai egeneto hote etelesen ho Iēsous tous logous toutous*); see Num. 16:31; Deut. 31:1 (LXX), 24; 32:45; Davies and Allison, *Commentary on Matthew*, 1:725; Harrington, *Gospel of Matthew*, 109. Neither commentary would speak of a direct comparison to Moses. Luz speaks of the need for caution on the matter: *Evangelium nach Matthäus*, 2:415–16.

136. Meier, *Law and History*, 35–37.

137. With the RSV.

138. In the Sayings Source (Q), the hymn form is found only in vv. 25–26. J. M. Robinson, "Die Hodajot-Formel in Gebet und Hymnus des Frühchristentums," in *Apophoreta: Festschrift für Ernst Haenchen*, ed. W. Eltester and F. H. Kettler, BZNW 30 (Berlin: A. Töpelmann, 1964), 194–235. I do not agree with Robinson, however, that Matt. 11:25–30 represents a polemic against the "official" *berachah*.

139. E.g., Wis. 2:13, 16, 18; 1QH 9.30–31, 11.35–36; Deutsch, *Hidden Wisdom*, 105–6.

140. On the content of Jesus' revelation in 11:25–27, in relationship to the literary context of the passage, see Christ, *Jesus Sophia*, 92–96. Doyle notes that while there is "no single obviously correct interpretation" of the significance of *tauta*, there is "considerable agreement with the general notion... of the divine design, especially as revealed in Jesus": "Matthew's Wisdom," 169.

141. Mark has his own motif of opposition as a context for the apocalyptic discourse: the parable of the tenants (12:1–12), the controversies (12:13–17, 18–27, 28–34, 35–37), the warning about the scribes (12:38–40), and the narrative of the widow's coin (12:41–44).

142. L. Sabourin notes the apocalyptic features of this text: "Traits apocalyptiques dans l'évangile de Matthieu," *Science et Esprit* 33 (1981): 364.

143. While Luz acknowledges Matthew's use of Daniel 7 in 24:30 and 26:64, and possibly 28:18–19, he generally minimizes apocalyptic influence on Matthew's use of "Son of Man": *Evangelium nach Matthäus*, 2:499–502.

144. E.g., 4 Ezra 10:57; *Jos. Asen.* 16:14; *T. Levi* 4:4, 6; *Mek. R. Simeon* I.ii.2; *t. Ḥag* 2:1–2; *j. Ḥag* 2.1; *b. Ḥag.* 14b; *Mek. R. Simeon.* Eleazar's mother and Abraham are declared "happy" on account of Eleazar; in *t. Ḥag, y. Ḥag, b. Ḥag* Abraham is called "happy" ('*šr*). See Gnilka, *Matthäusevangelium*, 2:57.

145. On Matt. 16:17–19 as the product of Matthean composition, see Gundry, *Matthew*, 330–31. Most view it as originating in pre-Matthean tradition, e.g., R. Brown, K. P. Donfried, J. Reumann, *Peter in the New Testament* (Minneapolis: Augsburg, 1973), 90–91; P. Hoffmann, "Der Petrus-Primat im Matthäusevangelium," in *Neues Testament und Kirche*, ed. Gnilka, 98; Nickelsburg, "Enoch, Levi, and Peter," 598; B. P. Robinson, "Peter and His Successors: Tradition and Redaction in Matthew 16.17–19," *JSNT* 21 (1984): 89.

146. On the apocalyptic nature of this material, see Orton, *Understanding Scribe*, 160; Nickelsburg, "Enoch, Levi, and Peter," 590–600.

147. Sabourin, "Traits apocalyptiques," 365.

148. See Smith, "Ascent to the Heavens," 403–24; M. Smith, "The Origin and History of the Transfiguration Story," *USQR* 36 (1980): 39–44. Smith argues convincingly that the transfiguration narrative reflects not a "misplaced resurrection story" but an experience of apocalyptic ascent during the ministry of the historical Jesus.

149. *1 Enoch* 18:6–16; *T. Levi* 2:5–6; *Apoc. Abr.* 12; see Donaldson, *Jesus on the Mountain*, 141–42.

150. Dan. 12:3; *2 Apoc. Bar.* 51:1–3, 10; 4 Ezra 7:97, 10:25; Rev. 1:16.

151. Dan. 10:5; *1 Enoch* 14:20, 62:15–16; *2 Enoch* 22:8–10; Rev. 3:4–5, 7:9.

152. E.g., Dan. 8:16; *1 Enoch* 14:8; *T. Levi* 18:6; Rev. 11:12.

153. Dan. 7:13; *1 Enoch* 14:8; Rev. 14:4.

154. For the acknowledgment of the Son of Man by God or the heavenly revealer, see *1 Enoch* 46:1–8, 62:1–16, 71:1–17. The last text is particularly significant because Enoch the seer actually becomes the Son of Man acknowledged by the heavenly revealer.

155. Regarding the relationship of Matthew's transfiguration narrative to apocalyptic thought, see Donaldson, *Jesus on the Mountain*, 141–42; Gnilka, *Matthäusevangelium*, 2:95–99; Luz, *Evangelium nach Matthäus*, 2:508–10.

156. See Dan. 12:3; *2 Apoc. Bar.* 51:1–3, 10; 4 Ezra 7:97, 10:25; Rev. 1:16.

157. With the RSV. On bright or white garments, see Dan. 10:5; *1 Enoch* 14:20, 62:15–16; *2 Enoch* 22:8–10; Rev. 3:4–5, 7:9.

158. Countenance: Of the righteous, 4 Ezra 7:97; Dan. 12:3; *2 Apoc. Bar.* 51:3; of God, *1 Enoch* 14:21; of Jesus, Rev. 1:16. Raiment: Of God, Dan. 7:9; *1 Enoch* 14:20.

159. The RSV, which we follow here, more closely parallels the biblical and Second Temple visionary texts.

160. Josh. 5:14; Judg. 13:20; 2 Chron. 7:3; Ezek. 2:1, 9:8; Dan. 8:17, 10:9; *1 Enoch* 14:24ff.; *Apoc. Abr.* 10:2.

161. Gen. 28:17; Dan. 8:17. Cf. Luke 1:29.

162. Gen. 15:1, 21:17, 26:24; Dan. 10:12, 19; *1 Enoch* 14:25–15:1; Luke 1:30.

163. Ezek. 2:1–2; Dan. 10:11; *1 Enoch* 15:1; *Apoc. Abr.* 10:4ff.

164. Exod. 24:9–18, 34:29–35; see Gnilka, *Matthäusevangelium*, 2:93; Donaldson, *Jesus on the Mountain*, 142–43; Davies, *Sermon on the Mount*, 50; Luz, *Evangelium nach Matthäus*, 2:507.

165. 1K 19:9–13; Davies, *Sermon on the Mount*, 50.

166. Davies, *Sermon on the Mount*, 51–52; Donaldson, *Jesus on the Mountain*, 149; Gundry, *Matthew*, 342–43.

167. Smith, "Origin and History," 42.

168. Davies and Allison would make the Sinai motifs the primary influence in Matt. 17:1–8, although they acknowledge some precedents in apocalyptic literature; *Commentary on Matthew*, 2:685–704. However, as we suggest in chapter 1, the Sinai theme is present in Second Temple and tannaitic materials, particularly in visionary accounts. It is very possible that it is apocalyptic traditions that mediate the Sinai motif in Matt. 17:1–9 as well as the Markan source.

169. Sabourin, "Traits apocalyptiques," 370.

170. *T. Levi* 3:9–4:1; *2 Apoc. Bar.* 27:7. Cf. Isa. 13:9–13, 24:17–23; Ḥag 2:6–7, 21–22.

171. Dan. 12:2–3; *2 Apoc. Bar.* 50:2–3, 75:7; *1 Enoch* 51:1–5; *Apoc. Adam and Eve* 10:2, 13:2–6; *Pss. Sol.* 2:31, 3:12; *Ps Phocylides* ll. 103ff.; *Sib. Or.* 4:179–92.

172. E.g., Zech. 1:7–6:8; Dan. 8:15–16; 10:2–14, 18; *1 Enoch* 60–61, 71:13–17; 4 Ezra 10:29–59; *Apoc. Abr.* 10:4–17:7. See Hengel, *Judaism and Hellenism*, 1:204; J. J. Collins, *The Apocalyptic Vision of the Book of Daniel* (Missoula, Mont.: Scholars Press, 1977): 86; Jansen, *Die Henochgestalt*, 116; Blenkinsopp, "Interpretation and Sectarian Tendencies," 10.

173. Many scholars have observed the similarities between these two texts: B. W. Bacon, "Jesus the Son of God," *HTR* 2 (1909): 279–85; B. J. Hubbard, *The Matthaean Redaction of a Primitive Apostolic Commissioning*, SBLDS 19 (Missoula, Mont.: Scholars Press, 1974), 79–80; Lührmann, *Redaktion*, 165–68; J. Reese, "How Matthew Portrays the Communication of Christ's Authority," *BTB* 7 (1977): 141.

174. See Betz, "Logion of the Easy Yoke," 24. Betz, however, parallels *praus kai tapeinos tē kardia* (11:28) with *panta hosa eneteila mēn* (28:20). Discussion of the similarities usually focuses on 11:27 (*Panta moi paredothē*) and 18:18b (*edothē moi pasa exousia*); e.g., Hubbard, *Matthaean Redaction*, 79.

175. Matt. 5:34–35; 6:10, 19; 11:25; 18:18; Strecker, *Der Weg der Gerechtigkeit*, 209; Zumstein, *La condition du croyant*, 88. The use of *ouranos* with *ge* is always pre-Matthean.

176. See Zumstein, *La condition du croyant*, 88.

177. Cf. 18:20; Strecker, *Der Weg der Gerechtigkeit*, 209.

178. E.g., *proselthōn* with a *verbum dicendi, elalēsen autois legōn* in v. 18a (13:3, 14:27, 23:1), the pleonastic use of *poreuesthai* (9:13, 10:7, 21:6), *oun, mathēteuein panta ta ethnē* in v. 19a (24:9, 14; 25:32), and *tereō, panta, entellesthai, kai idou,* and *synteleia tou aiōnos* in v. 20. On Matthean vocabulary and constructions present in 28:18–20, see Strecker, *Der Weg der Gerechtigkeit*, 209; Zumstein, *La condition du croyant*, 88; Barth, "Matthew's Understanding of the Law," 131.

179. Many have noticed the parallel between 28:18–20 and Dan. 7:14; e.g., Barth, "Matthew's Understanding," 133–34; Harrington, *Gospel of Matthew*, 415–16; Hill, *Gospel of Matthew*, 361; Hubbard, *Matthaean Redaction*, 80–82; Lohmeyer, *Evangelium des Matthäus*, 416–17; Lührmann, *Redaktion*, 65; Schweizer, *Matthäus und seine Gemeinde*, 348; Strecker, *Der Weg der Gerechtigkeit*, 209. A. Vögtle objected to the use of Dan. 7:14 to understand Matt. 28:18b–20: "Das christologische und ekklesiologische Anliegen von Mt 28:18–20," *SE* 2 (1964): 266–94. Meier, however, has successfully refuted his arguments in *Law and History*, 36–37.

180. Hubbard, *Matthaean Redaction*, 79; Bacon, "Jesus the Son of God," 279, 285. Bacon does not refer here to Dan. 7:14; he does state, however, that Matthew constructed 28:18 around 11:27.

181. For a summary of various positions, see Donaldson, *Jesus on the Mountain*, 175–78; Levine, *Social and Ethnic Dimension*, 176–77.

182. E.g., *T. Levi* 13:2, 9; *2 Apoc. Bar.* 76:2–5; see Orton, *Understanding Scribe*, 159–60.

183. Davies, *Sermon on the Mount*, 85–86; Donaldson, *Jesus on the Mountain*, 179–80. Both see the Moses typology as subordinated to "higher" christological patterns (Davies, 97; Donaldson, 180). Donaldson argues for the dominance of a Zion theme here and elsewhere in Matthew's use of the mountain motif (180–88). The analysis is helpful, although beyond the scope of this book. Moreover, I am not sure that one can truly say that "Whatever apocalyptic and Sinai overtones are present have been gathered up into this larger vision" (188).

184. Saldarini, "Delegitimation," 668. I arrived at this conclusion prior to reading Saldarini's material.

Chapter 4. Jesus-Wisdom, Disciples, and Sages

1. Suggs observed the relationship between Matthew's use of the Wisdom metaphor and his understanding of the scribal function of the disciples: *Wisdom Christology*, 120–27; see also Witherington, *Jesus the Sage*, 336–68.

2. There is an ongoing discussion over the designation of "disciple" in Matthew's Gospel. Some (Bornkamm, Luz, Pesch, Thompson) believe that the term designates primarily the members of the Matthean community. Others believe that the term refers primarily to the actual followers of the historical Jesus (Strecker). Still others consider the term to refer primarily to the "founders" of the community and subsequent leadership (Minear). For a summary and discussion of various positions, see G. Stanton, ed. *The Interpretation of Matthew*, IRT 3 (Philadelphia: Fortress, 1983), 8–9; Verseput, *Rejection of the Humble Messianic King*, 38–41; M. J. Wilkins, *The Concept of Disciple in Matthew's Gospel as Reflected in the Use of the Term MATHĒTĒS*, NovTSup 59 (Leiden: E. J. Brill, 1988), 168–69; Overman, *Matthew's Gospel*, 125. I believe the term to be multivalent, referring to historical figures, as well as representing members of the Matthean community. The latter includes a defined leadership group, as well as the community "at large." In this chapter I will use the term "disciple" to refer to the leaders of Matthew's community.

3. Davies, *Sermon on the Mount*, 96.

4. Strecker, *Der Weg der Gerechtigkeit*, 195.

5. Martin Hengel describes the context in the Greco-Roman world, Jewish and Gentile: *Charismatic Leader and His Followers*, 16–35. His theological assumptions, however, do not allow him to give sufficient appreciation to the religious content of the comparative materials.

6. Gnilka, *Matthäusevangelium*, 1:310.

7. E.g., J. D. Kingsbury, "On Following Jesus: The 'Eager' Scribe and the 'Reluctant' Disciple (Matthew 8.18–22)," *NTS* 34 (1988): 45–59; Luz, *Evangelium nach Matthäus*, 2:23; Davies and Allison, *Commentary on Matthew*, 2:41. Among those who hold forth the possibility that the scribe in 8:18–22 is a disciple or would-be disciple is Schweizer, *Matthäus und seine Gemeinde*, 148–49.

8. Gnilka, *Matthäusevangelium*, 1:310.

9. Kingsbury, "On Following Jesus," 51; Davies and Allison, *Commentary on Matthew*, 2:41.

10. Kingsbury, "On Following Jesus," 49.

11. J. Kiilunen, "Der nachfolgewillige Schriftgelehrte, Matthäus 8.19–20 im Verständnis des Evangelisten," *NTS* 37 (1991): 270.

12. Matthew's use here is traditional (Mark 10:17). Matthew uses *didaskalos* or *didaskale* redactionally only in 9:11, 12:38, and 22:36. In other places he takes it from Mark (22:16 ‖ Mark 12:14; 22:24 ‖ Mark 12:19; 26:18 ‖ Mark 14:14), Q (10:24–25 ‖ Q6:40) or M (17:24).

13. Kiilunen, "Der nachfolgewillige Schriftgelehrte," 274–75.

14. With the RSV.

15. Gundry, *Matthew*, 151–52; Orton, *Understanding Scribe*, 36; S. Légasse, "Scribes et disciples de Jésus," *RB* 68 (1961): 343. Légasse exceeds the possibilities offered by the text when he concludes that "disciples" here refers to a crowd surrounding Jesus, not to a group of his intimates.

16. Sanders, *Jesus and Judaism*, 177–79, 208, and *Jewish Law*, 92. While Sanders makes an important contribution to the conversation when he says that Jesus invited unrepentant and unreformed sinners to membership in the Reign of God, I do not understand how such an invitation would not also imply the call to repentance and restitution.

17. Kloppenborg, *Formation of Q*, 78; Luz, *Evangelium nach Matthäus*, 2:105.

18. Gnilka, *Matthäusevangelium*, 1:364.

19. E.g., Matt. 5:3, 10; 11:11, 12; 13:11; 19:14.

20. Luz, *Evangelium nach Matthäus*, 2:93.

21. In view of Matthew's expansion of this material, it is difficult to understand why Overman would speak of "the truncated version of the version of the mission in chapter 10," or state that in Matthew healings exorcisms and preaching are not essential to the disciples' ministry in Matthew: *Matthew's Gospel*, 120.

22. Gundry believes that this addition is a reference to the false prophets of 7:15–23 who are "ravenous wolves": *Matthew*, 186. I see no indication of this.

23. Mark 6:8 has Jesus tell the envoys to take nothing for the journey "except a staff."

24. With the RSV.

25. Luz, *Evangelium nach Matthäus*, 2:97.

26. Davies and Allison, *Commentary on Matthew*, 2:172; J. A. Fitzmyer, *The Gospel According to Luke (I-IX)*, AB 28 (Garden City, N.Y.: Doubleday, 1981), 754. See Witherington's nuanced discussion of the Markan and Q versions of this material, and their relationship to Cynic practice: *Jesus the Sage*, 126–27.

27. E.g., *The Cynic Epistles*, ed. and trans. A. J. Malherbe, Sources for Biblical Study 12 (Missoula, Mont.: Scholars Press, 1977), 55, 103, 161, 163.

28. DL 6:13; *Cynic Epistles*, ed. Malherbe, 83, 99, 163.

29. DL 6:13.

30. Hengel, *Charismatic Leader and His Followers*, 28–33.

31. E.g., 5:3 ‖ Luke 6:20b; 6:19–21 ‖ Luke 12:33–34. Gundry believes the intensified rigor of Matthew's missionary speech reflects a desire to expose false prophets who would not follow an ascetic way: *Matthew*, 187. He cites 6:16–18 and 9:14–17. However, neither of these texts supports his position; Matt. 6:16–18 exhorts community members to fast in secret and 9:14–17 gives reasons why Jesus' disciples do not fast.

32. The fact that 10:25b is a Matthean insertion suggests that the redactor is consciously paralleling the fate of the disciples to that of Jesus, also accused of exorcising through demonic power (12:22–27): Luz, *Evangelium nach Matthäus*, 2:121.

33. Matthew edits these verses substantially, taking v. 42 from Mark 9:41 and adding vv. 40–41, probably from M.

34. Doyle, "Matthew's Wisdom," 178; Pregeant, "Wisdom Passages," 482. The only other occurrence of *nēpioi* in the synoptic gospels is Matt. 21:16, which refers to those saluting Jesus as "Son of David." This confirms that the term refers to acceptance of Jesus, and not to learning or lack thereof.

35. Deutsch, *Hidden Wisdom*, 118–19.

36. Ibid., 98–99.

37. Gnilka, *Matthäusevangelium*, 1:439; Suggs, *Wisdom Christology*, 106–107.

38. Doyle understands the wise and understanding to represent the "self-proclaimed sages" in his community who insisted "on retention of Jewish law, customs and practices": "Matthew's Wisdom," 179.

39. Levine, *Social and Ethnic Dimension*, 247. Luz associates the *nēpioi* with the ordinary folk in contrast to the Jewish religious aristocracy: *Evangelium nach Matthäus*, 2:206.

40. Deutsch, *Hidden Wisdom*, 30–32.

41. Overman, *Matthew's Gospel*, 81.

42. On the relationship of the theme of understanding to Matthew's Wisdom speculation, see B. R. Doyle, "Matthew's Intention as Discerned by His Structure," *RB* 95 (1988): 44.

43. Barth, "Matthew's Understanding of the Law," 107; Lohmeyer, *Evangelium des Matthäus*, 200.

44. Luz, *Evangelium nach Matthäus*, 2:313–14.

45. Schweizer, *Das Evangelium nach Matthäus*, 194. Trilling, *Das Wahre Israel*, 77. The conjunction *hoti* emphasizes the crowd's culpability: Gundry, *The Use of the Old Testament in St. Matthew's Gospel, with Special Reference to the Messianic Hope*, NovTSup 18 (Leiden: Brill, 1967), 33–34.

46. The conjunction thus links the material which follows to the question *dia ti*; D. Wenham, "The Structure of Matthew XIII," *NTS* 25 (1979): 519; U. Wilckens, "Die Redaktion des Gleichniskapitals Mark 4 durch Matthäus," *TZ* 20 (1964): 208.

47. L. Cerfaux, "La connaissance des secrets du royaume d'après Matt. xiii.11 et parallèles," in *Recueil Lucien Cerfaux*, 3 vols. (Gembloux: J. Duculot, 1962), 3:129.

48. Barth, "Matthew's Understanding of the Law," 107; for analysis of the form of the text, which is Septuagintal except for the fact that *auton* is missing in the second clause, see Stendahl, *School of St. Matthew*, 129–32. The same form of the text is used in Acts 28:26–27; John 12:40 has a form closer to the MT. *Anaplēroutai . . . hē prophēteia* is found only here in Matthew's Gospel. Citations proper to Matthew are introduced regularly by *hina plērōthē to hrēthen* (1:22, 2:15, 4:14, 12:17, 21:4); *hopōs plērōthē to hrēthen* (2:23, 8:17, 13:35); *tote eplērōthē to hrēthen* (2:17, 27:9).

49. Zumstein, *La condition du croyant*, 210. Gundry has ignored the significance of Matthew's expansion, observing only that the fulfillment citation here is "obviously an editorial expansion of the allusive quotation in v. 13 and parallels": *Use of the Old Testament*, 197.

50. See *Pss. Sol.* 17:50; *b. Ḥag* 14b; Lohmeyer, *Evangelium des Matthäus*, 204.

51. Michaelis, *Evangelium nach Matthäus*, 1:200.

52. Wenham, "Structure of Matthew XIII," 520.

53. With the RSV.

54. Mark has simply *ho logos* (4:14–15).

55. Matthew prefers *ho ponēros* to "Satan," e.g., 5:37, 6:13, 13:38. He eliminates the Markan *Satanas* in 12:25, and changes it to *ho ponēros* here and to *diabolos* in 4:1.

56. Mark has "hear the word and accept it" (*akouousin ton logon kai paradechonta*, 4:20).

57. Barth, "Matthew's Understanding of the Law," 107.

58. Zumstein, *La condition du croyant*, 161–62.

59. Beyond the context of 11:2–13:58, Matthew also uses *suniēmi* in 16:12 to refer to Jesus' teaching about the leaven of the Pharisees and Sadducees, and 17:13 regarding Jesus' interpretation of John the Baptist as the apocalyptic Elijah figure.

60. In 15:10, Matthew takes *syniēmi* from his source (Mark 7:14), with a reference to the crowd. In 15:16 Matthew has Jesus exclaim to Peter regarding his, and his fellows', lack of understanding; they are *asynetoi* (‖ Mark 7:18). He follows this with the material about the relation between interiority and ritual purity (vv. 17–20), thus showing Jesus as leading his disciples to true understanding of ritual law through his instruction; U. Luz, "Die Jünger im Matthäusevangelium," *ZNW* 62 (1971): 149; Zumstein, *La condition du croyant*, 204–5. In 16:12, the verb occurs in a redactional conclusion to the pericope about the teaching of the Pharisees and Sadducees (16:5–12). And in 17:13, it occurs in a redactional conclusion to the saying about the coming of Elijah (Mark 9:11–13).

61. Luz, "Die Jünger im Matthäusevangelium," 149–50.

62. Ibid.; Overman, *Matthew's Gospel*, 128–29.

63. E.g., CD 6:2–3; 1QSa 1.28–2.3; 4Q403 I.i.1–29; 11QPsa 27.2–3; 4 Ezra 4:2, 10, 21–22; 5:22, 34, 39; 8:3; 13:53; *2 Apoc. Bar.* 46:5.

64. Cerfaux, "La connaissance," 133; Orton, *Understanding Scribe*," 148–51.

65. On whether 13:51–52 should be considered one of the series of parables about the Kingdom, see Wenham, "Structure of Matthew XIII," 516–22.

66. We have already noted the dispute over 8:18–22.

67. Michaelis, *Evangelium nach Matthäus*, 1:256; Luz, *Evangelium nach Matthäus*, 2:362; Davies and Allison, *Commentary on Matthew*, 2:444.

68. Lagrange, *Evangile selon s. Matthieu*, 280.

69. Orton, *Understanding Scribe*, 142.

70. Bultmann, *History of the Synoptic Tradition*, 103; Michaelis, *Evangelium nach Matthäus*, 1:256.

71. D. Zeller, "Zu einer jüdischen Vorlage von Mt. 13, 52," *BZ* 20 (1976): 223–24. Zeller raises the possibility that Matthew has constructed the entire parable. This is unlikely, for Matthew does not construct entire parables elsewhere.

72. Matt. 28:19; Acts 14:21; see A. H. McNeile, *Gospel According to Matthew*, 205; Luz, *Evangelium nach Matthäus*, 2:363. Luz believes that it signifies "to make disciples" in Matthew's Gospel.

73. Allen, *Commentary on Matthew*, 154; Trilling, *Das Wahre Israel*, 145.

74. Schweizer, *Matthäus und seine Gemeinde*, 148–51; Zumstein, *La condition du croyant*, 160–63; Hill, *Gospel of Matthew*, 240; Gnilka, *Matthäusevangelium*, 1:511; Orton, *Understanding Scribe*, 139–40. Although most believe 13:52 to reflect a function in the Matthean community, Légasse disputes that position: "Scribes et disciples," 494; for a similar position see Wilkens, "Redaktion," 323.

75. Zeller, "Zu einer jüdischen Vorlage," 224.

76. Gundry, *Matthew*, 281.

77. Orton, *Understanding Scribe*, 152.

78. O. L. Cope, *Matthew, a Scribe Trained for the Kingdom of Heaven*, CBQMS 5 (Washington, D.C.: Catholic Biblical Association, 1976), 25; Schweizer, *Matthäus und seine Gemeinde*, 44.

79. Michaelis, *Evangelium nach Matthäus*, 1:257. Viviano would understand "old" as referring only to the Hebrew Scriptures: *Study as Worship*, 167.

80. Cope, *Matthew*, 44–45.

81. Ibid., 25.

82. W. Trilling, "Amt und Amtverständnis bei Matthäus," in *Mélanges bibliques en hommage au R. P. Béda Rigaux*, ed. A. Descamps and R. D. A. de Halleux (Gembloux: Duculot, 1970), 34; Zumstein, *La condition du croyant*, 161–62. Zumstein restricts the content of old and new to Jesus' teaching and its interpretation: Gnilka, *Matthäusevangelium*, 1:511. Most neglect postbiblical Jewish tradition as being included in the referent of the expression.

83. Witherington, *Jesus the Sage*, 346.

84. See Davies and Allison, *Commentary on Matthew*, 2:448.

85. Witherington, *Jesus the Sage*, 347.

86. Overman, *Matthew's Gospel*, 116–17.

87. The future tense of the verb, *apostellō*, suggests that vv. 34–36 refer to Matthew's community: Garland, *Intention of Matthew 23*, 174. It would seem to me that this material pertains to members of the community with a teaching function. Doyle, however, in speaking of the appearances of Wisdom earlier in

the gospel, appears to equate the disciple-scribes with the Matthean community: "Matthew's Intention," 44.

88. The description of the fate of Wisdom's envoys in vv. 34–36 recalls the missionary speech (10:17b, 23). And, of course, it recalls the passion predictions (16:21 ‖ Mark 8:31; 17:22–23 ‖ Mark 9:31; 20:17–19 ‖ Mark 10:32–34).

89. Doyle, "Matthew's Wisdom," 425.

90. A. Sand, "Propheten, Weise und Schriftkundige in der Gemeinde des Matthäusevangelium," in *Kirche im Werden: Studien zum Thema Amt und Gemeinde in Neuen Testament*, ed. J. Hainz (Munich: Ferdinand Schöningh, 1976), 174–75.

91. Haenchen, "Matthäus 23," 53.

92. See 13:17.

93. Gnilka believes that Matthew's prophets may have exercised an office at the Eucharistic celebration, but there is nothing in the text to indicate this: *Matthäusevangelium*, 2:533.

94. Davies and Allison suggest that the prophets of 10:41 were itinerant teachers; *Commentary on Matthew*, 2:226.

95. Minear would subsume "scribe" and "wise man" under the category of "prophet": "False Prophecy," 76–77. The text, however, does not warrant this.

96. For an early consideration of the relationship between prophecy and Law, both in Matthew and in early Christianity, see E. Käsemann, "Sätze Heiligen Rechtes im Neuen Testament," *NTS* 1 (1954/55): 248–60.

97. Regarding the traditional nature of 23:8–10, see Bultmann, *History of the Synoptic Tradition*, 144, 146; Trilling, "Amt und Amtverständnis," 31; Zumstein, *La condition du croyant*, 157–58.

98. Contra Lohmeyer, *Evangelium des Matthäus*, 339.

99. J. T. Townsend, "Matthew XXIII.9," *JTS* 12 (1961): 59; K. Kohler, "Abba, Father: Title of Spiritual Leader and Saint," in *Exploring the Talmud*, ed. Dimitrovsky, 150–63.

100. Overman, *Matthew's Gospel*, 114, 123; Saldarini, "Delegitimation," 670–71.

101. The presence of similar sayings in various strata of the gospel material suggests that this too is traditional material (Matt. 18:4; Mark 9:35; Luke 9:48b; 14:11; 18:14; John 13:16); see Bultmann, *History of the Synoptic Tradition*, 143.

102. *Anawim* language was used in several communities following Jesus in the first century; e.g., Luke 14:11; 18:14; James 4:6, 10; 1 Pet. 5:5, 6; Phil. 4:12; 2 Cor. 10:1; Mark 9:42.

103. Matt. 10:1 ‖ Mark 6:7; 15:32 ‖ Mark 8:1; Matt. 18:32. Only in Matt. 15:10 ‖ Mark 7:14 does it refer to anyone other than disciples.

104. Luz believes that the *mikroi* of 10:42 are ordinary Christians; *Evangelium nach Matthäus*, 2:152. The context, however, at the end of a commissioning of missionaries, suggests a particular function in the community.

105. See 6:2–4, 5–6, 16–18.

106. See Kohler, "Abba, Father," 150–63.

107. One recalls the saying ascribed to Hillel: "My humiliation is my exal-

tation; my exaltation is my humiliation" (*Lev. Rab.* 1:5). A similar saying is attributed to R. Jose in *'Abot R. Nat. a* 11.

108. Urbach, *The Sages*, 1:396–99.

109. Levine, *Social and Ethnic Dimension*, 215–16. Contra Garland, who effectively recognizes only the community leaders as the "targets" of the critique in chapter 23: *Intention of Matthew 23*, 214–15. Doyle believes that the "Pharisees" may represent the Pharisees in Matthew's community who are causing difficulty through "judaizing" intentions; *Matthew's Wisdom*, 246. However, Matthew, as we have noted, has no difficulty with Torah observance in itself. He poses, rather, alternative interpretations to his community.

110. Renov, "Seat of Moses," 262–67.

111. Gnilka, *Matthäusevangelium*, 2:271.

112. Brooks, *Matthew's Community*, 116–17.

113. Saldarini, "Delegitimation," 670. In actual fact, beginning with the Hasmonean era, Pharisees were often members of the retainer class, sometimes functioning as bureaucrats for the court and government officials; see Saldarini, *Pharisees, Scribes and Sadducees*, 296–97.

114. Saldarini, *Matthew's Christian-Jewish Community*, 47–48.

115. E.g., 9:10–13, 14–17; 12:1–8; 19:10–12.

116. Saldarini, *Matthew's Christian-Jewish Community*, 134–41.

117. "Blind" is a favorite Matthean adjective for the Pharisees: e.g., 23:16, 17, 19, 24, 26.

118. E.g., 17:24–27; 18:21; 19:27 (Mark 10:28). Peter's role is legitimated in 16:17–19, as we will observe. See Gnilka, *Matthäusevangelium*, 2:68, 516; Overman, *Matthew's Gospel*, 137; A. F. Segal, "Matthew's Jewish Voice," in *Social History of the Matthean Community*, ed. Balch, 9–11; Luz, *Evangelium nach Matthäus*, 2:467–71.

119. Saldarini, *Matthew's Christian-Jewish Community*, 134. Observance of food laws was a matter of concern in several Christian communities: e.g., Mark 7:1–23; Acts 15:28–29; 1 Cor. 8:1–13; Rev. 2:14–15, 20.

120. Exod. 20:12; Deut. 5:16; Exod. 21:17; Lev. 20:9.

121. Here he alters the Markan list. Mark has "evil thoughts, fornication, theft, murder, adultery, coveting, wickedness, deceit, licentiousness, envy, slander, pride, foolishness" (7:22). Matthew's list reads "evil thoughts, murder, adultery, fornication, theft, false witness, slander" (15:19).

122. Overman, *Matthew's Gospel*, 83. Handwashing before daily meals was not required at this time; Sanders, *Jewish Law*, 39–40; Saldarini, *Matthew's Christian-Jewish Community*, 135–36.

123. This recalls chapter 23 where the scribes and Pharisees are also called "blind guides" (vv. 16, 24) and where the adjective *typhlos* also describes them in vv. 17, 19, 26. It also recalls indirectly the warning in 16:5–12 regarding the "leaven of the Pharisees and Sadducees" which Matthew applies in a redactional conclusion to their teaching.

124. On the tradition history of 16:17–19, see Bultmann, *History of the Synoptic Tradition*, 138–40; C. Kähler, "Zur Form- und Traditionsgeschichte von Matt. xvi, 17–19" *NTS* 23 (1976–77): 38–44; Gnilka, *Matthäusevangelium*, 2:48–57.

125. Hoffmann, "Petrus-Primat," 98; Orton, *Understanding Scribe*, 160, 237; Saldarini, "Delegitimation," 673–74; Wilkins, *Concept of Disciple*, 194–95.

126. Trilling, "Amt und Amtverständnis," 43; M. Wilcox, "Peter and the Rock: A Fresh Look at Matthew 16:17–19," *NTS* 22 (1975–76): 82; Brown et al. are unable to decide what is the referent of binding and loosing: *Peter in the New Testament*, 98–100, 106; also Nickelsburg, "Enoch, Levi, and Peter," 594; B. P. Robinson, "Peter and His Successors: Tradition and Redaction in Matthew 16:17–19," *JSNT* 21 (1984): 93–94.

127. Luz, *Evangelium nach Matthäus*, 2:465.

128. E.g., *m. Pesaḥ.* 4:5; *Ter.* 5:4; *t. Yebam.* 1:11; *j. Šabb.* 1.4, 59; *t. Yebam.* 4:6; *m. Pesaḥ.* 6:2; *j. Ber.* 4.27; Kähler, "Zur Form- und Traditionsgeschichte," 39; J. M. van Caugh and M. van Esbroeck, "La primauté de Pierre (Mt. 16,16–19) et son contexte judaïque," *RTL* 11 (1980): 321; J. Marcus, "The Gates of Hades and the Keys of the Kingdom (Matt. 16:18–19)," *CBQ* 50 (1988): 452.

129. Overman, *Matthew's Gospel*, 105–6. For later evidence, see *b. Mo'ed Qaṭ.* 16a; *Šabb.* 81b.

130. *Htîr* can also signify release from vows; e.g., *m. Ḥag* 1:8; *b. Ḥag* 10a; see Z. W. Falk, "Binding and Loosing," *JJS* 25 (1974): 92ff. However, this does not correspond to usage in Matthew.

131. E.g., *1 Enoch* 54:4–6; 69:28–29; *T. Levi* 18:12. See also *T. Jud.* 25:3; *T. Moses* 10:1; *Jub.* 23:29.

132. I prefer an inclusive interpretation of "binding and loosing" as more appropriate in the context of Matthew's Gospel as well as Second Temple and tannaitic thought than construing it as signifying *either* church discipline *or* halachic interpretation *or* exorcism.

133. Luz, "Die Jünger im Matthäusevangelium," 152; Strecker, *Der Weg der Gerechtigkeit*, 198–206.

134. H. Frankemölle, "Amtskritik im Matthäus-Evangelium," *Biblica* 54 (1973): 259. Some would say that the description of Peter in Matthew's Gospel refers only to the historical character and bears no trace of community office: e.g., Trilling, "Amt und Amtverständnis," 42; Hoffmann, "Petrus-Primat," 110; Wilkins, *Concept of Disciple*, 215.

While I would disagree with this position, I concur with those who observe that Peter is always within the circle of the disciples; while he does not have a station above other disciples, Matthew appears to consider him as "first among equals." See J. D. Kingsbury, "The Figure of Peter in Matthew's Gospel as a Theological Problem," *JBL* 98 (1979): 80.

135. Suggs, *Wisdom Christology*, 120–22. Suggs, however, considers 16:17–19 related to 5:11–12, and believes both to be commissionings of Christian scribes. However, the evidence does not support such a conclusion regarding 5:11–12.

136. Neh. 10:32; Exod. 30:11–16; Philo, *Spec.* 1:77; Josephus, *Ant.* 18:312; *War* 7:218. See Harrington, *Gospel of Matthew*, 261–62.

137. On the Temple tax and its continuation after 70 C.E., see Sanders, *Judaism*, 52–53.

138. See Sanders, *Jewish Law*, 49–51. The law refers to Exod. 30:13–16.

139. Harrington, *Gospel of Matthew*, 262; Saldarini, *Matthew's Christian-Jewish Community*, 143–47.

140. The NRSV translates *peri pantos pragmatos* as "anything," which does not convey the forensic connotation required by the context: Harrington, *Gospel of Matthew*, 269.

141. See Luke 17:3–4.

142. Matthew follows the LXX in the first clause but is closer to the Hebrew in the second.

143. Here Matthew follows Mark: 13:10ff. || Mark 4:10.

144. Matthew may here be referring to the entire community which understands itself in sectarian terms. On the sectarian nature of Matthew's community, see Saldarini, "Delegitimation," 665 n. 20.

145. J. Dupont, "La révélation du Fils de Dieu en faveur de Pierre (Mt 16,17) et de Paul (Gal 1,16)," *RSR* 52 (1964): 412–13; T. de Kruijf, *Der Sohn des lebendigen Gottes: Ein Beitrag zur Christologie des Matthäusevangeliums*, AnBib 16 (Rome: Pontifical Biblical Institute, 1962), 84–85; Orton, *Understanding Scribe*, 160.

146. Kähler, "Zur Form- und Traditionsgeschichte," 37; Robinson, "Peter and His Successors," 85–104.

147. Kähler, "Zur Form- und Traditionsgeschichte," 46.

148. Gundry, *Matthew*, 333. Both Dupont and de Kruijf also note the similarity; Luz, *Evangelium nach Matthäus*, 2:461.

149. Hubbard, *Matthaean Redaction*, 83; B. Malina, "The Literary Structure and Form of Matt. XXVIII.16–20," *NTS* 17 (1970): 89–90; J. Zumstein, "Matthieu 28:16–20," *RTP* 22 (1972): 25.

150. Barth, "Matthew's Understanding of the Law," 134.

151. Ibid., 134–35; Zumstein, "Matthieu 28:16–20," 28. Hubbard understands the use of *eneteilamēn* as a reiteration of the Moses motif (e.g., Exod. 34:28; Deut. 9:9, 11, 18): *Matthaean Redaction*, 92.

152. E. Fascher, "Jesus der Lehrer: Ein Beitrag zur Frage nach dem 'Quellort der Kirchenidee,'" *TLZ* 79 (1954): 333; Zumstein, "Matthieu 28:16–20," 28.

153. Wainwright, *Feminist Critical Reading of Matthew*, 317–18.

154. Cf. Mark 6:44, 8:9.

155. J. C. Anderson, "Matthew: Gender and Reading," *Semeia* 28 (1983): 9. J. P. Heil describes only Rahab and Ruth as Gentiles: "The Narrative Roles of the Women in Matthew's Genealogy," *Biblica* 38 (1992): 538–45. Raymond Brown has summarized the various interpretations of this aspect of the genealogy: *Birth of the Messiah*, 71–73, 590–96.

156. Wainwright, *Feminist Critical Reading of Matthew*, 160–71.

157. Anderson, "Matthew," 10–17.

158. See Luke 7:31–35.

159. A. C. Wire, "Gender Roles in a Scribal Community," in *Social History of the Matthean Community*, ed. Balch, 106.

160. Ibid.

161. With the RSV.

162. Regarding *akoloutheō* see J. D. Kingsbury, "The Verb *AKOLOUTHEIN* ('To Follow') as an Index of Matthew's View of His Community," *JBL* 97

(1978): 56–73. On *diakoneō*, see Wainwright, *Feminist Critical Reading of Matthew*, 296. *Diakoneō*, however, need not always indicate public ministry. It may simply indicate "service," particularly "table service"; e.g., 8:15. However, the usage in 25:44, as well as the fact that Matthew's Jesus, as Mark's, uses it to designate his own ministry (Mark 10:45; Matt. 20:28), indicates service in the community. And the occurrence of the two verbs together in 27:55 suggests that a more formal service is likewise understood here, as does the fact that in 27:55–56 the women are outside the bounds of the household.

163. Matthew exhibits a redactional tendency to heighten the apocalyptic tendency present in his sources, or to add it. See the discussion of this passage in chapter 3.

164. My translation.

165. Wainwright believes this may be the work of the redactor or come from the community tradition (M): *Feminist Critical Reading of Matthew*, 309–10. However, the way in which the text parallels vv. 1–8 suggests that it is redactional. It may, however, preserve a tradition about Jesus' commissioning women.

166. Wainwright holds that the story of the Canaanite woman, with its redactional "Have mercy on me, Lord, Son of David" (*eleēson me, kyrie, huios David*), could have "functioned as a legitimation of women's active role in liturgy, their participation in the community's theological reflection on the life and ministry of Jesus in the light of their scriptures and their leadership role": *Feminist Critical Reading of Matthew*, 245. Certainly the plea suggests participation in liturgy. However, there is no suggestion of the kind of specialized learning with which we are concerned in this study.

167. Regarding such appropriation in other contexts, see Wolfson, "Woman," and "Female Imaging of the Torah," 271–307. See also L. Irigaray, "Questions to Emmanuel Levinas on the Divinity of Love," trans. M. Whitford, in *Re-Reading Levinas*, ed. R. Bernasconi and S. Critchley (Bloomington: Indiana University Press, 1991), 109–11. For another interpretation of male appropriation of female metaphors, see the discussion of Julia Kristeva in T. Moi, *Sexual/Textual Politics; Feminist Literary Theory* (1985; rpt., London: Routledge, 1991), 166–67.

Chapter 5. Conclusions

1. On various kinds of sects, see B. Wilson, *Magic and the Millennium: A Sociological Study of Religious Movements of Protest among Tribal and Third-World Peoples* (London: Heinemann, 1973), 16–26; A. Saldarini, *Pharisees, Scribes and Sadducees*, 71–73.

Bibliography

Primary Sources

Aboth de Rabbi Nathan. Edited by S. Schechter. Vienna: Ch. D. Lippe, 1887.

The Apocrypha and Pseudepigrapha of the Old Testament. 2 vols. 1913; rpt., Oxford: Clarendon, 1963.

The Babylonian Talmud. 35 vols. General editor I. Epstein. London: Soncino, 1935–48.

Cicero. De Natura Deorum; Academica. Translated by H. Rackham. LCL. New York: Putnam's, 1933.

Cicero. Tusculan Disputations. Translated by J. E. King. LCL. New York: Putnam's, 1927.

The Cynic Epistles. Edited and translated by A. J. Malherbe. Sources for Biblical Study 12. Missoula, Mont.: Scholars Press, 1977.

The Dead Sea Scrolls in English. 4th ed., revised and extended. Edited and translated by G. Vermes. London: Penguin, 1995.

Diogenes Laertius: Lives of Eminent Philosophers. 2 vols. Translated by R. D. Hicks. LCL. Cambridge: Harvard University Press, 1925; rpt., 1980.

Discoveries in the Judaean Desert. Vol. 1: *Qumran Cave I*. Edited by D. Barthélemy and J. T. Milik. Oxford: Clarendon, 1955.

Discoveries in the Judaean Desert of Jordan. Vol. 3: *Les 'Petites Grottes' de Qumrân*. Edited by M. Baillet, J. T. Milik, and R. de Vaux, o.p. Oxford: Clarendon, 1962.

———. Vol. 4: *The Psalms Scroll of Qumrân Cave 11 (11QPsa)*. Edited by J. A. Sanders. Oxford: Clarendon, 1965.

———. Vol. 5: *Qumrân Cave 4 I(4Q158–4Q186)*. Edited by J. M. Allegro with A. A. Anderson. Oxford: Clarendon, 1968.

———. Vol. 7: *Qumrân Grotte 4 III(4Q482–4Q520)*. Edited by M. Baillet. Oxford: Clarendon, 1982.

Epictetus: The Discourses as Reported by Arrian, the Manual and Fragments. Translated by W. A. Oldfather. LCL. Cambridge: Harvard University Press, 1925; rpt., 1979.

The Fathers According to Rabbi Nathan. Edited and translated by J. Goldin. New Haven: Yale University Press, 1955; rpt., New York: Schocken, 1974.

Josephus. Translated by H. St. J. Thackeray (vols. 1–5), R. Marcus (vols. 5–8), and L. Feldman (vols. 9–10). LCL. Cambridge: Harvard University, 1926–65.

Mekilta de Rabbi Ishmael. 3 vols. Edited and translated by J. Z. Lauterbach. Philadelphia: Jewish Publication Society, 1933–35.

Midrash Rabbah. 2 vols. Wilna: Widow and Bros. Romm, 1878.

215

Midrash Rabbah. 10 vols. Edited and translated by H. Freedman and M. Simon. London: Soncino, 1939–51.

The Mishnah. Edited and translated by H. Danby. Oxford: Clarendon, 1933.

The Old Testament Pseudepigrapha. 2 vols. General editor J. H. Charlesworth. Garden City, N.Y.: Doubleday, 1983, 1985.

Oxyrhynchus Papyrii. Vol. 11. Edited and translated by B. P. Grenfell and A. S. Hunt. London: Oxford University Press, 1915.

Philo. Translated by F. H. Colson (vols. 1–10) and G. H. Whitaker (vols. 1–5). LCL. Cambridge: Harvard University, 1929–43.

Plutarch. Moralia. 14 vols. Edited and translated by F. C. Babbitt. LCL. Cambridge: Harvard University, 1927–76.

Shishah Sidre Mishnah. 6 vols. Edited by H. Albeck. Jerusalem: Mossad Bialik, 1952–57.

Sifre: A Tannaitic Commentary on the Book of Deuteronomy. Edited and translated by R. Hammer. Yale Judaica Series 24. New Haven: Yale University Press, 1986.

Sifre Debarim. Edited by L. Finkelstein and H. S. Horovitz. New York: Jewish Theological Seminary of America, 1969.

Songs of the Sabbath Sacrifice: A Critical Edition. Edited and translated by C. A. Newsom. HSS 27. Atlanta: Scholars Press, 1985.

Talmud Babli. Wilna: Widow and Bros. Romm, 1895–1908.

The Talmud of the Land of Israel: A Preliminary Translation and Explanation. 35 vols. General editor J. Neusner. Chicago: University of Chicago Press, 1983–90.

Talmud Yerushalmi. Venice: Daniel Bomberg, 1522.

Teles [the Cynic Teacher.] Edited and translated by E. O'Neil. SBL Texts and Translations 11. Missoula, Mont.: Scholars Press, 1977.

Tosefta. 4 vols. Edited by S. Lieberman. New York: 1955–73.

Tosefta. Edited by M. S. Zuckermandel. 1880; rpt., Jerusalem: Wehrman, 1963.

The Tosefta. 6 vols. Translated by J. Neusner. New York: KTAV, 1977.

Secondary Sources

Aletti, J. N. "Séduction en parole en Proverbes I–IX." *VT* 27 (1977): 129–44.

Alföldy, G. *The Social History of Rome.* Translated by D. Braund and F. Pollock. London: Croom Helm, 1985.

Allen, W. D. *A Critical and Exegetical Commentary on the Gospel According to St. Matthew.* ICC. New York: Scribner's, 1913.

Alt, A. "Solomonic Wisdom." In *Studies in Ancient Israelite Wisdom*, ed. J. L. Crenshaw, 102–12. New York: Ktav, 1976.

Anderson, J. C. "Matthew: Gender and Reading." *Semeia* 28 (1983): 3–28.

Auerbach, M. "The Change from a Standing to a Sitting Posture by Students after the Death of Rabban Gamaliel." In *Exploring the Talmud*, ed. Dimitrovsky, 1:165–74.

Aune, D. E. "Magic in Early Christianity." *ANRW* II.16.2 (1978): 1507–57.

———. "The Use of ΠΡΟΦΗΤΗΣ in Josephus." *JBL* 101 (1982): 419–21.

Axtell, H. L. *The Deification of Abstract Ideas in Roman Literature and Inscriptions*. Chicago: University of Chicago Press, 1907; rpt., New Rochelle, N.Y.: Aristilde D. Caralzas, 1987.

Bacon, B. W. "Jesus the Son of God." *HTR* 2 (1909): 277–309.

Baer, R. A. *Philo's Use of the Categories of Male and Female*. Leiden: Brill, 1970.

Bagnall, R. *Egypt in Late Antiquity*. Princeton: Princeton University Press, 1993.

Balch, D. L. *Let Wives Be Submissive: The Domestic Code in Peter*. Atlanta: Scholars Press, 1981.

———, ed. *Social History of the Matthean Community: Cross-Disciplinary Approaches*. Minneapolis: Fortress, 1991.

Banks, R. "Matthew's Understanding of the Law: Authenticity and Interpretation in Matthew 5:17–20." *JBL* 93 (1974): 226–42.

Barth, G. "Matthew's Understanding of the Law." In Bornkamm et al., *Tradition and Interpretation in Matthew*, 58–164.

Beauchamp, P. "Épouser la Sagesse ou n'épouser qu'elle? Une énigme du Livre de la Sagesse." In *La Sagesse de l'Ancien Testament*, ed. M. Gilbert, 347–69. Gembloux: Duculot, 1979.

Begrich, J. "Sōfēr und Mazkīr." *ZAW* 58 (1940): 1–29.

Berger, P. L. *The Sacred Canopy: Elements of a Sociological Theory of Religion*. Garden City, N.Y.: Anchor/Doubleday, 1969.

Berger, P. L., and T. Luckmann. *The Social Construction of Reality: A Treatise in the Sociology of Knowledge*. New York: Anchor Books, 1967.

Betz, H. D. "The Beatitudes of the Sermon on the Mount (Matthew 5:3–12): Observations on Their Literary Forms and Theological Significance." In *Essays on the Sermon on the Mount*, trans. Welborn, 17–36.

———. *Essays on the Sermon on the Mount*. Translated by L. L. Welborn. Philadelphia: Fortress, 1985.

———. "The Hermeneutical Principles of the Sermon on the Mount (Matthew 5:17–20)." In *Essays on the Sermon on the Mount*, trans. Welborn, 37–53.

———. "The Logion of the Easy Yoke and of Rest (Mt. 11:28–30)." *JBL* 86 (1967): 10–24.

———. "The Sermon on the Mount (Matthew 5:3–7:27): Its Literary Genre and Function." In *Essays on the Sermon on the Mount*, trans. Welborn, 1–16.

Bickerman, E. "La chaîne de la tradition pharisienne." *RB* 59 (1952): 44–54.

Black, M. *Models and Metaphors*. Ithaca, N.Y.: Cornell University Press, 1962.

Blenkinsopp, J. "Interpretation and Sectarian Tendencies: An Aspect of Second Temple History." In *Jewish and Christian Self-Definition*, ed. Sanders et al., 2:1–26.

———. "Prophecy and Priesthood in Josephus." *JJS* 25 (1974): 239–62.

———. "The Sage, the Scribe, and Scribalism in the Chronicler's Work." In *The Sage*, ed. Gammie and Perdue, 307–15.

Bokser, B. M. "Wonder-Working and the Rabbinic Tradition: The Case of Hanina Ben Dosa." *JSJ* 16 (1985): 42–92.

Boring, M. E. *Sayings of the Risen Jesus: The Prophecy in the Synoptic Tradition*. SNTSMS 46. Cambridge: Cambridge University Press, 1982.

Bornkamm, G. "End-Expectation and Church in Matthew." In Bornkamm et al., *Tradition and Interpretation in Matthew*, 15–51.

Bornkamm, G., G. Barth, and H. J. Held. *Tradition and Interpretation in Matthew*. Translated by P. Scott. London: SCM, 1963.

Bowersock, G. W. *Greek Sophists in the Roman Empire*. Oxford: Clarendon, 1969.

Brooke, G. J. "The Wisdom of Matthew's Beatitudes (4QBeat and Mt 5:3–12)." *Scripture Bulletin* 19, no. 2 (1989): 35–41.

Brooks, S. H. *Matthew's Community: The Evidence of His Special Sayings Material*. JSNTSS 16. Sheffield, England: JSOT Press, 1987.

Brown, P. *The Making of Late Antiquity*. Cambridge: Harvard University Press, 1978.

Brown, R. E. *The Birth of the Messiah: A Commentary on the Infancy Narratives in the Gospels of Matthew and Luke*. 2nd ed. AB Reference Library. New York: Doubleday, 1993.

———. *A Commentary on the Passion Narratives in the Four Gospels*. Vol. 1: *The Death of the Messiah: From Gethsemane to the Grave*. 2 vols. AB Reference Library. New York: Doubleday, 1994.

———. *The Gospel According to John (i–xii)*. AB. Garden City, N.Y.: Doubleday, 1966.

Brown, R. E., K. P. Donfried, and J. Reumann. *Peter in the New Testament*. Minneapolis: Augsburg, 1973.

Bultmann, R. "Der religionsgeschichte Hintergrund des Prologs zum Johannes-Evangelium." In *Eucharisterion: Studien zur Religion und Literatur des Alten und Neuen Testaments*, ed. H. Schmidt, 1–26. Göttingen: Vandenhoeck and Ruprecht, 1923.

———. *History of the Synoptic Tradition*. Translated by J. Marsh. New York: Harper and Row, 1963.

Burkert, W. *Greek Religion: Archaic and Classical*. Translated by J. Raffan. Cambridge: Harvard University Press, 1985.

Burnett, F. *The Testament of Jesus-Sophia: A Redaction Critical Study of the Eschatological Discourse in Matthew*. Washington, D.C.: University Press of America, 1981.

Bynum, C. W. "Women's Stories, Women's Symbols: A Critique of Victor Turner's Theory of Liminality." In *Anthropology and the Study of Religion*, ed. R. L. Moore and F. E. Reynolds, 105–25. Chicago: Center for the Scientific Study of Religion, 1984.

Cady, S., M. Ronan, and H. Taussig. *Sophia: The Future of Feminist Spirituality*. San Francisco: Harper and Row, 1986.

Camp, C. "The Female Sage in Ancient Israel and in the Biblical Wisdom Literature." In *The Sage*, ed. Gammie and Perdue, 185–203.

———. *Wisdom and the Feminine in the Book of Proverbs*. Bible and Literature 2. Decatur, Ga.: Almond Press, 1985.

———. "Woman Wisdom as Root Metaphor: A Theological Consideration." In *The Listening Heart: Essays in Wisdom and the Psalms in Honor of Roland E. Murphy, O Carm*, ed. K. Hogland et al., 45–76. Sheffield, England: JSOT Press, 1987.

Carlston, C. "Betz on the Sermon on the Mount: A Critique." *CBQ* 50 (1988): 47–57.

———. "Wisdom and Eschatology in Q." In *Logia: Les paroles de Jésus [The Sayings of Jesus]: Mémorial Joseph Coppens*, ed. Joël Delobel, 101–19. BETL 59. Leuven: Uitgeverij Peeters and Leuven University, 1982.

Cassirer, E. *Language and Myth*. Translated by S. Langer. New York: Dover, 1946.

Cerfaux, L. "La connaissance des secrets du royanne d'après Matt XIII et parallèles." In *Recueil Lucien Cerfaux*, 3:161–74. Gembloux: Duculot, 1962.

Chernus, I. *Mysticism in Rabbinic Judaism*. Berlin: de Gruyter, 1982.

———. "Visions of God in Merkabah Mysticism." *JSJ* 13 (1982): 123–46.

Chesnutt, R. D. "Revelatory Experiences Attributed to Biblical Women in Early Jewish Literature." In *"Women Like This,"* ed. Levine, 107–25.

Christ, F. *Jesus Sophia: Die Sophia-Christologie bei den Synoptikern*. ATANT 57. Zurich: Zwingli, 1970.

Cohen, S. J. D. *Josephus in Galilee and Rome: His Vita and His Development as an Historian*. Columbia Studies in the Classical Traditions 8. Leiden: Brill, 1979.

———. "Patriarchs and Scholarchs." *Proceedings of the American Academy for Jewish Research* 48 (1981): 57–85.

———. "The Significance of Yavneh: Pharisees, Rabbis, and the End of Jewish Sectarianism." *HUCA* 55 (1984): 27–53.

Cohn-Sherbok, D. M. "An Analysis of Jesus' Arguments Concerning the Plucking of Grain on the Sabbath." *JSNT* 2 (1979): 31–41.

Collins, J. J. "The Apocalyptic Technique: Setting and Function in the Book of Watchers." *CBQ* 44 (1982): 91–111.

———. *The Apocalyptic Vision of the Book of Daniel*. Missoula, Mont.: Scholars Press, 1977.

———. "Cosmos and Salvation: Jewish Wisdom and Apocalypse in the Hellenistic Age." *HR* 17 (1977): 121–42.

———. "Jewish Apocalyptic Against Its Hellenistic Near Eastern Environment." *BASOR* 220 (1975): 27–36.

———. "The Sage in the Apocalyptic and Pseudepigraphic Literature." In *The Sage*, ed. Gammie and Perdue, 343–54.

———. "The Son of Man in First-Century Judaism." *NTS* 38 (1992): 448–66.

Conzelmann, Hans. *1 Corinthians: A Commentary on the First Epistle to the Corinthians*. Translated by J. W. Leitch. Philadelphia: Fortress, 1975.

———. "The Mother of Wisdom." In *The Future of Our Religious Past*, ed. J. M. Robinson, trans. C. E. Carlston and R. P. Scharlemann, 230–43. London: SCM, 1971.

Cook, M. J. "Interpreting 'Pro-Jewish' Passages in Matthew" *HUCA* 54 (1983): 135–46.

Cope, O. L. *Matthew, a Scribe Trained for the Kingdom of Heaven*. CBQMS 5. Washington, D.C.: Catholic Biblical Association, 1976.

Coser, L. A. *The Functions of Social Conflict*. Glencoe, Ill.: Free Press, 1956.

———. "Social Conflict and the Theory of Social Change." In Coser, *Continuities in the Study of Social Conflict*, 17–35. New York: Free Press, 1967.

Coughenour, R. R. "The Wisdom Stance of Enoch's Redactor." *JSJ* 13 (1982): 47–55.

Crenshaw, J. L. "Education in Ancient Israel." *JBL* 104 (1985): 601–15.

Crocker, J. C. "The Social Functions of Rhetorical Forms." In *The Social Use of Metaphor: Essays on the Anthropology of Rhetoric*, ed. J. D. Sapir and J. C. Crocker, 33–66. Philadelphia: University of Pennsylvania Press, 1977.

Crosby, M. H. *House of Disciples: Church, Economics, and Justice in Matthew.* Maryknoll, N.Y.: Orbis Books, 1988.

Daube, D. *The New Testament and Rabbinic Judaism.* London: Athlone, 1956.

Davies, S. "The Christology and Protology of the *Gospel of Thomas*." *JBL* 111 (1992): 663–82.

———. *The Gospel of Thomas and Christian Wisdom.* New York: Seabury, 1983.

Davies, W. D. *Setting of the Sermon on the Mount.* Cambridge: Cambridge University Press, 1966.

Davies, W. D., and D. C. Allison Jr. *A Critical and Exegetical Commentary on the Gospel According to Saint Matthew.* Vol. 1: *Introduction and Commentary on Matthew I–VII.* ICC. Edinburgh: T. and T. Clark, 1988.

———. *A Critical and Exegetical Commentary on the Gospel According to Saint Matthew.* Vol. 2: *Commentary on Matthew VIII–XVIII.* ICC. Edinburgh: T. and T. Clark, 1991.

Davison, J. E. "*Anomia* and the Question of an Antinomian Polemic in Matthew." *JBL* 184 (1985): 617–35.

Desjardins, M. "Law in II Baruch and IV Ezra." *SR* 14 (1985): 25–38.

Deubner, L. "Personifikation abstrakter Begriffe." *Ausführliches Lexikon der griechischen und römischen Mythologie* 3, 2. Leipzig: B. G. Teubner, 1897–1907.

Deutsch, C. *Hidden Wisdom and the Easy Yoke: Wisdom, Torah and Discipleship in Matthew 11.25–30.* JSNTSS 18. Sheffield, England: Sheffield Academic Press, 1987.

———. "The Sirach 51 Acrostic: Confession and Exhortation." *ZAW* 94 (1982): 400–409.

———. "Transformation of Symbols: The New Jerusalem in Rv 21:1–22:5." *ZNW* 78 (1987).

———. "Wisdom in Matthew: Transformation of a Symbol." *NovT* 32 (1990): 13–47.

Di Lella, A. A. "Conservative and Progressive Theology: Sirach and Wisdom." *CBQ* 38 (1966): 139–54.

Dimitrovsky, H. Z., ed. *Exploring the Talmud.* Vol. 1: *Education.* New York: KTAV, 1976.

Dobschütz, E. von. "Matthäus als Rabbi und Katechet." *ZNW* 27 (1928): 338–48.

Dodd, C. H. *The Interpretation of the Fourth Gospel.* Cambridge: Cambridge University Press, 1968.

Donaldson, T. L. *Jesus on the Mountain: A Study in Matthean Theology.* JSNTSS 8. Sheffield, England: JSOT Press, 1985.

Douglas, M. *Natural Symbols: Explorations in Cosmology.* 2nd ed. London: Barrie and Jenkins, 1973.

Doyle, B. R. "Matthew's Intention as Discerned by His Structure." *RB 95* (1988): 34–54.

———. "Matthew's Wisdom: A Redaction-Critical Study of Matthew 11:1–14:3a." Ph.D. dissertation, University of Melbourne, 1984.

Duling, D. "Solomon, Exorcism, and the Son of David." *HTR* 68 (1975): 235–52.

———. "The Therapeutic Son of David: An Element in Matthew's Christological Apologetic." *NTS* 24 (1978): 392–410.

Dungan, D. L. *The Interrelations of the Gospels: A Symposium Led by M. E. Boismard, W. R. Farmer, F. Neirynck, Jerusalem 1984.* BETL 95. Macon, Ga.: Mercer University Press, 1990.

Dupont, J. "La révélation du Fils de Dieu en faveur de Pierre (Mt 16, 17) et de Paul (Gal 1, 16)." *RSR* 52 (1964): 411–20.

Eisenstadt, S. N. *The Political Systems of Empires.* New Brunswick, N.J.: Transaction, 1993.

Elbogen, I. *Der jüdische Gottesdienst in seiner geschichtlichen Entwicklung.* Leipzig: Gustav Fock, 1913.

Elder, L. B. "The Woman Question and Female Ascetics among Essenes." *BA* 57 (1994): 220–34.

Engelsman, J. C. *The Feminine Dimension of the Divine.* Philadelphia: Westminster, 1979.

Evans, G. " 'Gates' and 'Streets': Urban Institutions in O.T. Times." *JRH* 2 (1963/63): 1–12.

Fascher, E. "Jesus der Lehrer: Ein Beitrag zur Frage nach dem 'Quellort der Kirchenidee.' " *TLZ* 79 (1954): 325–42.

Fawcett, T. *The Symbolic Language of Religion: An Introduction.* London: SCM, 1970.

Fears, J. R. "The Cult of Virtues and Roman Imperial Ideology." *ANRW* II.17.2 (1981): 827–948.

Finkelstein, L. "The Development of the Amidah." *JQR* n.s. 16 (1925–26): 1–43, 127–70.

Finley, M. I. *The Ancient Greeks.* New York: Penguin, 1991.

Fitzmyer, J. *The Gospel According to Luke (I–IX).* AB 28. Garden City, N.Y.: Doubleday, 1981.

———. "The Use of Explicit Old Testament Quotations in the Qumran Literature and in the New Testament." In *Essays on the Semitic Background of the New Testament,* ed. Fitzmyer, 3–58. Sources for Biblical Study 5. Missoula, Mont.: Scholars Press, 1975.

Flusser, D., and S. Safrai. "The Essene Doctrine of Hypostasis and Rabbi Meir." *Immanuel* 14 (1982): 47–57.

Fournier-Bidoz, A. "L'arbre et la demeure: Siracide XXIV 10–17." *VT* 34 (1984): 1–10.

Fraade, S. D. "Ascetical Aspects of Ancient Judaism." In *Jewish Spirituality*, vol. 1: *From the Bible to the Middle Ages*, ed. A. Green, 253–88. New York: Crossroad, 1986.

———. *From Tradition to Commentary: Torah and Its Interpretation in the Midrash Sifre to Deuteronomy*. Albany: State University of New York Press, 1991.

Frankemölle, H. "Amtskritik im Matthäus-Evangelium." *Biblica* 54 (1973): 247–62

Fraser, P. M. *Ptolemaic Alexandria*. 3 vols. Oxford: Clarendon, 1972.

Freyne, S. "The Disciples in Mark and the Mashilim in Daniel." *JSNT* 16 (1983): 7–23.

———. *Galilee from Alexander the Great to Hadrian, 323 B.C.E. to 135 C.E.: A Study of Second Temple Judaism*. Wilmington, Del.: Michael Glazier, 1980.

Frye, N. *The Great Code: The Bible and Literature*. San Diego: Harvest/HBJ, 1983.

Frymer-Kensky, T. *In the Wake of the Goddesses: Women, Culture, and the Biblical Transformation of Pagan Myth*. New York: Free Press, 1992.

Gager, J. G. *Kingdom and Community: The Social World of Early Christianity*. Englewood Cliffs, N.J.: Prentice-Hall, 1975.

———. *The Origins of Anti-Semitism: Attitudes Toward Judaism in Pagan and Christian Antiquity*. New York: Oxford University Press, 1985

Gammie, J. G. "The Classification, Stages of Growth and Changing Intentions in the Book of Daniel." *JBL* 95 (1976): 91–204.

———. "The Sage in Sirach." In *The Sage*, ed. Gammie and Perdue, 355–72.

Gammie, J. G., and L. G. Perdue, eds. *The Sage in Israel and the Ancient Near East*. Winona Lake, Ind.: Eisenbrauns, 1990.

Garland, D. *The Intention of Matthew 23*. NovTSup 52. Leiden: Brill, 1979.

Geertz, C. "Ethos, World View and the Analysis of Sacred Symbols." In Geertz, *Interpretation of Cultures*, 126–41.

———. *The Interpretation of Cultures: Selected Essays by Clifford Geertz*. New York: Basic Books, 1973.

———. "Religion as a Cultural System." In Geertz, *Interpretation of Cultures*, 87–125.

———. "Ritual and Social Change: A Javanese Example." In Geertz, *Interpretation of Cultures*, 142–69.

Gellner, E. "Patrons and Clients." In *Patrons and Clients in Mediterranean Societies*, ed. Gellner and Waterbury, 1–6.

Gellner, E., and J. Waterbury, eds. *Patrons and Clients in Mediterranean Societies*. London: G. Duckworth, 1977.

Georgi, D. "Weisheit Salomos." In *Jüdische Schriften aus hellenistisch-römischer Zeit*, bd. 3, t. 4., ed. W. G. Kümmel et al., 391–478. Gütersloh: Gütersloher Verlagshaven Gerd Mohn, 1980.

Gerhardsson, B. "The Seven Parables in Matthew XIII." *NTS* 19 (1972–73): 16–37.

Gervaryahu, H. M. "Privathäuser als Versammhungstälten von Meister und Jüngern." *ASTI* 12 (1983): 5–12

Gilbert, M. "Le discours de la Sagesse en Proverbes, 8. Structure et cohérence." In *La sagesse de l'Ancien Testament*, ed. M. Gilbert, 202–18. Gembloux: Duculot, 1979.

Glatzer, N. *Hillel the Elder: The Emergence of Classical Judaism.* New York: Schocken, 1970.

Glombitza, O. "Das Zeichen des Jona (zum Verständnis von Matth. xii. 38–42." *NTS* 8 (1961–62): 359–66.

Gnilka, J. *Das Matthäusevangelism.* 2 vols. Freiburg: Herder, 1986, 1988.

———. "Die Kirche des Matthäus und die Gemeinde von Qumran." *BZ* 7 (1963): 43–63.

Goldberg, A. M. *Untersuchungen über die Vorstellung von der Schekinah in der frühen rabbinischen Literatur.* StJud 5. Berlin: de Gruyter, 1969.

Goldin, J. "A Philosophical Session in a Tannaitic Academy." In *Exploring the Talmud*, ed. Dimitrovsky, 1:357–77.

———. "Several Sidelights of a Torah Education in Tannaitic and Early Amoraic Times." In *Exploring the Talmud*, ed. Dimitrovsky, 1:176–91.

Goodblatt, D. "The Beruriah Traditions." *JJS* 26 (1975): 68–85.

Goodenough, E. R. *By Light, Light: The Mystic Gospel of Hellenistic Judaism.* New Haven: Yale University Press, 1935.

Gordis, R. *The Book of God and Man.* Chicago: University of Chicago Press, 1965.

———. *The Book of Job: Commentary, New Translation and Special Studies.* New York: Jewish Theological Seminary of America, 1978.

Gottwald, Norman K. *The Hebrew Bible — A Socio-Literary Introduction.* Philadelphia: Fortress, 1985.

Grant, M. *From Alexander to Cleopatra: The Hellenistic World.* New York: Scribner's, 1982.

Green, W. S. "Palestinian Holy Men: Charismatic Leadership and Rabbinic Tradition." *ANRW* II.19.2 (1979): 619–47.

Greenfield, J. C., and M. E. Stone. "The Books of Enoch and the Traditions of Enoch." *Numen* 26 (1979): 89–103.

Grelot, P. "La légende d'Hénoch dans les apocryphes at dans la bible: origine et significance." *RSR* 46 (1958): 5–26, 181–210.

———. "Sur cette pierre je bâtirai mon Eglise (Mt 16, 186)." *NRT* 109 (1987): 641–59.

Gruenwald, I. *Apocalyptic and Merkavah Mysticism.* Leiden: Brill, 1980.

———. *From Apocalypticism to Gnosticism.* Frankfurt: Peter Lang, 1988.

Grözinger, K. E. "Singen und Ekstatische Sprache in der frühen jüdische Mystik." *JSJ* 11 (1980): 66–77.

Gundry, R. H. *Matthew: A Commentary on His Literary and Theological Art.* Grand Rapids, Mich.: Eerdmans, 1982.

———. *The Use of the Old Testament in St. Matthew's Gospel, with Special Reference to the Messianic Hope.* NovTSup 18. Leiden: Brill, 1967.

Gutman, S. "The Synagogue at Gamla." In *Ancient Synagogues Revealed*, ed. L. I. Levine, 30–34. Jerusalem: Israel Exploration Society, 1981.

Guttmann, A. "The Significance of Miracles for Talmudic Judaism." *HUCA* 20 (1947): 363–406.

Habel, N. C. "The Symbolism of Wisdom in Proverbs 1–9." *Int* 26 (1972): 131–57.

Hadas, M. and M. Smith. *Heroes and Gods.* New York: Harper and Row, 1965.

Haenchen, E. "Matthäus 23." *ZTK* 48 (1951): 38–63.

Halivni, D. "Whoever Studies Laws." *Proceedings of the Rabbinical Assembly* 41 (1979): 298–303.

Halperin, D. J. *The Faces of the Chariot: Early Jewish Responses to Ezekiel's Vision.* Texte und Studien zum Antiken Jüdischen 16. Tübingen: Mohr/ Siebeck, 1988.

———. *The Merkabah in Rabbinic Literature.* American Oriental Series 62. New Haven: American Oriental Society, 1980.

———. "Merkabah Midrash in the Septuagint." *JBL* 101 (1982): 351–63.

Halpern-Amaru, B. "The Killing of the Prophets: Unraveling a Midrash." *HUCA* 54 (1983): 153–80.

———. "Portraits of Women in Pseudo-Philo's *Biblical Antiquities.*" In *"Women Like This,"* ed. Levine, 83–106.

Hamdorf, F. W. *Griechischen Kultpersonifikationen der vorhellenistischen Zeit.* Mainz: Philipp von Zabern, 1964.

Hamerton-Kelly, R. G. "Attitudes to the Law in Matthew's Gospel: A Discussion of Matthew 5:18." *BR* 17 (1972): 23.

———. *Pre-Existence, Wisdom and the Son of Man: A Study of the Idea of Pre-Existence in the New Testament.* SNTSMS 21. Cambridge: Cambridge University Press, 1973.

Haran, M. "Behind the Scenes of History: Determining the Date of the Priestly Source." *SBL* 100 (1981): 321–33.

———. "Book-Scrolls in Israel in Pre-Exilic Times." *JJS* 33 (1982): 161–73.

Hare, D. R. A. *The Theme of Jewish Persecution of Christians in the Gospel According to St. Matthew.* SNTSMS 6. Cambridge: Cambridge University Press, 1967.

Harnack, A. *Sprüche und Reden Jesu: die zweite Quelle des Matthäus und Lukas.* BENT 2. Leipzig: Hinrichs, 1907.

Harrelson, W. "Wisdom Hidden and Revealed According to Baruch (Baruch 3.9–4.4)." In *Priests, Prophets and Scribes: Essays on the Formation and Heritage of Second Temple Judaism in Honour of Joseph Blenkinsopp,* ed. E. Ulrich et al., 158–71. JSOTSS 149. Sheffield, England: JSOT Press, 1992.

Harrington, D. J. *The Gospel of Matthew.* Sacra Pagina 1. Collegeville, Minn.: Michael Glazier/Liturgical Press, 1991.

Harris, S. L. "Wisdom or Creation? A New Interpretation of Job XXVIII:27." *VT* 33, no. 4 (1983): 419–27.

Harris, W. V. *Ancient Literacy.* Cambridge: Harvard University Press, 1989.

Hartmann, L. F., and A. A. Di Lella. *The Book of Daniel.* Garden City, N.Y.: Doubleday, 1978.

Haspecker, J. *Gottesfurcht Bei Jesus Sirach: Ihre Religiöse Struktur und Ihre Literarische und Doktrinäre Bedeutung.* AnBib 30. Rome: Pontifical Biblical Institute, 1969.

Heil, J. P. "The Narrative Roles of the Women in Matthew's Genealogy." *Biblica* 38 (1992): 538–45.

Heinemann, J. *Prayer in the Talmud.* StJud 9. Berlin: de Gruyter, 1977.

Held, H. J. "Matthew as Interpreter of the Miracle Stories." In Bornkamm et al., *Tradition and Interpretation in Matthew*, 165–299.

Hengel, M. *The Charismatic Leader and His Followers.* Translated by James Greig. New York: Crossroad, 1981.

———. "Jesus als messianischer Lehrer der Weisheit und die Anfänge der Christologie." In *Sagesse et Religion, Colloque de Strasbourg, 1976*, 147–90. Travaux de Centre d'Études Supérieures spécialisé d'Histoire des Religions de Strasbourg. Paris: Presses Universitaires de France, 1979.

———. *Judaism and Hellenism: Studies in Their Encounter in Palestine during the Early Hellenistic Period.* 2 vols. Translated by J. Bowden. Philadelphia: Fortress, 1974.

———. "Zur matthäische Bergpredigt und ihrem jüdische Hintergrund." *TRu* 52 (1987): 327–400.

Henle, P. "Metaphor." In *Language, Thought and Culture*, ed. Henle, 173–95. Ann Arbor: University of Michigan Press, 1958.

Hicks, J. M. "The Sabbath Controversy in Matthew: An Exegesis of Matthew 12:1–14." *ResQ* 27 (1984): 79–91.

Hill, D. "ΔIKAIOI as a Quasi-Technical Term." *NTS* 11 (1964/65): 296–302.

———. "False Prophets and Charismatics: Structure and Interpretation in Matthew 7, 15–23." *Biblica* 57 (1976): 327–48.

———. *The Gospel of Matthew.* New Century Bible. Grand Rapids, Mich.: Eerdmans, 1972.

———. *New Testament Prophecy.* London: Marshall, Morgan and Scott, 1979.

Himmelfarb, M. *Ascent to Heaven in Jewish and Christian Apocalypses.* New York: Oxford University Press, 1993.

Hoffman, L. *The Canonization of the Synagogue Service.* CSJCA 4. Notre Dame, Ind.: University of Notre Dame Press, 1979.

Hoffmann, P. "Der Petrus-Primat im Matthäusevangelism." In *Neues Testament und Kirche: für Rudolf Schmachenburg*, ed. J. Gnilka, 94–114. Freiburg: Herder, 1974.

———. *Studien zur Theologie der Logienquelle.* NTAbh 8. Münster: Aschendorff, 1972.

Holladay, C. R. *THEIOS ANER in Hellenistic Judaism: A Critique of the Use of This Category in New Testament Christology.* SBLDS 40. Missoula, Mont.: Scholars Press, 1977.

Hoppe, L. *The Synagogues and Churches of Ancient Palestine.* Collegeville, Minn.: Michael Glazier/Liturgical Press, 1994.

Horsley, R. A. " 'Like One of the Prophets of Old': Two Types of Popular Prophets at the Time of Jesus." *CBQ* 47 (1985): 435–63.

———. "Spiritual Marriage with Sophia." *VC* 33 (1979): 30–54.

Hubbard, B. J. *The Matthaean Redaction of a Primitive Apostolic Commissioning.* SBLDS 19. Missoula, Mont.: Scholars Press, 1974.

Idel, M. *Kabbalah: New Perspectives.* New Haven: Yale University Press, 1988.

Ingelaere, J. C. "L'inspiration prophétique dans le judaisme: Le démoignage de Flavius Josèphe." *ETR* 62 (1987): 237–45.

Irigaray, L. "Questions to Emmanuel Levinas on the Divinity of Love." Translated by M. Whitford. In *Re-Reading Levinas*, ed. R. Bernasconi and S. Critchley, 109–18. Bloomington: Indiana University Press, 1991.

Isenberg, S. R. "Power Through Temple and Torah in Greco-Roman Palestine." In *Christianity, Judaism and Other Graeco-Roman Cults*, pt. 2, *Early Christianity*, ed. J. Neusner, 24–52. Leiden: Brill, 1975.

Jacobson, A. D. "The Literary Unity of Q." *JBL* 101 (1982): 365–89.

Jansen, H. L. *Die Henochgestalt: Eine vergleichende religionsgeschichtliche Untersuchung*. Oslo: Kommisjon Hos Jacob Dybwad, 1939.

Jeremias, J. *Jerusalem in the Time of Jesus: An Investigation into Economic and Social Conditions during the New Testament Period*. Translated by F. H. Cave and C. H. Cave. London: SCM, 1969.

Johnson, E. A. *She Who Is: The Mystery of God in Feminist Theological Discourse*. New York: Crossroad, 1992.

Johnson, L. T. "The New Testament's Anti-Jewish Slander and the Conventions of Ancient Polemic." *JBL* 108 (1989): 419–41.

Johnson, M. D. "Reflections on a Wisdom Approach to Matthew's Christology." *CBQ* 36 (1974): 44–64.

Judge, E. A. "The Early Christians as a Scholastic Community." *JRH* 1 (1960–61): 4–15, 125–37.

Kähler, C. "Zur Form- und Traditionsgeschichte von Matt xvi, 17–19." *NTS* 23 (1976–77): 36–58.

Käsemann, E. "The Beginning of Christian Theology." In *New Testament Questions of Today*, trans. W. J. Montague, 1–22. Philadelphia: Fortress, 1969.

———. "Sätze Heiligen Rechtes im Neuen Testament." *NTS* 1 (1954/55): 248–60.

Katz, S. "Issues in the Separation of Judaism and Christianity after 70 C.E.: A Reconsideration." *JBL* 103 (1984): 43–76.

Kautsky, J. H. *The Politics of Aristocratic Empires*. Chapel Hill: University of North Carolina Press, 1982.

Kayatz, C. *Studien zu Proverbien 1–9: eine form und motivgeschichtliche Untersuchung Einbeziehung ägyptischen Vergleichsmaterials*. WMANT 22. Neukirchen-Vluyn: Neukirchener Verlag, 1966.

Kiilunen, J. "Der nachfolgewillige Schriftgelehrte: Matthäus 8.19–20 im Verständnis des Evangelisten." *NTS* 37 (1991): 268–79.

Kilpatrick, G. D. *The Origins of the Gospel According to St. Matthew*. Oxford: Clarendon, 1950.

Kimelman, R. "*Birkat ha-Minim* and the Lack of Evidence for an Anti-Christian Jewish Prayer in Late Antiquity." In *Jewish and Christian Self-Definition*, ed. Sanders et al., 2:226–44.

Kingsbury, J. D. "The Figure of Peter in Matthew's Gospel as a Theological Problem." *JBL* 98 (1979): 80.

———. *Matthew: Structure, Christology, Kingdom*. Philadelphia: Fortress, 1975.

———. "On Following Jesus: The 'Eager' Scribe and the 'Reluctant' Disciple (Matthew 8.18–22)." *NTS* 34 (1988): 45–59.

————. "The Verb *AKOLOUTHEIN* ('To Follow') as an Index of Matthew's View of His Community." *JBL* 97 (1978): 56–73.

Kirk, G. S. *The Nature of Greek Myths.* Baltimore: Penguin Books, 1974.

Kloppenborg, J. *The Formation of Q: Trajectories in Ancient Wisdom Collections.* Studies in Antiquity and Christianity. Philadelphia: Fortress, 1987.

————. "Isis and Sophia in the Book of Wisdom." *HTR* 75 (1982): 57–84.

————. "Wisdom Christology in Q." *LTP* 34 (1978): 129–47.

Klostermann, E. *Das Matthäusevangelium.* 4th ed. HNT 4. Tübingen: J. C. B. Mohr, 1971.

Knibb, M. "Apocalyptic and Wisdom in Fourth Ezra." *JSJ* 13 (1982): 56–79.

Knox, W. L. "The Divine Wisdom." *JTS* 38 (1937): 230–37.

Koester, H. *Ancient Christian Gospels: Their History and Development.* Philadelphia: Trinity Press International, 1990.

————. *Introduction to the New Testament.* Vol. 2: *History and Literature of Early Christianity.* Hermeneia Foundations and Facets. Philadelphia: Fortress, 1982.

————. *TDNT,* s.v. "ὑπόστασις."

Kohler, K. "Abba, Father: Title of Spiritual Leader and Saint." In *Exploring the Talmud,* ed. Dimitrovsky, 1:150–63.

Kraemer, R. S. *Her Share of the Blessings: Women's Religions among Pagans, Jews, and Christians in the Greco-Roman World.* New York: Oxford University Press, 1992.

————. "Monastic Jewish Women in Greco-Roman Egypt: Philo of Alexandia on the *Therapeutrides.*" *Signs* 14 (1989): 345–80.

————. "Women's Authorship of Jewish and Christian Literature in the Greco-Roman Period." In *"Women Like This,"* ed. Levine, 221–42.

Kruijf, T. de. *Der Sohn des lebendigen Gottes: Ein Beitrag zur Christologie des Matthäusevangeliums.* AnBib 16. Rome: Pontifical Biblical Institute, 1962.

Lagrange, M. J. *L'évangile selon s. Matthieu.* 4th ed. Paris: J. Gabalda, 1927.

Lang, B. *Frau Weisheit: Deutung einer biblischen Gestalt.* Düsseldorf: Patmos, 1975.

————. *Wisdom and the Book of Proverbs: A Hebrew Goddess Redefined.* New York: Pilgrim, 1986.

Larcher, C. *Études sur le livre de la Sagesse.* EBib. Paris: J. Gabalda, 1969.

Leach, E. *Culture and Communication: The Logic by Which Symbols Are Connected.* Cambridge: Cambridge University Press, 1976.

Lebram, J. C. H. "The Piety of the Jewish Apocalyptists." In *Apocalypticism in the Mediterranean World and the Near East,* ed. D. Hellholm, 171–210. 2nd ed. Tübingen: J. C. B. Mohr (Paul Siebeck), 1989.

Leeuwen, R. C. Van. "Liminality and Worldview in Proverbs 1–9." *Semeia* 50 (1990): 111–44.

Lefkowitz, M. "Did Ancient Women Write Novels?" In *"Women Like This,"* ed. Levine, 199–219.

Légasse, S. *Jésus et l'Enfant: "Enfants," "Petits," et "Simples" dans la tradition synoptique.* EBib. Paris: J. Gabalda, 1969.

————. "Scribes et disciples de Jésus." *RB* 68 (1961): 321–45, 481–506.

Lehmann, M. R. "11 Q Psa and Ben Sira." *RevQ* 11 (1983): 239–51.

Leivestad, R. "Das Dogma von der prophetenlose Zeit." *NTS* 19 (1972/73): 288–99.

Lemaire, André. "The Sage in School and Temple." In *The Sage*, ed. Gammie and Perdue, 165–81.

———. "Sagesse et écoles." *VT* 34 (1984): 270–81.

Lénhardt, P. "Voies de la continuité juive: Aspects de la relation maître-disciple d'après la littérature rabbinique ancienne." *RSR* 66 (1978): 489–516.

Lenski, G. *Power and Privilege: A Theory of Social Stratification.* New York: McGraw-Hill, 1966.

Lévi-Strauss, C. *Structural Anthropology.* Translated by C. Jacobson and B. Grundfest Schoepf. New York: Basic Books, 1963.

Levine, A.-J. *The Social and Ethnic Dimension of Matthean Salvation History: 'Go Nowhere Among the Gentiles...' (Matthew 10:6).* Lewiston, N.Y.: Mellen, 1988.

———. "Who's Catering the Q Affair? Feminist Observations on Q Paraenesis." *Semeia* 50 (1990): 145–61.

———, ed. *"Women Like This": New Perspectives on Jewish Women in the Greco-Roman World.* SBL Early Judaism and Its Literature 1. Atlanta: Scholars Press, 1991.

Levine, E. "The Sabbath Controversy According to Matthew." *NTS* 22 (1976): 480–83.

Levine, L. I. *The Rabbinic Class of Roman Palestine in Late Antiquity.* New York: Jewish Theological Seminary of America, 1989.

Lichtenberger, H. "Eine weisheitlichte Mahnrede in der Qumranfunder (4Q185)." In *Qumran: Sa piété, sa théologie et son milieu,* ed. M. Delcor, 151–62. Paris: Gembloux, 1978.

Lightstone, J. N. *The Commerce of the Sacred: Mediation of the Divine among Jews in the Graeco-Roman Diaspora.* BJS 59. Chico, Calif.: Scholars Press, 1984.

Lind, L. R. "Roman Religion and Ethical Thought: Abstraction and Personification." *CJ* 69 (1972): 108–19.

Lips, H. von. *Weisheitliche Traditionen in Neuen Testament.* WMANT 64. Neukirchen-Vluyn: Neukirchener Verlag, 1990.

Lohfink, N. "Der Messiaskönig und seine Armen Kommen zum Zion: Beobachtungen zu Mt 21,1–17." In *Studien zum Mattäusevangelium: Festschrift für Wilhelm Pesch,* ed. Ludger Schenke, 177–200. Stuttgart: Katholisches Bibelwerk, 1988.

Lohmeyer, E. *Das Evangelium des Matthäus.* Göttingen: Vandenhoeck and Ruprecht, 1956.

Lohse, E. "Ich aber sage auch." In *Der Ruf Jesu und die Antwort der Gemeinde: Exegetische Untersuchungen Joachim Jeremias,* ed. Lohse, 189–203. Göttingen: Vandenhoeck and Ruprecht, 1970.

Lührmann, D. *Die Redaktion der Logienquelle.* WMANT 33. Neukirchen-Vluyn: Neukirchener Verlag, 1969.

Luz, U. *Das Evangelium nach Matthäus.* 2 vols. EKKNT. Neukirchen: Neukirchener Verlag, 1985, 1990.

———. "Die Jünger im Matthäusevangelium." *ZNW* 62 (1971): 141–71.

————. *Matthew 1–7: A Commentary.* Translated by Wilhelm C. Linss. Minneapolis: Augsburg, 1989.

McCreesh, T. P. "Wisdom as Wife: Proverbs 31:10–31." *RB* 92 (1985): 25–46.

McEleney, N. J. "The Principles of the Sermon on the Mount." *CBQ* 41 (1979): 552–70.

McFague, S. *Metaphorical Theology: Models of God in Religious Language.* Philadelphia: Fortress, 1982.

————. *Speaking in Parables: A Study in Metaphor and Theology.* Philadelphia: Fortress, 1975.

Mack, B. L. *Logos und Sophia: Untersuchungen zur Weisheitstheologie im hellenistischen Judentum.* SUNT 10. Gottingen: Vandenhoeck and Ruprecht, 1973.

————. "Wisdom and Apocalyptic in Philo." In *Studia Philonica Annual 1991*, ed. David T. Runia, 3:21–39. Studies in Hellenistic Judaism. Atlanta: Scholars Press, 1991.

————. "Wisdom Myth and Myth-ology." *Int* 24 (1970): 46–60.

McKane, W. *Proverbs: A New Approach.* Philadelphia: Westminster, 1970.

MacMullen, R. *Roman Social Relations, 50 B.C. to A.D. 284.* New Haven: Yale University Press, 1974.

McNeile, A. H. *The Gospel According to St. Matthew.* New York: Macmillan, 1915; rpt., Grand Rapids, Mich.: Baker, 1980.

Malherbe, A. J. *Moral Exhortation: A Greco-Roman Sourcebook.* Library of Early Christianity 4. Philadelphia: Westminster, 1989.

————. *Paul and the Popular Philosophers.* Minneapolis: Fortress, 1989.

Malina, B. "The Literary Structure and Form of Matt. XXVIII.16–20." *NTS* 17 (1970): 87–103.

————. *The New Testament World: Insights from Cultural Anthropology.* Atlanta: John Knox, 1981.

————. "The Social Sciences and Biblical Interpretation." In *The Bible and Liberation: Political and Social Hermeneutics*, ed. N. K. Gottwald, 11–25. Maryknoll, N.Y.: Orbis, 1983.

Manson, T. W. *The Sayings of Jesus.* London: SCM, 1949.

Marbock, J. "Gesetz und Weisheit: Zum Verständnis des Gesetzes bei Jesus Ben Sira." *BZ*, n.f. 20 (1976): 1–21.

Marcus, J. "The Gates of Hades and the Keys of the Kingdom (Matt 16:18–19)." *CBQ* 50 (1988): 443–55.

Marrou, H.-I. *Histoire de l'éducation dans l'antiquité.* 2nd edition. Paris: Éditions du Seuíl, 1950.

Mason, S. *Flavius Josephus on the Pharisees: A Composition-Critical Study.* Leiden: Brill, 1990.

————. "Priesthood in Josephus and the 'Pharisaic Revolution.'" *JBL* 107 (1988): 657–61.

Meeks, W. A. *The First Urban Christians: The Social World of the Apostle Paul.* New Haven: Yale University Press, 1983.

————. "The Image of the Androgyne: Some Uses of a Symbol in Earliest Christianity." *HR* 13 (1974): 165–208.

————. *The Moral World of the First Christians*. Library of Early Christianity 6. Philadelphia: Westminster, 1986.

Meeks, W. A., and R. A. Wilken. *Jews and Christians in Antioch in the First Four Centuries of the Common Era*. Missoula, Mont.: Scholars Press, 1978.

Meier, J. *Law and History in Matthew's Gospel*. AnBib 71. Rome: Pontifical Biblical Institute, 1976.

————. *The Vision of Matthew: Christ, Church and Morality in the First Gospel*. New York: Paulist Press, 1979.

Michaelis, W. *Das Evangelium nach Matthäus*. 2 vols. Zürich: Zwingli, 1949.

Middendorp, T. *Die Stellung Jesu Ben Siras zwischen Judentum und Hellenismus*. Leiden: Brill, 1973.

Mielziner, M. *Introduction to the Talmud*. 5th ed. New York: Bloch, 1968.

Miller, R. J. "The Rejection of the Prophets in Q." *JBL* 107 (1988): 225–40.

Minear, P. S. "False Prophecy and Hypocrisy in the Gospel of Matthew." In *Neues Testament und Kirche: für Rudolf Schnackenburg*, ed. J. Gnilka, 76–93. Freiburg: Herder, 1974.

————. *Matthew: The Teacher's Gospel*. New York: Pilgrim Press, 1982.

Moi, T. *Sexual/Textual Politics: Feminist Literary Theory*. 1985; rpt., London: Routledge, 1991.

Moore, G. F. *Judaism in the First Centuries of the Christian Era: The Age of the Tannaim*. 3 vols. Cambridge: Harvard University Press, 1927, 1930; rpt., New York: Shocken, 1971.

Morenz, S. *Egyptian Religion*. Translated by Ann E. Keep. London: Methuen, 1973.

Morosco, R. E. "Matthew's Formation of a Commissioning Type-Scene." *JBL* 103 (1984): 539–56.

Muraska, T. "Sir 51: 13–30: An Erotic Hymn to Wisdom?" *JSJ* 10 (1979): 166–78.

Murphy, F. J. "Sapiential Elements in the Syriac Apocalypse of Baruch." *JQR* 48 (1986): 311–27.

————. *The Structure and Meaning of Second Baruch*. SBLDS 78. Atlanta: Scholars Press, 1985.

Murphy, R. E. "Wisdom's Song: Proverbs 1:20–33." *CBQ* 48 (1986): 456–60.

Myers, J. M. *I Chronicles*. AB 12. Garden City, N.Y.: Doubleday, 1965.

————. *II Chronicles*. AB 13. Garden City, N.Y.: Doubleday, 1965.

————. *Ezra, Neremiah*. AB 14. Garden City, N.Y.: Doubleday, 1965.

————. *I and II Esdras*. AB 42. Garden City, N.Y.: Doubleday, 1974.

Neusner, J. *Development of a Legend: Studies on the Traditions Concerning Yohanan ben Zakkai*. Leiden: Brill, 1970.

————. *First-Century Judaism in Crisis: Johanan ben Zakkai and the Renaissance of Torah*. Nashville: Abingdon, 1975.

————. "'First Cleanse the Inside': The 'Halakhic' Background of a Controversy-Saying." *NTS* 22 (1976): 486–95.

————. *There We Sat Down: Talmudic Judaism in the Making*. Nashville: Abingdon, 1972.

Newman, B. "The Pilgrimage of Christ-Sophia." *Vox Benedictina* 9 (1992): 9–37.

Newsom, C. A. "The Development of 1 Enoch 6–19: Cosmology and Judgment." *CBQ* 42 (1980): 310–29.

———. "Merkabah Exegesis in the Qumran Sabbath Shirot." *JJS* 38 (1987): 11–30.

———. "The Sage in the Literature of Qumran." In *The Sage*, ed. Gammie and Perdue, 373–82.

———. *Songs of the Sabbath Sacrifice: A Critical Edition.* HSS 27. Atlanta: Scholars Press, 1985.

———. "Woman and the Discourse of Patriarchal Wisdom: A Study of Proverbs 1–9." In *Gender and Difference in Ancient Israel*, ed. Peggy L. Day, 142–60. Minneapolis: Fortress, 1989.

Nickelsburg, G. W. E. "The Apocalyptic Message of 1 Enoch 92–105." *CBQ* 39 (1977): 309–28.

———. "Enoch, Levi, and Peter: Recipients of Revelation in Upper Galilee." *JBL* 100 (1981): 575–600.

———. "The Epistle of Enoch and the Qumran Literature." *JJS* 33 (1982): 333–48.

———. *Jewish Literature between the Bible and the Mishnah: A Historical and Literary Introduction.* Philadelphia: Fortress, 1981.

———. "Riches, the Rich and God's Judgment in Enoch 92–105 and the Gospel According to Luke." *NTS* 25 (1978–79): 324–44.

Niditch, S. "The Visionary." In *Ideal Figures in Ancient Judaism: Profiles and Paradigms*, ed. J. J. Collins and G. W. E. Nickelsburg, 153–79. Chico, Calif.: SBL, 1980.

Nilsson, M. P. *Geschichte der griechischen Religion.* Vol. 2: *Die hellenistische und römische Zeit.* Munich: C. H. Beck'sche Buchhandlung, 1950.

———. "Kultische Personifikationen." *Eranos* 50 (1952): 31–40.

Nock, A. D. *Conversion: The Old and the New in Religion from Alexander the Great to Augustine of Hippo.* Oxford: Oxford University Press, 1963.

———. "The Cult of Heroes." In *Essays on Religion and the Ancient World*, ed. Stewart, 2:575–602.

———. "The Emperor's Divine Comes." In *Essays on Religion and the Ancient World*, 2:653–75.

———. *Essays on Religion and the Ancient World.* 2 vols. Edited by Zeph. Stewart. Cambridge: Harvard University Press, 1972.

———. "Notes on Ruler-Culture I–IV." In *Essays on Religion and the Ancient World*, ed. Stewart, 1:134–57.

———. "Religious Attitudes of the Ancient Greeks." In *Essays on Religion and the Ancient World*, ed. Stewart, 2:534–50.

———. "Ruler-Worship and Syncretism." In *Essays on Religion and the Ancient World*, ed. Stewart, 2:551–58.

Norden, E. *Agnostos Theos: Untersuchungen zur Formengeschichte religiöser Reden.* Leipzig: Teubner, 1913.

Olivier, J. P. J. "Schools and Wisdom Literature." *JNSL* 4 (1975): 49–60.

Orton, D. E. *The Understanding Scribe: Matthew and the Apocalyptic Ideal.* JSNTSS 25. Sheffield, England: Sheffield Academic Press, 1989.

Overman, J. A. *Matthew's Gospel and Formative Judaism: The Social World of the Matthean Community.* Minneapolis: Fortress, 1990.

Pamment, M. "The Son of Man in the First Gospel." *NTS* 29 (1983): 116–29.

Pautrel, R. "Ben Sira et le stoïcisme." *RSR* 51 (1963): 535–49.

Peek, Werner. *Der Isishymnus von Andros: und verwandte Texte.* Berlin: Weidmannsche Buchhandlung, 1930.

Pembroke, S. "Women in Charge: The Function of Alternatives in Early Greek Tradition and the Ancient Idea of Matriarchy." *Journal of the Warburg and Courtauld Institutes* 30 (1967): 1–35.

Perdue, L. G. "Liminality as a Social Setting for Wisdom Instructions." *ZAW* 93 (1981): 114–26.

Perrin, N. *Jesus and the Language of the Kingdom: Symbol and Metaphor in New Testament Interpretation.* Philadelphia: Fortress, 1976.

———. *Rediscovering the Teaching of Jesus.* New York: Harper and Row, 1976.

Perrine, L. *Sound and Sense: An Introduction to Poetry.* 6th ed. San Diego: Harcourt Brace Jovanovich, 1982.

Pervo, R. I. "Aseneth and Her Sisters: Women in Jewish Narrative and in the Greek Novels." In *"Women Like This,"* ed. Levine, 145–60.

Plöger, O. *Sprüche Salomos (Proverbia).* BKAT 17. Neukirchen-Vluyn: Neukirchener Verlag, 1984.

Plummer, A. *An Exegetical Commentary on the Gospel According to S. Matthew.* London: Elliott Stock, 1909.

Pomeroy, S. B. *Women in Hellenistic Egypt: From Alexander to Cleopatra.* New York: Schocken, 1984.

Pope, M. *Job.* AB 15. Garden City, N.Y.: Doubleday, 1965.

Pregeant, R. "The Wisdom Passages in Matthew's Story." *SBL Seminar Papers* (1990): 469–93.

Preiss, T. "Jésus et la Sagesse." *ETR* 28 (1953): 69–75.

Puech, E. "Un hymne essénien en partie retrouvé et les béatitudes, 1 QH V 12–VI 18 (= col XIII–XIV 7) et 4QBeat." *RevQ* 13 (1988): 59–88.

Rad, G. Von. *Wisdom in Israel.* Translated by J. D. Martin. Nashville: Abingdon, 1981.

Ramlot, F. M. "Autour de la mystique juive du thrône divin." *ETR* 59 (1984): 71–76.

Rawson, E. *Intellectual Life in the Late Roman Republic.* Baltimore: Johns Hopkins University Press, 1985.

Reddit, P. L. "The Concept of *Nomos* in Fourth Maccabees." *CBQ* 45 (1983): 249–70.

Reese, J. M. *Hellenistic Influence on the Book of Wisdom and Its Consequences.* AnBib 41. Rome: Pontifical Biblical Institute, 1970.

———. "How Matthew Portrays the Communication of Christ's Authority." *BTB* 7 (1977): 141.

Reider, J. *The Book of Wisdom.* New York: Harper and Brothers, 1957.

Reiling, J. "The Use of ΨΕΥΔΟΠΡΟΦΗΤΗΣ in the LXX, Philo and Josephus." *NovT* 13 (1971): 147–56.

Reinhardt, K. "Personifikation und Allegorie." In *Vermächtnis der Antike: Gesammelte Essays zum Philosophie und Geschichtschreiburg*, ed. C. Becker, 7–40. Göttingen: Vandenhoeck and Ruprecht, 1960.

Renov, I. "The Seat of Moses." *IEJ* 5 (1955): 262–67.

Riaud, J. "Quelques réflexions sur les Thérapeutes d'Alexandrie à la lumière de De Vita Mosis II, 67." *Studia Philonica Annual* 3 (1991): 184–91.

Richards, I. A. *The Philosophy of Rhetoric*. New York: Oxford University Press, 1936.

Ricoeur, P. *La métaphore vive*. Paris: Éditions du Seuil, 1975.

Ringgren, H. "Hypostasen." *RGG* 4 (1959), vol. 3, cols. 504–6.

———. *Word and Wisdom: Studies in the Hypostatization of Divine Qualities and Functions in the ANE*. Lund: Hakan Ohlssons Bokmyekeri, 1947.

Robinson, B. P. "Peter and His Successors: Tradition and Redaction in Matthew 16.17–19." *JSNT* 21 (1984): 85–104.

Robinson, J. "Basic Shifts in German Theology." *Int* 16 (1962): 76–97.

———. "Die Hodajot-Formel in Gebet und Hymnus des Frühchristentums." In *Apophoreta: Festschrift für Ernst Haenchen*, ed. W. Eltester and F. H. Kettler, 194–235. BZNW 30. Berlin: A. Töpelmann, 1964.

———. "Jesus as Sophos and Sophia." In *Aspects of Wisdom in Judaism and Early Christianity*, ed. R. L. Wilken, 1–16. CSJCA 1. Notre Dame, Ind.: University of Notre Dame Press, 1975.

———. "Very Goddess and Very Man: Jesus' Better Self." In *Images of the Feminine in Gnosticism*, ed. K. King, 113–27. Studies in Antiquity and Christianity. Philadelphia: Fortress, 1988.

Rosaldo, M. Zimbalist. "Woman, Culture and Society: A Theoretical Overview." In *Woman, Culture and Society*, ed. M. Zimbalist Rosaldo and L. Lamphere, 17–42. Stanford, Calif.: Stanford University Press, 1974.

Rose, H. J. *A Handbook of Greek Mythology*. New York: Dutton, 1959.

Rowland, C. "The Visions of God in Apocalyptic Literature." *JSJ* 10 (1979): 137–54.

Russell, D. S. *The Method and Message of Jewish Apocalyptic*. The Old Testament Library. Philadelphia: Westminster, 1976.

Sabourin, L. "Traits apocalyptiques dans l'évangile de Matthieu." *Science et Esprit* 33 (1981): 357–72.

Safrai, S. "Elementary Education, in Religious and Social Significance in the Talmudic Period." *Cahiers d'Histoire Mondiale* 11 (1968): 148–68.

Safrai, S., and M. Stern. *The Jewish People in the First Century: Historical Geography, Political History, Social, Cultural and Religious Life and Institutions*, vol. 1. Compendia Rerum Iudaicarum ad Novum Testamentum. Philadelphia: Fortress, 1974.

Saldarini, A. "Apocalypses and 'Apocalyptic' in Rabbinic Literature." *Semeia* 14 (1979): 187–205.

———. "Delegitimation of Leaders in Matthew 23." *CBQ* 54 (1992): 659–80.

———. "The Gospel of Matthew and Jewish-Christian Conflict." In *Social History of the Matthean Community*, ed. Balch, 38–61.

———. *Matthew's Christian-Jewish Community*. Chicago: University of Chicago Press, 1994.

————. *Pharisees, Scribes and Sadducees in Palestinian Society: A Sociological Approach*. Wilmington, Del.: Michael Glazier, 1988.

————. *Scholastic Rabbinism: A Literary Study of the Fathers According to Rabbi Nathan*. BJS 14. Chico, Calif.: Scholars Press, 1982.

Sand, A. "Propheten, Weise und Schriftkundige in der Gemeinde des Matthäusevangelium." In *Kirche im Werden: Studien zum Thema Amt und Gemeinde in Neuen Testament*, ed. J. Hainz, 167–84. Munich: Ferdinand Schöningh, 1976.

Sanders, E. P. *Jesus and Judaism*. Philadelphia: Fortress, 1985.

————. *Jewish Law from Jesus to the Mishnah: Five Studies*. Philadelphia: Trinity Press International, 1990.

————. *Judaism: Practice and Belief, 63 B.C.E.–66 C.E.* Philadelphia: Trinity Press International, 1992.

Sanders, E. P., A. I. Baumgarten, and A. Mendelson, eds. *Jewish and Christian Self-Definition*: Vol. 2, *Aspects of Judaism in the Graeco-Roman Period*. Philadelphia: Fortress, 1981.

Sapir, J. D. "The Anatomy of Metaphor." In *The Social Use of Metaphor: Essays on the Anthropology of Rhetoric*, ed. J. D. Sapir and J. C. Crocker, 3–32. Philadelphia: University of Pennsylvania Press, 1977.

Sayler, G. *Have the Promises Failed? A Literary Analysis of 2 Baruch*. SBLDS 72. Chico, Calif.: Scholars Press, 1984.

Schiffman, L. "Tannaitic Perspectives on the Jewish-Christian Schism." In *Jewish and Christian Self-Definition*, ed. Sanders et al., 2:115–56.

Schmidt, T. E. "Hostility to Wealth in Philo of Alexandria." *JSNT* 19 (1983): 85–97.

Schniewind, J. *Das Evangelium nach Matthäus*. NTD 2. Göttingen: Vandenhoeck and Ruprecht, 1960.

Scholem, G. E. *Jewish Gnosticism, Merkabah Mysticism and Talmudic Tradition*. New York: Jewish Theological Seminary, 1965.

————. *Major Trends in Jewish Mysticism*. New York: Scholem, 1960.

Schubert, K. "Einige Beobachtungen zum Verständnis des Logosbegriffs im frührabbinischen Schrifttum." *Judaica* 9 (1953): 65–80.

Schuler, P. L. "Philo's Moses and Matthew's Jesus: A Comparative Study in Ancient Literature." *Studia Philonica Annual* 2 (1990): 86–103.

Schuller, E. M. "Women in the Dead Sea Scrolls." In *Methods of Investigation of the Dead Sea Scrolls and the Khirbet Qumran Site: Present Realities and Future Prospects*, ed. M. O. Wise et al., 114–31. Annals of the New York Academy of Sciences 722. New York: New York Academy of Sciences, 1994.

Schürmann, H. "Wer daher eines dieser geringsten Gebote auflöst...Wo fand Matthäus das Logion Mt 5:19?" *BZ* 4 (1960): 246.

Schüssler-Fiorenza, E. *In Memory of Her: A Feminist Theological Reconstruction of Christian Origins*. New York: Crossroad, 1983.

————. *Jesus: Miriam's Child, Sophia's Prophet: Critical Issues in Feminist Christology*. New York: Continuum, 1994.

————. "The Phenomenon of Early Christian Apocalyptics: Some Reflections on Method." In *Apocalypticism in the Mediterranean World and the Near*

East, ed. D. Hellholm, 295–316. Tübingen: J. C. B. Mohr (Paul Siebeck), 1983.

Schutz, A., and T. Luckmann. *The Structures of the Life-World.* Translated by R. M. Zaner and H. T. Engelhardt Jr. Evanston, Ill.: Northwestern University Press, 1973.

Schweizer, E. *Das Evangelium nach Matthäus.* NTD 2. Göttingen: Vandenhoeck and Ruprecht, 1976.

———. *Matthäus und seine Gemeinde.* Stuttgart: KBW, 1974.

Scott, J. "Patronage or Exploitation?" In *Patrons and Clients in Mediterranean Societies*, ed. Gellner and Waterbury, 21–39.

Scott, R. B. Y. *Proverbs, Ecclesiastes.* AB 18. Garden City, N.Y.: Doubleday, 1965.

———. "Solomon and the Beginnings of Wisdom." In *Studies in Ancient Israelite Wisdom*, ed. J. L. Crenshaw, 262–79. New York: KTAV, 1976.

———. *The Way of Wisdom in the Old Testament.* New York: Macmillan, 1971.

Scroggs, R. "The Earliest Christian Communities as Sectarian Movement." In *Christianity, Judaism and Other Graeco-Roman Cults*, pt. 2, *Early Christianity*, ed. J. Neusner, 1–23. Leiden: Brill, 1975.

———. "Eschatological Existence in Matthew and Paul: *Coincidentia Oppositorum.*" In *The Text and the Times: New Testament Essays for Today*, ed. Scroggs, 234–56. Minneapolis: Fortress, 1993.

———. "The Political Dimensions of Anti-Judaism in the New Testament." Unpublished paper.

Segal, A. F. "Heavenly Ascent in Hellenistic Judaism, Early Christianity and Their Environment." *ANRW* II.2 (1980): 1333–94.

———. "Matthew's Jewish Voice." In *Social History of the Matthean Community*, ed. Balch, 3–37.

———. *Rebecca's Children: Judaism and Christianity in the Roman World.* Cambridge: Harvard University Press, 1986.

Setzer, C. *Jewish Responses to Early Christians: History and Polemics, 30–150 C.E.* Minneapolis: Fortress, 1994.

Sevenster, J. *The Roots of Pagan Anti-Semitism in the Ancient World.* NovTSup 41. Leiden: Brill, 1975.

Sheppard, G. T. "The Epilogue to Qoheleth as Theological Commentary." *CBQ* 39 (1977): 182–89.

———. *Wisdom as Hermeneutical Construct: A Study in the Sapientializing of the Old Testament.* BZAW 151. Berlin: de Gruyter, 1980.

Shuler, P. L. "Philo's Moses and Matthew's Jesus: A Comparative Study in Ancient Literature." *Studia Philonica Annual* 2 (1990): 86–103.

Shupak, N. "The 'Sitz im Leben' of Proverbs in the Light of a Comparison of Biblical and Egyptian Wisdom Literature." *RB* 94 (1987): 98–119.

Silverman, S. "Patronage as Myth." In *Patrons and Clients in Mediterranean Societies*, ed. Gellner and Waterbury, 7–19.

Sjoberg, Erik. *Der Menschensohn im Äthiopischen Henochbuch.* Acta Reg. Societatis Humaniorum Litterarum Lundensis 51. Lund: Gleerup, 1946.

Skehan, P. W. "Structures in Poems on Wisdom: Proverbs 8 and Sirach 24." *CBQ* 41 (1979): 365–79.

———. *Studies in Israelite Poetry and Wisdom*. CBQMS 1. Washington, D.C.: Catholic Biblical Association of America, 1971.

Skehan, P. W., and A. A. Di Lella. *The Wisdom of Ben Sira*. AB 39. New York: Doubleday, 1987.

Sly, D. *Philo's Perception of Women*. BJS 209. Atlanta: Scholars Press, 1990.

Smallwood, M. *The Jews under the Roman Rule*. Leiden: Brill, 1976.

Smith, J. Z. "Wisdom and Apocalyptic." In *Visionaries and Their Apocalypses*, ed. P. D. Hanson, 101–20. Philadelphia: Fortress, 1983.

Smith, M. "Ascent to the Heavens and the Beginnings of Christianity." *Eranos-jahrbuch* 50 (1981): 403–24.

———. *Clement of Alexandria and a Secret Gospel of Mark*. Cambridge: Harvard University Press, 1973.

———. *Jesus the Magician*. San Francisco: Harper and Row, 1978.

———. "On the Differences Between the Culture of Israel and the Major Cultures of the Ancient Near East." *JANESCU* 5 (1973): 389–95.

———. "The Origin and History of the Transfiguration Story." *USQR* 36 (1980): 39–44.

———. "Palestinian Judaism in the First Century." In *Israel: Its Role in Civilization*, ed. M. Davis, 67–81. New York: Jewish Theological Seminary of America, 1956.

———. *Tannaitic Parallels to the Gospels*. SBLDS 6. Philadelphia: SBL, 1968.

Stadelmann, H. *Ben Sira als Schriftgelehrter: eine Untersuchung zum Berufsfbild des vor-makkabäischen Söfēr unter Berüchsichtigung seines Verhältnisses zu Priester-Propheten-und Weisheitlehrtum*. WUNT, 2nd ser., 6. Tübingen: J. C. B. Mohr (Paul Siebeck), 1980.

Stadelmann, R. *Syrisch-Palästinensische Gottheitenin Ägypten*. Leiden: Brill, 1967.

Stanton, G. "5 Ezra and the Matthean Christianity in the Second Century." *JTS* 28 (1977): 67–83.

———, ed. *The Interpretation of Matthew*. IRT 3. Philadelphia: Fortress, 1983.

Steck, O. *Israel und das gewaltsame Geschick der Propheten: Untersuchungen zur Überlieferung des deuteronomistischen Geschichtsbildes im Alten Testament, Spätjudentum und Urchristentum*. WMANT 320. Neukirchen-Vluyn: Neukirchener Verlag, 1967.

Stendahl, K. *The School of St. Matthew and Its Use of the Old Testament*. 2nd ed., with new introduction by the author. Philadelphia: Fortress, 1968.

Stone, M. E. "The Book of Enoch and Judaism in the Third Century B.C.E." *CBQ* 40 (1978): 479–92.

———. "Lists of Revealed Things in the Apocalyptic Literature." In *Magnalia Dei: The Mighty Acts of God: G. Ernest Wright in Memoriam*, ed. F. M. Cross et al., 414–52. Garden City, N.Y.: Doubleday, 1976.

———. "Reactions to Destructions of the Second Temple." *JSJ* 12 (1981): 195–204.

———. *Scriptures, Sects and Vision: A Profile of Judaism from Ezra to the Jewish Revolts*. Philadelphia: Fortress, 1980.

Strecker, G. *Die Bergpredigt: ein exegetischer Kommentar.* Göttingen: Vanden-hoeck and Ruprecht, 1984.

———. "The Concept of History in Matthew." *JAAR* 25 (1967): 219–30.

———. *Der Weg der Gerechtigkeit.* FRLANT 82. Göttingen: Vandenhoeck and Ruprecht, 1962.

Strugnell, J. "Notes sur le No 184 des 'Discoveries in the Judean Desert of Jordan.' " *RevQ* 7 (1969–71): 163–276.

Suggs, M. J. *Wisdom Christology and Law in Matthew's Gospel.* Cambridge: Harvard University Press, 1970.

———. "Wisdom of Solomon 2.10–15: A Homily on the Fourth Servant Song." *JBL* 76 (1957): 26–33.

Suter, D. *Tradition and Composition in the Parables of Enoch.* SBLDS 47. Missoula, Mont.: Scholars Press, 1979.

Theissen, G. *The Gospels in Context: Social and Political History in the Synoptic Tradition.* Minneapolis: Fortress, 1991.

———. "The Sociological Interpretation of Religious Traditions: Its Method-ological Problems as Exemplified in Early Christianity." In *The Bible and Liberation: Political and Social Hermeneutics*, ed. N. K. Gottwald, 38–48. Maryknoll, N.Y.: Orbis, 1983.

Tiede, D. L. *The Charismatic Figure as Miracle Worker.* SBLDS 1. Missoula Mont.: SBL, 1972.

Tobin, T. H. "4Q 185 and Jewish Wisdom Literature." In *Of Scribes and Scrolls: Studies on the Hebrew Bible, Intertestamental Judaism and Christian Origins*, ed. H. W. Attridge, J. J. Collins, and T. H. Tobin, 145–52. College Theology Society Resources in Religion 5. Lanham, Md.: University Press of America, 1990.

Townsend, J. T. "Matthew XXIII.9." *JTS* 12 (1961): 59.

Trenchard, W. C. *Ben Sira's View of Women: A Literary Analysis.* BJS 38. Chico, Calif.: Scholars Press, 1982.

Trilling, W. "Amt und Amtverständnis bei Matthäus." In *Mélanges bibliques en hommage au R. P. Béda Rigaux*, ed. A. Descamps and R. D. A. de Halleux, 29–44. Gembloux: Duculot, 1970.

———. *Das Wahre Israel: Studien zur Theologie des Matthäus-Evangeliums.* 3rd ed. SANT 10. Munich: Kösel, 1964.

Tsevat, M. *The Meaning of the Book of Job and Other Biblical Studies.* New York: Ktav, 1980.

Turner, V. "Metaphors of Anti-Structure in Religious Culture." In *Changing Per-spectives in the Scientific Study of Religion*, ed. A. W. Eister, 63–84. New York: John Wiley and Sons, 1974.

———. *The Ritual Process: Structure and Anti-Structure.* Ithaca, N.Y.: Cornell University Press, 1969.

Urbach, E. "Class Studies and Leadership in the World of the Palestinian Sages." *Proceedings of the Israel Academy of Science and Humanities* 2 (1968): 38–74.

———. *The Sages: Their Concepts and Beliefs.* 2 vols. Translated by I. Abra-hams. Jerusalem: Magnes Press (Hebrew University), 1975.

———. "The Talmudic Sage — Character and Authority." *Cahiers d'Histoire Mondiale* 11 (1968): 116–47.

van Caugh, J. M., and M. van Esbroeck. "La primauté de Pierre (Mt. 16,16–19) et son contexte judaïque." *RTL* 11 (1980): 321.

Vander Kam, J. *Enoch and the Growth of an Apocalyptic Tradition.* CBQMS 16. Washington: Catholic Biblical Association of America, 1984.

van der Kwaak, H. "Der Klage über Jerusalem (Matth. xxiii 37–39)." *NovT* 8 (1966): 156–70.

van Segbroeck, F. "Jesus rejeté par sa patrie (Mt. 13:54–58)." *Biblica* 49 (1968): 167–98.

Vawter, B. "Prov. 8:22: Wisdom and Creation." *JBL* 99 (1980): 205–16.

———. "Yahweh: Lord of the Heavens and the Earth." *CBQ* 48 (1986): 461–67.

Vermes, G. *Jesus the Jew: A Historian's Reading of the Gospels.* Philadelphia: Fortress, 1973.

Verseput, D. *The Rejection of the Humble Messianic King.* Frankfurt: Peter Lang, 1986.

Viviano, B. T. *Study as Worship: Aboth and the New Testament.* SJLA 26. Leiden: Brill, 1978.

Wainwright, E. M. *Towards a Feminist Critical Reading of the Gospel According to Matthew.* BZNW 60. Berlin: de Gruyter, 1991.

Weber, M. *Ancient Judaism.* Translated and edited by H. H. Garth and Don Martindale. New York: Free Press, 1952.

Webster, E. C. "Strophic Patterns in Job 3–28." *JSOT* 26 (1983): 33–60.

Webster, T. B. L. "Personification as a Mode of Greek Thought." *Journal of the Warburg and Courtauld Institutes* 17 (1954): 10–21.

Wegner, J. R. "Philo's Portrayal of Women — Hebraic or Hellenic?" In *"Women Like This,"* ed. Levine, 41–66.

Weingrod, A. "Patronage and Power." In *Patrons and Clients in Mediterranean Societies,* ed. Gellner and Waterbury, 41–51.

Weiss, J. "Das Logion Mt. 11, 25–30." In *Neutestamentliche Studien: Georg Heinrici zu seinem 70. Geburtstag,* 120–29. Leipzig: Hinrich, 1914.

Wengst, K. *Humility: Solidarity of the Humiliated: The Transformation of an Attitude and Its Social Relevance in Graeco-Roman, Old Testament-Jewish and Early Christian Tradition.* Translated by J. Bowden. Philadelphia: Fortress, 1988.

Wenham, D. "The Structure of Matthew XIII." *NTS* 25 (1979): 516–22.

Wheelwright, P. *The Burning Fountain: A Study in the Language of Symbolism.* Bloomington: Indiana University Press, 1954.

———. *Metaphor and Reality.* Bloomington: Indiana University Press, 1964.

Whybray, R. N. *The Intellectual Tradition in the Old Testament.* BZAW 135. Berlin: de Gruyter, 1974.

———. *Wisdom in Proverbs: The Concept of Wisdom in Proverbs 1–9.* Studies in Biblical Theology. London: SCM, 1965.

Wilcox, M. "Peter and the Rock: A Fresh Look at Matthew 16:17–19." *NTS* 22 (1975–76): 73–88.

Wilckens, U. "Die Redaktion des Gleichniskapitals Mark 4 durch Matthäus." *TZ* 20 (1964): 208.

———. *TDNT*, s.v. "σοφία."

———. *Weisheit und Torheit: Eine exegetisch-religionsgeschichtliche Untersuchung zu 1.Kor.1 und 2.* BHT 26. Tübingen: J. C. B. Mohr (Paul Siebeck), 1959.

Wilkins, M. J. *The Concept of Disciple in Matthew's Gospel as Reflected in the Use of the Term MATHĒTĒS.* NovTSup 59. Leiden: Brill, 1988.

Williams, N. P. "Great Texts Reconsidered: Matthew xi 25–27 = Luke x 21–22." *Exp Tim* 51 (1939–40): 182–86, 215–20.

Wilson, B. *Magic and the Millennium: A Sociological Study of Religious Movements of Protest among Tribal and Third-World Peoples.* London: Heinemann, 1973.

Winston, D. "The Sage as Mystic in the Wisdom of Solomon." In *The Sage*, ed. Gammie and Perdue, 383–97.

———. *The Wisdom of Solomon.* AB 43. Garden City, N.Y.: Doubleday, 1979.

———, ed. *Philo of Alexandria: The Contemplative Life, the Giants, and Selections.* Classics of Western Spirituality. New York: Paulist, 1981.

Winter, P. "Matthew xi:27 and Lk x.22 from the First to the Fifth Century: Reflections on the Development of the Text." *NovT* 1 (1956): 112–48.

Wire, A. C. "Gender Roles in a Scribal Community." In *Social History of the Matthean Community*, ed. Balch, 87–121.

Witherington, B. *Jesus the Sage: The Pilgrimage of Wisdom.* Minneapolis: Fortress, 1994.

———. *Wisdom's Gospel: A Sapiential Reading of the Beloved Disciple's Testimony.* Louisville, Ky.: Westminster/John Knox, forthcoming.

Witt, R. E. *Isis in the Graeco-Roman World.* Ithaca, N.Y.: Cornell University Press, 1971.

Wolfson, E. "Female Imaging of the Torah: From Literary Metaphor to Religious Symbol." In *From Ancient Israel to Modern Judaism: Intellect in Quest of Understanding: Essays in Honor of Marvin Fox*, ed. J. Neusner, E. S. Frerichs, and N. M. Sarna, 2:271–307. BJS 173. Atlanta: Scholars Press, 1989.

———. "Woman — The Feminine as Other in Theosophic Kabbalah: Some Philosophical Observations on the Divine Androgyne." In *The Other in Jewish Thought and History*, ed. L. Silberstein and R. Cohn. New York: New York University, 1994.

Yee, G. A. "An Analysis of Prov 8:22–31 According to Style and Structure." *ZAW* 94 (1982): 58–66.

Zahn, T. *Das Evangelium des Matthäus.* KNT 1. Leipzig: A. Deichert, 1903.

Zeller, D. "Zu einer jüdischen Vorlage von Mt. 13, 52." *BZ* 20 (1976): 223–27.

Zerafa, P. P. *The Wisdom of God in the Book of Job.* Studia Universitatis S. Thomae in Urbe 8. Rome: Herder, 1978.

Zumstein, J. *La condition du croyant dans l'évangile selon Matthieu.* OBO 16. Fribourg: Éditions Universitaires, 1977.

———. "Matthieu 28:16–20." *RTP* 22 (1972): 25.

Index of Texts

OTHER ANCIENT LITERATURE

General Index